A Poet's Ear

BOOKS BY ANNIE FINCH

Poetry
The Encyclopedia of Scotland
Eve
Calendars
Among the Goddesses
Spells

Prose
The Ghost of Meter
The Body of Poetry
A Poet's Craft/A Poet's Ear

Translation
The Complete Poetry of Louise Labé

Editor
Villanelles (with Marie-Elizabeth Mali)
Multiformalisms (with Susan M. Schultz)
Lofty Dogmas: Poets on Poetics (with Deborah Brown and Maxine Kumin)
Carolyn Kizer: Perspectives (with Johanna Keller and Candace McClelland)
An Exaltation of Forms (with Kathrine Varnes)
After New Formalism
A Formal Feeling Comes: Poems in Form by Contemporary Women

A Poet's Ear

A HANDBOOK OF
METER AND FORM

Annie Finch

THE UNIVERSITY OF MICHIGAN PRESS

ANN ARBOR

Published in the United States of America by
The University of Michigan Press
Manufactured in the United States of America
⊗ Printed on acid-free paper

2016   2015   2014   2013   4   3   2   1

A CIP catalog record for this book is available from the British Library.

Library of Congress Cataloging-in-Publication Data

Finch, Annie, 1956–
    A poet's ear : a handbook of meter and form / Annie Finch.
        p.   cm.
    ISBN 978-0-472-07066-4 (cloth : acid-free paper) —ISBN 978-0-
472-05066-6 (pbk. : acid-free paper)
    1. Poetry   Authorship.   I. Title.
PN1059.A9F564   2011
808.1—dc23   2012000978

The ear is the only true writer and the only true reader.
—ROBERT FROST

Preface

A Poet's Ear is an introduction to form: the art of structuring a poem through the repetition of line, accent, syllable, rhyme, stanza, and other elements and procedures. A longer book, *A Poet's Craft,* is being published simultaneously with this book for readers interested in a more comprehensive guide to writing poetry. It includes everything here as well as chapters on additional aspects of writing poetry, such as inspiration, imagery, diction, tropes, syntax, revision, and publishing and performing your work.

For decades, I have been fascinated and compelled by poetic form. In a poetic culture dominated almost exclusively by free verse, I often found myself in the minority among friends and colleagues in my excitement about the potential contributions of form to the poetics of the late twentieth and twenty-first centuries. Now a tide is turning, and poets of all kinds—narrative, exploratory, and performance-based, as well as so-called formalist poets—are increasingly hungry to understand how meter and form work. As this wonderful diversity of sophisticated and eager poets arrive at the gates of form, there have been few up-to-date, thorough, and accessible resources there to meet them. This book is an offering, an attempt to give back some of the joy and excitement that writing in form has provided me. It distills just about everything I have learned over my life as a practicing formal poet and longtime teacher of formal poetics.

A Poet's Ear focuses on the aspect of writing poetry that tends to be most challenging to the contemporary writer. It offers the findings of three exploratory journeys. The first has been my nearly lifelong central journey as a poet, from writing in form as a child, to free verse, and then back to a more culturally and aesthetically inclusive formalism, which I call "multiformalism." The second has been an intellectual journey, as student and then as scholar, critic, editor, and teacher, thinking about how meter and form work in poetry and developing my own ideas about poetic form, including the idea I call "metrical diversity"—the profound importance of nourishing a full range of metrical possibilities in English. And then there has been an interpersonal journey, along with other poets, students, readers, and listeners, in person and through essays, books, lectures, panels, reviews, online forums, and listserv and blog posts—an ongoing conversation about form and its role in contemporary poetry.

Whether your motivation for learning to write in form is to become more adept at free verse or to explore the complexities of formal poetry, or whether you are simply curious, you will find that *A Poet's Ear* offers a more comprehensive and varied introduction to poetic form in English than any other handbook. In addition to the basic meters and traditional European forms, such as the ballad and sonnet, discussed in most handbooks, the topics included here encompass the pantoum, blues, ghazal, and other forms brought to English from cultures worldwide, as well as postmodern forms and techniques such as the paradelle and procedural verse.

And true to the idea of "metrical diversity," the meters explored here are a wider variety than you will find discussed in other handbooks. Not only do they include a thorough discussion of iambic meter; this book also goes into detail about how to write in the noniambic meters—trochees, anapests, and dactyls—and classical metrical patterns such as sapphics, amphibrachs, and hendecasyllabics. The information given here, based on firsthand experience writing and reading, is in most cases the first discussion in print of how to vary and modulate these meters. I hope and expect that others will eventually add their own discoveries to this preliminary discussion.

The beginning of the twenty-first century marks a time of liberation for formal poetics. The ancient art of metrical poetry is stirring, calling to us, and poets are hearing its voice, answering with a greater variety of forms than have ever existed simultaneously in English before. For those contemporary poets who have devoted even a minimal amount of time to writing in form, the reason for the resurgence may be palpable. The art of patterning poetry connects speech and dance and song, wordlessness and word, constraint and liberation, exercise and flight. For many of us, there is nothing like it; to write poetry this way seems a profoundly human art, bringing verbal reason and physical emotion into more intimacy than any other craft makes possible. It creates tangible connections among ourselves and between ourselves and our environment— all in a way that resonates with human traditions across cultures and eras and resists mightily being adulterated or commodified. A poem crafted in structures that have evolved especially to embody and express the cyclical patterns of body, voice, memory: what gift can be shared more often, more freely, and still remain completely itself? It is my hope that this book will help you know better how to write and read such poems, to give and receive such gifts.

Acknowledgments

With love and thanks to all my teachers, especially my mother Margaret Rockwell Finch—my first and best teacher of poetry—and to all my students, especially those in the Stonecoast MFA program, with whom I have learned so much.

For thoughts on the manuscripts of *A Poet's Craft* and *A Poet's Ear,* for ideas for poems, exercises, and topics, and for various other kinds of knowledge, encouragement, and inspiration, I would like to offer my thanks to Kelli Russell Agodon, Charles Alexander, Michael Alexander, Kazim Ali, Tanya Allen, Amy Alvarez, Cathleen Bailey, Charles Bernstein, Robert Bly, Marie Borroff, Anne Bowman, Glen Brand, Julian Brand, Stephen Burt, Marci Buschner, Tom Cable, Janine Canan, Julie Carr, Caroline Casey, Kathleen Ceveny, Mike Chasar, Fred Courtright, Joel Davis, Josh Davis, Solana D'Lamont, Francesca deGrandis, Leigh DiAngelo, Camille Dungy, Jilly Dybka, Martin Earl, Moira Egan, Jill Essbaum, Patricia Fargnoli, Marta Rijn Finch, Althea Finch-Brand, Ann Fisher-Worth, Gary B. Fitzgerald, Kathleen Flenniken, Ruth Foley, Soyini Ford, Diane Gage, Dana Gioia, David Graham, Vince Gotera, Arielle Greenberg, Cindy Guttierrez, R. S. Gwynn, Marilyn Hacker, Patricia Hagge, Alyssa Harad, Joy Harjo, Charles Hartman, Mary Harwood, Farideh Hasanzadeh, Terrance Hayes, Kate Hibbard, Tanya Higgins, Holly Hinkle, Richard Hoffman, John Hollander, Gray Jacobik, Kathleen Jesme, Judy Jones, Julie Kane, Robin Kemp, Diane Kendig, Penelope Laurans, Andrea Levin, Emily Lloyd, Rosemary Lloyd, Diane Lockward, Julia Manship, Ken Markee, Charles Martin, Bernadette Mayer, Janet McCann, Cynthia MacDonald, Shanna Miller McNair, Mark Melnicove, Diane Middlebrook, Peggy Miller, Christina Mock, Ellen Moody, Indigo Moor, Richard Mullen, Ross Murfin, Rochelle Namaroff, C. J. Sage, Ann Silsbee, Laurel Snyder, Jeff Oaks, D. G. Nanouk Okpik, Alexandra Oliver, Jena Osman, Alicia Ostriker, Kathleen Ossip, Christina Pacosz, Danielle Pafunda, Janet Passehl, Michael Peich, Jessica Piazza, Stanley Plumly, Fran Quinn, Christina Rau, Tad Richards, Adrian Richwell, Elizabeth Robinson, Fred Robinson, Sonia Sanchez, Susan M. Schultz, Ntozake Shange, Don Share, John Shaw, Ron Silliman, Beth Simon, John Oliver Simon, Evie Shockley, Patricia Smith, Tracy K. Smith, Laurel Snyder, Kevin St. Jarre, A. E. Stallings, Sue Standing, Lisa Storie, Chris Stroffolino, Cheryl Boyce Taylor, Susan Tichy, John Tranter, Sina Queyras, Colin Ward, Karrie Waarala, Baron Wormser, Ingrid Wendt, Anne Witty, Wynn Yarbrough, and Lady Zen. My grateful appreciation also goes to all the others who are not listed here but should be.

Special thanks to Ruth Gundle of Eighth Mountain Press for her moral support and extensive hands-on editing help in the very earliest stages of this book, which even now includes some of her words and phrases; to Kathleen Clancy, for useful suggestions on the drafts of several chapters; to Daniel Tobin, for going far beyond the call of duty as a manuscript reader; to my talented graduate research assistant Teal Gardella for her invaluable work on the final round of corrections; to Ellen Bauerle and Marcia LaBrenz at the University of Michigan Press for their patience and care; to my supportive family, especially my daughter, Althea, for crucial photocopying; and to my sister, Marta Rijn Finch, who donated her extraordinary poetic and scholarly knowledge and her copyediting skills with such dedication and generosity.

Contents

PART 1: METER

1. *Forms of Free Verse*   3

    GEORGE HERBERT, *The Collar*   4

Six Types of Free Verse   5

    WALT WHITMAN, Sections 8 and 9 from *Crossing Brooklyn Ferry*   6

    WILLIAM CARLOS WILLIAMS, *Nantucket*   8

    NAOMI SHIHAB NYE, *Blood*   9

    ANNE CARSON, from *Book of Isaiah*   10

    GWENDOLYN BROOKS, from *Boy Breaking Glass*   10

    AUDRE LORDE, from *Coal*   11

    ROBERT DUNCAN, from *The Torso*   11

    LINDA GREGERSON, from *Sold*   13

Prose Poems   13

    SUSAN SCHULTZ, from *Before the next war*   13

    RUSSELL EDSON, *You*   14

    SAWAKO NAKAYASU, *A field of fried umbrellas*   14

The Line in Free Verse   15

    WILLIAM CARLOS WILLIAMS, *To a Poor Old Woman*   16

    E. ETHELBERT MILLER, *Breakfast with Naomi Ayala*   16

    GALWAY KINNELL, *Daybreak*   17

    DIANE DIPRIMA, *and where thou art I am*   18

    GLORIA FRYM, from *Homeless at Home* (2 lines)   18

    DENISE LEVERTOV, from *Our Bodies*   19

    LUCINDA ROY, from *The Humming Birds*   19

    TIM SEIBLES, from *Hardie* (2 lines)   19

LORINE NIEDECKER, *Margaret Fuller*   19

SUE STANDING, from *Waking up in the Swamp* (3 lines)   20

HAYDEN CARRUTH, from *Five Short Shorts* (3 lines)   20

ROBERT CREELEY, The Europeans   20

HEATHER MCHUGH, from *A*   21

KEVIN YOUNG, from *Aubade*   21

JUNE JORDAN, from *Lullaby*   21

LANGSTON HUGHES, *The Negro Speaks of Rivers*   22

W. S. MERWIN, from *Native Trees*   22

W. H. AUDEN, from *Musée des Beaux Arts*   23

SHARON OLDS, from *I Go Back to May 1937*   23

LUCI TAPAHONSO, from *Leda and the Cowboy*   24

FARIDEH HASSANZADEH, from *Isn't It Enough*   24

Rhythm in Free Verse   25

ADRIENNE RICH, *Tonight No Poetry Will Serve*   25

W. B. YEATS, from *Easter 1916*   26

H.D., from *The Walls Do Not Fall*   27

Questions for Meditation or Discussion   28

Quotes   28

Poetry Practices   29

2. Hearing the Beat: Accent and Accentual Poetry   31

Accent and Emotion   34

Syllabic Poetry   35

MARIANNE MOORE, *She Trimmed the Candles Like One
Who Loves the Beautiful*   35

DYLAN THOMAS, *Fern Hill*   37

DONALD JUSTICE, *The Thin Man*   38

PETER MEINKE, *Zinc Fingers*   39

Accentual Poetry   40

GILDA RADNER (Roseanne Roseannadanna), *Jeans*   41

ANONYMOUS, trans. Annie Finch, *The Seafarer*   41

MOS DEF, from *Respiration*   42

ELIZABETH BISHOP, *The Moose*   44

LANDIS EVERSON, *Famine*   50

ELIZABETH WOODY, from *The Girlfriends* (2 lines)   50

W. B. YEATS, from *Easter 1916*   51

Questions for Meditation or Discussion   52
   ANNIE FINCH AND ALTHEA FINCH-BRAND, *Up the Tallest Tree*   52
   ROBERT LOUIS STEVENSON, *From a Railway Carriage*   52
   ANONYMOUS, Scottish proverb   53

Quotes   53
   WALT WHITMAN, *I Sing the Body Electric* (2 lines)   53

Poetry Practices   54

3. *Meter: A Language for the Body*   56

Prosody and History   57
   THE GAWAIN POET, from *Sir Gawain and the Green Knight*   58
   THE GAWAIN POET, trans. Marie Borroff, from *Sir Gawain*
     and the Green Knight   59
   GEOFFREY CHAUCER, from *The Wife of Bath's Tale*   59
   GEOFFREY CHAUCER, trans. Sinan Kökbugur, from
     The Wife of Bath's Tale   60

Scansion Marks   62

The Four Most Common Metrical Patterns   63
   HENRY WADSWORTH LONGFELLOW, from *The Song of Hiawatha*   63
   ANNE BRADSTREET, *To My Dearest and Loving Husband*   64
   HENRY LIVINGSTON JR., from *The Night Before Christmas*   64
   HENRY WADSWORTH LONGFELLOW, from *Evangeline*   65

Meter, Rhythm, and the Metrical Foot   66

Meter in Contemporary Poetry   68
   LISA JARNOT, *Hound Pastoral*   68
   ALLISON JOSEPH, from *Parable*   69
   RACHEL LODEN, *Nineveh Fallen*   70

The Line in Free Verse and Metrical Poetry   71

How to Scan a Poem   72
   EDNA ST. VINCENT MILLAY, from *Love is not all* (2 lines)   73

A Note on Scansion and Subjectivity: The 80/20 Rule   75

Why Bother?   76

Questions for Meditation or Discussion   77

Quotes   78

ALEXANDER POPE, from *Essay on Criticism* (2 lines)   78

DOROTHY PARKER, *Fighting Words*   78

Poetry Practices   79

4. The Many Voices of Iambic Meter   83

  R. S. GWYNN, *Approaching a Significant Birthday, He Peruses
  The Norton Anthology of Poetry*   84

Blank Iambic Verse, Enjambment, and Caesura   85

  ALFRED, LORD TENNYSON, *Ulysses*   86

The Five Basic Metrical Variations in Iambic Pentameter   89

  Anapests as Variations   89

    CHARLES MARTIN, from *Breaking Old Ground*   89

    EDNA ST. VINCENT MILLAY, *Sonnet 30*   89

    WILLIAM MEREDITH, *The Illiterate*   91

  Trochees as Variations   92

    W. B. YEATS, from *Among School Children*   92

    WILLIAM WORDSWORTH, from *I Wandered Lonely as a Cloud*   93

  Spondees and Pyrrhics as Variations   93

    GWENDOLYN BROOKS, *The Pool Players, Seven at the
    Golden Shovel*   94

    GEORGE PEELE, *Bathsheba's Song*   94

    DYLAN THOMAS, from *Do Not Go Gentle into
    That Good Night* (2 lines)   94

    HART CRANE, from *To Brooklyn Bridge*   95

    SUZANNE DOYLE, from *Some Girls*   96

    ALEXANDER POPE, from *Essay on Criticism*   97

  Headless and Extra-Syllable Lines   97

    ROBERT HAYDEN, from *Those Winter Sundays* (1 line)   97

    GEOFFREY CHAUCER, from *Prologue* to The Canterbury Tales (1 line)   98

    BENJAMIN ALIRE SAENZ, from *To the Desert* (1 line)   99

    WILLIAM SHAKESPEARE, from *Hamlet*   101

    EDNA ST. VINCENT MILLAY, *Sonnet 30*   102

    MARILYN NELSON, *Chosen*   103

    ROBERT FROST, from *Birches*   103

  Expressive Variation and Keeping Your Balance   105

    ANNE FINCH, *The Apology*   106

JOHN DONNE, *Batter My Heart*   107

WILLIAM SHAKESPEARE, *Sonnet 116*   108

ALEXANDER POPE, from *Essay on Criticism* (2 lines)   109

Iambic Dimeter, Trimeter, Tetrameter, and Fourteeners   109

THEODORE ROETHKE, from *Open House*   110

JOHN KEATS, *I Had a Dove*   110

THEODORE ROETHKE, *My Papa's Waltz*   111

CHRISTINA ROSSETTI, from *Under the Rose*   111

LANGSTON HUGHES, *Justice*   112

GEORGE HERBERT, *Love (III)*   112

OVID, trans. Arthur Golding, from *Metamorphoses*   113

Iambic Pentameter in the Twenty-First Century   115

Questions for Meditation or Discussion   116

THEODORE ROETHKE, *Four for Sir John Davies*   116

Quotes   117

Poetry Practices   118

5. *The Metrical Palette: Beyond Iambic Pentameter*   120

Trochaic Meter   121

WILLIAM SHAKESPEARE, from *Macbeth*   121

WILLIAM BLAKE, *Tyger! Tyger!*   122

HENRY WADSWORTH LONGFELLOW, from *Hiawatha*   123

SARAH JOSEPHA HALE, from *Iron*   126

ROBERT HERRICK, *Upon a Child*   127

WILLIAM SHAKESPEARE, from *A Winter's Tale*   129

CAROLYN KIZER, from *Mud Soup*   130

GWENDOLYN BROOKS, from *The Anniad*   130

W. H. AUDEN, *Lullaby*   131

Anapestic Meter   133

CIRILO F. BAUTISTA, trans. José Edmundo Ocampo Reyes,
Questions and Answers   133

SARA TEASDALE, *I Would Live in Your Love*   133

HENRY WADSWORTH LONGFELLOW, from *Paul Revere's Ride*   134

JOHN GREENLEAF WHITTIER, from *The Quaker Alumni*   135

ALFRED NICOL, from *Mother's Side*   136

OLIVER WENDELL HOLMES, from *The Boys*   136

JAMES RUSSELL LOWELL, from *A Fable for Critics*   136

ALFRED, LORD TENNYSON, from *Maud*   137

GEORGE GORDON, LORD BYRON, from *The Destruction of Sennacharib*   137

ALGERNON CHARLES SWINBURNE, from *Atalanta in Calydon*   138

ROBERT BROWNING, from *How They Brought the Good News
from Ghent to Aix*   138

R. J. YEATMAN AND W. C. SELLAR, *How I brought the good news
from Aix to Ghent (or Vice Versa)*   138

LEWIS CARROLL, from *The Hunting of the Snark*   139

EDGAR ALLAN POE, *Annabel Lee*   139

ALGERNON CHARLES SWINBURNE, from *A Song in Time
of Revolution*   140

HENRY LIVINGSTON JR., from *The Night Before Christmas*   141

INDIGO MOOR, from *Halo in Decline*   141

THOMAS HARDY, from *Under the Waterfall*   142

JAMES DICKEY, from *The Lifeguard*   142

Dactylic Meter   143

HENRY WADSWORTH LONGFELLOW, from *Evangeline*   144

SYLVIA PLATH, from *Mushrooms*   146

ROBERT BROWNING, from *The Lost Leader* (2 lines)   146

A. E. STALLINGS, *Arachne Gives Thanks to Athena*   146

CHRISTINA ROSSETTI, from *Goblin Market*   147

GENEVIEVE TAGGARD, *At Last the Women Are Moving*   148

RACHEL HADAS, *The Slip*   149

R. S. GWYNN, *The Denouement*   150

Mixed Meters   151

GEORGIA DOUGLAS JOHNSON, *Your World*   151

JUDITH MOFFETT, from *Mezzo Cammin*   152

JOHN DRYDEN, from *A Hymn for St. Cecilia's Day*   152

Amphibrachs, Dipodics, and Hendecasyllabics   156

ANNA AKHMATOVA, trans. Annie Finch with George Kline,
The White Bird   156

SAMUEL WOODWORTH, from *The Old Oaken Bucket*   157

ERNEST LAWRENCE THAYER, from *Casey at the Bat*   159

RUDYARD KIPLING, from *The Galley-Slave*   159

ARIELLE GREENBERG, *The Meter of the Night Sky*   160

ALGERNON CHARLES SWINBURNE, from *Hendecasyllabics*   160

PATRICIA SMITH, *The Reemergence of the Noose*   161

Meter and Meaning   162

   ANONYMOUS, from *Dr. Seuss Tech Support*   162

   JULIA ALVAREZ, *What Could it Be*   163

Questions for Meditation or Discussion   164

Quotes   164

Poetry Practices   165

PART 2: FORM

6. *Paradigms of Rhyme*   169

Definitions   169

Rhyme's Roots   169

Kinds of Rhyme   171

   RITA DOVE, from *Blown Apart by Loss* (2 lines)   171

   JOHN DONNE, from *The Calm* (2 lines)   171

   WILFRED OWEN, *Futility*   172

   SANDRA CISNEROS, from *The Poet Reflects on Her Solitary Fate*   172

   EMILY DICKINSON, *Poem 1078*   173

   KIM ADDONIZIO, *Blues for Dante Alighieri*   173

   JOSEPH BRODSKY, from *December in Florence*   174

   DIXON LANIER MERRITT, *The Pelican*   174

   PHILIP LARKIN, from *Churchgoing*   175

   W. B. YEATS, *He Wishes for the Cloths of Heaven*   175

   RANDALL MANN, *The Heron*   176

   EDGAR ALLAN POE, from *The Raven*   177

   ANNIE FINCH, *Brigid*   178

   SYLVIA PLATH, from *Black Rook in Rainy Weather*   179

   JOHN SKELTON, from *Colin Clout*   180

   ROBERT FROST, *After Apple-Picking*   180

Rhyme and Emphasis   182

   WILLIAM WORDSWORTH, *She dwelt among the untrodden ways*   182

   ALEXANDER POPE, from *The Rape of the Lock* (2 LINES)   182

   SONIA SANCHEZ, from *Song No. 2*   183

   WILLIAM SHAKESPEARE, from *Macbeth*   183

Rhyme and Meaning   183

   WILLIAM SHAKESPEARE, *Sonnet 73*   184

   LANGSTON HUGHES, *Casualty*   184

MOLLY PEACOCK, *Of Night*   185
ROBERT FROST, *Bereft*   185
PAUL MULDOON, *The Outlier*   186
MARGARET DANNER, *The Painted Lady*   188
THOM GUNN, *The Night-Piece*   188
ALEXANDER POPE, from *Essay on Criticism*   189
AARON SHURIN, *If the judgment's cruel*   189

Advice on Rhyming   190
GWENDOLYN BROOKS, *Beverly Hills, Chicago*   191

Questions for Meditation or Discussion   193
BEN JONSON, from *A Fit of Rime Against Rime*   193
ROBERT FROST, *The Most of It*   193
SEAMUS HEANEY, from *History*   194

Quotes   193
MAJOR JACKSON, from *Letter to Brooks*   195

Poetry Practices   196

7. *Stanzas: A Poem's Breathing Rooms*   198

The Stanza in Free Verse and Shaped Poems   199
WILLIAM BLAKE, *London*   199
ROBERT FROST, *To Earthward*   200
MALKA HEIFETZ TUSSMAN, trans. Marcia Falk, *Last Apple*   202
COLE SWENSEN, from *June 2*   202
GEORGE HERBERT, from *Easter-Wings*   203
MAY SWENSON, *Bleeding*   204

Two- and Three-Line Stanzas   206
ALEXANDER POPE, from *Essay on Man*   206
ALEXANDER POPE, from *Essay on Criticism*   206
MARGARET CAVENDISH, *Nature's Cook*   207
ELIZABETH BARRETT BROWNING, *from* A Vision of Poets   208
DANTE ALIGHIERI, trans. Michael Palma, from *The Inferno*   209
PERCY BYSSHE SHELLEY, from *Ode to the West Wind*   210
DEREK WALCOTT, from *The Bounty*   211

Four-Line Stanzas   211
MOTHER GOOSE, *Three Children*   212
W. H. AUDEN, from *As I Walked Out One Evening*   212

COUNTEE CULLEN, *Incident* — 213

GEORGE GORDON, LORD BYRON, from
    The Destruction of Sennacherib — 214

ALFRED, LORD TENNYSON, from *In Memoriam* — 215

RICHARD WILBUR, *Advice to a Prophet* — 216

SAPPHO, trans. John Myers O'Hara, *Moon and Stars* — 218

SAPPHO, trans. Annie Finch, *Household of the Muses* — 218

ALGERNON CHARLES SWINBURNE, *Hymn to Aphrodite* — 219

WILLIAM MEREDITH, *Effort at Speech* — 219

MARILYN HACKER, from *Dusk: July* — 221

MARY SIDNEY, from *Psalm 120* — 222

WILLIAM BLAKE, from *Evening* — 222

ROBIN SKELTON, from *The Garden at Dawn* — 222

MARILYN HACKER, from *Going Back to the River* — 223

Longer Stanzas — 223

PHILIP LARKIN, *Home is So Sad* — 223

WILLIAM SHAKESPEARE, from *Venus and Adonis* — 224

ANNE BRADSTREET, from "Contemplations" — 224

GEOFFREY CHAUCER, from *Troilus and Criseyde* — 225

MAJOR JACKSON, from *Letter to Brooks* — 225

GEORGE GORDON, LORD BYRON, from *Don Juan* — 226

W. B. YEATS, from *Among School Children* — 227

EDMUND SPENSER, from *The Faerie Queene* — 228

JOHN KEATS, from *The Eve of St. Agnes* — 228

PERCY BYSSHE SHELLEY, from *Adonais: An Elegy on the
    Death of John Keats* — 229

GEORGE SANTAYANA, *Decima* — 230

The Dynamic Stanza — 231

EMILY GALVIN, *Light Warning* — 231

Questions for Meditation or Discussion — 232

Quotes — 233

Poetry Practices — 233

8. *Worth Repeating: Forms Based on Repetition* — 235

KING JAMES BIBLE, from *Song of Solomon* — 236

WALT WHITMAN, from *Out of the Cradle, Endlessly Rocking* — 236

OLENA KALYTIAK DAVIS, *O Great Slacker*   237

CHRISTOPHER SMART, from *Jubilate Agno*   238

JOY HARJO, *Ah, Ah*   240

MURIEL RUKEYSER, *Looking at Each Other*   241

The Blues   244

    LANGSTON HUGHES, *The Weary Blues*   245

    LEADBELLY, from *Good Morning Blues*   246

    SONIA SANCHEZ, *Song No. 2*   246

    NATASHA TRETHEWEY, *Graveyard Blues*   248

The Villanelle   248

    THEODORE ROETHKE, from *The Waking* (2 lines)   249

    DYLAN THOMAS, from *Do Not Go Gentle into That Good Night* (2 lines)   249

    ELIZABETH BISHOP, from *One Art* (2 lines)   249

    EDWIN ARLINGTON ROBINSON, *The House on the Hill*   250

    MICHAEL RYAN, *Milk the Mouse*   251

    ELIZABETH BISHOP, *One Art*   251

    DYLAN THOMAS, *Do Not Go Gentle into That Good Night*   252

    MENDI OBADIKE, *Contagion*   253

The Sestina and Canzone   254

    SIR PHILIP SIDNEY, from *Ye Gote-heard Gods*   255

    RUDYARD KIPLING, from *Sestina of the Tramp-Royal*   256

    ELIZABETH BISHOP, *Sestina*   257

    ANTHONY HECHT, *The Book of Yolek*   259

    MARILYN HACKER, *Untoward Occurrence at an Embassy Poetry Reading*   260

    HELEN FROST, *my choice . . . KATIE*   262

    ALGERNON CHARLES SWINBURNE, from *Sestina*   264

    AGHA SHAHID ALI, *Lenox Hill*   265

The Rondeau, Triolet, Kyrielle, and Tritina   267

    AUSTIN DOBSON, from *The Same Imitated*   268

    PAUL LAURENCE DUNBAR, *We Wear the Mask*   268

    MARILYN HACKER, from *Love, Death, and the Changing of the Seasons*   269

    G. K. CHESTERTON, *Triolet*   270

    A. E. STALLINGS, *Triolet on a Line Apocryphally Attributed to Martin Luther*   270

    MARIE PONSOT, *Roundstone Cove*   270

The Paradelle   271

    BILLY COLLINS, from *Paradelle for Susan*   271

    HENRY TAYLOR, *Paradelle: Nocturne de la Ville*   272

The Ghazal   273

  ROBERT BLY, *Call and Answer*   273

  JOHN DRURY, *Ghazal of the Lagoon*   275

  MIMI KHALVATI, *Ghazal*   275

Pantoum   276

  NELLIE WONG, *Grandmother's Song*   277

  ELAINE EQUI, from *A Date with Robbe-Grillet*   278

  PAUL MULDOON, *The Mountain Is Holding Out*   279

Refrain in Free Verse and Form   280

  LUCIA TRENT, *Breed, Women, Breed*   280

  JANE KENYON, *Otherwise*   281

  HENRY WADSWORTH LONGFELLOW, from *A Boy's Will*   282

Questions for Meditation or Discussion   284

  WESLI COURT, *Sestina*   285

Quotes   286

Poetry Practices   288

9. *Chaos in Fourteen Lines: The Sonnet*   290

  WILLIAM WORDSWORTH, *Nuns Fret Not*   290

  CLAUDE MCKAY, *If We Must Die*   291

The Italian and English Sonnet   295

  MARK JARMAN, *Unholy Sonnet*   295

  JOHN BERRYMAN, *Sonnet 115*   296

  EDNA ST. VINCENT MILLAY, *I will put Chaos into fourteen lines* 296

  EMMA LAZARUS, *The New Colossus*   297

  WILLIAM SHAKESPEARE, *Sonnet 12*   298

  ROBERT FROST, *The Silken Tent*   298

Writing Sonnets   299

  LOUISE BOGAN, *Single Sonnet*   299

  RUTH PADEL, *Tiger Drinking at Forest Pool*   300

  KAREN VOLKMAN, *Sonnet*   301

  JUNE JORDAN, *Something Like a Sonnet for Phillis Miracle Wheatley* 302

Sonnets and Sequences   303

Reclaiming the Sonnet   304

  LOUISE LABÉ, trans. Annie Finch, *Sonnet 18*   304

  OWEN DODSON, *Midnight Bell*   305

  JOHN DONNE, *Batter My Heart*   306

Variations and Deformations of the Sonnet   306

GERARD MANLY HOPKINS, *Pied Beauty*   307

GWENDOLYN BROOKS, *the sonnet-ballad*   308

ROBERT LOWELL, *History*   309

TED BERRIGAN, *In Joe Brainard's collage its white arrow*   310

Questions for Meditation or Discussion   312

JOHN KEATS, *If By Dull Rhymes Our English Must Be Chain'd*   312

Quotes   313

Poetry Practices   313

10. Deep Story: The Ballad   315

ANONYMOUS, *Tiranti, My Son*   316

ANONYMOUS, from *Clerk Saunders*   318

ANONYMOUS, *The Willow Tree*   318

HELEN ADAM, *I Love My Love*   320

LANGSTON HUGHES, *Madam and the Census Man*   323

DUDLEY RANDALL, *Ballad of Birmingham: On the Bombing of a Church in Alabama, 1963*   324

SAMUEL TAYLOR COLERIDGE, from *The Rime of the Ancient Mariner*   326

ELIZABETH BISHOP, from *The Burglar of Babylon*   327

LEE ANN BROWN, from *Ballad of Susan Smith*   329

Questions for Meditation or Discussion   329

Quotes   330

Poetry Practices   331

ANONYMOUS, *Lady Isabel and the Elf-Knight*   331

11. Procedural Poetry   336

Procedural and Nonce Poems   336

HARRYETTE MULLEN, from *Dim Lady* (2 lines)   338

JOAN RETALLACK, *AID/I/SAPPEARANCE*   339

JACKSON MACLOW, *Call Me Ishmael*   341

DAN ZIMMERMAN, from *Isotopes*   342

CHRISTIAN BOK, from *Eunoia*   343

Found and Genre Poems   346

JEN BERVIN, Shakespeare's *Sonnet 15*   346

MICHAEL MAGEE, *Pledge: 1*   347

CATHY BOWMAN, *Wedding Invitation III*   348

Questions for Meditation or Discussion   349

Quotes   349

Poetry Practices   349

Afterword: Form and Inspiration   351

A Poet's Bookshelf on Form: For Further Reading   353

Appendix: Scansions   357

Credits   405

Index   409

PART 1

Meter

CHAPTER 1

Forms of Free Verse

The free-verse line break is the first and often the only formal poetic device that contemporary readers of poetry may know. It's easy to make fun of bad free verse as "just cut-up prose," but in fact, as greeting-card writers know, the process of cutting up prose—any prose—into lines does surround it with an aura of special attention and poetic dignity. Why? Because the line breaks are a repeated device completely independent from the meaning of the language. The line breaks, through their repeating rhythm, lend the prose that sculptural, structured, formal quality that distinguishes poetry from any other kind of writing.

Virtually any element of language can be repeated in order to structure language into a poem, to give it form. Besides the line break, the repeated, structuring element that makes us recognize a "poem" can be a word sound (in which case the poem rhymes); a rhythmic pattern (in which case the poem is metrical); or a number of accents (in which case the poem is accentual). The repeated element can also be a phrase (making the poem a chant), or sentences (giving the poem a refrain, like a blues poem). It can even be an invisible process (like incorporating every fortieth word in the dictionary), making the poem a procedural poem.

In all these cases, it is the structuring capacity of repetition that lends a poem its distinctively poetic power. The word "structure" is the key. Prose may be decorated with the occasional repetition of alliteration, rhyme, or rhythm. As long as the repetition is random and unpredictable, however lyrical the language may be, it remains lyric prose. But when one repeated element, including the line break, becomes predictable and actually structures the language, then the text becomes a poem.

> Line break: the break where a line of poetry ends, indicated by a slash (/) when the poem is reproduced in a prose context. In prose paragraphs (including prose poems) line breaks change according to the margins of the printed text, but in poetry line breaks are always intentional and are always respected by the printer.

Free verse is the way many of us came to appreciate the power of repetition in poetry and the importance of the poetic line. At the beginning of the twentieth century, in her preface to an anthology of Imagist poets, Amy Lowell advocated increased respect for free verse, which she defined as "writing whose cadence is more marked, more definite, and closer knit than that of prose, but which is not so violently nor so obviously accented as the so-called 'regular verse.'" A century later, free verse has become so pervasive that it is somewhat invisible: a sonnet or blues is considered to be a form, while free verse is just accepted as "poetry." But in fact, free verse is a form, with certain poetic shapes, and it has been around in English since long before Amy Lowell. The word "verse" comes from the Latin word *versus,* meaning "the turning of a plow at the end of a furrow." This turning back to create lines gives free verse its repeating pattern. If you ever feel that free verse is more modern than traditional forms, consider the following free verse poem:

"The Collar," George Herbert (1585)

I struck the board, and cried, No more.
I will abroad.
What? Shall I ever sigh and pine?
My lines and life are free; free as the road,
Loose as the wind, as large as store.
Shall I be still in suit?
Have I no harvest but a thorn
To let me blood, and not restore
What I have lost with cordial fruit?
Sure there was wine
Before my sighs did dry it: there was corn
Before my tears did drown it.
Is the year only lost to me?
Have I no bays to crown it?

No flowers, no garlands gay? all blasted?
All wasted?
Not so, my heart: but there is fruit,
And thou hast hands.
Recover all thy sigh-blown age
On double pleasures: leave thy cold dispute
Of what is fit, and not. Forsake thy cage,
Thy rope of sands,
Which petty thoughts have made, and made to thee
Good cable, to enforce and draw,
And be thy law,
While thou didst wink and wouldst not see.
Away; take heed:
I will abroad.
Call in thy death's head there: tie up thy fears.
He that forbears
To suit and serve his need,
Deserves his load.
But as I raved and grew more fierce and wild
At every word,
Me thoughts I heard one calling, Child:
And I replied, My Lord.

Composed in 1585, this poem moves unpredictably among varying (albeit mostly iambic) rhythms and line lengths. Some lines have no countable pattern of stresses; others are in more regular rhythmic patterns, such as lines 6 through 9, which also use rhyme. But the overall effect of the poem is uniquely rhythmic, the internal changes of the speaker's voice creating a dialectic between outward movement and drawing inward, rushes of passion and hesitant thought. Each line of the poem is "free" to follow the shape of the speaker's voice at any point, from the weary, brief enervation of "All wasted?" to the long surge of "But as I raved and grew more fierce and wild."

Six Types of Free Verse

While free verse by definition resists classification, with each poem theoretically being free to jump between any sorts of lines, in practice it tends to fall into distinctive kinds of patterns which are often lumped together. When you write free verse, it is helpful to know which of these traditions you are working in, since they each have different histories, different aims, and different methods.

Long-lined, oral-based free verse is the most ancient type. It descends from Old Testament psalms, which inspired such poets as William Blake, Christopher Smart, and eventually Walt Whitman and Allen Ginsberg. Long-lined free verse usually aims to move readers through their ears, or their internal ears (how your brain "hears" words when you read silently). It lends itself to long sentences, waves and surges of sound, public or political situations, rolling rhythms, repeated phrases, especially at the beginnings of lines, where they are called "anaphora" (as in Whitman's "catalogs"), high rhetoric, and grand gestures.

> Catalog, in poetry, means a list, whether a litany or simply a list of places, body parts, equipment, etc.

The line breaks in long-lined free verse are determined by rhythmic units or breath patterns, but not by any visual factors. If you read aloud these poems by Walt Whitman, you will notice your voice following out the contrasting lengths and energetic patterns of each line:

From "Crossing Brooklyn Ferry," Walt Whitman (1856)

8

Ah, what can ever be more stately and admirable to me than
　　mast-hemm'd Manhattan?
River and sunset and scallop-edg'd waves of flood-tide?
The sea-gulls oscillating their bodies, the hay-boat in the
　　twilight, and the belated lighter?

What gods can exceed these that clasp me by the hand, and with
　　voices I love call me promptly and loudly by my nighest name as I
　　approach?
What is more subtle than this which ties me to the woman or man that
　　looks in my face?
Which fuses me into you now, and pours my meaning into you?

We understand then do we not?
What I promis'd without mentioning it, have you not accepted?
What the study could not teach—what the preaching could not
    accomplish is accomplish'd, is it not?

9

Flow on, river! flow with the flood-tide, and ebb with the ebb-tide!
Frolic on, crested and scallop-edg'd waves!
Gorgeous clouds of the sunset! drench with your splendor me, or the
    men and women generations after me!
Cross from shore to shore, countless crowds of passengers!
Stand up, tall masts of Mannahatta! stand up, beautiful hills of
    Brooklyn!
Throb, baffled and curious brain! throw out questions and answers!
Suspend here and everywhere, eternal float of solution!
Gaze, loving and thirsting eyes, in the house or street or public
    assembly!
Sound out, voices of young men! loudly and musically call me by my
    nighest name!

"Crossing Brooklyn Ferry," like almost all Whitman's poems, cries out to be declaimed, perhaps from the prow of a ship. It doesn't matter whether the audience is the reader, the waves, the passengers, the clouds, the river, the hills; what matters is the voice of the poet speaking. The long lines, often corresponding to sentences, allow a voice to gather force and momentum. This tendency is so ingrained in long-lined free verse that it can be used ironically for the opposite effect. The very long lines of contemporary poet C. K. Williams's intimate confessions add a disconcerting element of universality and nakedness to his personal ruminations.

    Short-lined free verse, on the other hand, aims for the eye rather than the ear of the reader. This type of free verse entered the English language in the early twentieth century through the work of such Imagist poets as H.D. and Ezra Pound, influenced by the avant-garde Vorticist movement and by translations of traditional Chinese poetry. They were struck by the power of the Chinese ideogram, at once both a picture and a letter, and wanted to create a similar contemplative, self-contained objectivity in their free verse poems. Imagists, most notably H.D., cultivated a cool, impersonal style of presenting images.

This style of short-lined free verse aims for a hyper-awareness of every word on the part of the reader:

"Nantucket," William Carlos Williams (1934)

Flowers through the window
lavender and yellow

changed by white curtains—
Smell of cleanliness—

Sunshine of late afternoon—
On the glass tray

a glass pitcher, the tumbler
turned down, by which

a key is lying—And the
immaculate white bed

Unlike in long- and medium-lined free verse, these breaks tend to happen at unnatural places, such as in the middle of a phrase. The visual impact of the line breaks is crucial. It is hard to imagine this kind of free verse existing before the invention of the typewriter, since the spacing of letters, and which words end up under which words, is all-important—just as the contemplation of the calligraphy of a traditional painted Chinese poem is a key part of the experience. Simplicity is key in this central twentieth-century tradition. Anything that appears artificial or clumsy can ruin the effect, including rhetoric, any kind of cliché, too much rhyme or word-music, and repeated or insistent rhythms. The ideal audience for this type of poetry is not a listener in a crowd but a solitary reader contemplating the poem on the page. You wrap yourself around these poems; they don't sweep you away.

Literary or medium-lined free verse tends to aim for the mind rather than the ear or eye. This kind of poem often seems closely linked to metered poetry, and sometimes it hovers around meter. The lines tend to follow syntactic units, breaking at natural pauses between phrases. Often, such poems cultivate immediacy of tone and a plain, conversational style; the main goal is to create an emotional persona for the speaker with whom the reader can identify:

"Blood," Naomi Shihab Nye

"A true Arab knows how to catch a fly in his hands,"
my father would say. And he'd prove it,
cupping the buzzer instantly
while the host with the swatter stared.

In the spring our palms peeled like snakes.
True Arabs believed watermelon could heal fifty ways.
I changed these to fit the occasion.

Years before, a girl knocked,
wanted to see the Arab.
I said we didn't have one.
After that, my father told me who he was,
"Shihab"—"shooting star"—
a good name, borrowed from the sky.
Once I said, "When we die, we give it back?"
He said that's what a true Arab would say.

Today the headlines clot in my blood.
A little Palestinian dangles a truck on the front page.
Homeless fig, this tragedy with a terrible root
is too big for us. What flag can we wave?
I wave the flag of stone and seed,
table mat stitched in blue.

I call my father, we talk around the news.
It is too much for him,
neither of his two languages can reach it.
I drive into the country to find sheep, cows,
to plead with the air:
Who calls anyone civilized?

Where can the crying heart graze?
What does a true Arab do now?

Often, as in this poem, medium-lined free verse uses regular rhythm for extra effect, at the climax or in the last line. In "Blood," the last three lines fall into
a   strong,   incantatory   three-beat   rhythm: "WHO   calls   ANyone
CIVilized?/WHERE can the/CRYing heart GRAZE? / What DOES a true A-rab
do NOW?" (When listening for beats, remember that stress is relative; you may
hear beats on "heart," "true," and "now," but notice that they are lighter than the
capitalized beats. They add texture and slow down the line, but they don't cancel out the regularity of the pattern.)

George Herbert's poem above may be called **variable-lined free verse** because of the great variation in the length of the lines. Variable line free verse is
sometimes used for a whole poem, and sometimes just for certain passages that
make strong expressive use of the contrast between line-lengths, as in the following couplet:

From "Book of Isaiah," Anne Carson

There is a kind of pressure in humans to take whatever is most beloved by
    them and smash it.

Some of the most powerful variable-length free verse is strongly influenced by
jazz and has a kinetic, musical drive:

From "Boy Breaking Glass," Gwendolyn Brooks

A mistake.
A cliff.
A hymn, a snare, and an exceeding sun.

The best free verse is alert and conscious of the regular rhythm underlying
it, and keeps its head above the rhythmical water. This fluent passage by Audre
Lorde segues a dactylic rhythm at the opening of the first line into a trochaic
rhythm, which continues through the second line and into the third line, which
then emerges as a headless iambic pentameter:

From "Coal," Audre Lorde

Some words are open like a diamond
on glass windows
singing out within the crash of sun

This kind of tension against other meters is crucial when using iambic pentameter in a free verse poem; iambic pentameter is so hackneyed and familiar-
sounding that, inserted into prosy free verse without strong counterbalancing
rhythms, its presence (especially in the final line of a poem, where it is most
likely to appear) can add a smug, flaccid, or pedestrian quality to otherwise
good free verse.

A fifth common kind of free verse, called **open field** or **projective free
verse,** moves away from the line altogether. A subspecies of graphic poetry, this
kind of free verse takes the entire blank space of the page for a visual field, as in
this poem:

From "The Torso," Robert Duncan

At the axis of his mid hriff

the navel, for in the pit of his stomach the chord from
Which first he was fed has its temple

At the root of the groin

the pubic hair, for the torso is the stem in which the man
Flowers forth and leads to the stamen of flesh in which
His seed rises

A wave of need and desire over   taking me

Cried out my name

(This was long ago;   It was another life)

and said,

What do you want of me?

I do not know, I said.   I have fallen in love.   He
    Has brought me into heights and depths my heart
        would fear   without him.   His look

    pierces my side   fire eyes

I have been waiting for you, he said:
                    I know what you desire

    you do not know but through me

And I am with you everywhere.

Duncan's use of the page is almost three-dimensional, like a hologram: the visual and auditory elements work so seamlessly together that it is impossible to separate them, and the reader is drawn into entering the page on its own terms. The spacings themselves take on the character of words; for example, in the lines

I do not know, I said.   I have fallen in love.   He
    Has brought me into heights and depths my heart
        would fear   without him.   His look

the confusion and fear described in the first and third line are reflected in the spacings, contrasted with the confident beautiful surge of the second line, with its regular five-beat rhythm, and in the lines

I have been waiting for you, he said:
                    I know what you desire

Here the visual indentation makes the second line read subtly, quietly, as if in a visual depiction of an "undertone."

In the last few decades, open-field poetry has influenced all of free verse so that it is now not uncommon for poets such as Adrienne Rich, Jorie Graham, Frank Bidart, and Tim Seibles to use long spaces in the middle of a line, to arrange margins across the page, to move lines or bits of lines away from the rest of the poem, or otherwise to make free use of the full range of the page and the visual impacts of lines across it. Again, these techniques can add a dramatic visual and narrative dimension to a poem, in addition to the effect of the line breaks on the meanings of the words and lines. For example, in this passage, the short lines and staggering margin create multiple layers of meaning:

From "Sold," Linda Gregerson

"The delicious part," he said, is when
　　　I get her
　　to strip the bed. This is my opening

gambit: she's vacuumed the living room carpet
　　　with whatever
　　she's been using till now,

and I've run the Electrolux over it once and come up
　　　with a fistful
　　of dirt, God's truth—we use

white linen filters and she's watched
　　　me put
　　a new one in. The woman is amazed."

The lineation helps highlight certain phrases, creating a comical subtext alongside the vacuum cleaner sales story.

Prose Poems

Prose poems, our sixth type of free verse, are technically not free verse at all, since they don't use a break at the end of a line. Prose poems don't concern themselves with the line:

From "Before the next war," Susan Schultz

The worms make pieces. Washstand or wasteland, his life a loaded one.
　　Girls for guns (don't check statistics). Bag slung over his shoulder, he

runs awkwardly toward the orange or the red slide. Casualties kill war fever. *Watch out for the baby.* The language of Wall Street must more closely approximate ordinary language (if not its philosophy), he says. Builds a tower of legos and a plastic flower...

The lack of deliberate line breaks creates a relentlessness to this rush of prose. Much in these words feels like a lyric poem: the verbal interest, the clash of dictions, the amused attention to idiomatic language, and the high level of imagery. Some prose poems have a more clearly narrative coherence. This one is by Russell Edson, a writer who has referred to himself as "Little Mister Prose Poem" because of his consistent use of the form:

"You," Russell Edson

Out of nothing there comes a time called childhood, which is simply a
    path leading through an archway called adolescence. A small town
    there, past the arch called youth.
Soon, down the road, where one almost misses the life lived beyond the
    flower, is a small shack labeled, you.
And it is here the future lives in the several postures of arm on windowsill,
    cheek on this; elbows on knees, face in the hands; sometimes the
    head thrown back, eyes staring into the ceiling . . . This into nothing
    down the long day's arc

The last line of this prose poem is in iambic pentameter; like much free verse, many of Edson's prose poems achieve closure through the use of meter.

Unlike Edson's poem, which uses a meditative mood to unite its thoughts and images, this prose poem, originally published simultaneously in Japanese and English, is focused entirely on one image. The steady attention to one scene unites the text with remarkable focus and concentration.

"A field of fried umbrellas," Sawako Nakayasu

They are arranged so neatly that one wonders if there are small children
    beneath them, holding hands so as to keep the rows intact and the
    columns true, in spite of whatever kind of weather may come.

Enough fresh oil was used in the frying of these umbrellas that
theoretically they should repel any sort of fluid which takes a shot at
the field, and in fact this is true, but the unfortunate inherent shape
of the umbrella encourages the rain to slip inside the crevices
between one fried umbrella and another, getting the toes of the
children wet, whether they are there or not.

Because of the lack of line breaks, some writers classify prose poems as
"lyric prose," not as poetry. Lewis Turco makes such an argument in his *New
Book of Forms*. Yet those who write them usually insist they are poetry because
of their lyrical use of language. Some prose poems are structured by repeating
patterns in the numbers of sentences, a strategy evident in two classics of prose
poetry whose sections are too long to excerpt here: Ron Silliman's *Tjantjing*,
with numbers of sentences based on the numbers in the Fibonacci series, and
Lyn Hejinian's *My Life*, written in 37 sections of 37 sentences each when she was
37, and then revised into 45 sections of 45 lines each eight years later.

One also might see the repetition of the ending of the prose poem as a sort
of ultimate line break which happens once at the end of each prose poem and
serves as a repeating structural element. After all, some contemporary poetry
does not concern itself with endings at all; this is generally true of poems whose
written embodiments are considered to be transcripts of performances, such as
the poetry of David Antin. So the ending in a prose poem shouldn't be taken for
granted, and if you read a number of prose poems in a row, you begin to get a
sense for the repeating rhythm of what I call the "terminal hiatus" at the end of
each one. In my opinion, brief length, defined by the terminal hiatus, is what
distinguishes a "prose poem" from lyric prose.

The Line in Free Verse

As you will know if you are used to writing and/or reading free verse, a free
verse poem can slip into random prosiness if the line breaks are not carefully
varied and controlled—just as you will see that formal verse can slip into singsong doggerel if the meter is not carefully varied and controlled. The line breaks
in a free verse poem are the primary way that a poet determines pauses, tension,
and emphasis.

Notice how the line breaks can change the feeling of a phrase:

"To a Poor Old Woman," William Carlos Williams (1935)

munching a plum on
the street a paper bag
of them in her hand

They taste good to her
They taste good
to her. They taste
good to her

You can see it by
the way she gives herself
to the one half
sucked out in her hand

Comforted
a solace of ripe plums
seeming to fill the air
They taste good to her

On one level, the line breaks change the meaning of the phrase repeated in the second stanza; "they taste good to her" means what we would expect it to mean; "they taste good / to her" brings us more into the experience of the woman and emphasizes the taste; and "they taste / good to her" is almost a pun, as if the plums are being good to her, or doing her good, by tasting good. On another level that is harder to paraphrase, the line breaks also change the physical reaction we have to reading the words. In other words, line breaks create not only different kinds of meaning, but also different kinds of experience.

When you work on line breaks you become aware that, as Roethke is supposed to have said, "Each line in a poem must be a poem." This state of "poemness," this fullness or completeness to each line, can be achieved in innumerable ways in free verse. In this poem, the abrupt line breaks on "practicing," "old," and "Yusef" add a sort of deadpan humor:

"Breakfast with Naomi Ayala," E. Ethelbert Miller

I guess you'll eat your bagel
after I'm gone. Saturday morning
and we meet at Tryst on 18th street.
It's not my favorite place. Something
about it reminds me of South Africa
before Nelson Mandela started practicing
law. Every time I see you I write a poem.
It's like the sun never setting on the old
empire. I kiss you good-bye before the
check arrives. When I get home I'll
read something by Lucille Clifton or Yusef
Komunyakaa. I want to know what the
other poets are doing these days.

Or the line can play against the sentence for expressive or descriptive effect, in
a sort of syntax picture, as in this poem:

"Daybreak," Galway Kinnell

On the tidal mud, just before sunset,
dozens of starfishes
were creeping. It was
as though the mud were a sky
and enormous, imperfect stars
moved across it as slowly
as the actual stars cross heaven.
All at once they stopped,
and, as if they had simply
increased their receptivity
to gravity, they sank down
into the mud, faded down
into it and lay still, and by the time
pink of sunset broke across them
they were as invisible
as the true stars at daybreak.

When the starfish begin to sink into the mud in lines 9–13, the lines also begin to sink down through the poem. The heavy enjambment and the midline commas create a palpable effect of resistance and descent, which evens out into horizontal motion as the last three lines describe the streaks of the sunset.

The focus point of a free-verse line can be a returning (though not predictable) rhythm. Half of the lines in this poem have a five-beat rhythm:

"and where thou art I am," Diane DiPrima

astride the wind. or held
by two hoodlums under a starting truck.
crocheting in the attic.
striding forever out of the heart of quartz
immense, unhesitant, monotonous
as galaxies, or rain; or
lost cities of the dinosaurs now sunk
in the unopening rock.

who keeps the bats from flying in your window?
who rolls the words you drop back into seed?
                              who picks
sorrows like lice from your heart & cracks them
                              between her teeth?
who else blows down your chimney with the moon
scattering ashes from your dismal hearth to show
the sleeping Bird in the coals, or is it
garnet you lost?

                    What laughter spins you
    Around in the windy street?

Or the focus can be a surprising enjambment. This enjambment focuses not on a word, as in the Miller line breaks, but on a syntactical unit:

From "Homeless at Home," Gloria Frym

You wore half a smile and I
Wore the other.

The focus can be the impact of a word:

From "Our Bodies," Denise Levertov

a line or groove I love
runs down
my body from breastbone
to waist. It speaks of
eagerness, of
distance.

Almost every line here includes a word that anchors the line with vividness
or surprise, and the last line *is* such a word.

It can be a punch line, with visual as well as aural impact:

From "The Humming Birds," Lucinda Roy

There.
      It's yours.
            The key to me.

Go on.

Lick it.

Or a revelation:

From "Hardie," Tim Seibles

I was a child. You think I don't remember?!
You think it's easy keeping all this innocence pent up inside?!

Or each line of the poem can center on a new aspect of an image:

"Margaret Fuller," Lorine Niedecker

She carried books
and chrysanthemums

to Boston
into a cold storm.

Or a phrase full of repeating vowel and consonant sounds:

"Waking up in the Swamp," Sue Standing

Like the old blue sleigh
Up to its runners

In moss and hot, soft needles.

Or the repetition of a word in a fresh way:

From "Five Short Shorts," Hayden Carruth

Why speak of the use
of poetry? Poetry
is what uses us.

Or a dramatic role the line needs to play within the poem as a whole, as in the last line of the following poem:

"The Europeans," Robert Creeley

Or me wanting another man's
wife, etc.
        History.

Unable to keep straight
generations.

Telling them all about
myself.

Whether that identity arises on the meaning level, the visual level, or the sound level, every line in a free verse poem needs to have some reason for being a line. Line breaks can play against expectations; they can be used to emphasize a rhyme or repeating sound, or to mute it:

From "A," Heather McHugh

Partly
Fungal outburst, viral
Outburst, burst

Of life (what are
We turning
To? Remember, numbers
Brought to grief

Make greater grief, as surely as they make
Great names . . .

In this passage, the repeating words "burst" and "grief" are muted but present because of their position midline; imagine the difference in effect if they were repeated at the ends of the lines every time.

Line breaks have a strong effect on the way a reader perceives a poem's logic. A line break can enable the *line* to suggest something very different from the *sentence,* or even to contradict it.

From "Aubade," Kevin Young

There is little else
I love; the small

of yr back, yr thick
bottom

lip stuck out.

From "Lullaby," June Jordan

The evening burns a low
red
line occasional with golden glass
across the sky

On the other hand, sometimes the line breaks occur consistently at the end of sentences or phrases. This is particularly true of long-lined free verse, but it can also be an effective strategy for short-lined or variable line-length free verse:

"The Negro Speaks of Rivers," Langston Hughes (1921)

I've known rivers:
I've known rivers ancient as the world and older than the
    flow of human blood in human veins.

My soul has grown deep like the rivers.

I bathed in the Euphrates when dawns were young.
I built my hut near the Congo and it lulled me to sleep.
I looked upon the Nile and raised the pyramids above it.

I heard the singing of the Mississippi when Abe Lincoln
    went down to New Orleans, and I've seen its muddy
    bosom turn all golden in the sunset.

I've known rivers:
Ancient, dusky rivers.

My soul has grown deep like the rivers.

In this stanza, line breaks function instead of all the elements of punctuation: commas, periods, question marks, and quotation marks:

From "Native Trees," W. S. Merwin

Neither my father nor my mother knew
the names of the trees
where I was born
what is that
I asked and my
father and mother did not

hear they did not look where I pointed
surfaces of furniture held
the attention of their fingers
and across the room they could watch
walls they had forgotten
where there were no questions
no voices and no shade

A poem that always breaks in the middle of a sentence or phrase (enjambment) can create a sense of unbroken flow, or a sense of urgency. The excerpt from Auden's poem uses the broken phrase to create a sense of meditative urgency:

From "Musée des Beaux Arts," W. H. Auden (1938)

About suffering they were never wrong,
The Old Masters: how well, they understood
Its human position; how it takes place
While someone else is eating or opening a window or just walking dully
    along . . .

The poem below uses the same technique to create a sense of emotional urgency:

From "I Go Back to May 1937," Sharon Olds

I see my father strolling out
under the ochre sandstone arch, the
red tiles glinting like bent
plates of blood behind his head, I
see my mother with a few light books at her hip
standing at the pillar made of tiny bricks with the
wrought-iron gate still open behind her, its
sword-tips black in the May air,
they are about to graduate, they are about to get married . . .

And this excerpt uses the broken phrase to create a sense of narrative urgency:

From "Leda and the Cowboy," Luci Tapahonso

Even then, as they danced, the things he told her
Were fleeting. Leda smiled and a strange desperation
Engulfed him.

In the following poem, the technique of breaking the line in the middle of
a phrase is used only once, at the end of the middle stanza, where it creates a
poignant sense of resignation and sadness.

From "Isn't It Enough," Farideh Hassanzadeh

Night by night
more and more,
I feel real.

Like the bloody sound of alarms,
Like the roaring anti-aircraft rounds,
Like the falling bombs and rockets,
which turn the ruins and ashes
into eternal reality;
I feel night by night more real
and old,

so old and real that in the mirror
I see nothing anymore
but an aisle of empty chairs.

Especially after the self-contained line, "I feel real," the addition of the phrase
"and old" after the line break seems to be happening in the poet's mind at the
minute we are reading, giving it great urgency.

Sometimes it's mysterious what makes a line break work. I began writing
free-verse poems in the early 1970s, long before personal computers. Each time
I wanted to change a line break I would need to type my entire poem over to get
the full effect, but I rarely remember feeling it was a waste of time. It can be
hard for a poet to explain such choices; we may need to see it, hear it, almost
smell it—to weigh it physically—to decide where the line breaks should go.
Though you may not know exactly why or how, after some practice you will be-

gin to recognize a satisfying free verse line when you see it. Ideally, as said above, every line in your free verse poem should have some reason for being a line, whether that identity arises on the sound level, the meaning level, the visual level, or in some other way that is harder to pin down.

Rhythm in Free Verse

Some free verse is unabashedly rhythmic. The rhythm is sometimes created by the dynamic between lines, as in this poem:

"Tonight No Poetry Will Serve," Adrienne Rich

Saw you walking barefoot
taking a long look
at the new moon's eyelid
later spread
sleep-fallen, naked in your dark hair
asleep but not oblivious
of the unslept unsleeping
elsewhere

Tonight I think
no poetry
will serve

Syntax of rendition:

verb pilots the plane
adverb modifies action
verb force-feeds noun
submerges the subject
noun is choking
verb disgraced goes on doing

there are adjectives up for sale

now diagram the sentence

The parallelism of syntax and lines knits the poem together as it conveys the poet's grief, fury, and frustration over the context of war, in which she and the person addressed are living their lives.

Some passages of the most admired twentieth-century free verse, including sections of Yeats and of Elizabeth Bishop's wonderful "The Moose," included in chapter 2, on accent, have an even stronger rhythmic unity, with virtually the same number of strong accents in every line. Try reading them aloud and listen for stronger syllables. As you will see in chapter 7, technically these parts of the poems could work as accentual poetry:

From "Easter 1916," W. B. Yeats (1916)

Hearts with one purpose alone
Through summer and winter seem
Enchanted to a stone
To trouble the living stream.
The horse that comes from the road.
The rider, the birds that range
From cloud to tumbling cloud,
Minute by minute they change;
A shadow of cloud on the stream
Changes minute by minute;
A horse-hoof slides on the brim,
And a horse plashes within it;
The long-legged moor-hens dive,
And hens to moor-cocks call;
Minute by minute they live:
The stone's in the midst of all.

This regularity can work well in a particular passage, but generally when writing free verse, it is best to make sure you don't slip into any regular rhythm for very long. Save that for your accentual poetry. The best free verse is constantly aware of its own lack of predictability, discovering a unique rhythmic energy within each line, and never allowing itself to become comfortable with any shape or rhythm. The following passage by H.D. conveys, both in its rhythms and in its imagery, the excitement and the uncertainty, the sense of risk and even danger, of the most effective free verse:

From "The Walls Do Not Fall," H.D. (1944)

through doors twisted on hinges,
and the lintels slant

cross-wise;
we walk continually

on thin air
that thickens to a blind fog,

then step swiftly aside,
for even the air

is independable,
thick where it should be fine

and tenuous
where wings separate and open,

and the ether
is heavier than the floor,

and the floor sags
like a ship floundering;

we know no rule
of procedure,

we are voyagers, discoverers
of the not-known,

the unrecorded;
we have no map;

possibly we will reach haven,
heaven.

Since free verse often relies to an extra extent on imagery, and since it tries to defamiliarize familiar language with the most minimal tools, practicing free verse for a while can strengthen your eye for imagery and your ear for idiomatic diction even if you are committed to metrical poetry. On the other hand, if you are committed to free verse poetry, practicing meter will teach and strengthen your ear so you can create free verse rhythms that are alive and interesting. Many poets go through phases when they only want to write in free verse or periods when they only want to write in meter. Each of these phases can be good for your poetry and can help you write the other way. Writing free verse is an excellent way to understand what goes into writing a strong poetic line, whether that line is in free verse or meter.

QUESTIONS FOR MEDITATION OR DISCUSSION

Paul Lake claims in his essay "The Verse That Print Bred" that free verse is primarily a visual art. Do you agree or disagree? Here is one suggestion to deepen your thought on this question: Listen to a reading of free verse by the poet, or ask someone to read free verse aloud to you in a natural way, the way they would read it at a poetry reading. Mark down on a piece of paper each time you hear a line break (one simple way to do this is to write down the word just before the break). Then look at the text of the poem and compare the line breaks. How many of them did you hear correctly? How did you recognize them? Read some free verse of your own to someone else. Do they recognize your line breaks? Does it matter to you whether they can? Why or why not?

Ever since Ezra Pound talked about "breaking the pentameter," some people have felt that free verse posed a threat to metrical verse, or that metrical verse posed a threat to free verse, even though many poets write in both modes. Do you think there is any reason that one kind of poetry might threaten the other? Do you have an emotional response to the idea of free verse, or to the idea of metrical verse? If so, what experiences of yours do you think contributed to this feeling?

QUOTES

We believe that the individuality of a poet may often be better expressed in free-verse than in conventional forms.
    —Amy Lowell

I am not at all clear what free verse is anymore. That's one of the things you learn not to know.
   —Howard Nemerov

Free verse is *not* the poetic equivalent of "free parking" or "free beer" . . . [It] is still organized, like all poems, around technical constraints.
   —Michelle Boisseau

I could not use the long line because of my nervous nature.
   —William Carlos Williams

In sound and sense it is the music of inner relationships that moves me.
   —Robert Duncan

No verse is free for the man [*sic*] who wants to do a good job.
   —T. S. Eliot

POETRY PRACTICES

Group (Trading Breaks). Divide into pairs and trade free verse poems. Take 15 minutes to change each other's line breaks to be the way you would want them to be if it were your poem. Meet up again and discuss.

Self-Self-Portrait. Copy the following words, the text of a poem by Jane Hirshfield called "Late Self-Portrait by Rembrandt": "The dog, dead for years, keeps coming back in the dream. We look at each other there with the old joy. It was always her gift to bring me into the present—which sleeps, changes, awakens, dresses, leaves. Happiness and unhappiness differ as a bucket hammered from gold differs from one of pressed tin, this painting proposes. Each carries the same water, it says." Lineate the text into a free verse poem. Only after you are finished, look at Hirshfield's version. Write about what you learn from this experience.

Explorations in Free Verse. Take one of your free-verse poems and rewrite it several times, changing only the line breaks. Try it as long-line free verse, short-lined free verse, medium-lined free verse, variable-lined free verse, and open-field verse. Pick your favorite line breaks from each version and combine them into one favorite version. Try to justify each line break to yourself.

Free Verse Waves. Much free verse gains its power from repetition. Take one of your free verse poems and make it three times longer. Don't add any new words; just incorporate as many repetitions as you like of any of the words already in the poem.

Scroll. Write a contemplative poem in short-lined free verse and inscribe it by hand on a scroll. A rolled-up sheet of typing paper will do if you write it very nicely. Feel free to illustrate it if you like. For inspiration, look at haiku, the lyrics of William Carlos Williams, H.D.'s first book *Sea Garden,* and the work of George Oppen. Hang your scroll on your wall or present it to a friend.

End-Stop versus Enjambment. Write a poem with the line breaks at the ends of sentences or phrases, so that each line is completely self-contained. Now rewrite the poem with enjambment at the end of each line, so that it keeps you tumbling from line to line as you read. For ideas, look at some of Sharon Olds's poems with their breathless rush of line breaks. If you want to take it a little further, try using the "hinge" technique of Audre Lorde and Matthea Harvey.

Howl Redux. Write a public poem in long-lined free verse and read it aloud. For inspiration, look at Robinson Jeffers's "Shine, Perishing Republic" in chapter 1 or Whitman's "Crossing Brooklyn Ferry" in this chapter. For examples of free verse poems that have had public impact, you can look at Allen Ginsberg's "Howl," which caused a sensation when it was first read on October 7, 1955, and became a sort of anthem for the Beat generation. For more recent examples of public free verse, look at the longer-lined sections of Amiri Baraka's controversial "Somebody Blew Up America" and Maya Angelou's poem for Bill Clinton's inauguration, "On the Pulse of the Morning."

Embedding Rhyme. Write a poem including some rhymes that coincide with line breaks. Rewrite it so the rhymes are embedded within lines.

Line Break as Punctuation. Write a poem with no punctuation, using line breaks as the only clues to syntax. You might want to look at Merwin's "Native Trees" as a model. Then take one of your existing free verse poems that does use punctuation and simply remove the punctuation. Compare the two poems. Did writing without punctuation change the way you thought of the line?

CHAPTER 2

Hearing the Beat: Accent and Accentual Poetry

Hazrat Inayat Khan wrote that "motion is the significance of life, and the law of motion is rhythm." A metrical poem is a poem with a regular pattern of rhythm, and the heartbeat of rhythm underlies all patterns of regular poetic meter. Since accent is the basis of rhythm in English, accent forms the beat, the lifeblood of a metrical poem. As we have seen, even some of the best-known passages of free verse are written in accentual meter—in lines with a regular pattern of accents.

What is an accent? It is an essential part of language that we all use every day. Anyone can distinguish the identical-looking noun and verb in these two sentences: "If you love this old record, then record it." "A desert is a bad place to desert someone." If you understand English, you can easily understand the difference in accent between the words; moreover, you rely on those accents for meaning.

Accent (marked / in many dictionaries and when marking poems, and sometimes signified with capital letters) is a technical term for stress or emphasis. The way accents are placed on certain syllables and not others as we speak is central to our understanding of everyday English. Say THIS sentENCe with THE acCENTS in unusUal placES. If you put the accents on the wrong syllables when you speak, it will sound as if you are not familiar with the language, as if you have a foreign "accent."

Although pauses and the lengths of syllables play a part in rhythm, accent is the most pervasive and clearest aspect of rhythm in English. The pattern of accents in a word or phrase speaks to our body, not just our mind. You can test this idea by thinking about the accented and unaccented syllables of your name. Notice how intimate and familiar you are with your name's accentual pattern, how it feels when you say it. Try changing it on purpose; instead of "maHALia JACKson," say "MA-halia jackSON." Notice how strange it sounds and feels.

With the aid of computers, linguists have isolated three elements that go into making a syllable sound accented. Stop reading for a minute and guess what they might be. You may have guessed loudness. That's one of them. The second is the length of the syllable—how long it takes to pronounce it. If you stretch out the time it takes to say a syllable, you will emphasize it even if you don't say it any louder than the other syllables in the sentence; try it and see. The final element is pitch: how high or low the syllable sounds compared to other syllables in the word (for example, syllables containing the sound "ee" sound higher-pitched than syllables containing the sound "uh," so "beet" sounds more accented than "but" in the phrase "but I like beets!"). Accent can be created by any of these three factors—loudness, length, and pitch—or by any combination of them, depending on the speaker and the situation.

When you start listening to the accents in a sentence or line of poetry, you may notice that some accented syllables have bigger accents than others. After all, all syllables have some accent; if they didn't, we couldn't hear them. One trick for telling which syllable has the strongest accent is to hold the back of your hand under your chin while saying the word (it helps to say the word loudly). When your chin drops the lowest, that's the most strongly accented syllable.

How to Hear Accent

When you first become aware of hearing accents, it is easy to get nervous or confused about which syllable is actually carrying the accent. Here are some handy tricks to help figure out where an accent belongs. If you ever find yourself at a loss, try these, in this order:

1. When confused by which syllable to accent in a word, use my method of "reverse exaggeration": say a two-syllable word aloud to yourself, whispering one syllable and practically shouting the other so that there is a strong contrast. Then try the other way. Which sounds right?
2. Try the "single-syllable shout method," developed by Jessica Piazza: "Imagine you are trying to convey a word to someone across a room, but are forbidden to shout more than ONE syllable of the word at a time. Which syllable would you shout? . . . For example, try it with the word 'meter.' When you must shout only one syllable, you get either 'MEEE-ter'—which sounds pretty good or 'me-TEEER' which sounds pretty awkward. You can see, in this case, that the first syllable is the stressed one. . . . If two syllables sound right, chances are they aren't

next to each other, and both might hold a stress in the word. Trying the shout method on the word 'enemy,' for example, you'll find that shouting the first AND third syllables will both sound somewhat right—at least a whole lot better than shouting the second."

3. Insert the word or phrase into regular speech: if you are confused by the accent on "planet" in Keats's lines "Then felt I like some watcher of the skies / when a new planet swims into his ken," instead try saying, "I went to the planetarium to see a show about planets." (Thanks to Karrie Waarala for this idea.)

4. Get a few people to say the word aloud with you in unison. The group will exaggerate the difference between the stressed and unstressed syllables. If none of these works, try the reverse exaggeration or single-syllable shout method as a group! Look the word up in a dictionary to check your answer. The stressed syllable will have an accent mark.

Certain linguists mark every syllable in a line of poetry on a scale of 1 to 4. While it can help you appreciate the beauty of a line to notice so many levels of accent, it can also become confusing. Don't let yourself get too distracted. Sometimes I imagine a line of poetry as a riverbed full of rocks of different sizes. All of the syllables, like all of the rocks, have height, but some are higher than others. Once your ear decides where the water level is, you will know that any syllables that rise above that particular level are thought of as "accented," and those underwater are not. It doesn't mean they have no accent, but for our purposes, we can consider the smaller rocks that are hidden under the water as unaccented (and if you find that *all* the syllables in a line seem accented to you, just imagine that it rains for a while and the water rises till only the highest of them are showing). Generally, any word of two syllables will have one stressed syllable; words of four syllables will have two. Among one-syllable words, more important words—nouns, verbs, adjectives, or adverbs—tend to be stressed, as in "Jack and Jill went up the hill / to fetch a pail of water."

Accentual poetry is poetry that has a regular pattern of accents in every line. Much of the first poetry we learn as children is accentual: "Janey and Johnny, up in a tree,/ K-I-S-S-I-N-G./ First comes love, then comes marriage, / then comes Johnny with a baby carriage." "MY mother SAYS to PICK the VEry best ONE and YOU are NOT it." Sometimes your ear will tell you that a syllable in a line of poetry is accented or not accented, but your mind will try to talk you out of it.

You may find it hard to believe that a tiny part of a word, like the suffix *-ly*, or an insignificant word, like "and," can be accented. No matter what your mind says, always trust your ear. One way accentual poems work is by playing against our expectations of where the accent should fall. (The scholar of accentual poetry Derek Attridge uses the helpful terms "promotion" and "demotion" to describe what happens when a stress falls on an unexpected syllable, or doesn't fall on an expected syllable.) A helpful principle to keep in mind is that *stress is relative:* a stressed syllable is considered to be one with more emphasis than the syllables around it. For example, the word "and" is unstressed in George Herbert's line "my HAND was NEXT to THEM, and THEN my HEART," where it falls between two heavier syllables. But in Emily Dickinson's line "The ADmirAtions AND conTEMPTS of TIME, "and" is stressed, because it falls between two lighter syllables.

In poetry there are three ways that a syllable can be accented. *Lexical accent* is what is marked in the dictionary; every word of two syllables or more has a lexical accent that never changes. With words of one syllable, other factors come into play. *Phrasal accent* is created by a grammatical situation, where more important words (usually nouns and verbs) are accented more: "house" is stressed more than "to the" in the sentence: "I RUN to the HOUSE." *Performative accent* is created by the speaker's meaning and can override normal phrasal stress: "She lives in the GREEN house, not the blue one!" Because of performative accent, the same syllable can be accented if you mean one thing ("I SAID, get over here!") but not in others ("I said, get over HERE!"). As you'll see in later chapters, metrical poetry has the ability to control exactly how performative accent falls—a marvelous capacity unique to metrical poetry among all types of literature.

Accent and Emotion

If you heard someone saying, "I SAID, get over here!" and couldn't hear the words, your body might tense up anyway, simply from the physical recognition of anger in the accentual patterns. Because of this direct, emotional line of communication to our bodies, accentual patterns are one of poetry's most potentially powerful tools. Children and crowds, perhaps because they are not very interested in reason, are particularly attuned to this bodily aspect of poetry. Nursery rhymes, jump rope songs, teasing songs, and childhood poems are usually composed in a rhythm based on accents, as are the slogans chanted during political rallies. Though it is impossible to isolate accentual patterns entirely from the way a poem is performed, we can hear how different accentual patterns soothe, incite, or cause anxiety. The staccato rhythm of the antiwar chant "Hell, no! We won't go!" in which every single syllable is accented, raises defiant energy. The quick, frantic rhythm of "Baby, baby, stick your head in gravy" causes anxiety. The civil rights slogan "We shall overcome" has a "falling rhythm," progressing more slowly from accented to nonaccented syllables; even without its traditional rolling melody, this pattern of accents sounds both peaceful and persistent. Poems built on these powerful kinds of accent-based rhythm are known as accentual poems.

If we think of language as made up of syllables, some of them accented and some not, and we want to make countable, repeatable, easy-to-remember patterns out of these syllables as we turn them into lines of poetry, there are three choices. We could choose patterns based on the number of accents, the number of syllables, or a combination of the two. And in fact, these are the three basic systems of poetic lines, or meter, that can be found in English: accentual meter, syllabic meter, and accentual-syllabic meter. We'll take up accentual-syllabic poetry—it's the most common metered poetry in English—in the next few chapters, but first we will discuss the others.

Syllabic Poetry

Syllabic poetry is based on a consistent number of syllables in each line, without any regard to accent. This is the main organizing principle of poetry in French, Italian, and other Romance languages. But in English, no well-known poet has used this system predominantly except Marianne Moore:

"She Trimmed the Candles Like One Who Loves the Beautiful," Marianne Moore (1917)

It was right that such light
    As there was in the room should burn before her. She
Made me think of Diana—monkeys and penguins and white

Bears and herons: of wood
    Covered ravines cut by waterfalls, of mountains
With streaks of white smoke across them, of knife blades set in good

> Syllabic poetry is poetry with lines that follow a repeating pattern of syllables.

African ivory
    Hafts: of white and blue foxes on the confines of
The icy sea." But when she spoke of externality

She flouted it and called
    Good looks, mortality decked out in circumstance:
She said: You speak of death and are respectfully appalled.

Things that one can suffer
    Without the appearance of a surface scratch, put
Dying far away. Death is not unique in character:

Always overrated,
    It is a needful happening like lighting these—
Or like reiterating to the deaf what has been said.

Moore's typical syllabic practice, which we can call "corresponding syllabics," matches up each stanza to the same template: there are a certain number of syllables in each of the first lines, a certain number in each of the second lines, and so on. The combination of syllabic consistency and regularly indented lines lends a ceremonial quality to this poem. Unlike an accentual pattern, evident primarily to the ear and transcribed onto the page as an afterthought, a syllabic pattern becomes evident during the process of reading on the page. Because its form is so dependent on the reader's interpretative process, corresponding syllabics conveys the cryptic quality of a secret language. This almost ironic, literary type of meter is well suited to Moore's refined musings on an object in a museum. On the other hand, poems like Dylan Thomas's "Fern Hill" and "Poem in October," also written in corresponding syllabics, are very much poems for the ear; in these poems, the syllabic pattern structures the strong rhythms and intense word-music while keeping it from becoming *too* lush and predictable.

"Fern Hill," Dylan Thomas (1946)

Now as I was young and easy under the apple boughs
About the lilting house and happy as the grass was green,
The night above the dingle starry,
Time let me hail and climb
Golden in the heydays of his eyes,
And honoured among wagons I was prince of the apple towns
And once below a time I lordly had the trees and leaves
Trail with daisies and barley
Down the rivers of the windfall light.

And as I was green and carefree, famous among the barns
About the happy yard and singing as the farm was home,
In the sun that is young once only,
Time let me play and be
Golden in the mercy of his means,
And green and golden I was huntsman and herdsman, the calves
Sang to my horn, the foxes on the hills barked clear and cold,
And the sabbath rang slowly
In the pebbles of the holy streams.

All the sun long it was running, it was lovely, the hay
Fields high as the house, the tunes from the chimneys, it was air
And playing, lovely and watery
And fire green as grass.
And nightly under the simple stars
As I rode to sleep the owls were bearing the farm away,
All the moon long I heard, blessed among stables, the nightjars
Flying with the ricks, and the horses
Flashing into the dark.

And then to awake, and the farm, like a wanderer white
With the dew, come back, the cock on his shoulder: it was all
Shining, it was Adam and maiden,
The sky gathered again
And the sun grew round that very day.

So it must have been after the birth of the simple light
In the first, spinning place, the spellbound horses walking warm
Out of the whinnying green stable
On to the fields of praise.

And honoured among foxes and pheasants by the gay house
Under the new made clouds and happy as the heart was long,
In the sun born over and over,
I ran my heedless ways,
My wishes raced through the house high hay
And nothing I cared, at my sky blue trades, that time allows
In all his tuneful turning so few and such morning songs
Before the children green and golden
Follow him out of grace.

Nothing I cared, in the lamb white days, that time would take me
Up to the swallow thronged loft by the shadow of my hand,
In the moon that is always rising,
Nor that riding to sleep
I should hear him fly with the high fields
And wake to the farm forever fled from the childless land.
Oh as I was young and easy in the mercy of his means,
Time held me green and dying
Though I sang in my chains like the sea.

Another type of syllabic poem uses the same number of syllables in every line:

"The Thin Man," Donald Justice

I indulge myself
In rich refusals.
Nothing suffices.
I hone myself to
This edge. Asleep, I
Am a horizon.

This appropriately thin poem about renunciation builds interest in part by re-
nouncing any audible pattern (until the last line). Each line is different; only

lines 2 and 6 have the same pattern of word lengths, and even that is counter-balanced by a difference in the stress patterns of the first two syllables (the accent on the second syllable of "in rich" and on the first syllable of "am a"). Though the rhythms until the end are deliberately prosy, the last line achieves closure in part by adhering to the well-known rhythm of the adonic line, described in chapter 7, "Stanzas."

The following poem uses syllabics to keep a narrative thrust going, the 11-syllable lines like half-noticed signposts as the story moves along past them:

"Zinc Fingers," Peter Meinke

Though scientists inform us that criminals
have insufficient zinc I've always believed
it's insufficient gold and silver that gets
them going. The man who slipped his hand into
my front pocket on the jammed Paris Metro
wasn't trying to make friends. His overcoat
smelled greasy and it was unpleasant holding
hands above my wallet pressed in on all sides
like stacked baguettes. There was no way to move or
take a swing. Still some action on my part seemed
to be called for. We stood nose to nose. I tried
to look in his eyes but he stared at my chin
shy on our first date so after a while as
we rattled along toward the Champs-Elysees

I lost concentration and began to think

of our scholarly daughter working at Yale
on a project called Zinc Fingers scanning a
protein with pseudopods each with a trace of
zinc that latch onto our DNA and help
determine what we become. This brought me back
to *mon ami* the pickpocket. I wondered
how he chose his hard line of work and if as
a boy he was good at cards for example
or sewing and for that matter what choice did
I have either so when we reached our stop and

he looked up from my chin at last I smiled at
him and his eyes flashed in fear or surprise and
I called *It's OK* as he scuttled away
Tout va bien! though I held tight to my wallet

Though every line has 11 syllables, this poem reads like free verse until you start counting the syllables. As a result, the poem achieves a subtler kind of control than the audible obviousness of accentual or accentual-syllabic meter would allow. The poet has written about the composition of this poem, "One advantage of syllabic poetry is that it's kind of a regulated free verse, giving some shape but still being pretty loose." Balancing between these two forces, syllabic verse can achieve an intriguing tension.

When writing syllabic verse, one of the most important things to keep in mind is to avoid falling into accentual-syllabic meter. For this reason, it is a good idea to use an irregular number of syllables in each line. If Meinke had used ten rather than eleven syllables, it would have been much harder for him to avoid distracting readers with accidental meter.

Accentual Poetry

While syllabic poetry in English is an arcane practice, carried out consciously by sophisticated poets in relatively recent times, accentual poems have been composed in English since the beginning of the spoken language. **Accentual poetry** is the most common form for folk poetry, popular poetry, and poetry meant to be heard not read. This makes sense, because the nature of each poetic meter is closely related to its language. Accent is an important feature of English, as it is of all Germanic-based languages.

An accentual poem can have any number of syllables per line, but it must have the same number of accents in each line. Unlike syllabic poetry, which can vary the number of syllables in each line of a stanza as long as it keeps to a pattern, accentual poetry works best if each line has a predictable number of accents. It would be confusing to have a "corresponding accentual" poem, because accent patterns are *alive* in a way that syllabic patterns are not; they can sound different in different contexts, and the pattern of one line influences the way we hear the next line. (That's why a lot of people emphasize the last syllable of "water" when they hear "Jack and Jill went up the hill / to fetch a pail of water.")

Legend says the poem below was written by comedian Gilda Radner for an early episode of *Saturday Night Live.* Childish and exaggerated, it is a perfect choice of theme for an accentual poem:

"Jeans," Roseanne Roseannadanna (Gilda Radner)

Jeans jeans the magical pants	(seven syllables)
the more they itch the more you dance	(eight syllables)
the more you dance the more people watch	(nine syllables)
to see how you scratch that itch in your crotch.	(ten syllables)

Can you hear the four strong accents in each line? Accents override the differences in the number of syllables. Maneuvering through this tension is part of the fun of hearing accentual poetry.

Accentual poems in English predate writing. In fact, accentual meter may be thought of as our earliest form of communicative technology, because it is designed, at least in part, to make it possible to remember poems that could take days to recite, such as the epic poem *Beowulf.* "The Seafarer," below, is another long accentual poem, first written down in A.D. 950 but probably composed earlier as an oral poem. Like *Beowulf* and much other Anglo-Saxon poetry, it was composed in **accentual alliterative verse.**

The term **alliteration** means that a sound or cluster of sounds is repeated at the beginning of two or more words of a line (track and true, sob and sea). So in accentual alliterative verse each line has the same number of accents, and alliteration links two or more of the stressed syllables. The alliteration may work along with the accentual pattern to make the poem easier to memorize. Although accentual alliterative poems can have any number of accents per line, the most common number is four, as in the poem below. The layout of the poem reflects the **medial pause** that divides each line of this kind of poem in half. Notice how the alliterations link the two halves in the Anglo-Saxon.

"The Seafarer" (ninth century AD), trans. Annie Finch

MÆG ic be me sylfum	soðgied wrecan
siþas secgan	hu ic geswincdagum
earfoðwile	oft þrowade
bitre breostceare	gebidan hæbbe
gecunnad in ceole	cearselda fela

atol yþa gewealc	þær mec oft bigeat
nearo nihtwaco	æt nacan stefnan
þonne he be clifan cnossað	calde geþrungen
wæron mine fet	forste gebunden
caldum clommum	þær þa ceare seofedun
hate ymb heortan	hungor innan slat
merewerges mod	

From "The Seafarer" (ninth century A.D.) (trans. Annie Finch)

I keep the track	of a song true of me,
to tell of trials,	struggling times,
hard days,	how I endured.
I have carried	bitter cares,
had on ships	a house of cares;
terrible sea-waves	tossed when I kept
narrowed watches	on the stern at night
and the ship thrust at cliffs.	Thronged in cold
were my feet,	bound in frost,
with chains of cold,	while hunger cut
my ocean-weary mood.	

The strength and simplicity of the accentual pattern gives the poem an air of inevitability and dignity. The fittingness of that feeling to the poem's themes, of loneliness and courage in exile, may be the reason this remains one of the most-loved poems of the Anglo-Saxon era.

Most more recent accentual poems rely on a regular accentual pattern, but without alliteration. Rap poetry is composed in an accentual pattern, often with some lines linked together by rhyme:

From "Respiration," Mos Def

This ain't no time where the usual is suitable
Tonight alive, let's describe the inscrutable
The indisputable, we New York the narcotic
Strength in metal and fiber optics
where mercenaries is paid to trade hot stock tips

for profits, thirsty criminals take pockets
Hard knuckles on the second hands of workin' class watches
Skyscrapers is colossus, the cost of living
is preposterous, stay alive, you play or die, no options
No Batman and Robin, can't tell between
the cops and the robbers, they both partners, they all heartless
With no conscience, back streets stay darkened
Where unbeliever hearts stay hardened
My eagle talons stay sharpened, like city lights stay throbbin'
You either make a way or stay sobbin', the Shiny Apple
is bruised but sweet and if you choose to eat
You could lose your teeth, many crews retreat
Nightly news repeat, who got shot down and locked down
Spotlight to savages, NASDAQ averages
My narrative, rose to explain this existence
Amidst the harbor lights which remain in the distance

So much on my mind that it can't recline
Blastin' holes in the night 'til she bled sunshine
Breathe in, inhale vapors from bright stars that shine
Breathe out, weed smoke retrace the skyline
Heard the bass ride out like an ancient mating call
I can't take it y'all, I can feel the city breathin'
Chest heavin', against the flesh of the evening
Sigh before we die like the last train leaving . . .

Almost all the lines have four beats, with a few exceptions for emphasis and variety. Since the lines vary in length from 9 syllables (STRENGTH in METal and FIBer optics) to 15 syllables (my EAGle talons stay SHARPened, like CITy lights stay THROBbing), it can take intense energy to rap out the beat on the longer lines. The more strong syllables, like "lights" or the "tal" in "talons," need to be overridden, the more tension the rapping voice needs to resolve. A rap poem is meant to be performed, and the performance helps to manifest the poem's form.

Rap is often improvised and uses some of the same composition techniques as ancient oral poetry, including the accentual beat, word-music such as alliteration to hold the poem tighter together, and a technique called a **formula,** which is a piece of language the poet has used before, one that already fits the poem's accentual pattern and can be inserted as necessary. Repetition of phrases allows improvisation to gather steam. Rhyme emphasizes the connections between lines and provides markers that remind your ear of the poem's overall progression. I have heard rap poets make up brilliant raps on the spur of the moment using these techniques.

When writing a rap or rap-influenced poem, it's important to keep in mind that sometimes what works in performance may not work well on the page—and vice versa. Poems that perform well generally keep a strong sense of the line breaks. Their language is direct and their emotional mood clear. They work especially well when they build to a particular dramatic point in the poem that allows you to really let loose as a climax to your performance. Reading aloud as you go will help you do a better job with writing *any* kind of poetry, but with rap and other performance poetry, of course, it is an absolute must. For a poem to work well on the page, it also needs a certain amount of subtlety and complexity. The best poems, like many in this book, have always worked well both on *and* off the page.

Dramatically effective free verse often gains some of its power from passages with a strong, regularly accented rhythm, basically identical to accentual poetry:

"The Moose," Elizabeth Bishop

For Grace Bulmer Bowers

From narrow provinces
of fish and bread and tea,
home of the long tides
where the bay leaves the sea
twice a day and takes
the herrings long rides,

where if the river
enters or retreats
in a wall of brown foam
depends on if it meets
the bay coming in,
the bay not at home;

where, silted red,
sometimes the sun sets
facing a red sea,
and others, veins the flats'
lavender, rich mud
in burning rivulets;

on red, gravelly roads,
down rows of sugar maples,
past clapboard farmhouses
and neat, clapboard churches,
bleached, ridged as clamshells,
past twin silver birches,

through late afternoon
a bus journeys west,
the windshield flashing pink,
pink glancing off of metal,
brushing the dented flank
of blue, beat-up enamel;

down hollows, up rises,
and waits, patient, while
a lone traveller gives
kisses and embraces
to seven relatives
and a collie supervises.

Goodbye to the elms,
to the farm, to the dog.
The bus starts. The light
grows richer; the fog,
shifting, salty, thin,
comes closing in.

Its cold, round crystals
form and slide and settle

in the white hens' feathers,
in gray glazed cabbages,
on the cabbage roses
and lupins like apostles;

the sweet peas cling
to their wet white string
on the whitewashed fences;
bumblebees creep
inside the foxgloves,
and evening commences.

One stop at Bass River.
Then the Economies—
Lower, Middle, Upper;
Five Islands, Five Houses,
where a woman shakes a tablecloth
out after supper.

A pale flickering. Gone.
The Tantramar marshes
and the smell of salt hay.
An iron bridge trembles
and a loose plank rattles
but doesn't give way.

On the left, a red light
swims through the dark:
a ship's port lantern.
Two rubber boots show,
illuminated, solemn.
A dog gives one bark.

A woman climbs in
with two market bags,
brisk, freckled, elderly.
"A grand night. Yes, sir,

all the way to Boston."
She regards us amicably.

Moonlight as we enter
the New Brunswick woods,
hairy, scratchy, splintery;
moonlight and mist
caught in them like lamb's wool
on bushes in a pasture.

The passengers lie back.
Snores. Some long sighs.
A dreamy divagation
begins in the night,
a gentle, auditory,
slow hallucination. . . .

In the creakings and noises,
an old conversation
—not concerning us,
but recognizable, somewhere,
back in the bus:
Grandparents' voices

uninterruptedly
talking, in Eternity:
names being mentioned,
things cleared up finally;
what he said, what she said,
who got pensioned;

deaths, deaths and sicknesses;
the year he remarried;
the year (something) happened.
She died in childbirth.
That was the son lost
when the schooner foundered.

He took to drink. Yes.
She went to the bad.
When Amos began to pray
even in the store and
finally the family had
to put him away.

"Yes . . ." that peculiar
affirmative. "Yes . . ."
A sharp, indrawn breath,
half groan, half acceptance,
that means "Life's like that.
We know *it* (also death)."

Talking the way they talked
in the old featherbed,
peacefully, on and on,
dim lamplight in the hall,
down in the kitchen, the dog
tucked in her shawl.

Now, it's all right now
even to fall asleep
just as on all those nights.
—Suddenly the bus driver
stops with a jolt,
turns off his lights.

A moose has come out of
the impenetrable wood
and stands there, looms, rather,
in the middle of the road.
It approaches; it sniffs at
the bus's hot hood.

Towering, antlerless,
high as a church,
homely as a house

(or, safe as houses).
A man's voice assures us
"Perfectly harmless. . . .",

Some of the passengers
exclaim in whispers,
childishly, softly,
"Sure are big creatures."
"It's awful plain."
"Look! It's a she!"

Taking her time,
she looks the bus over,
grand, otherworldly.
Why, why do we feel
(we all feel) this sweet
sensation of joy?

"Curious creatures,"
says our quiet driver,
rolling his r's.
"Look at that, would you."
Then he shifts gears.
For a moment longer,

by craning backward,
the moose can be seen
on the moonlit macadam;
then there's a dim
smell of moose, an acrid
smell of gasoline.

The long, thin jolt of the lines toward and away from their core of three accents reminds us of the jolt of the bus through the night. Much of the mystery of this poem comes from its rhythm, which creates an ongoing basic template of time and darkness along which the brief, illuminated described occurrences come and go.

While it's fun to focus on the hypnotic intensity of much accentual poetry, some poems use accentual prosody in a subtler way:

"Famine," Landis Everson

In the middle of the night at least twenty deer
Came out upon my pillow to graze,
Gazing down at me with sad, round eyes,
Their pointed hooves quilting my pillow.

And I thrashed gently in sleeplessness,
Moving not to disturb them, wondering
At the famine this year that forces so many
To roam to poor, unfamiliar pastures.

The moon through the window throws cold light
Upon their curved backs, making a forest
Of crossed antler shadows on sheets
That until now have been flawless and starved.

Rather than forcing the accent to fall in a certain place, this poem allows it to hover over the words. The poem is too prosodically delicate to commit to any meter, yet it is a formal poem, with the same number of accents in every line, and so it is accentual almost by default, without the rocking, forward drive that underlies most accentual poems.

By contrast, these two lines from a free-verse poem each have four strongly perceptible accents, though they have very different rhythmic patterns and numbers of syllables:

From "The Girlfriends," Elizabeth Woody

Filled with old lovers, in the clutch of the chair,
you are a bloom of uncombed hair.

As you read accentual poems, you may notice that sometimes the rhythm makes you not stress words you normally would stress (such as "old" in Woody's poem above) and stress words you normally wouldn't stress (such as "to" in the third line of the Yeats passage below). That is normal, and part of the power and fun of accentual poetry. You may also notice that you and others may not always agree on which syllables are stressed. That is also normal. Sometimes these disagreements arise from regional or generational differences in speech. Probably you will agree on the basic number of syllables per line, and on how most of the lines in the poem work. But hearing accents is not a completely exact science. That's okay. A disagreement here and there doesn't invalidate the entire system of meter; it just means that there are a few places where people hear things differently. When in doubt, just shrug, read aloud, don't think too much, trust your ear and your body, read aloud again, and remember to enjoy—after all, the point of understanding poetry's rhythms is to enjoy poetry more.

Scanning Exercises. Read the following passages aloud (reading aloud under your breath is ok if necessary). As you read, mark a little accent mark (´) with a pencil over the places where you notice an accent. When in doubt about a particular syllable, just write a quick question mark and move on, following your body's response to the words:

From "Easter 1916," W. B. Yeats (1916)

Hearts with one purpose alone
Through summer and winter seem
Enchanted to a stone
To trouble the living stream.
The horse that comes from the road,
The rider, the birds that range
From cloud to tumbling cloud,
Minute by minute they change;
A shadow of cloud on the stream
Changes minute by minute;
A horse-hoof slides on the brim,
And a horse plashes within it;
The long-legged moor-hens dive,
And hens to moor-cocks call;
Minute by minute they live:
The stone's in the midst of all.

Each of these lines has three accents. The number of syllables varies from six to eight; though the number doesn't vary as widely as in the rap poem, the order and pattern of accents and syllables still changes greatly from line to line. The result is a chant-like, mesmerizing feeling, as if the rhythmic pattern, like the stone, is so strong that it withstands any syllabic obstacles in its way.

QUESTIONS FOR MEDITATION OR DISCUSSION

Many of the most memorable accentual poems are written for children, and there is much that such poems can teach us about how accentual meter works. Mark the rhythmical pattern in the three children's poems below by putting an accent mark over each syllable you think is accented. Remember that *accent is relative*. The lines may have lots of stresses. You don't need to mark every stress; just mark the strongest ones. If you read the poem aloud, it will help you to "get in the groove." Then you can check your scansion against the ones in the back of the book.

"Up the Tallest Tree," Annie Finch and Althea Finch-Brand (on the model of the children's book Chicka Chicka Boom Boom!*)*

I told you and you told me,
I'll meet you at the top of the tallest tree.
So we climbed and we climbed till we could see
The highest mountain and the deepest sea.
Rat a tat a tat tat!
What do you think of that!

"From a Railway Carriage," Robert Louis Stevenson (1913)

Faster than fairies, faster than witches,
Bridges and houses, hedges and ditches;
And charging along like troops in a battle
All through the meadows the horses and cattle:
All of the sights of the hill and the plain
Fly as thick as driving rain;
And ever again, in the wink of an eye,
Painted stations whistle by.

Here is a child who clambers and scrambles,
All by himself and gathering brambles;
Here is a tramp who stands and gazes;
And here is the green for stringing the daisies!
Here is a cart runaway in the road
Lumping along with man and load;
And here is a mill, and there is a river:
Each a glimpse and gone forever!

Scottish proverb, Anonymous, ca. 1726

If wishes were horses, beggars would ride.
If turnips were watches, I would wear one by my side.
And if "ifs" and "an's" were pots and pans,
There'd be no work for tinkers' hands.

QUOTES

Limitations are a form of understanding, and we should not so easily treat them as stop signs. A limitation is often like the pivot point for a pole-vaulter. It is that place you hope to put down your pole, but only so that it will carry you up, much higher and farther than where the pole has stopped, so long as you have run fast and far enough to make this confrontation work.
   —Alberto Rios

All is a procession,
The universe is a procession with measured and perfect motion.
   —Walt Whitman

Words in themselves do not convey meaning . . . let us take the example of two people who are talking on the other side of a closed door whose voices can be heard but whose words cannot be distinguished. Even though the words do not carry, the sound of them does, and the listener can catch the meaning of the conversation.
   —Robert Frost

A poem with a strong accentual meter . . . can be "heard" as a poem even if it is printed out as prose.
—Marilyn Hacker

POETRY PRACTICES

Group (Electropoetrygram). While one person reads aloud a text of prose or poetry, someone else graphs it on the board like an electrocardiogram, marking the "highs" of intensity and the "lows." (Based on Alan Zeigler, *The Writing Workshop.*)

Group (Power Marking). Read aloud a free-verse poem to a partner while they mark the accents they hear in each line. Switch places. Do you hear any regularly recurring accents? Solo variation: Make an audio recording of one of your free-verse poems. Play it back several times, listening for and marking the patterns of the accents.

Accentual Poem. Write a poem of at least 20 lines that has the same number of accents in each line. The poem should not fall into a regular, "singsong" meter; instead, the accents should dominate the syllables—as in a rap poem. In other words, the poem should not necessarily have the same number of syllables in each line the way a metrical poem does. Accentual poetry is basically an oral form. Try yours out by reading it aloud to a friend or roommate, and see if they can hear how many accents are in each line.

Shape-shifting: Syllabic to Accentual. Write a poem of at least 12 lines with the same number of syllables in each line. Then revise it into an accentual poem. How does your poem change?

Song Stanzas. Think of a song you know by heart that has a strong beat. Make up two new stanzas of your own for the song without writing them down until they're finished. Sing them to a friend.

Symbolic Syllables. Write a poem in corresponding syllabics in which each line has a number of syllables that is meaningful to you in some way. Maybe the numbers tell a story, like your birth month followed by the age you were when you moved, followed by your lucky number. See if you can weave awareness of these numbers into your lines.

Make Your Own Nursery Rhyme. Think of a short poem from the oral tradition (maybe a nursery rhyme or playground rhyme), preferably one you know by heart with a rhythm that you enjoy. Say it aloud several times in a row. (*a*) Use that rhythmic momentum to help you compose a new poem in the exact same pattern of accents and syllables. The words don't have to make any sense at all (it's fine to write nonsense like, "hats are green and make a tax, winter wakes us on our backs"); all that matters here is accentual sense. As with the song, try to compose two stanzas *before* you copy it down. If it rhymes, feel free to use the original rhyme pattern or discard it. (*b*) Check the accentual pattern by marking the accents and counting the syllables in both your poem and the original to see if they match up. (*c*) Write a few more "stanzas" in the same pattern. (*d*) Revise to make more sense, if you want to.

Being Beowulf. Write a poem in accentual-alliterative meter of at least 12 lines. Don't forget to include the medial pause and to link the half-lines with alliteration. Try to use the Anglo-Saxon mood evoked by the meter to your advantage: tell a heroic story, or evoke an archetypal setting.

You the Rapper. Write and perform a rap poem of at least 12 lines. Feel free to go way over the top in your performance.

CHAPTER 3

Meter: A Language for the Body

Whether in a single accentual poem or in its more complex, developed incarnation, meter remains the traditional transporting power, the intoxicant, hypnotic drumbeat of poetry. Meter can manifest the language of the body, the beating of the wings of Pegasus; it can become a direct channel to the blood beating through a reader's veins. Meter is, after all, the reason that poets have been compared to drunkards, priests, shamans, the reason that Shakespeare wrote, "The lunatic, the lover and the poet / are of imagination all compact." To write in meter for me can be an experience so intense that it feels like a joyful secret, at once physical and private and a publicly shared gift.

Writing in meter is the skill most unique to writing poetry. Novels, stories, and plays in prose all make use of images, metaphors, word-music, tone of voice, and story, and sometimes of metrical and rhythmic passages, but poetry is the only kind of literature that can be completely structured by meter.

Some kind of meter has been central to poetry, has defined poetry, for most of remembered time in every culture. In the twentieth century, after the typewriter made it possible for poets to control their spacing exactly, the free verse movement blossomed and led many to think that the time of meter was over. But meter persisted and has begun to appeal to younger poets more and more alongside free verse, as the novelty of free verse has worn off and the popularity of rap and slam poetry has brought poems back off the page and into the ear.

When babies are starting to learn a language, long before they understand the meanings of words, they wiggle and move in response to a language's physical contours; an adult talking to an infant will exaggerate the physical elements of the language that are meaningful: "You're so *cute*! Look at your little *toes*!!" Meter works in a similarly physical way. By organizing and emphasizing the English language's inherent accents, meter talks to the body in us, communicates in a way that can be understood prior to our understanding of the words' meanings.

The word **meter** comes literally from the Greek word for "measure." Its basic meaning is simple: it refers to any kind of repeating, countable pattern within lines of poetry. In the last chapter we discussed syllabic meter, patterns based on the number of syllables in a line, and accentual meter, patterns based on the number of accents in a line. In this chapter and the two that follow, we'll be looking at accentual-syllabic meter, patterns based on both accents and syllables. Accentual-syllabic meter is the heart of metrical poetry in English.

Slam poetry: poetry performed, usually from memory, at oral competitions called "poetry slams," where judges rank poets for the quality of their poems and performance.

Writing in accentual-syllabic meter, according to one of my students who composes music, is similar to the process of writing music. In both cases, "It is crucial to keep the structure (meter in poetry, time signatures in music) you are working with in the background. First hum or say the rhythm aloud to yourself a few times, then put it out of your mind" while you use your imagination to lay the foundation of the poem. Finally, "delve into" the meter and vary it to strengthen the poem.

Sometimes, I notice myself humming a tune at random—and then realize it's not random at all: the words of the tune connect with something that has just happened in my life. In the same way, a poem can arrive as a tune that has a certain physical wisdom to it. If you let the tune lead the way, it can take you to words you may not have realized you wanted to say. If you are conversant with the meters, or tunes, of poetry, you will know better how to dance with the rhythm and allow the words to follow.

Poems can be written according to various kinds of meter, as we have seen with syllabic and accentual meter. This is because various features of the language can be counted or made into patterns. Any system of such counted elements is called a **prosody.**

Prosody and History

A durable prosody is always based on key elements that are meaningful to ordinary speakers of the language. Accent is central to meaning in Germanic languages. Old English, being a Germanic language, had an accentual prosody: a line of Anglo-Saxon or Old English poetry was based on a certain number of accents. Accent is not as meaningful in French words, and it is not part of French prosody. Instead French has a syllabic prosody: a line of French poetry is based on a certain number of syllables. Chinese meter incorporates pitch and tone because, in Chinese, pitch and tone are meaningful elements that change the definitions of words. A meter based on pitch and tone would have no meaning to English speakers.

> Prosody: a general term for the metrical structure of poetry. Theoretically, anything that can be repeated or counted—words, syllables, accented syllables, sentences, even line breaks—can be experimented with as an element in prosody.

The accentual-syllabic meter which is now the mainstay of English prosody came about through a historical event. England had a purely accentual prosody until the Norman Conquest in 1066, when the French conquered the Germanic-speaking tribes of England. Over centuries, with the addition of more and more French-derived words into the language, the four-beat bedrock line of accentual verse gradually evolved into an iambic tetrameter or iambic pentameter line in which there is a regular pattern of syllables in addition to accents, and the number of syllables in a line is almost (not quite!) as important as the number of accents. The fourteenth-century narrative poem "Sir Gawain and the Green Knight" gives a sense of this transition. Like the Anglo-Saxon poem "The Seafarer" in the last chapter, "Gawain" maintains four strong beats and the alliterative pattern; but it has much more regularity in terms of syllables, and the caesura in the middle of the line is less pronounced:

From "Sir Gawain and the Green Knight," The Gawain Poet (fourteenth century AD)

From Þe lorde ful lowde with lote and laȝter myry,
When he seȝe Sir Gawayn, with solace he spekez;
Þe goude ladyez were geten, and gedered þe meyny,
He schewez hem þe scheldez, and schapes hem þe tale
Of þe largesse and þe lenþe, þe liþernez alse

Of þe were of þe wylde swyn in wod þer he fled.
Þat oþer knyȝt ful comly comended his dedez,
And praysed hit as gret prys þat he proued hade,
For suche a brawne of a best, þe bolde burne sayde,
Ne such sydes of a swyn segh he neuer are.

From "Sir Gawain and the Green Knight" (trans. Marie Borroff)

The lord laughed aloud, with many a light word.
When he greeted Sir Gawain—with good cheer he speaks.
They fetch the fair dames and the folk of the house;
He brings forth the brawn, and begins the tale
Of the great length and girth, the grim rage as well,
Of the battle of the boar they beset in the wood.
The other man meetly commended his deeds
And praised well the prize of his princely sport,
For the brawn of that boar, the bold knight said,
And the sides of that swine surpassed all others.

Many of the four-beat accentual lines in the original (for example, each of the last four lines) could be scanned as iambic pentameter; you can try it after you've read the next chapter. From there it is not far to Chaucer's line, which is generally accepted as the earliest consistent iambic pentameter in English (a "gossip" means a woman's female friend):

From "The Wife of Bath's Tale," Geoffrey Chaucer (ca. 1390)

My fifthe housbonde, God his soule blesse,
Which that I took for love and no richesse,
He somtyme was a clerk of Oxenford,
And hadde left scole, and wente at hom to bord
With my gossib, dwellynge in oure toun,
God have hir soule! hir name was Alisoun.
She knew myn herte and eek my privetee
Bet than oure parisshe preest, as moot I thee.
To hir biwreyed I my conseil al,
For hadde myn housbonde pissed on a wal,

Or doon a thyng that sholde han cost his lyf,
To hir, and to another worthy wyf,
And to my nece, which that I loved weel,
I wolde han toold his conseil every deel.
And so I dide ful often, God it woot,
That made his face ful often reed and hoot
For verray shame, and blamed hym-self, for he
Had toold to me so greet a pryvetee.

From "The Wife of Bath's Tale" (trans. Sinan Kökbugur)

My fifth husband, may God his spirit bless!
Whom I took all for love, and not riches,
Had been sometime a student at Oxford,
And had left school and had come home to board
With my best gossip, dwelling in our town,
God save her soul! Her name was Alison.
She knew my heart and all my privity
Better than did our parish priest, s'help me!
To her confided I my secrets all.
For had my husband pissed against a wall,
Or done a thing that might have cost his life,
To her and to another worthy wife,
And to my niece whom I loved always well,
I would have told it—every bit I'd tell,
And did so, many and many a time, knows God,
Which made his face full often red and hot
For utter shame; he blamed himself that he
Had told me of so deep a privity.

Just as the two languages have combined (Chaucer uses French-based words
such as "conseil" and "pryvetee"), the native, Germanic accentual system of
prosody has combined with the conquerers' French syllabic system, producing
a metrical system that takes into account both number of syllables and number
of accents. The iambic tetrameter line remained important in English poetry,
especially in Scotland, and accentual prosody never really lost its core relationship to English; Suzanne Wood claims that even the *Canterbury Tales* is based

---

Metrical feet

u/	iamb
/u	trochee
uu	pyrrhic
//	spondee
uu/	anapest
/uu	dactyl
u/u	amphibrach
/u/	cretic (also called amphimacer)
u//	bacchius
//u	antibacchius
uuu	tribrach
///	molossos
/uuuu	first paeon
u/uu	second paeon
uu/u	third paeon
uuu/	fourth paeon
uu//	double iamb (also called minor iambic)
//uu	major ionic
u//u	antispast
u/u/	diamb
u///	first epitrite
/u//	second epitrite
//u/	third epitrite
///u	fourth epitrite
/uu/	choriamb
uuuu	tetrabrach (also called proceleus or maticus)
////	dispondee

---

mostly in the older four-beat accentual line, and Derek Attridge's *Poetic Rhythm* uses a system based in scanning accentual verse to scan all poetry in English. But by the Renaissance, along with the evolution of the language into the English we speak today, the longer, iambic pentameter line evolved into the dominant position. English now is built on a base of about 25 percent Germanic (including Anglo-Saxon and some Old Norse words) words and 60 percent

Latinate (about half French and half Latin) words. Because of its hybrid nature, our accentual-syllabic system of prosody combines strength and fluidity; it is one of the unique and magnificent strengths of poetry in English.

This chapter introduces a few key terms of accentual-syllabic meter and the four most common metrical patterns. The important thing, at first, is to begin to hear these different patterns and to get a sense of how they change a poem's energy, how they affect readers, and especially how they affect you as a poet. I recommend that you read the passages in meter aloud slowly and with attention to any physical sensations you have as you read (heart racing, sense of excitement in stomach, heart slowing, relaxing of shoulders, sense of calm, etc.). Reading aloud, loudly if possible or under your breath if necessary, is important because meters are meant for your internal or external ear, not your brain. Enjoy them as much as you can. It's okay if you don't remember all the names and terms right away; they will be repeated in other chapters. But I hope you will stay with this chapter, rereading the poems and looking for others in the same meters throughout the book, until you have a solid sense of the four basic patterns.

Scansion Marks

The process of marking the metrical patterns in a poem is called **scansion**. (At the end of the last chapter, when you were asked to mark the rhythmical pattern of some accentual poems, you were scanning the poems as you marked the accents.)

In accentual-syllabic meter, we pay attention to both the number of accents *and* the number of syllables. Also, unlike in both accentual and syllabic poems, where it's simply the counting that matters, here we are noticing not only the number but also the recurring *pattern* of stressed and unstressed syllables— noticing it, and marking it. How can you mark such a pattern? There are many possible ways, from the numbers 1 to 4 to musical notation (quarter notes, half notes, and whole notes) to capital letters, which we have used occasionally in this book. But from now on, we will be using the symbols u, /, \, and I, which are the standard and most common scansion marks. Here is what they mean: u is used for an unstressed syllable or breve (from the Greek word for "short"); / is used for a stressed syllable or ictus (from the Greek word for "accent"). \ is optional and can be used for a lighter stress, or "half-stress"; I is used to mark the boundary between repeating units, called a "foot break." To refer to these symbols, rather than the arcane words "breve" and "ictus" or the unwieldy terms "accented syllable" and "unaccented syllable," we will use two terms that have proven useful in my own teaching because they are so visual and easy to remember: the **cup** (u) and the **wand** (/) Don't worry—by the end of the chapter these four symbols—cup, wand, half-accent, and foot boundary—should be quite familiar to you.

The Four Most Common Metrical Patterns

When we speak conversational English, an accent naturally falls every two or three syllables. The most common metrical patterns in poetry are ones where the accent happens every two syllables (**duple meter**) or every three syllables (**triple meter**).

In **trochaic** meter, the accent always comes first (/ u), so the pattern sounds as if it is **falling:** TUM ta TUM ta TUM ta TUM ta. Read the poem below aloud. We'll be coming back to it more closely, but this time, just read it aloud to feel the meter physically in your throat and/or your ear.

From The Song of Hiawatha, *Henry Wadsworth Longfellow (1855)*

/ ˘ / ˘ / ˘ / ˘
YE who LOVE the HAUNTS of NATure,
Love the sunshine of the meadow,
Love the shadow of the forest,
Love the wind among the branches,
And the rain-shower and the snow-storm,
And the rushing of great rivers
Through their palisades of pine-trees,
And the thunder in the mountains,
Whose innumerable echoes
Flap like eagles in their eyries;—
Listen to these wild traditions,
To this Song of Hiawatha!

Did you find yourself accenting "and" and "to" slightly? Longfellow chose this meter, which he had heard used in ancient Finnish epic poetry, because it reminded him of drumbeats and seemed appropriate to the stateliness and power he found in Native American culture. The meter is very regular, though sometimes there are variations, as in line 6, where he changes the rhythm to a **rising** font ("of great") instead of staying with the trochaic, falling pattern.

In **iambic** meter, the unstressed syllable comes before the accent (u /), so the pattern sounds as if it is rising: ta TUM ta TUM ta TUM ta TUM. Read this poem aloud and experience the meter:

From "To My Dearest and Loving Husband," Anne Bradstreet (1678)

⌣ ′ ⌣ ′   ⌣   ′   ⌣ ′ ⌣ ′
If EVer TWO were ONE, then SUREly WE.
If ever man were loved by wife, then thee;
If ever wife was happy in a man,
Compare with me ye women if you can.
I prize thy love more than whole mines of gold,
Or all the riches that the East doth hold.
My love is such that rivers cannot quench,
Nor ought but love from thee give recompense.
Thy love is such I can no way repay;
The heavens reward thee manifold, I pray.
Then while we live, in love let's so persever,
That when we live no more we may live ever.

One of the United States' first published poets, Bradstreet chose this dignified, rational-sounding meter to lend her words the authority of the British poetic tradition. The familiar metrical pattern echoes Shakespeare, Milton, and other powerful poets, and the rising rhythm's insistent regularity lends force to the argument about love's power and persistence. One of the most interesting aspects of the poem is the varying of the rising pattern with extra syllables at the end of the last two lines, a variation we will discuss in the next chapter.

The **anapestic** meter is a rising triple meter (u u /): ta ta TUM ta ta TUM ta ta TUM ta ta TUM. Here is the an excerpt from the most famous anapestic poem in English:

From "The Night Before Christmas," Henry Livingston Jr. (ca. 1822)

⌣ ⌣ ′ ⌣ ⌣   ′   ⌣ ⌣ ′   ⌣ ⌣   ′
Twas the NIGHT before CHRISTmas, and ALL through the HOUSE,
not a creature was stirring, not even a mouse.
The stockings were hung by the chimney with care,
in hopes that St. Nicholas soon would be there.

The children were nestled all snug in their beds,
while visions of sugarplums danced in their heads,
and mamma in her 'kerchief, and I in my cap,
had just settled down for a long winter's nap,
when out on the lawn there arose such a clatter,
I sprang from the bed to see what was the matter.
Away to the window I flew like a flash,
tore open the shutters and threw up the sash.
The moon on the breast of the new-fallen snow
gave the lustre of mid-day to objects below . . .

The anapest is like an extended iamb with an extra unaccented syllable; anapests are often found in iambic lines and vice versa. Do you notice any places where Livingston varies the anapests with iambs? Notice especially the beginnings of lines. But the overall lilt of the triple pattern, each anapest skating over two syllables at a time on its way to the accent, lends speed and a light, whimsical touch to the poem.

In **dactylic** meter the accent comes before two unstressed syllables, making it a falling triple meter (/uu): TUM ta ta TUM ta ta TUM ta ta TUM ta ta, almost like an extended trochee with an extra unstressed syllable. The pattern resembles that of a waltz:

From Evangeline, *Henry Wadsworth Longfellow (1850)*

/ ᵛ ᵛ   / ᵛ   ᵛ / ᵛ   ᵛ   /   ᵛ ᵛ   /   ᵛ ᵛ
THIS is the FORest primEval. The MURmuring PINES and the

/   ᵛ
HEMlocks,
Bearded with moss, and in garments green, indistinct in the twilight,
Stand like Druids of eld, with voices sad and prophetic,
Stand like harpers hoar, with beards that rest on their bosoms.
Loud from its rocky caverns, the deep-voiced neighboring ocean
Speaks, and in accents disconsolate answers the wail of the forest.

This is the forest primeval; but where are the hearts that beneath it
Leaped like the roe, when he hears in the woodland the voice of the
        huntsman?
Where is the thatch-roofed village, the home of Acadian farmers?

Men whose lives glided on like rivers that water the woodlands,
Darkened by shadows of earth, but reflecting an image of heaven?
Waste are those pleasant farms, and the farmers forever departed!
Scattered like dust and leaves, when the mighty blasts of October
Seize them, and whirl them aloft, and sprinkle them far o'er the ocean.
Naught but tradition remains of the beautiful village of Grand-Pré.

While dactyls, like any meter, can lend themselves to any mood, this falling triple meter is well suited for solemn, thoughtful passages such as the opening of Longfellow's epic poem *Evangeline,* once so famous it was memorized by schoolchildren throughout the United States. Longfellow's American epic is a story of love, not war, but he copied his lines of dactylic meter from the meter of classical epics, the *Iliad, Odyssey,* and *Aeneid.* Like classical dactylic meter, *Evangeline* intersperses many trochees (the two-syllable pattern used in *Hiawatha*) with the dactyls. Each line moves through a series of falling patterns, until at the end it seems to complete itself, resolving in a kind of meditative balance before the next line begins.

That's it. The four patterns you have just learned—two triple, two double, two falling, two rising—are the basis of almost all metrical poetry in English.

Practice: Go back over the four poems and scan them by marking with a wand (/) where you hear a strong accent. Remember to mark only the accents that are stronger than the syllables around them. If you hear an accent that is not as strong as the others, you may use a half-accent to mark it (\). Don't worry if the words don't match up exactly with the patterns. Later you will go back and finish your scansions.

Meter, Rhythm, and the Metrical Foot

We've discussed syllable and accent (sometimes called stress, beat, or strong syllable). The next key term you need to know is **foot.** A foot is the repeating pattern of accents and unaccented syllables that moves a line of meter along. It pays no attention to words, only syllables. Each iamb, trochee, anapest, or dactyl (along with other, less common feet we'll get to later) is called a foot. A straight vertical line, the **foot break,** is used to indicate where one foot stops and another starts. A foot break can happen between words or in the middle of a word.

Most metrical lines have either three feet, four feet, or five feet, but a line could have as many as nine feet.

> 1 foot monometer
> 2 feet dimeter
> 3 feet trimeter
> 4 feet tetrameter
> 5 feet pentameter
> 6 feet hexameter
> 7 feet heptameter
> 8 feet octameter
> 9 feet nonameter

Let's look at the first lines of each of the four poems above:

This line of trochaic meter has four feet, so it's trochaic tetrameter:
YE who I LOVE a I NAtion's I LEgends, /u I /u I / I /u

This line of iambic meter has five feet, so it's iambic pentameter:
If EVIer TWO I were ONE, I then SUREIly WE. u/ I u/ I u/ I u/ I u/

This line of anapestic meter has four feet, so it's anapestic tetrameter:
Twas the NIGHT I before CHRISTImas, and ALL I through the HOUSE,
uu/ I uu/ I uu/ I uu/

This line of dactylic meter has six feet, so it's dactylic hexameter:
THIS is the I FORest primIEval. The I MURmuring I PINES and the I HEMlocks,
/uu I /uu I /uu I /uu I /uu I /u

Notice that the last foot above, HEMlocks, is not the same as the others. In fact, go back and re-read the four poems above one more time. If you listen carefully, you'll see that none of them is perfectly regular. Each has some variations, such as an initial syllable of the first word of a line or the final syllable of the last word left off; some lines slip in another kind of foot besides the basic foot of the poem. When metrically accomplished poets write in meter, they almost always vary it. In fact, it's often this interplay between the basic foot, which the reader comes to expect, and the variations from it, that carries the tension and expression of the poem. We'll explore this further in the next chapters.

For now, it may help to understand that meter and **rhythm** are two different things. Meter is a predictable structure of stressed and unstressed syllables in a clear pattern. It's a scaffolding, a skeleton, like the framework of a house. Rhythm is an expressive movement of energy that can change. Rhythm, the underlying life-pulse of the poem, derives not only from patterns of stress and unstress but also from other elements including word length, word-music, line breaks in free verse, and syntax and phrasing.

I have a student who grew up reading "The Night Before Christmas" aloud expressively in family poetry-reading competitions. Because of the strong, predictable anapestic meter of the poem, she was able to read the poem in any rhythm she chose for dramatic effect: a racing galloping, or a long suspenseful hush after "not a creature was stirring." Whatever she did, it wouldn't change the underlying meter.

Meter is by definition predictable, and rhythm is not. That's why different poets, or poems, using the exact same meter can sound so very different in their pacing and overall effect. But meter is the most fundamental, powerful, conspicuous, and distinctive tool that poets have available to create, and break, rhythm, and to mark a poem with their own uniquely recognizable rhythmic pulse.

Meter in Contemporary Poetry

Beginning writers are often leery of meter, associating it with "old" poems and believing that forward-looking contemporary poetry is not concerned with it. This is far from the case. The following poems were all written during the last few years. Read them aloud, first just to enjoy them and then a second time to identify their meters. Listen for the predominant meter and notice with your ear any variations from it. How does the meter add to the effect of each poem? You'll note that in the Jarnot poem, the ends of the metrical feet may not correspond exactly with the ends of the lines. This is an unusual strategy, but it doesn't change the meter of the poem.

"Hound Pastoral," Lisa Jarnot

Of the hay in the barn
and the hound in the field

of the bay in the sound, of the
sound of the hound in the field

of the back of the field of the
bay and the front of the field

of the back of the hound and the
front of the hound and the sound
of the hound when he bays at
the sound in the field

with the baying of hounds in the
baying of arms in the field

of the hound on the page in the
sound of the hound in the field

of the hay that unrests near
the hound in the barn in the field

of the bend in the barn in the
sound of the hound in the bay
by the barn in the field.

From "Parable," Allison Joseph

Sweep the walk and cook the dinner,
have his babies but stay thinner.

Raise his children, feed them knowledge,
clean the house with spit and polish.

Wipe their noses, scrub their fingers,
do their laundry, tweeze their splinters,

buy the groceries, sew on patches,
while your hair falls out in thatches.

Chop the veggies, fry the bacon,
tell your girlfriends they're mistaken

when you see your husband straying,
though his hair is dull and graying.

Wash the windows, weed the garden,
feel yourself begin to harden

as your husband packs his suitcase,
shines his shoes then ties each shoelace . . .

"Nineveh Fallen," Rachel Loden

Kuyunjik, palace mound

Nineveh fallen. My
Ghostly battalion
Silver-bell ankle rings
Tatterdemalion

Babylon Cadillac. Black
Candle guttering
Nettle-leav'd bellflowers
Sweet-faced American

Elvis in Cuneiform
Black-winged deity
Fifteen-gate city of
Mooncalf & talisman

Nineveh fallen. My
Ghostly battalion
Daughters of Sargon
Be carried away

The Line in Free Verse and Metrical Poetry

Writing free verse can give us the habit of thinking of the line as something to "break," for cleverness's or surprise's sake or to build energy in the poem. But a line in metrical poetry needs to be treated with more respect; it has a stronger inherent identity than the line in free verse. As we saw in the chapter on free verse, free-verse poems tend to break the line based on visual effect, not on sound. But metrical poems use the line as a unit of sound, of voice.

When poets who are used to writing in free verse first begin writing in meter, sometimes they break lines in a visual manner, as if they were breaking lines of free verse. For example, a student in a beginning meter class opened an iambic pentameter poem with these lines: "He walks in late again and sits his little / girl on the tiny plastic chair. She starts / to cry . . ." These might be interesting free-verse line breaks, but in a metrical poem they tend to undermine the aural integrity of the line. She was happier with the opening of her poem after she had rewritten it to break the lines in accord with the natural sound of their phrasing: "He walks in late and sits his little girl / on the tiny plastic chair. She starts to cry. . ." As a basis for a metrical line, the habit of keeping phrases together is much more effective; if the poet did decide to break one line against the natural phrase-sounds for a special effect, the line break would be much more dramatic by contrast.

For those used to reading and writing free verse, here's something else to keep in mind: lines of metrical poetry should break in places where the syntax provides a natural break. This is not at all the case for most types of free verse (except for incantatory or accent-based free verse). But for metrical poetry, though you can vary this principle for expressive purposes, it should always be the general rule. Why? Because meter creates the same kind of kinetic surprise and energy throughout an entire poetic line that free verse creates at the line breaks; it's as if each foot break is a miniature line-break, with the same potential for syntactical surprise, enjambment into the next foot, and meaningful variation that line breaks provide in free verse. As a result, by the end of each line of a good metrical poem, a reader's rhythmic attention has already had quite a workout. If you break lines in metrical poetry with the freedom and casualness regarding syntax that you might use in free verse, your reader will become at best rhythmically confused, and at worst seasick.

How to Scan a Poem

Now go back through each group of poems, the old and the new, and scan them. It is important not to skip steps but to follow each step in turn (you have already done step 1 for the group of old poems). Follow this system until you know a particular meter inside out, and your foundation will remain accurate.

Step 1. Mark the accents: listen to where you hear an accent and mark it with a wand over the syllable, just as you did for accentual poetry in the last chapter. Use a reversed wand if you need to. Remember, your ear, not your brain, is the ultimate authority. It may help to read the poem aloud while emphasizing the strongest accents and reducing the emphasis on any secondary accents.

Step 2. The remaining syllables are unstressed. Mark them with cups over the syllables.

Step 3. Look for repeating patterns. Mark the foot breaks between repeating patterns with a vertical line (if the foot break falls in the middle of a word, put the foot break line right through the middle of the word). Sometimes there will be two correct ways to divide the feet, say, into anapestic tetrameter or iambic pentameter. If you have a choice, always choose the meter that gives the same number of feet as the other lines in the poem.

Step 4. Some scanners like to mark "promoted" syllables—places where the meter creates a stress where there would not be one in speech—with a special mark: an accent over a cup. This makes you more aware of how the line works, and you can do this if you like.

As you go, savor how the process of scanning helps you appreciate each syllable of the poem and its particular, unique weight at this spot in the poem. Feel the delicious differences between lines that scan identically but have very different words. Feel the effects of any contrasts between your expectation and the actual pattern, as you move through the lines. This is the pleasure of scansion: it helps you to feel a poem's physical presence more attentively, more deeply.

Hints:

Look at the context of the poem for clues about the line length. In an iambic pentameter poem, every line will have five feet, even if the poet has used variation so that some of those feet are not iambs. As a good rule of thumb, remember that there is usually at least one accent per foot; so, if you know from the other lines that a poem is written in pentameter, your scansion of each line should have at least five accents in it.

While most lines scan quite straightforwardly, some lines are difficult to scan. There are even a few lines that critics have spent decades arguing over the correct way of scanning. So, if you get confused about a particular line, don't worry too much about it. The following advice will help with tricky lines:

1. When in doubt, read the poem aloud again in a relaxed manner. The stressed syllables may seem to "pop out" at you. Listen for the swing of the meter.

2. Go back and check your scansion to make sure that you marked the accents first, before bothering with cups and foot breaks, and that you marked the accents your ear was actually hearing. Many scansion problems come from trying to force a poem into a meter we *think* it should have, instead of *listening* to the actual rhythm.

3. Hear the line you have doubts about in the context of the rest of the poem.

4. Remind yourself that if other lines in the poem have a certain number of feet, your scansion of this line probably should have at least that number of accents (for example, in iambic pentameter, each line generally has at least five accents). Maybe you are missing a light accent that is actually supposed to be promoted (made stronger) by the meter. Or maybe there is a variation, such as a spondee (which we will discuss in the next chapter).

5. If a line has more accents than other lines in the poem, remember that though every syllable in speech is somewhat accented, you only need to mark the *strong* accents.

6. Get a friend or two (or a big group!) to say the poem aloud with you. Combined voices usually decide quite clearly where the accents should fall.

7. If you are still confused about whether a syllable is accented or not, consider using the half-accent, marked by the reverse wand (\), a symbol that has resolved many metrical arguments. For example, listen to the meter in the following lines from an iambic pentameter sonnet by Edna St. Vincent Millay:

Love is not all: it is not meat nor drink,
Nor slumber nor a roof against the rain.

Most people would be comfortable scanning the second "nor" in the second line as an accent (making the second foot an iamb), but others might hear it as so lightly stressed compared to "roof" that they would prefer to scan it with a cup (making the second foot a pyrrhic). For still others, neither of those would feel accurate; they could use a compromise symbol, the reversed wand. None of these is the "right" scansion of this foot—it's a matter of individual preference. Some other choices, such as, for example, scanning the first line as a footless dactylic tetrameter, would in fact be "wrong" scansions, since they would violate the metrical contract between the poet and reader that says the poem is in iambic pentameter and each line has five feet. But in the case of the scansion of "nor," any of the three choices would be reasonable and would preserve the metrical contract and maintain the poem's overall scansion as iambic pentameter.

One word of caution: I would advise you to use half-accents sparingly, as they are rarely necessary and can make scansions look like a confusing thicket—but if using one will allow you to move on and enjoy the sound of a poem instead of worrying over whether a syllable is accented or not, it is well worth it.

If you are very confused about how to scan a particular line, consider starting your scanning at the end of the line instead of at the beginning. I remember vividly that when I was a young poet and first met the formalist poet Dana Gioia, Dana showed me some notebooks that he kept solely to practice scansion in, filled with metrically tricky poems copied out in his extremely neat handwriting and then scanned. One line, which happened to be the opening of one of my favorite poems by Yeats, had given him particular trouble:

Suddenly I saw the cold and rook-delighting heaven

He explained that after repeated attempts, he had only figured out how to scan the line by starting at the end of the line. To do that, he had ignored the extra-syllable ending and then marked all the iambs, since he knew from the context of the rest of the poem that the line was iambic. That process had made it clear to him that the line was in iambic heptameter with the first syllable of the first iamb left off (such a "headless" line is not uncommon).

Don't get too focused on the idea of the meter. That will ruin your enjoyment and lead to mistakes. Your ear and/or your body are the final metrical authority. So, when in doubt, read aloud! Pleasure is the ultimate aim of scansion—to help you hear better where the rhythms of a poem lie, to distinguish between subtle degrees of emphasis that can poignantly affect meaning, and to appreciate and learn from the exquisite skill of a poet who may have spent decades perfecting the subtle art of metrical writing.

A Note on Scansion and Subjectivity: The 80/20 Rule

When people first learn how to scan, sometimes they are dismayed to discover the subjective component of meter and scansion. Two people in a group may disagree, for example, on whether a certain syllable in a poem should be stressed or not. Maybe one person has a different pronunciation of the word based on a regional dialect, or a different emotional interpretation of the line. It is not uncommon to feel frustrated at such moments, and perhaps even to be tempted to give up the entire effort. After all, prosody is sometimes dubbed a "science," and if you are going to go to all the trouble to learn it, shouldn't there be a guarantee of solid answers? If there's no clear answer to the simple question, "Is this syllable stressed or not?" does that mean there aren't any clear answers? Maybe the whole business of scanning a poem is subjective, so then who's to say that a line is iambic? Why not just call it dactylic? Who could stop me if I said that's how I hear it?

If you are having such thoughts, it may help to remember the 80/20 rule. As a rule, a group of people hearing a given poem will all agree on at least 80 percent of its scansion—and the proportion is usually higher. The area for disagreement will be 20 percent or less of syllables in the poem. Furthermore, even in those cases, it's likely the disagreement won't affect the overall scansion of the poem, but only the foot in question. For example, people who hear "fire" pronounced with two syllables will hear the second foot as an anapest in the line, "I fire the smoke and let the heat resound," while people who hear "fire" pronounced with one syllable will hear that foot as an iamb. But whether the second foot is an iamb or an anapest, both groups can still agree that the line is iambic pentameter. Or, in this line by Charles Martin, "Tired of earth, they dwindled on their hill," some will hear "tired" as one syllable and the first line as a headless iambic pentameter; others will hear the first foot as a trochee. But either way, the rest of the line is not affected.

The 80/20 rule assumes a shared basic level of knowledge about meter. You may occasionally encounter people who are so unfamiliar with a certain meter that they are physically unable to hear it; because of the long-reigning dominance of iambic meter in poetry, this sometimes happens with noniambic meters. As with any field of which someone is truly ignorant, in that case discussion may not be possible since even the 80 percent may not be shared. But in general, you can rest assured that the 20 percent or less of scansion that is subjective, while it allows for individual variations in linguistic background, speech patterns, personality, mood, and interpretation of the poem, does not make it necessary to throw the validity of the shared, objective 80 percent of scansion into question, nor to forgo the innumerable benefits of scansion.

Knowing how to scan puts you on an intimate basis with poems so that you can feel the ear and the body of the poets at work, not only in the choice of what meter they used but in how and why they varied it. In the Millay poem quoted above, for example, scanning the poem will remind you that the word "love" which opens the poem should not be accented at all, metrically speaking. The fact that Millay does accent the word, in the context of the poem's overall meaning, lends the opening of the poem a poignant and touching bravado. As you begin to hear such effects in other poets, your own metrical writing will become increasingly assured and effective. And in the process of becoming proficient at scanning, you will broaden the repertoire of meters that come naturally to you.

Why Bother?

Some poets who aren't used to writing in meter are afraid that it will be constricting. It is. It requires the sacrifice of infinite choices, and a possible commitment to spending extra time on a poem, to yield meter's benefits: increased rhythmical, musical, and performative control over your lines; surprising discoveries of words and phrases you would never have found on your own; the potential for powerful impact on the reader and for remarkable beauty. These fruits are more than worth the trouble to those poets willing to put in some metrical practice (usually only a month or two is sufficient to learn the basics). And once you've learned the basics, the skill will be with you forever. It's like playing music. As *The Jazz Piano Book* says: "When McCoy Tyner is playing a million notes a minute, he is not thinking, 'Left hand 3-5-7-9, 7th down a half step.' He's done that already, many years ago. He knows what the chord looks like and feels like when he plays it. Aim for the state of grace where you no longer have to think about theory. In order to reach that point, you'll have to think about theory a great deal."

QUESTIONS FOR MEDITATION OR DISCUSSION

Recently, scientists in Germany experimented with the effect of meter on heart rate. They found that reading aloud poetry in dactylic hexameter for 15 minutes was much better for synchronizing people's heart rate with their breath after a heart attack than either regular breathing or controlled breathing. Researchers have also found that reading aloud metrical poetry helps stroke victims and autistic people talk when nothing else can. Think about your own experience reading metrical poetry. Do you experience any physical effects?

For centuries there has been an ongoing discussion about whether certain meters are better suited for certain moods or subjects. What do you think? Experiment with different phrases and meanings and see if it is harder for you to express certain kinds of things in certain rhythms.

Derek Attridge's books *Rhythms of English Poetry* and *Poetic Rhythm* sparked something of a controversy in the world of prosody. Attridge, a linguist who has worked extensively with accentual poetry, proposes a system of scansion that does away with the foot altogether and concentrates on the relation between the expectation of a certain number of stresses in a line and the occurrence (or nonoccurrence) of those stresses.

By contrast, *A Poet's Craft* focuses on the traditional accentual-syllabic system of scansion for three reasons: it is still by far the most commonly known and accepted system; the terminology seems to me simpler and more graceful than Attridge's; and, most importantly, I find the foot indispensable to understanding the rhythms of poetry. The foot marks out a certain period of time, a kind of "waiting" place in which a stress can occur as expected, or occur unexpectedly lightly, or unexpectedly heavily, or occur not at all, in relation to the other feet in analogous places in other lines in the poem. For example, when we read the excerpt from Anne Bradstreet's poem above, the stress on the word "whole" at the beginning of the third foot strikes us intensely, if we are reading carefully, because unconsciously we are aware of the grid of the poem and are registering the fact that the previous three lines have not had a stress in the corresponding foot of the line. To me, the foot breaks are like the "warp" in weaving, a strong framework of parallel threads that the rest of the poem can be woven across, like a "weft" of lines ducking in and out through the warp-threads. Without the feet, awareness of that important spatial aspect of the poem's rhythmic tapestry is completely lost.

That said, Attridge's theories have passionate proponents who think the concept of the foot is unnecessary. A useful project for readers interested in prosody would be to read some of Attridge's work and come to their own conclusions.

QUOTES

Poetry is emotion put into measure. The emotion must come by nature, but the measure can be acquired by art.
—Thomas Hardy

I think that a poet who doesn't know anything about metrics, who hasn't really practiced the discipline of formal metrics is at a great loss.... You can be free in heroic couplets. In completely unconfined, unrestrained verse, one is a prisoner of infinity; that is the worst kind of bondage because there is no escape from it.
—Stanley Kunitz

True Ease in Writing comes from Art, not Chance,
As those move easiest who have learn'd to dance.
—Alexander Pope

However minute the employment may appear, and whatever ridicule may be incurred by a solemn deliberation upon accents and pauses, it is certain that without this petty knowledge no man [sic] can be a poet.
—Samuel Johnson

"Fighting Words," Dorothy Parker (1927)

Say my love is easy had,
Say I'm bitten raw with pride,
Say I am too often sad—
Still behold me at your side.

Say I'm neither brave nor young,
Say I woo and coddle care,
Say the devil touched my tongue—
Still you have my heart to wear.

But say my verses do not scan,
And I get me another man!

I approach a poem in just the same way a free-verse writer does. What matters is the subject and the words that are going to be found for conveying and exploring the subject. The only difference is that I include meters and rhymes in my free-verse proceeding.
　—Richard Wilbur

Verse form literally embodies theme. If you think of form as the outside of an Inside, that's only half the truth. Verse form is also inside the Inside. It acts as a skeleton as well as a skin. It is a body.
　—Molly Peacock

Jettison ornament gaily but keep shape.
　—Basil Bunting

Poetry begins to atrophy when it gets too far from the music.
　—Ezra Pound

On the matter of song: I believe there must be a return toward the musical structure of poetry, just as there must be, for certain people at least, a return to warmth within a relationship.
　—Paul Blackburn

POETRY PRACTICES

(Group) Name Dance. Scan your names and those of your friends.

(Group) Dada Meter Hat. With a group of poets, or even alone, try my metrical version of the famous Dada hat game. It's a great way to bypass the compulsion to make sense, opening yourself to the sheer fun of meter. Each person

writes down a dozen of their favorite words, cuts them apart, and puts the separated words in a communal basket. Individually or in small groups, pull out
several words from the basket and arrange groups of words into lines of iambs,
trochees, dactyls, and anapests. Share the lines with the rest of the group. If you
write lines on a board, notice how all the lines in a certain meter can combine
into surprising poems that are held together by their common metrical pattern.
Also be sure to notice how any word, of any length and rhythm, can be used in
a line of any meter; you may think at first, for example, that the word "beautiful" can only be used in a dactylic line, since it is a dactylic word, but if you play
this game correctly you should find yourself using it in lines of all four meters:
not only the dactylic "beautiful fun in the teeth of the infinite," but also the
anapestic "in the teeth of the beautiful infinite fun," the iambic "in fun the teeth
of beautiful the infinite," and the trochaic "beautiful the teeth in fun of infinite
the" (nobody said these phrases had to make sense). This lesson is one of the
most important things you can learn about meter.

(Group) Call and Response.   One person reads a metrical line (regular or, later
on, with variations) and everyone else needs to write down a line in the identical, syllable-by-syllable rhythm of accented and unaccented syllables. The response lines can be read aloud separately, or combined into one poem. This is
a good method of ear training, since it makes you focus on every syllable.

(Group) Metrical Mad Libs. Pick a poem in a regular meter and cross out certain words. Solicit words in the same metrical pattern from the group, and fill
in the blanks before you read the result aloud, as in Mad Libs.

(Group) Metrical Talking. Form conversational-size groups and practice talking
in one meter of the four basic meters at a time. The rule is that you can only speak
if you talk in the appropriate meter. You may want to rotate meters so each group
has a chance to try all four. Then have a large group conversation with one of
these variations: (*a*) conversation stays in one meter until someone calls "switch"
or otherwise signals a change to another meter; (*b*) any meter is allowed, and each
person says which meter the last sentence was before they say their own sentence;
(*c*) any meter is allowed and everyone talks the best they can.

(Group or individual) Drumming on the Table. Drumming in different meters is an excellent way to become familiar with the patterns. Use your palms on
the table or your feet on the floor, or even better, get a drum and use patterns of
loud and soft drumming. See if you can identify meters someone taps out. Or

accompany yourself or someone else reciting a metrical poem, like an Anglo-Saxon **scop**. The recitation should be slow enough that you can drum once per syllable. Practice at least a few times before performing.

Metrical Compass. (This exercise is recommended as a foundation in addition to any of the others.) Write nine unrhymed lines in trochaic tetrameter. (Tetrameter is a good line-length to start with because it is long enough to get momentum going but short enough to stay focused.) Don't worry about making any sense at first; just focus on the rhythm (if you want to write nonsense like "Sting the open roses happy, springing follicles rely," that's fine). Try using your ear to guide you. My advice is to read a poem in the same meter aloud before you start, to "entrain" the rhythm in your ear. A drum can have the same effect. Just absorb the rhythm through reading the poem or listening to the drum, and then keep going on your own ("entraining" is a term developed by my student Patricia Hagge, a yoga teacher, who has a strong sense of the physical reality of meter).

When you think you have done it, scan the lines following the three steps on page 322 to make sure the meter is exact. If you have trouble hearing the meter, it can help to ask someone else to read it aloud. First mark the stresses and then fill in the unstressed syllables. You can use the standard method, u and / on your keyboard, or write marks in by hand above the words, or use boldface or capital letters for stressed syllables. But whatever marks you use, *be sure to do the final step—after the syllables are marked, add foot breaks to show where the pattern repeats. Use pencil at first, until you get the hang of it.* Making decisions about foot breaks will force you to listen to the underlying heartbeat of the line—the norm from which variation occurs—and will deepen the quality of your attention: not only your awareness of the contrasts between varying lines, but also even of the way passages that look metrically identical are using the meter in different ways.

Don't worry if the process seems mechanical at first, and you find yourself exaggerating or counting on your fingers. You'll get beyond that soon enough. Keep scanning and rewriting until your words fit the pattern. Then use the same technique to write at least nine lines each in unrhymed anapestic tetrameter, iambic tetrameter, and dactylic tetrameter. Don't forget to scan each one, including foot breaks, to show the meter. Ideally, you will review the sections on each meter in this chapter, and in the "Metrical Palette" chapter up ahead if you like, noting common variations and so forth, before you engage with each of the four meters. Switching between meters can be tiring the first time or two, but the metrical flexibility that is your goal is well within reach.

After you have the basics of each point of the metrical compass down, you will learn in the next few chapters about how to vary the meter and aim for a more complex, natural sound.

Note: if you have any trouble with this exercise, or if you feel inhibited or stuck when you try to write in meter, please do the next exercise, "Meter Moving," first, and then return to the "Metrical Compass."

Meter Moving. Using a drum or your voice chanting to mark the rhythms, dance or move to the four different meters learned in this chapter. A simple way is to choose a line of your own, or one from another poem, that you like and that you know is in the correct meter. Recite the line aloud as many times as you like while dancing in a rhythmic way, perhaps moving in a circle. When you feel confident, stop saying the line and start making up new lines in the same meter and saying them aloud while you continue dancing. Lay a notebook open, and pause to write the lines down.

Advanced dancing: The ancient Greek choruses used to use special steps to dance parts of verse plays in various meters. I will never forget seeing poet and classicist A. E. Stallings dancing meters out in the ancient manner. She lowered her arms and took a long step for the long (stressed syllable), raised her arms and took short steps for the short (cupped) syllable. Try this method, or develop your own vocabulary of dance steps or hand gestures to dance out a favorite metrical passage.

CHAPTER 4

The Many Voices of Iambic Meter

Just as skilled saxophone players can make distinct and different voices sound through the same musical instrument, skilled poets can make distinct and different voices sound through the same metrical instrument. The basic iambic pentameter pattern, the most common iambic line-length, can encompass lines as simple as "I work all day, and get half-drunk at night" or as convoluted as "the sceptred terror of whose sessions rends"; as gentle as "How do I love thee? Let me count the ways" or as intense as "gusty emotions on wet roads on autumn nights"; as light as "I hold my honey and I store my bread" or as heavy as "rocks, caves, lakes, fens, bogs, dens, and shades of death"; as direct as "Shall I compare thee to a summer's day?" (or as the title of this chapter) or as arcane as "Dead locked with them, taking root as cradles rock." These lines (by Philip Larkin, Hart Crane, Elizabeth Barrett Browning, Wallace Stevens, Gwendolyn Brooks, John Milton, William Shakespeare, Alexander Pope, and Sylvia Plath), are all just simple 10-syllable iambic pentameters, most of them consisting of five iambs in a row. Even without any rhythmic variation, they are astonishingly different in voice. When you add in the numerous possibilities of metrical variation through substitution—the central subject of this chapter—the rhythmic options of iambic pentameter are inexhaustible. And even that is without the variation of actual words themselves, the way the lengths of syllables and play of vowels and consonants also change the rhythms of words.

Even after a century dominated by free verse, it is still true to say that the vast bulk of respected, literary poetry written in English over the last five hundred years has been written in iambic pentameter. This is one of the reasons the following poem is so wryly funny:

"*Approaching a Significant Birthday, He Peruses* The Norton Anthology of Poetry," *R. S. Gwynn*

All human things are subject to decay.
Beauty is momentary in the mind.
The curfew tolls the knell of parting day.
If Winter comes, can Spring be far behind?
Forlorn! the very word is like a bell
And somewhat of a sad perplexity.
Here, take my picture, though I bid farewell,
In a dark time the eye begins to see
The woods decay, the woods decay and fall—
Bare ruined choirs where late the sweet birds sang.
What but design of darkness to appall?
An aged man is but a paltry thing.
If I should die, think only this of me:
Crass casualty obstructs the sun and rain
When I have fears that I may cease to be,
To cease upon the midnight with no pain
And hear the spectral singing of the moon
And strictly meditate the thankless muse.
The world is too much with us, late and soon.
It gathers to a greatness, like the ooze.
Do not go gentle into that good night.
Fame is no plant that grows on mortal soil.
Again he raised the jug up to the light:
Old age hath yet his honor and his toil.
Downward to darkness on extended wings,
Break, break, break, on thy cold gray stones, O sea,
And tell sad stories of the death of kings.
I do not think that they will sing to me.

Each of these lines is taken from a famous poem in iambic pentameter. Gwynn's clever use of their rhymes to link them across poets and centuries underscores their disarming rhythmic kinship. You can get a related effect by skimming the index of first lines in an older anthology such as the classic *Palgrave's Golden Treasury of Poetry*. Most of the index will be in iambic pentameter, and those lines that are not will be mostly in the runner-up meter, iambic tetrameter.

(Please note that this is not true of contemporary anthologies of formal verse such as the often-used *Strong Measures,* which include many poems that do *not* scan regularly.)

Louise Bogan called iambic pentameter "the large carrier of English poetry." Iambic pentameter is so common in English-language poetry, so familiar, that if people want to evoke the idea of meter in general, often they will murmur in this pattern: ta-TUM-ta-TUM-ta-TUM-ta-TUM-ta-TUM. Even with Dickinson, Whitman, and the major free verse poets of the twentieth century taken into account, the majority of the so far-acknowledged great poets of the English language wrote much or all of their poetry in iambic pentameter, among them Chaucer, Spenser, Shakespeare, Milton, Donne, Pope, Wordsworth, Coleridge, Keats, Shelley, Tennyson, both Brownings, and in the twentieth-century Yeats, Frost, Auden, Crane, Millay, Stevens, Hayden, Heaney, and Walcott.

Blank Iambic Verse, Enjambment, and Caesura

A note on terminology: The technical term for unrhymed poetry in meter is **blank verse.** You should be aware that, since such a huge majority of metrical poetry is in iambic pentameter, some books use the term blank verse to mean simply "unrhymed iambic pentameter." (Of course, iambic pentameter can also be combined into many kinds of rhyme patterns, from the basic "heroic couplet" of two rhymed lines on up to 10-line stanzas.) But in this book, which acknowledges the importance of noniambic meters, I will specify **blank iambic verse** when discussing unrhymed iambic pentameter specifically, to distinguish this prevalent meter of English poetry from **blank dactylic verse, blank trochaic verse,** and so on.

Much of the most influential iambic pentameter poetry, from Shakespeare's plays to *Paradise Lost,* is blank iambic verse. Unlike rhymed stanzas which tend to make a reader stop at the ends of lines, all blank verse is a fluid, flexible medium in which the sentences tend to roll over from line to line. Skillful blank verse poets manipulate not only the meter within each line but also the play of language over the lines. The poem below, according to family stories, was a favorite poem of my great-aunt Jessie Hughan—a brave woman who ran for office before U.S. women even had the vote. I feel I know more about her whenever I read this famous poem told in the voice of Ulysses, after the adventures of the *Odyssey* were over. The poem is designed to sound well aloud and to be

enjoyable to read aloud; in those days before television, a favorite poem would
be read aloud to friends and family often in the evenings. Read it aloud, and notice the variety of sentence lengths in the poem, beginning with the contrast between the first two sentences (and while you're at it, keep an eye out for the line
that appears in Gwynn's parody above):

"Ulysses," Alfred, Lord Tennyson (1842)

It little profits that an idle king,
By this still hearth, among these barren crags,
Match'd with an aged wife, I mete and dole
Unequal laws unto a savage race,
That hoard, and sleep, and feed, and know not me.
I cannot rest from travel; I will drink
Life to the lees. All times I have enjoy'd
Greatly, have suffer'd greatly, both with those
That loved me, and alone; on shore, and when
Thro' scudding drifts the rainy Hyades
Vext the dim sea. I am become a name;
For always roaming with a hungry heart
Much have I seen and known:—cities of men
And manners, climates, councils, governments,
Myself not least, but honor'd of them all,—
And drunk delight of battle with my peers,
Far on the ringing plains of windy Troy.
I am a part of all that I have met;
Yet all experience is an arch wherethrough
Gleams that untravell'd world whose margin fades
For ever and for ever when I move.
How dull it is to pause, to make an end,
To rust unburnish'd, not to shine in use!
As tho' to breathe were life! Life piled on life
Were all too little, and of one to me
Little remains: but every hour is saved
From that eternal silence, something more,
A bringer of new things; and vile it were
For some three suns to store and hoard myself,
And this gray spirit yearning in desire

To follow knowledge like a sinking star,
Beyond the utmost bound of human thought.
This is my son, mine own Telemachus,
to whom I leave the sceptre and the isle—
Well-loved of me, discerning to fulfill
This labor, by slow prudence to make mild
A rugged people, and thro' soft degrees
Subdue them to the useful and the good.
Most blameless is he, centred in the sphere
Of common duties, decent not to fail
In offices of tenderness, and pay
Meet adoration to my household gods,
When I am gone. He works his work, I mine.
There lies the port; the vessel puffs her sail;
There gloom the dark, broad seas. My mariners,
Souls that have toil'd, and wrought, and thought with me,—
That ever with a frolic welcome took
The thunder and the sunshine, and opposed
Free hearts, free foreheads,—you and I are old;
Old age hath yet his honor and his toil.
Death closes all; but something ere the end,
Some work of noble note, may yet be done,
Not unbecoming men that strove with Gods.
The lights begin to twinkle from the rocks;
The long day wanes; the slow moon climbs; the deep
Moans round with many voices. Come, my friends.
'Tis not too late to seek a newer world.
Push off, and sitting well in order smite
The sounding furrows; for my purpose holds
To sail beyond the sunset, and the baths
Of all the western stars, until I die.
It may be that the gulfs will wash us down;
It may be we shall touch the Happy Isles,
And see the great Achilles, whom we knew.
Tho' much is taken, much abides; and tho'
We are not now that strength which in old days
Moved earth and heaven, that which we are, we are,—
One equal temper of heroic hearts,

Made weak by time and fate, but strong in will
To strive, to seek, to find, and not to yield.

One of the manifestations of Tennyson's considerable skill here is the variety of ways he uses **enjambment** (from the French for "jumping off," this refers to a sentence that jumps off the end of one line and continues in the next) to keep the lines from being monotonous: for example, one line ends between a verb and its object ("I will drink / Life to the lees"), another between the addressees and the address ("Come, my friends. / 'Tis not too late").

In addition to the variations in sentence length and enjambment, Tennyson also uses another subtle method of modulating the language across lines in this poem. Each line contains a **caesura,** or pause, created by grammatical phrases and/or punctuation. The caesura's position within the line changes constantly (Alexander Pope said it should never occur in the same place for three lines in a row), and creates a rhythm of phrases that counterpoints the metrical rhythm, adding still another layer of complexity on top of the natural speech rhythms.

If you read a poem aloud, you can hear the caesuras as the places where your voice naturally pauses. Most lines that are pentameter or longer have at least one caesura, and some have two—or sometimes even three or four. The caesura in line 2 of "Ulysses" is easy to spot, since it is created by a comma. In line 1, the caesura is subtler: it is the brief pause created by the end of the verb phrase "it little profits" (subject-adverb-verb)—in line 1. Line 3 has a caesura marked and accentuated by a comma. Line 4 has a caesura after the end of the noun phrase "unequal laws" (adjective-noun). Line 5 has three caesuras marked by punctuation, the last of them the strongest. Line 6 has one caesura at the semicolon. Read the poem again, noticing caesuras, and how Tennyson balances the strength of the caesuras against the strength of the line endings. If the caesuras were too strong in comparison to the line endings, the whole orientation of the poem would be skewed, undermining the foundation of the lines.

When scanning a poem, it is customary to mark the caesuras with a double vertical line (‖-like a double foot-break). If you are scanning the poem, you will notice that some caesuras occur in the middle of a metrical foot, and some between metrical feet. Traditionally, the former is called a **feminine caesura** and the latter a **masculine caesura**. Look for at least two examples of each kind of caesura in "Ulysses." Do you find that they have different effects?

The Five Basic Metrical Variations in Iambic Pentameter

Like a kaleidoscope that shifts a few pieces of color into infinite patterns, a metrical line can create innumerable rhythmic patterns by means of only a few basic changes. Because iambic pentameter is by far the most commonly used meter, the possible variations in this meter are well understood. The rest of this chapter will explore the most common of those changes—the basic vocabulary of rhythmic variation in a line of iambic pentameter. Though you will recognize the names of some meters from the previous chapter, the information here only applies to when those feet appear as variations in iambic meter.

Anapests as Variations

You will remember anapestic meter from "The Night Before Christmas." In iambic pentameter, anapests are used to vary the rhythm. Adding an anapest in place of one of the iambs in an iambic line is often said to have the effect of speeding up the line, and lightening it. Since more syllables have to fit in the same space, or time, they seem to need to be read, or spoken, more quickly. For example, scan this passage of iambic pentameter from Charles Martin's "Breaking Old Ground," and notice how the anapest in the first foot of the last line gives a feeling of lightness and casualness:

> It really seems to want to be our friend,
> Returning, is it, out of sympathy
> Or just to see how everything will end?
> Waiting, in either case, for one like me
> To show up some morning at the backyard fence.

In the following sonnet, Edna St. Vincent Millay uses only one anapest in the entire poem. Scan the poem and see if you can find it. The foot where it appears has a freedom and lightness that is eloquent in the context of the rest of the poem.

"Sonnet 30," Edna St. Vincent Millay (1923)

> I shall go back again to the bleak shore,
> And build a little shanty on the sand

In such a way that the extremest band
Of brittle seaweed will escape my door
But by a yard or two. And nevermore
Shall I return to take you by the hand.
I shall be gone to what I understand,
And happier than I ever was before.
The love that stood a moment in your eyes,
The words that lay a moment on your tongue,
Are one with all that in a moment dies,
A little undersaid and oversung.
But I shall find the sullen rocks and skies
Unchanged from what they were when I was young.

Of course, meter is just as complex as language, and metrical effects can't be labeled all that easily. Sometimes, the effect of an anapest is not of quickness or lightness, but of struggle where three syllables try to fit in the space of two, as in the fourth foot of this iambic pentameter line:

Your DYIing WAS | a DIFIficult ENIterPRISE

Please note that to hear the iambic pentameter pattern in this line, you need to recognize that though the accent on the last syllable of "enterprise" is softer than the accent on the first syllable, it is still accented. (Remember the principle of relative stress: it doesn't matter how accented an accented syllable is, only that it is more accented than the syllable[s] next to it.) The third syllable of "difficult," however, is not accented, because it is in the same anapest with the much stronger syllable *en* (some people might prefer to scan "cult" as a half-stress, and this is no problem, since it doesn't change the basic pattern of the line).

The anapest can also create an effect of bending, as our expectation of a two-syllable iamb in the second and third foot in this line bends to accept a three-syllable anapest instead:

And WHETIher she BENDS | or STRAIGHTIens TO | each BUSH

or of slowness and peace, as a two-syllable foot relaxes to hold three syllables in the second and third foot of this line:

DesPAIR | of our DAYS | and the CALM | MILK-GIVIer WHO

In each of these cases, of course, the meter is not working alone to create the effect. Meaning plays a part, and other aspects of the words—such as the unstressed, suppressed second syllable of "whether" followed by the quick short word "bend" and the contrasting, strong high-pitched syllable "straight," or the two murmuring "m's" of "calm" and "milk" next to each other—have a role as well.

In the following poem, the anapests carry a lot of emotional weight:

"The Illiterate," William Meredith

Touching your goodness, I am like a man
Who turns a letter over in his hand
And you might think this was because the hand
Was unfamiliar but, truth is, the man
Has never had a letter from anyone;
And now he is both afraid of what it means
And ashamed because he has no other means
To find out what it says than to ask someone.

His uncle could have left the farm to him,
Or his parents died before he sent them word,
Or the dark girl changed and want him for beloved.
Afraid and letter-proud, he keeps it with him.
What would you call his feeling for the words
That keep him rich and orphaned and beloved?

There are many remarkable things about this sonnet, including the use of identical words for rhymes and the last syllable which perhaps answers the poem's question in a hidden way. Meredith spent his life as a closeted gay man, a situation which perhaps adds intensity to the hidden feelings of shame and elation conveyed so subtly and skillfully in this poem. The poem is equally remarkable on the metrical level (if you scan the poem and are confused by line 12, don't worry, we'll discuss it below). Every one of the four anapests in this poem adds to the meaning. The first one, in line 5, delays a stress and so forces us to give a stronger accent to the word "anyone," pronouncing it with the exact surprise that the man must have felt. This ability to force the reader to use performative stress of particular kinds is, to my mind, one of the most marvelous capacities of metrical poetry. After this first anapest, each one in the poem emphasizes the man's confused emotions at exactly the points of most heightened poignancy: his embarrassment at the thought of asking someone, his fear about his parents, and his elation over love. Not a single metrical variation is wasted.

As in the sonnets by Meredith and Millay, ideally any variation from the basic pattern of your own metrical poems should have a sense of inevitability. When you are writing meter well and are comfortable with it, you may not even notice that you are varying the meter as you write—but when you go back and revise your poems, the sense of inevitability is something you can look for. It is a high standard to uphold, but one that will repay your attention. In a way, the skillful use of variation gets at the essence, the point, of meter, which is to make it impossible to separate the rhythm from the words, the form from the function, or, to use a phrase of Yeats', the "dancer from the dance."

Trochees as Variations

When trochees are used to vary iambic pentameter, there is an additional factor to take into account. It's easy for an anapest to fit anywhere in an iambic line without undermining the rhythm, since anapests and iambs are both rising feet: when we read Elizabeth Bishop's iambic line "some realms I owned, two rivers, a continent," the anapest in the fourth foot doesn't disturb our momentum. But a trochee is a falling foot. Since it moves in the opposite direction from an iambic line, it can cause the line to stumble. If the iambic pentameter line were, "a deep river and realms and continents," the trochee in the second foot would confuse the meter as we read the line aloud, tempting a reader to pronounce "river" as "rivER" or to stop suddenly after "deep." (If you don't notice this happening, try reading Bishop's line directly after a completely regular iambic pentameter, such as Alexander Pope's maxim "A little learning is a dangerous thing," to accentuate the effect.)

Linguists have discovered that, probably for this reason, a trochee usually occurs in iambic poems only where there is time to brace yourself and catch your balance to get ready for it: when you've had a whole line break to prepare, as in the first foot of a line (the first line below is an example), or after a caesura, as in the third foot of the third line below:

From "Among School Children," W. B. Yeats (1928)

Labour is blossoming or dancing where
The body is not bruised to pleasure soul,
Nor beauty born out of its own despair.

A trochee in the first foot, as in the word "labour," is an extremely common variation, probably the most common in iambic poetry. Trochees in the middle of a line often occur after periods or commas; in the third line of this poem, though, the phrase "nor beauty born" is followed by a strong grammatical caesura that prepares us for the trochee "out of." Unlike my hypothetical trochee "river" above, this trochee does not disturb the rest of the line; though the rhythm of "out of" surprises our ears, because of the grammatical pause, we have no trouble hearing it almost as if it were the first foot of a line, which makes it easier to reestablish the meter and hear "its own despair" as two iambs.

Because of the trochee's tendency to catch you up short, one effect of a trochee in iambic pentameter, especially at the beginning of a line, can be a sense of immediacy or surprise:

From "I Wandered Lonely as a Cloud," William Wordsworth (1804)

I wander'd lonely as a cloud
That floats on high o'er vales and hills,
When all at once I saw a crowd,
A host of golden daffodils,
Beside the lake, beneath the trees,
Fluttering and dancing in the breeze!

Though the daffodils are described as appearing suddenly, it is not until the word "Fluttering" that we feel the immediacy of their effect on the poet, the sudden vividness of the sight. This trochee, cited by Paul Fussell in his classic book *Poetic Meter and Poetic Form,* is a good illustration of how much can be accomplished with just a little metrical variation. This single foot is the only variation from strict iambic pentameter in six lines of poetry, and yet the two syllables have such an impact that I doubt the poem would be half as famous without it.

Spondees and Pyrrhics as Variations

The **spondee** (//), a foot with two stresses, and the **pyrrhic** (uu), a foot with two light syllables, are two feet that are only used to vary other meters. Given the accentual nature of English, it would be impossible to write a poem all in pyrrhics or spondees. The closest I have ever seen are Gwendolyn Brooks's great poem that begins "We real cool" and George Peele's poem below; still, notice how the spondees tend to turn into trochees as you read:

"The Pool Players, Seven at the Golden Shovel," Gwendolyn Brooks

We real cool. We
Left school. We

Lurk late. We
Strike straight. We

Sing sin. We
Thin gin. We

Jazz June. We
Die soon.

"Bathsheba's Song," George Peele *(1599)*

Hot sun, cool fire, tempered with sweet air,
Black shade, fair nurse, shadow my white hair,
Shine, sun, burn, fire, breathe, air, and ease me,
Black shade, fair nurse, shroud me and please me;
Shadow, my sweet nurse, keep me from burning,
Make not my glad cause, cause of mourning.
    Let not my beauty's fire
    Inflame unstaid desire,
    Nor pierce any bright eye
    That wandereth lightly.

From this unusual and extreme example, you can see that spondees are *intense*. They leave no room for breathing. When we speak in spondees, we do so out of urgency: "*Stop that!*" So when Dylan Thomas wants to hold his father back from dying, he speaks in spondees instead of iambs for four out of the poem's first six feet:

Do not go gentle into that good night,
Rage, rage against the dying of the light.

Some people may hear "Do not" as a trochee, rather than a spondee. Others will feel that it is a spondee because the expected metrical stress on "not" (because it is the second syllable of an iamb) helps give the word as much stress as "do." Others may hear it as an iamb. It doesn't really matter; the scansion of monosyllables often varies in different readers' ears because of performative accent. If you are in a group and there is disagreement over scanning, you can always compromise and mark "do" or "not" with a reversed wand (\) to signify a half-accent, which will still convey the urgency of the phrase.

Once you have the sound of a regular meter deeply established in your ear, it is humbling how deeply you can be moved by just one variation in it. For 30 years I have had the same intense response to the spondee that opens the first line of Hart Crane's "To Brooklyn Bridge," the balance and shock of whose stresses moves me just as it did when I used to carry the old paperback edition of his book *The Bridge* with me on the subway to my first job in New York City, reading the line over and over as the train jostled:

How many dawns, chill from his rippling rest
The seagull's wings shall dip and pivot him,
Shedding white rings of tumult, building high
Over the chained bay waters Liberty—

This famous opening line of Crane's epic is enhanced not just by the spondee but also by the trochee that follows the caesura, "chill from." Imagine if the line read, "How many dawns that from his rippling rest." The impact of the word "how," with its urgent, poignant dipthong defiantly stressing the first syllable like a seagull balancing on a powerful air current, would be far weaker.

A spondee and pyrrhic frequently occur together in the same line, and very often the spondee immediately follows the pyrrhic. Since the pyrrhic loses an accent, and the spondee immediately replaces it, the combination has the effect of righting the rhythm almost immediately, so the ear expecting iambs is not confused for long. This is such a common pattern that it is sometimes called by its own name, the **double iamb.** It is a favorite and distinctive trick of Shakespeare's. Can you find one double iamb in each of these lines from his sonnets?

I summon up remembrance of things past

And beauty making beautiful old rhyme

If this be error and upon me proved

That I in your sweet thoughts would be forgot

In very metrically regular poems, a single substitution can have a large effect. The following poem has one spondee in the last line, which single-footedly elevates the subtlety and impact of the whole poem.

From "Some Girls," Suzanne Doyle

The risk is moral death each time we act,
And every act is whittled by the blade
Of history, pared down to brutal fact . . .
We are a different kind of tough; we hawk
Our epic violence in bleak bars, in bed, in art.

The spondee is "bleak bars," giving an additional intensity and urgency to the bleakness Doyle describes. (If you had trouble finding it, it may have been hard to find because Doyle uses a longer line, iambic hexameter instead of pentameter, for the last line of the poem.)

One of the following lines has two spondees; the others have one each. See if you can find them:

We crept in the tall grass and slept till noon

With his damned hoobla-hoobla-hoobla-how

There is a wide, wide wonder in it all

Slowly the poison the whole blood stream fills

Usually, the spondee has the effect of slowing down an iambic line by making it hold more accents (remember, one of the aspects of an accented syllable is length, so a line with more accented syllables will probably seem to last longer). Alexander Pope's famous passage about metrical effects shows how spondees and anapests can create the effects of slowness and speed, respectively:

From "Essay on Criticism," Alexander Pope (1711)

But when loud surges lash the sounding shore,
The hoarse, rough verse should like the torrent roar;
When Ajax strives some rock's vast weight to throw,
The line too labors, and the words move slow;
Not so, when swift Camilla scours the plain,
Flies o'er the unbending corn, and skims along the main.

Pope is actually making fun here of poets who use too much expressive varia-tion. He makes it easy for us to notice the spondees and anapests by describing the line slowing down and the words moving slow in lines including the spon-dees "loud surge," "rough verse," "some rocks'" "vast weight," "too lab," and "move slow." The last line speeds up with the anapest "the unbend" as well as with an extra iamb.

Though a skillful poet can use a rhythm to create virtually any effect, still, the standard accepted "meanings" of the feet are valid enough, enough of the time, that it is worth repeating them one more time: spondee-slowness, anapest-quickness, trochee-surprise.

Headless and Extra-Syllable Lines

The two variations in iambic pentameter that remain for us to discuss are quite simple. One variation cuts off the first unstressed syllable from the line, and the other adds a final extra syllable. A line with a missing first syllable is given the gruesome name **headless pentameter** (a translation of the technical Greek term *akephalos,* meaning a "headless" line). Here are two examples from the first feet of two very famous iambic pentameter poems:

From "Those Winter Sundays, " Robert Hayden

Sundays too my father got up early

From "Prologue" to The Canterbury Tales, *Geoffrey Chaucer*

When that Aprille with his showres soote

This variation can look like an initial trochee, but the effect is different—because the first foot it is not a trochee but half of an iamb, this opening seems to catch the reader in midsentence, as if we are coming in on the middle of a conversation. To show what is happening, we scan the line by indicating the missing syllable in parentheses:

(u) /]   u   / l   u   / l u   / l u / l (u)
  Sundays too my father got up early

(u) /   ]   u   / l   u   / l u   / l u   / l (u)
  When that Aprille with his showres soote

The line from Hayden is not only headless; it also has an extra syllable at the end. Parentheses are also used to indicate such an extra unstressed syllable at the end of the line, an effect that used to be called a "feminine ending" but is now more properly called an **extra-syllable ending.** It might seem that Hayden's line would scan more simply as a trochaic line, and one prosodist, James MacAuley, would in fact scan it that way. But most would agree that it is most important to recognize a poem's metrical consistency wherever possible, and that because all the rest of Hayden's poem is iambic, not trochaic, and this line can be scanned as iambic with two common variations, that is the correct scansion. Another well-known example of an extra-syllable ending occurs in this line from *Hamlet:*

/   l u / l u   / l /   u l u   / l (u)
  To be, or not to be, that is the question

The extra-syllable ending can create a lingering, falling, meditative effect and can be very beautiful, like a minor key in music. Again, we show the extra syllable in parentheses, to indicate that it is not part of the underlying metrical pattern of the line. Usually an extra-syllable ending involves a very unimportant syllable, like the last syllable of "question." There is a remarkable exception in "The Illiterate" by William Meredith above, where the man's secretive hiding of the letter is conveyed by the hiding of the important word "him" within an extra-syllable ending.

To recap, here are the most important basic variations in iambic pentameter:

1. The anapest, a metrical foot with a stress followed by two unaccented syllables (uu/) such as "on the way," can be substituted for an iamb anywhere in the line.
2. The trochee, a metrical foot with a stress followed by an unaccented syllable (/u) such as "open," can be substituted after a caesura in the line, or at the beginning of the line.
3. The pyrrhic, a metrical foot with two light syllables (uu) such as "in the," or the spondee, a metrical foot with two stressed syllables (//) such as "airplane," can be substituted for an iamb anywhere in the line, as long as the line as a whole keeps at least five accents.
4. An extra syllable can be added at the end, an effect simply referred to as an "extra-syllable ending."
5. The first, unstressed syllable can be dropped, making a "headless" line.

If you ever hear a definition of iambic pentameter as a 10-syllable line, ignore it. With four anapests and an extra-syllable ending, an iambic pentameter line could have as many as fourteen syllables. With a missing unstressed syllable (a rare variation sometimes called a *rest*), it could have as few as eight syllables. The nine-syllable line below has a rest or omitted unstressed syllable at the first syllable of the third foot, before "I," which adds force to the rest of the line:

From "To the Desert," Benjamin Alire Saenz

And keep me warm. I was born for you

Rarely, there is a two-syllable rest where a whole foot is missing, as happens in the extra-long caesura before the trochee in line 13 of Hamlet's soliloquy below:

Must give us pause: there's the respect

It is unlikely that Shakespeare would have paused this line for so long without such a self-conscious verbal warning!

Helpful Tip. While many lines of iambic pentameter do not have 10 syllables, it *is* true that almost all iambic pentameter lines will have at least five strong stresses. If you write a line of iambic pentameter and can hear only four strong stresses, it is likely that your line is not metrical.

Another Helpful Tip. The second foot of a line of iambic pentameter is especially sensitive and can upset the rhythm of a line. When in doubt about whether one of your lines scans, start by making sure the second foot is an iamb.

Scansion Exercise: Expressive Variation

Expressive variation is the term used to describe changes in the basic metrical pattern that are not random or at odds with the poem but work with the poem, emphasizing the feelings conveyed in the words. The amazing thing about expressive variation is that so many factors besides meter can be brought into play—including meaning, as in the line in the anapest section of this chapter about dying being difficult; imagery, as in the word "bend"; and word-music, as in the juxtaposition of "m's" in "calm milk-giver." As you will see in the chapter "The Metrical Palette," a skillful poet can literally make any meter create any effect, and still have it seem as if no other meter could have done the job. Nonetheless, meters do have strong tendencies. Anapestic speed and lightness, like spondaic slowness and intensity, are well-known effects for a good reason. When starting out writing in meter, it's a good idea to respect these commonly acknowledged metrical tendencies at first. It's too easy to write an unintentional joke if you choose a meter whose mood undermines the mood of your poem. Save your anapestic dirges until you have had more practice.

The poems below contain many exquisite examples of expressive variation, from the heaviness of the branches "loaded with ice a sunny winter morning" to the obsessive drivenness of "I might be driven to sell your love for peace." They show how natural and inevitable metrical variations seem when they connect seamlessly with the meaning of the line. At such points, it is impossible to tell whether the meter holds the meaning or the meaning holds the meter, and the old cliché of poetic form as a vessel or container into which the meaning of the poem is poured seems a very clumsy analogy. I prefer, instead, a paradoxical metaphor used by the Buddhist monk Thich Nhat Hanh: "Form is the wave, emptiness the water." Just as the water of the ocean can only come to us in the shape of the waves that embody and make it real, the emptiness of reality can only come to us in the shapes of the multiple forms we experience, which make it real. And just so, the meaning of lines of poetry can only come to us in the rhythms that embody and make them real. Though Thich Nhat Hanh was talking about the nature of our perception of reality, not about poetry, I have never found a closer approximation to my experience of the mystery of expressive variation.

Hamlet's soliloquy is one of the most famous iambic pentameter passages in our literature. Yet not one of the first five lines is a simple iambic pentameter made of five iambs. Read it aloud, enjoying and experiencing the meter, and noticing the variations.

From Hamlet, *William Shakespeare (1602)*

To be, or not to be: that is the question:
Whether 'tis nobler in the mind to suffer
The slings and arrows of outrageous fortune,
Or to take arms against a sea of troubles,
And by opposing end them? To die: to sleep;
No more; and by a sleep to say we end
The heart-ache and the thousand natural shocks
That flesh is heir to. 'Tis a consummation
Devoutly to be wish'd. To die, to sleep;
To sleep: perchance to dream: ay, there's the rub;
For in that sleep of death what dreams may come
When we have shuffled off this mortal coil,
Must give us pause: there's the respect
That makes calamity of so long life;
For who would bear the whips and scorns of time,
The oppressor's wrong, the proud man's contumely,
The pangs of despised love, the law's delay,
The insolence of office, and the spurns
That patient merit of the unworthy takes,
When he himself might his quietus make
With a bare bodkin? who would fardels bear,
To grunt and sweat under a weary life,
But that the dread of something after death,
The undiscover'd country from whose bourn

No traveller returns, puzzles the will
And makes us rather bear those ills we have
Than fly to others that we know not of?
Thus conscience does make cowards of us all;
And thus the native hue of resolution
Is sicklied o'er with the pale cast of thought.

Now scan the passage (if you want to see how I would scan it, look in the back of the book). Notice how the variations build in frequency as the mood of the passage intensifies. The interplay between the expected meter and the actual rhythm of the syllables is a powerful relationship. The memory or expectation of a metrical pattern becomes an active force in the line, adding its rueful or delicate or wry or enthusiastic twist to whatever is happening rhythmically in that line.

Read the following poem out loud, and notice how just a few variations can have dramatic impact in a poem that is so metrically regular.

Sonnet 30, Edna St. Vincent Millay (1931)

Love is not all: it is not meat nor drink
Nor slumber nor a roof against the rain;
Nor yet a floating spar to men that sink
And rise and sink and rise and sink again;
Love can not fill the thickened lung with breath,
Nor clean the blood, nor set the fractured bone;
Yet many a man is making friends with death
Even as I speak, for lack of love alone.
It well may be that in a difficult hour,
Pinned down by pain and moaning for release,
Or nagged by want past resolution's power,
I might be driven to sell your love for peace,
Or trade the memory of this night for food.
It well may be. I do not think I would.

Now scan it (again, to check your scanning against mine, look in the back). Notice the defiance in the spondee "Love can" and the pain in "pinned down." What is the effect on you of the extreme regularity of the meter in line 4? Notice how the anapests, increasing in frequency toward the end of the poem, interweave with certain consonant sounds that help them to echo anapests earlier in the poem.

"Chosen," Marilyn Nelson

Diverne wanted to die, that August night.
His face hung over hers, a sweating moon.
She wished so hard, she killed part of her heart.

If she had died, her one begotten son,
her life's one light, would never have been born.
Pomp Atwood might have been another man:

born with a single race, another name.
Diverne might not have known the starburst joy
her son would give her. And the man who came

out of a twelve-room house and ran to her
close shack across three yards that night, to leap
onto her cornshuck pallet. Pomp was their

share of the future. And it wasn't rape.
In spite of her raw terror. And his whip.

Only three spondees vary this historical poem, all involving the slave Diverne's son and his importance to her life: "Pomp At-," "born with," "burst joy." There are also three trochees expressing the excitement of Pomp's father: "out of," "onto," and "share of." There are no other substitutions, and no extra syllables. This sonnet, like Millay's, does a lot with very few variations.

By contrast, read aloud this passage from Frost's "Birches," and you will see how far a poem can move in the other direction—away from regularity—without crashing. Notice how Frost uses an occasional perfectly regular line to reestablish the rhythm after especially wild variations.

From "Birches," Robert Frost (1915)

When I see birches bend to left and right
Across the lines of straighter darker trees,

I like to think some boy's been swinging them.
But swinging doesn't bend them down to stay
As ice-storms do. Often you must have seen them
Loaded with ice a sunny winter morning
After a rain. They click upon themselves
As the breeze rises, and turn many-colored
As the stir cracks and crazes their enamel.
Soon the sun's warmth makes them shed crystal shells
Shattering and avalanching on the snow-crust—
Such heaps of broken glass to sweep away
You'd think the inner dome of heaven had fallen.
They are dragged to the withered bracken by the load,
And they seem not to break; though once they are bowed
So low for long, they never right themselves:
You may see their trunks arching in the woods
Years afterwards, trailing their leaves on the ground . . .

Now scan the poem and if you want to, check your scansion against mine in the back of the book. Notice how trochees enter the poem with the surprise of the ice-storm, how spondees can convey excitement (breeze rises, stir cracks) and also slowness, as in the three spondees in a row in line 10. Frost is good enough to break rules and make it work; not only does he use a stressed syllable for an extra-syllable ending; he manages to make anapests convey slowness in line 14 and pushes trochees almost to the brink of confusion in line 11, slightly over the brink in line 18.

Scanning poems written by poets skilled in variations on iambic meter can be challenging. It's easy to get disoriented. Don't forget your foot breaks! And one more thing: when scanning, bear in mind the simplicity principle. Like Occam's razor, the medieval philosophical idea that, all other things being equal, it's best to choose the simplest explanation, this principle reminds us always to stay as close to the basic metrical pattern as possible. In other words, where the base foot is iambic, keep as many iambic feet as you can. So it is better to scan Frost's line, "As the stir cracks and crazes their enamel," as pyrrhic | spondee | iamb | iamb | iamb | extra-syllable ending:

u u | /   / | u   /|u   / |u /(u)
as the stir cracks and crazes their enamel

than as anapest-trochee-trochee-trochee-trochee:

```
u  u  / | /   u |  / u|  /  u|/ u
as the stir cracks and crazes their enamel
```

In this case, the simpler scansion gives you three iambs, manifesting both the line's underlying metrical expectation and its rhythmic kinship with other lines in the poem. The simplicity principle applies not only to the kind of feet but also to the number of feet. If you are scanning a poem you know is basically in iambic pentameter, first do your best to scan each line with five feet before you decide that a line is longer or shorter, as it is at the ending of "Some Girls." In a nutshell, here is the simplicity principle: *The simplest (accurate) scansion is always best!*

Expressive Variation and Keeping Your Balance

Like learning to ride a bicycle, writing in meter is a skill that gets better with a little practice. At first, you're so afraid of falling over that you ride only in a straight line and always keep your wheels straight up and down. But after a while, you get a sense of how far you can lean at an angle and still keep your balance. When you are starting to write iambic pentameter, it's fine to start with a very regular basic line, trying out new combinations of syllables one by one to see how you can change the rhythm through substitutions. After you are more comfortable with meter, you will be riding your bicycle with full control, able to veer around corners and hop over curbs without worrying about balance. You won't have to think about varying the rhythm; it will happen by itself as you write.

Just as a bicycle going around a curve is balancing between momentum and gravity, a metrical line moving through a poem is balancing between the metrical pattern and ordinary, nonmetrical speech. Which angle to strike between these two rhythms is, up to a point, a matter both of fashion and of individual taste. In the eighteenth century, metrical poetry had a steady regularity that would have sounded dull in the Renaissance or the late nineteenth century. The common eighteenth-century term for metrical verse was "numbers," and each line of iambic pentameter did keep to "numbers": each line had 10 syllables, after the French model, and to add extra syllables was a sign of poor taste or poor skill. To avoid extra syllables, poets used **elisions** such as "wand'ring" and "ev'ry," as in this poem:

"The Apology," Anne Finch, Countess of Winchilsea (1685)

'Tis true I write and tell me by what Rule
I am alone forbid to play the fool,
To follow through the Groves a wand'ring Muse
And fain'd Idea's for my pleasures chuse.
Why shou'd it in my Pen be held a fault
Whilst Mira paints her face, to paint a thought?
Whilst Lamia to the manly Bumper flys
And borrow'd Spiritts sparkle in her Eyes,
Why should it be in me a thing so vain
To heat with Poetry my colder Brain?
But I write ill and there-fore should forbear.
Does Flavia cease now at her fortieth year
In ev'ry Place to let that face be seen
Which all the Town rejected at fifteen?
Each Woman has her weaknesse; mine indeed
Is still to write tho' hopeless to succeed.
Nor to the Men is this so easy found;
Ev'n in most Works with which the Wits abound
(So weak are all since our first breach with Heav'n)
Ther's less to be Applauded then forgiven.

Some poets today continue to prefer to write very regular iambic pentameter that always stays close to the basic ta-TUM ta-TUM ta-TUM ta-TUM ta-TUM pattern. Sometimes known as the "plain style," this type of meter was championed by the poet-critic Yvor Winters and his students at Stanford University in the middle of the twentieth century, such as Timothy Steele and Thom Gunn. Other contemporary poets prefer a dense and rhythmically complex iambic pentameter line (we might call it the "clotted style"), full of spondees, anapests, and caesuras, that stretches the pattern as far as it will go, more like the style of John Donne. If you scan this poem, you will discover numerous trochees, spondees, and anapests that clot and slow and complicate the underlying iambic beat:

"Batter My Heart," John Donne (1635)

Batter my heart, three-person'd God; for you
As yet but knock, breathe, shine, and seek to mend;
That I may rise and stand, o'erthrow mee, and bend
Your force to break, blow, burn, and make me new.
I, like an usurp'd town to'another due,
Labor to'admit you, but Oh, to no end;
Reason, your viceroy in mee, mee should defend,
But is captiv'd, and proves weak or untrue.
Yet dearly I love you, and would be lov'd fain,
But am betroth'd unto your enemie;
Divorce mee, untie, or breake that knot again,
Take me to you, imprison mee, for I,
Except you'enthrall mee, never shall be free,
Nor ever chaste, except you ravish me.

Experimenting with stretching the basic pattern is fun, and it's one of my own favorite ways to write in meter. But if your variations end up undermining the rhythm instead of stretching it, you can involve your readers in a bike crash and lose their trust for the rest of the poem. If you read a lot of metrical poems, scanning lines that sound unusual so you can really understand their rhythms, you will begin to develop an ear for which variations threaten the iambic pentameter and which ones stretch or tease it.

How to Avoid a Metrical Crash

As you are developing your ear, here are two tricks that can be used for a quick metrical check of iambic pentameter:

1. Make sure there are no trochees except at the beginnings of lines (and, if you are feeling confident, after punctuation or another strong caesura in the line).
2. Make sure the line has at least five strong accents.

How much substitution should you use in your metrical poems? Three factors, at least, will come into play. The first is your own aesthetic taste combined with your own skill level (even if you are drawn to a style with lots of variation, it's probably best to try only a few simple substitutions until you really get the hang of keeping your balance). The second is the expressive need at any particular moment in the poem—which variations will express the feeling or idea or aesthetic effect you want to get across. The third factor, which in a way implies the others, is your overall "metrical contract" with the reader. In a nutshell, you should vary the meter when it will be expressive and when it won't confuse or betray the reader's ear.

Metrical contract is a term, coined by John Hollander, for the understanding that reader and poet share about a poem's meter. The reader comes to count on a certain meter in a particular poem; if the poem suddenly breaks the meter, it is a violation of this unspoken contract. The metrically literate reader may respond in different ways: by feeling betrayed, getting bored, getting distracted, or just deciding the poet doesn't know how to use meter. Poets who want to honor the metrical contract and reap the full benefits of meter have more or less leeway to stretch the meter depending on how far the reader's ability to keep the meter in mind has already been tried at that point in the poem. For example, if you scan the first six lines of the following poem, you will see that the opening is very irregular, but there is a certain point where the meter has been stretched to the breaking point and, just then, the poet brings it back to exact regularity again—almost as if to say, "See, I was only teasing!"—before adding one extra variation for good measure. (When you are done, check the scansion against the one at the back of the book.)

Sonnet 116, William Shakespeare (1609)

Let me not to the marriage of true minds
Admit impediments. Love is not love
Which alters when it alteration finds,
Or bends with the remover to remove:
O no! it is an ever-fixed mark
That looks on tempests and is never shaken;
It is the star to every wandering bark,
Whose worth's unknown, although his height be taken.
Love's not Time's fool, though rosy lips and cheeks
Within his bending sickle's compass come:

Love alters not with his brief hours and weeks,
But bears it out even to the edge of doom.
If this be error and upon me proved
I never writ, nor no man ever loved.

As you write in meter and especially as you read aloud in meter, you will begin to get a sense of when to push and play and when to reassure. Working creatively with your reader's metrical expectations (and of course, at the same time with your own!) is one of the deep satisfactions of writing in meter. This chapter sets out rules and conventions that are generally accepted today for maintaining the iambic meter and keeping the "metrical contract" with a reader. However, it is worth keeping in mind that, as we noted above, ideas of meter change over time, and the line between expressing one's personal aesthetic and breaking the metrical contract is not always clear-cut. In the eighteenth century, as we have seen, anapestic substitutions were considered to break the meter, so poets such as Anne Finch and Alexander Pope used elisions to avoid them, as Pope does in this couplet:

At ev'ry Trifle scorn to take Offence,
That always shows Great Pride, or Little Sense.

A century and a half later, poets began to use anapests in iambic pentameter again, haltingly—and now they are common. But like anything that changes as our society changes, prosody can be controversial. Donne's more prosodically conservative contemporary Ben Jonson, presumably not just taking offense at a trifle, wrote that "Donne for not keeping of accent deserved hanging." And every century since has had its own prosodic controversies.

Iambic Dimeter, Trimeter, Tetrameter, and Fourteeners

With all the attention to iambic pentameter, we shouldn't overlook the other common iambic meters. Iambic tetrameter is the next most common meter after iambic pentameter. This shorter line can create an effect of openness and directness, used by Theodore Roethke, below:

From "Open House," Theodore Roethke (1941)

My secrets cry aloud.
I have no need for tongue.
My heart keeps open house,
My doors are widely swung.

Sometimes a line that could scan as iambic pentameter in an iambic pentameter poem needs to be scanned differently in iambic tetrameter. Scan this poem, paying particular attention to lines 3, 8, and 10:

"I Had a Dove," John Keats (1817)

I had a dove and the sweet dove died;
And I have thought it died of grieving:
O, what could it grieve for? Its feet were tied,
With a silken thread of my own hand's weaving;
Sweet little red feet! why should you die—
Why should you leave me, sweet bird! why?
You liv'd alone in the forest-tree,
Why, pretty thing! would you not live with me?
I kiss'd you oft and gave you white peas;
Why not live sweetly, as in the green trees?

There are many triple feet in the poem, contributing a casualness and innocence of tone, and also giving several lines in the poem 10 syllables. Each of lines 3, 8, and 10 could be scanned as iambic pentameter in another context. But Keats hurriedly skips over a syllable involving the bird directly ("it," "you," "live") in each of these lines, forcing it to fit the tetrameter pattern instead. The cumulative effect is chilling, as awareness of the bird's identity is repeatedly erased in order to keep the poem's almost flippant tone. This is a remarkably subtle example of creative use of the interplay between two possible scansions.

Iambic trimeter is not nearly as common as iambic tetrameter, but has been used for some memorable poems. This three-foot meter can have a strong waltzing effect, like the dance with a strong triple rhythm which was considered scandalous when it was first introduced in the nineteenth century. Here, the poet plays directly with the dance association:

"My Papa's Waltz," Theodore Roethke (1942)

The whiskey on your breath
Could make a small boy dizzy;
But I hung on like death:
Such waltzing was not easy.

We romped until the pans
Slid from the kitchen shelf;
My mother's countenance
Could not unfrown itself.

The hand that held my wrist
Was battered on one knuckle;
At every step you missed
My right ear scraped a buckle.

You beat time on my head
With a palm caked hard by dirt,
Then waltzed me off to bed
Still clinging to your shirt.

Roethke emphasizes the waltzing rhythm with strategically placed anapests and extra-syllable endings. By contrast, in the following poem, the speaker's determination to stand her ground feels even more dogged because the poem is successfully resisting the dancing tendency of the meter:

From "Under the Rose," Christina Rossetti (1866)

I think my mind is fixed
On one point and made up:
To accept my lot unmixed;
Never to drug the cup
But drink it by myself.
I'll not be wooed for pelf;
I'll not blot out my shame
With any man's good name;

But nameless as I stand,
My hand is my own hand,
And nameless as I came

I go to the dark land.

The single anapest in this passage (in the third line) is immediately balanced by a powerful trochee/iamb combination in the following line, and the rest of the lines never waver from iambic.

Even in a relatively short line, the contrast between irregularity and regularity can be used for strong effects. This four-line poem was the first one in a pamphlet Hughes put together to raise money for a legal defense fund:

"Justice," Langston Hughes (ca. 1931)

That Justice is a blind goddess
Is a thing to which we black are wise:
Her bandage hides two festering sores
That once perhaps were eyes.

Each line until the last has an irregularity in the iambic meter: A trochee ends the first line and a single anapest lightens each of the second and third lines. So the startling regularity of the last, shorter line, which brings the iambic meter into clear focus at the same time it brings the metaphor into focus, makes a strong contrast. Not a syllable of this poem is wasted.

Iambic poems also sometimes mix lines of different lengths, as George Herbert mixes pentameter and trimeter in this famous poem:

"Love (III)," George Herbert (1633)

Love bade me welcome; yet my soul drew back,
Guilty of dust and sin.
But quick-eyed Love, observing me grow slack
From my first entrance in,
Drew nearer to me, sweetly questioning
If I lacked anything.

"A guest," I answered "worthy to be here";
Love said, "You shall be he."
"I, the unkind, ungrateful? Ah, my dear,
I cannot look on Thee."
Love took my hand and smiling did reply,
"Who made the eyes but I?"

"Truth, Lord; but I have marr'd them: let my shame
Go where it doth deserve."
"And know you not," says Love, "who bore the blame?"
"My dear, then I will serve."
"You must sit down," says Love, "and taste my meat."
So I did sit and eat.

A minister who wrote poetry only about his complex relationship with God, Herbert skillfully uses the short line to draw the reader into the intimate spiritual space of the poem, with the alternating long and short lines capturing the approach and retreat, trust and mistrust, of this spiritual courtship.

The **ballad stanza,** discussed at length in another chapter, consists of alternating lines of iambic tetrameter and trimeter. It is the other central meter in English-language poetry besides iambic pentameter. A literary version is called **fourteeners**—a seven-foot line, once extremely popular, which simply combines two lines of ballad stanza into one line of seven iambs (iambic heptameter). The best-known poem ever written in fourteeners is Arthur Golding's translation of Ovid's *Metamorphoses* (1567), which includes the following description of Daphne being turned into a laurel tree to save herself from Apollo's pursuit. Since Apollo was the god of poetry in classical Greece, it also provides an explanation of why a laurel crown is the legendary ceremonial decoration worn by poets. Notice that you may have to pronounce some words in the old-fashioned way to keep the meter (e.g., "hanged" with two syllables in line 3, and "advised" with three syllables in line 7); the meter will guide you:

And as she ran the meeting windes hir garments backewarde blue,
So that hir naked skinne apearde behinde hir as she flue,
Hir goodly yellowe golden haire that hanged loose and slacke,
With every puffe of ayre did wave and tosse behinde hir backe.

Hir running made hir seeme more fayre, the youthfull God therefore
Coulde not abyde to waste his wordes in dalyance any more.
But as his love advysed him he gan to mende his pace,
And with the better foote before, the fleeing Nymph to chace.
And even as when the greedie Grewnde doth course the sielie Hare,
Amiddes the plaine and champion fielde without all covert bare, . . .
Both twaine of them doe straine themselves and lay on footemanship,
Who may best runne with all his force the tother to outstrip,
The t'one for safetie of his lyfe, the tother for his pray,
The Grewnde aye prest with open mouth to beare the Hare away,
Thrusts forth his snoute and gyrdeth out and at hir loynes doth snatch,
As though he would at everie stride betweene his teeth hir latch:
Againe in doubt of being caught the Hare aye shrinking slips
Upon the sodaine from his Jawes, and from betweene his lips:
So farde Apollo and the Mayde: hope made Apollo swift,
And feare did make the Mayden fleete devising how to shift. . . .
Howebeit he that did pursue of both the swifter went,
As furthred by the feathred wings that Cupid had him lent,
So that he would not let hir rest, but preased at hir heele
So neere that through hir scattred haire she might his breathing feele.
But when she sawe hir breath was gone and strength began to fayle,
The colour faded in hir cheekes, and ginning for to quayle,
Shee looked to Penaeus streame and sayde: Nowe Father dere,
And if yon streames have powre of Gods then help your daughter here.
O let the earth devour me quicke, on which I seeme too fayre,
Or else this shape which is my harme by chaunging straight appayre. . . .
This piteous prayer scarsly sed: hir sinewes waxed starke,
And therewithall about hir breast did grow a tender barke.
Hir haire was turned into leaves, hir armes in boughes did growe,
Hir feete that were ere while so swift, now rooted were as slowe.
Hir crowne became the toppe, and thus of that she earst had beene,
Remayned nothing in the worlde, but beautie fresh and greene.
Which when that Phoebus did beholde (affection did so move)
The tree to which his love was turnde he coulde no lesse but love,
And as he softly layde his hande upon the tender plant,
Within the barke newe overgrowne he felt hir heart yet pant. . . .
And in his armes embracing fast hir boughes and braunches lythe,

He proferde kisses to the tree, the tree did from him writhe.
Well (quoth Apollo) though my Feere and spouse thou can not bee,
Assuredly from this tyme forth yet shalt thou be my tree.
Thou shalt adorne my golden lockes, and eke my pleasant Harpe,
Thou shalt adorne my Quyver full of shaftes and arrowes sharpe.
Thou shalt adorne the valiant knyghts and royall Emperours:
When for their noble feates of armes like mightie conquerours,
Triumphantly with stately pompe up to the Capitoll,
They shall ascende with solemne traine that doe their deedes extoll. . . .
Before Augustus Pallace doore full duely shalt thou warde,
The Oke amid the Pallace yarde aye faythfully to garde,
And as my heade is never poulde nor never more without
A seemely bushe of youthfull haire that spreadeth rounde about,
Even so this honour give I thee continually to have
Thy braunches clad from time to tyme with leaves both fresh and brave.

Golding's skill with fourteeners is still famous after all these centuries because it is hard to equal; such long lines tend to break in the middle and sound clumsy. But Golding brings out their suppleness and their usefulness for telling stories and developing the dramatic situation; seven feet allow the momentum to build so that, for example, the reader's heart beats fast during the chase scene as Apollo closes in on his victim.

Iambic Pentameter in the Twenty-First Century

Because of the charged history of iambic pentameter during the twentieth century, it seems appropriate to pause and consider some of the implications of writing in this meter today. After all, Ezra Pound and the Imagists declared very early in the twentieth century that "to break the pentameter" was the "first heave" toward developing a new poetry. During much of the twentieth century, poets in the United States took their cue from this attitude, and to scoff at the artificiality or old-fashionedness of poets who wrote in meter eventually became fashionable. Meter seemed too mechanical, too easy, too expected a way to achieve that mysterious thing we call true poetry; "real" poetry, as opposed to mere verse, was bound to come in an original, unique, and unexpected shape and size.

In the innovation-weary twenty-first century, that attitude has been changing. Perhaps it is because technology is making it possible for audiences to experience regular rhythm through the ear again; or perhaps it is because, at a time when many of us are prone to feel helpless in the face of sobering realities, poets are rediscovering that this deeply grounded meter can give to a poem a satisfying solidity, a grace, and a strength and energy that can feel, at any rate, akin to power. And of course, in the wake of a full century of free verse, iambic pentameter no longer seems as constricting as it did. The great iconoclastic poet Robert Creeley's last book of poetry, which I heard him read from a few weeks before he died in 2005, was written largely in iambic pentameter couplets. He remarked to me that day that meter "had been there all along" for him. Now a younger generation of poets, even some of the most experimental stripe, are beginning to write iambic pentameter as well, whether plain style iambic like Karen Volkman, or a looser, more Donne-like iambic like Joshua Mehigan.

However, now that meter is beginning to seep back into contemporary poetry again, it is essential not to forget modernism's lessons. As Timothy Steele's book *Missing Measures* shows, the modernists did not mean to banish all meter permanently, but only to break down the dominance of iambic pentameter and to open the way for different kinds of metrical patterns. The centuries-long domination of meter by iambic pentameter proved stifling, and it's important to keep other metrical options available. Some noniambic meters are the subject of the next chapter.

QUESTIONS FOR MEDITATION OR DISCUSSION

Theodore Roethke wrote in his poem "Four for Sir John Davies,"

> I take this cadence from a man named Yeats;
> I take it, and I give it back again:
> For other tunes and other wanton beats
> Have tossed my heart and fiddled through my brain.
> Yes, I was dancing-mad, and how
> That came to be the bears and Yeats would know.

Read some poems by Yeats in this book and elsewhere. Is this passage really in the cadence of Yeats? If so, by what specific strategies do you think Roethke achieved this effect? Write your own iambic pentameter quatrain that attempts to capture another poet's cadence exactly.

How does it feel to read iambic pentameter? How does it feel to write it? Do you find that using this meter affects the "voice" in your poems? How?

Marilyn Nelson, in her essay "Owning the Masters," enters an ongoing conversation about the use of European-based meters by contemporary poets of color. Nelson writes, "Yes, writing in traditional form is taxing. But it is also liberating. . . . As we own the masters and learn to use more and more levels of this language we love, for whose continued evolution we share responsibility, the signifiers become ours." What do you think a contemporary writer gains or loses by engaging with poetic tradition?

When you read this line, you may have noticed a trochee in the middle of the line. Since trochees break the rhythm of iambic pentameter, why is this one here?

```
 /   ]  u  /|  u  /  |/u|u/   |(u)
To be, or not to be, that is the question
```

Look for other examples, in the poems throughout this book, of iambic lines that include trochees. In each case, how does it affect the momentum of the iambic line? Is there a rhythmic factor (having to do with syntax, grammar, punctuation, speech emphasis, or word-music) that influences the effect? In each case, is there a relation between this rhythmic change and the meaning or emotion of the poem at that point?

Richard Hoffman points out that a single anapest moves through the iambic lines of Robert Frost's famous poem "The Road Not Taken." Trace this anapest through the poem and meditate on its meaning. If it is ever missing, can you find a place where it appears again, in counterbalance?

Timothy Steele writes, "English iambic versification has greatly benefited from the historical tendency towards monosyllabism in our language . . . monosyllabic words are wonderfully handy." Do you agree? Look for examples of iambic pentameter lines that use monosyllabic words to support your claim.

QUOTES

Iambic pentameter goes da dum da dum da dum da dum da dum. And it shouldn't do that too often.
    —Howard Nemerov, via Charles Martin

Good blank verse does not sound like a series of identically measured lines. It sounds like a series of subtle variations on the same theme.
  —James Fenton

Writing about the iambic pentameter is like writing a defense of breathing. When I was a child I had severe asthma. I would lie perfectly still and concentrate on the production of the next breath. So I have never since been able to take breathing for granted. It is both the most natural and the most concentrated activity I know. One breath and the pentameter line have the same duration.
  —Carolyn Kizer

The more art is controlled, limited, worked over, the more it is free. . . . The more constraints one imposes, the more one frees oneself of the chains that shackle the spirit.
  —Igor Stravinsky

POETRY PRACTICES

(Group) Variation Sampler. Each person writes 15 lines in iambic pentameter that include at least two spondees, two pyrrhics, two anapests, and two trochees, as well as one headless line and one extra-syllable ending. Either look at everyone's as a group, or trade in pairs, and scan the poems to spot each other's variations. Copy your favorite line from the poem you have been scanning on the blackboard.

(Group) Group Blank Iambics. Pass a piece of paper around the group (or a subgroup). Each person writes one line of iambic pentameter and folds the paper so the next person can't see the previous line. Option: the first person can leave a clue ("verb," "plural noun," etc.) for the beginning of the next line. Circulate, and share the finished product.

Blank Iambic Verse. Write a poem of 20 lines in blank iambic verse. Write it in at least three drafts. Draft 1: Say what you want to say. Draft 2: Deepen the meaning and/or sound, and add word-music. 3. Build and focus the emotional coherence. In each draft, try these strategies: move the caesura as much as you can from line to line to add variety, including feminine and masculine caesuras. Change from long to short sentences to play off sentence length against the line length. Experiment with long and short syllables. Use a variety of metrical variations to help express the mood you want. Use at least three spondees, three anapests, three trochees, and two extra-syllable endings in your poem.

Caesura Thread. Read Tennyson's "Ulysses," or another passage of blank iambic verse, slowly and mark the caesura in each line. You may find that some lines have one stronger caesura and also some weaker ones. It's okay to mark only the strongest caesuras. Connect the caesuras in one line down the poem to notice how the caesura changes position as the poem proceeds. If the caesura occurred in the same place in every line, we would be likely to find the poem terribly monotonous. The modulation of caesuras is an important aspect of writing any poem in lines, whether in meter or free verse.

Meter Mimicry. Choose a passage in iambic pentameter that you admire or even love, from the poems in this book or elsewhere. Write an exact metrical copy of the passage, in different words but with the same metrical variations, syllable by syllable. Don't forget the line beginnings and endings, and any other substitutions or changes. Once you know the line's rhythm well, you may want to go further and also reproduce the relative weight of the different accents in the line, as well as the caesuras (whether caused by punctuation or simply by the meanings of the phrases in the line).

Pentameter Pastiche. Along the model of R. S. Gwynn's "Approaching a Significant Birthday," choose lines in iambic pentameter from a number of poems in this book and combine them into one poem. (Optional: See if others in the group can recognize where the lines came from.) Advanced variation: use the rhymes to arrange them into heroic couplets or into a sonnet (you can include lines from poems outside the book if necessary).

Iambic Pentameter Dialogue. With one other poet, practice your metrical chops by taking turns telling each other a line of iambic pentameter with variations. The other poet has to imitate the rhythmic pattern exactly in their own line. This will probably go more quickly if you decide that making sense is optional. Experiment with writing the lines down as you hear them and with keeping it oral. Is there a difference in how easily you pick up the rhythm?

CHAPTER 5

The Metrical Palette: Beyond Iambic Pentameter

Just as music has other time signatures besides 4/4 time, and painting has other ranges of color besides greens and yellows, poetry has other meters besides iambic. Yet for hundreds of years, almost all serious poetry in English meter has been written in iambs. One of the most exciting aspects of being a poet today is our access to a fascinating and almost unexplored landscape of metrical possibilities: the "noniambic" meters. In teaching a variety of meters to my students, I have found that certain poets come alive in trochees, dactyls, or anapests, writing poems that they could never have written in iambic meter.

Iambic meter can seem inevitable, if only because of its pervasiveness. Poets and critics have sometimes quoted phrases like, "I'll have a shake, a burger and some fries" (quoted by Robert Hass) or "a glass of California chardonnay" (quoted by Marilyn Hacker) to prove that iambs are simply "natural" to English speech. But in fact, it turns out that all meters with stresses every two or three syllables are equally natural to English. I have learned from conversation with linguists that, since English has a stress every second or third syllable no matter what the syntax is doing, anapests, trochees, and dactyls are just as likely to arise in English as iambs. This thought was confirmed for me years ago, when I was returning from a conference where I had heard a talk asserting the naturalness and centrality of iambic meter. Just as I was thinking that other meters could be natural as well, we hit some choppy skies and my idea was confirmed by some flawless anapests that may be familiar to you as well: "Please return to your seats and make sure that your seatbelts are fastened securely."

And it's not just rising meters. We also talk in trochees: "Pass the salt and pepper, sweetie." "Did you see what she was wearing?" "Have I got a story for you!" And in dactyls: "After you buy it, you need to assemble it." "Do you have time? Take a look at your calendar!" "When did she tell you that I couldn't be there?" Any regular rhythmic pattern that involves a stress every two or three syllables will turn up routinely in the everyday modulations of English. While writing this chapter, I stepped out to the post office. I was waiting in line looking at the placards on the walls when I found myself idly reading not only a phrase in iambic pentameter (with one anapest, which by now you should be able to find)—"Wherever you see this symbol, you'll find stamps"—but also a trochaic pentameter followed by a dactylic tetrameter: "Are you shipping something liquid, fragile, / perishable or potentially dangerous?"

I was once taught by a poet who had little experience with scansion but felt confident in solemnly assuring her students that "English falls naturally into iambics" (a sentence which scans as perfect dactyls). Still, I'm convinced by now that the real reason so many poets find iambic the inevitable meter is not ignorance or stubbornness, but simply the force of collective habit. After reading and being taught to venerate so many thousands of cherished iambic lines from so many centuries, and rarely hearing any other meters, naturally our ears have become attuned to recognize and imitate iambic meter. And that is exactly why noniambic meters have such fresh, exciting expressive riches to offer, not only as patterns used for substitution in iambic meter, but as rhythmic patterns of their own. This chapter will explore a few of their possibilities, building on the basic introduction to meter in the chapter before last.

Trochaic Meter (/u)

> Double, double, toil and trouble,
> Fire burn and cauldron bubble . . .
> Eye of newt, and toe of frog,
> Wool of bat, and tongue of dog,
> Adder's fork, and blind-worm's sting,
> Lizard's leg and owlet's wing;
> For a charm of powerful trouble,
> Like a hell-broth boil and bubble.

It is no coincidence that Shakespeare chose trochaic meter to help the witches brew up their "charm of powerful trouble" in act 4 of *Macbeth*. For almost as long as iambic meter has been the meter of logic, reason, power, and civilization, trochaic meter has tended to be associated with the uncanny and subversive. The most well-known lyric poem in trochees evokes a powerful creature of the wilderness in such a way as to make it seem to call into question all the ideas about God that were prevalent in Blake's time:

"Tyger! Tyger!" William Blake (1794)

Tyger! Tyger! burning bright
In the forests of the night
What immortal hand or eye
Could frame thy fearful symmetry?

In what distant deeps or skies
Burnt the fire of thine eyes?
On what wings dare he aspire?
What the hand dare seize the fire?

And what shoulder, & what art,
Could twist the sinews of thy heart?
And when thy heart began to beat,
What dread hand? & what dread feet?

What the hammer? what the chain?
In what furnace was thy brain?
What the anvil? what dread grasp
Dare its deadly terrors clasp?

When the stars threw down their spears
And water'd heaven with their tears,
Did he smile his work to see?
Did he who made the Lamb make thee?

Tyger! Tyger! burning bright
In the forests of the night,
What immortal hand or eye
Dare frame thy fearful symmetry?

Though several of these lines are iambic, the overwhelming power of the trochaic meter is what lends this poem its compelling vitality and its rare memorability. The trochee's power is not limited to lyric poetry: one of the most popular narrative poems, Edgar Allan Poe's "The Raven," is trochaic. Like the witches' song and "The Tyger," "The Raven" also invokes spooky subject matter. The long-standing association of trochees with the uncanny is the reason that witches' spells in popular culture—in movies or on television shows such as *Sabrina* or *Buffy the Vampire Slayer*—are usually written in trochees.

But there's no need to restrict your trochees only to spooky subjects. The mysterious power of this meter can be used for many different moods. When Longfellow chose trochaic meter for *Hiawatha,* his inspiration was not Shakespeare's witches but a completely different source: the meter of ancient Finnish oral poetry, the captivating, push-pull rhythm I describe in the introduction to this book. This rhythm, with pulsating stronger and weaker stresses in alternating feet, seems to have developed to accompany the pull of oars through rivers and fjords of northern Finland, where perhaps the ancient stories collected in the *Kalevala,* like the Native American legends gathered by Longfellow, were recounted for hours on end to entertain the rowers. Even in its English version, the meter can convey the lulling motion of oars. Try reading this excerpt aloud:

From Hiawatha, *Henry Wadsworth Longfellow (1855)*

And Nokomis, the old woman,
Pointing with her finger westward,
Spake these words to Hiawatha:
"Yonder dwells the great Pearl-Feather,
Megissogwon, the Magician,
Manito of Wealth and Wampum,
Guarded by his fiery serpents,
Guarded by the black pitch-water.
You can see his fiery serpents,
The Kenabeek, the great serpents,
Coiling, playing in the water;
You can see the black pitch-water
Stretching far away beyond them,
To the purple clouds of sunset!
"He it was who slew my father,
By his wicked wiles and cunning,
When he from the moon descended,

When he came on earth to seek me.
He, the mightiest of Magicians,
Sends the fever from the marshes,
Sends the pestilential vapors,
Sends the poisonous exhalations,
Sends the white fog from the fen-lands,
Sends disease and death among us!
"Take your bow, O Hiawatha,
Take your arrows, jasper-headed,
Take your war-club, Puggawaugun,
And your mittens, Minjekahwun,
And your birch-canoe for sailing,
And the oil of Mishe-Nahma,
So to smear its sides, that swiftly
You may pass the black pitch-water;
Slay this merciless magician,
Save the people from the fever
That he breathes across the fen-lands,
And avenge my father's murder!"
Straightway then my Hiawatha
Armed himself with all his war-gear,
Launched his birch-canoe for sailing;
With his palm it sides he patted,
Said with glee, "Cheemaun, my darling,
O my Birch-canoe! leap forward,
Where you see the fiery serpents,
Where you see the black pitch-water!"
. . . Then he took the oil of Nahma,
And the bows and sides annointed,
Smeared them well with oil, that swiftly
He might pass the black pitch-water.
All night long he sailed upon it,
Sailed upon that sluggish water,
Covered with its mould of ages,
Black with rotting water-rushes,
Rank with flags and leaves of lilies,
Stagnant, lifeless, dreary, dismal,

Lighted by the shimmering moonlight,
And by will-o'-the-wisps illumined,
Fires by ghosts of dead men kindled,
In their weary night-encampments.
All the air was white with moonlight,
All the water black with shadow,
And around him the Suggema,
The mosquito, sang his war-song,
And the fire-flies, Wah-wah-taysee,
Waved their torches to mislead him;
And the bull-frog, the Dahinda,
Thrust his head into the moonlight,
Fixed his yellow eyes upon him,
Sobbed and sank beneath the surface;
And anon a thousand whistles,
Answered over all the fen-lands,
And the heron, the Shuh-shuh gah,
Far off on the reedy margin,
Heralded the hero's coming.

As you were reading this passage, did you find yourself unnaturally stressing certain syllables at the beginnings of lines, such as "and" at the beginning of line 8, or "in" at the beginning of line 10? Readers commonly read noniambic meters in this unnatural way, simply because we are not as used to their variations as we are to the variations in iambic meter. But to do a good passage of noniambic poetry justice, we should read it with the same respect for its variations from the base meter as we read iambic meter. An educated reader of metrical poetry would not pronounce Shakespeare's line "to BE, or NOT to BE, that IS the QUESTion." Nor should you pronounce Longfellow's line, "AND aROUND him THE sshuhSHUHgah." Instead, read the lines with natural word-emphasis, simply pausing for a split second at the end of each line, but otherwise accenting them as if each line were prose. The meter will take care of itself; just listen, and appreciate the way Longfellow creates beauty and interest by varying from the basic trochaic meter, just as Shakespeare varies from the basic iambic meter.

Of course, sometimes a poet wants to create a pounding, intense trochaic rhythm, as Sara Josepha Hale does in the middle of the following passage.

From "Iron," Sarah Josepha Hale (1823)

... Then a voice, from out the mountains,
As an earthquake shook the ground,
And like frightened fawns the fountains,
Leaping, fled before the sound;
And the Anak oaks bowed lowly,
Quivering, aspen-like, with fear—
While the deep response came slowly,
Or it must have crushed mine ear!
"Iron! Iron! Iron!" crashing,
Like the battle-axe and shield;
Or the sword on helmet clashing,
Through a bloody battle-field:
"Iron! Iron! Iron!" rolling,
Like the far-off cannon's boom;
Or the death-knell, slowly tolling,
Through a dungeon's charnel gloom!
"Iron! Iron! Iron!" swinging,
Like the summer winds at play;
Or as bells of Time were ringing
In the blest Millennial Day!

Hale, who was not only the author of "Mary Had a Little Lamb" but also the person who spearheaded the movement to make Thanksgiving a national holiday, understood the value of public language and rhetoric. She starts this passage by building the trochaic rhythm slowly, interspersing clearly trochaic feet like "earthquake" and "frightened" after pyrrhics ("and the") or even iambs ("and like"). Because of this subtle buildup, when the poem reaches its climax with the word "Iron," the release of pent-up energy is dramatic and energetic, a movement similar to that in Claude McKay's "If We Must Die," which will be discussed in the chapter on the sonnet. (Locate Hale's entire poem online for the full effect.)

A skilled writer of noniambic meter, like a skilled writer of iambic meter, will develop a sense of the "metrical contract" with the reader and be sure not to push the variations too far. One fascinating example of how this works in trochaic meter is William Blake's revision of the beginning of stanza 2 of "The Tyger." An earlier version of the stanza began,

Burnt in distant deeps or skies
The cruel fire of thine eyes?

But Blake revised it to read,

In what distant deeps or skies
Burnt the fire of thine eyes?

The new version saves the powerful word "Burnt" for later in the sentence, giving the reader a chance to prepare for it and appreciate it. It also moves the trochaic phrase "burnt the" to a place where the grammar strengthens the emphasis on "burnt" even further, reconfirming the trochaic meter. In the first version, the second line starts with a strong iamb, continuing the iambs that began the last lines of the first stanza. In the new version, both lines start with trochees, the second with an extremely strong one. This reconfirmed trochaic meter resounds through the entire poem, making the sound of the meter indisputable at just the point where it might have been about to weaken.

These lines are a good reminder that the trochaic line is not simply the opposite of an iambic line. You will remember that it is common for a trochee to appear as the first foot of an iambic line, but the opposite is not true, because an iamb in the first foot of a trochaic line is harder to recover from. When writing trochees, it's a good idea to keep a trochee in the first foot whenever possible, unless you have a very good reason to vary it. This moving little poem does have a good reason; it would sound mechanical were it not for the variation at the beginning of the last line:

"Upon A Child," Robert Herrick (1648)

Here a pretty baby lies
Sung asleep with lullabies:
Pray be silent, and not stir
Th'easy earth that covers her.

Partly because iambs are so unusual at the beginnings of trochaic lines, this half-iamb surprises us, slows the line, makes us literally gasp a bit, just on the brink of realizing the true theme of the poem. (I say "half-iamb" because of the apostrophe, which would make most readers slur the first syllable and pronounce it very lightly.) This bone-chillingly casual effect is accomplished entirely through this single, subtle substitution in the trochaic meter.

You may have noticed that many of the lines in these trochaic poems—including every other line of "Iron" and all the lines of "The Tyger"—seem to be missing the final unstressed syllable. In lines of "falling meter"—trochees and dactyls—it is a common variation to leave off one or both of the last two unstressed syllables. I call such lines **footless** when leaving off one syllable, and **double footless** when leaving off two syllables. Correspondingly, just as the end of a line in falling meter can commonly lose syllables, the beginning of a line in falling meter can commonly add syllables; I call this the **running start.** These are the inverse variations to the common conventions for iambic and anapestic meter, where it's the end of the line that commonly adds unstressed syllables (the extra-syllable ending) and the beginning that loses them (the "headless" line).

The way to scan a "footless" trochaic line is, as with the headless iambic line, to mark the missing unstressed syllables in parentheses:

′ ˘ | ′ ˘ | ′ ˘ | ′ (˘)
Tyger, Tyger, burning bright

In "The Tyger," the missing final unstressed syllables are a key part of the beating rhythm which helps create this poem's physical and emotional impact. The meter is intertwined with the imagery of the forge, anvil, and hammer that builds gradually through the poem and is fully expressed in the fourth stanza.

When you are writing in a falling meter, remaining aware of running starts and footless lines can help reconcile your ear and your eye. For example, if you write,

I will write a lot of meter
Because it makes my poems sweeter,

your ear may say the lines sound fine together, but your eye may think there is a problem. In fact, the first syllable of "because" is part of a running start; readers won't hear it as interfering with the line. You'd scan the second line with parentheses around the extra-syllable beginning, like this:

(u) I /   u I   /   u I / u   I /   u
be cause it makes my poems sweeter

Notice how the parentheses make it very clear exactly how this line matches up with the line before it, and also how they differ. Such awareness of sameness and difference is one of the basic aims of scansion.

The subtle variations possible in a meter are among its delights and glories. Still, when you are starting out in any new meter, be careful not to overdo the variations. Too many running starts will turn your trochees into iambs and your dactyls into anapests. So start out by sticking very closely to the basic pattern. After you've read, and written, a lot of poems in a certain meter, you'll gain a surer sense of how much variation will work in a given spot without tipping things over the edge. A good rule of thumb, as in anything involving writing poetry, is: don't do something just because you can do it; do it only when other aspects of the poem demand it.

In addition to varying the meter with dactyls, footless lines, and perhaps an occasional running start, when writing trochees, keep the following two guidelines in mind to help you modulate the meter in subtle ways:

1. Vary the placement of the caesura
2. Not all stresses are equal; contrast light and strong stresses within your lines.

The word "trochee" (/u) comes from the Greek word for "running," and sometimes trochees, especially when they use the final unstressed syllables consistently, can have a very light, playful quality, as in this peddler's call from Shakespeare's *A Winter's Tale*:

Gloves as sweet as damask roses;
Masks for faces and for noses;
Bugle bracelet, necklace amber,
Perfume for a lady's chamber . . .

Or even funnier, as in Carolyn Kizer's wonderful parody of *Hiawatha*, "Mud Soup":

From "Mud Soup," Carolyn Kizer

Dice the pork and chop the celery,
Chop the onions, chop the carrots,
Chop the tender index finger.
Put the kettle on the burner,
Drop the lentils into kettle:
Two quarts water, two cups lentils.
Afternoon is wearing on . . .

So it is important to remember that trochees do not always have to be intense or heavy. Like any meter, they can really be used for any mood or subject. Still, awareness of the history and connotations of trochees as a clear alternative to the dominant meter of iambics can help you use them well. It is especially interesting to note that, as mentioned in the sonnet chapter, trochees have developed a tradition among African American poets in the twentieth century, including two important, ambitious, and self-consciously African American poems, Gwendolyn Brooks's epic *The Anniad* and Countee Cullen's lyric "Heritage." Here is a passage from the opening of *The Anniad*:

From The Anniad, *Gwendolyn Brooks (1949)*

Think of sweet and chocolate,
Left to folly or to fate,
Whom the higher gods forgot,
Whom the lower gods berate;
Physical and underfed
Fancying on the featherbed
What was never and is not . . .

In addition to the common footless line, FEATHerBED, Brooks also uses variations such as the substitution of a dactyl for a trochee, both at the end of a line (SWEET and CHOColate) and in the middle (FANCYing ON the). Occasionally an iamb can be substituted, such as "and is" in the last line (WHAT was NEVer and IS NOT); just like substituting a trochee in an iambic line, this usually happens after a caesura or pause in the grammar, in this case the grammatical pause after "never." Read the last line aloud. The momentum of the line might tempt you to read the line in an unnaturally accented way and pronounce "and is" as a trochee: "WHAT was NEVer AND is NOT," but I would urge you to resist this temptation. In fact, "and is" is most definitely an iamb, since "is" is a much more important monosyllable than "and" and would get more stress in any context. The correct way to read this line aloud, as with any line of metrical poetry, is to find a balance between the expected stress and the actual stress, so that you simultaneously remind your hearers of the underlying pattern and let them enjoy the pleasure of the variation from it. I would probably read the line with a half-stress on "is," less of a stress than on "not" but still more perceptible than on "and."

At a time when even iambic meter is mysterious to most poets, noniambic meters have been truly flying under the conscious radar of poetics. For example, I have not seen recent discussion of the common variations in noniambic meter outside of my own writings. Nor have I ever seen any mention in writing of such issues as the importance of trochaic meter in twentieth-century African American poetry. Yet for poets whose internal ears are fully attuned to meter, a meter such as trochees speaks a distinct language available to anyone who cares to notice it. Like Poe's purloined letter, meter is a secret left out in plain sight:

"Lullaby," W. H. Auden (1940)

Lay your sleeping head, my love,
Human on my faithless arm;
Time and fevers burn away
Individual beauty from
Thoughtful children, and the grave
Proves the child ephemeral:
But in my arms till break of day
Let the living creature lie,
Mortal, guilty, but to me
The entirely beautiful.

Soul and body have no bounds:
To lovers as they lie upon
Her tolerant enchanted slope
In their ordinary swoon,
Grave the vision Venus sends

Of supernatural sympathy,
Universal love and hope;
While an abstract insight wakes
Among the glaciers and the rocks
The hermit's sensual ecstasy.

Certainty, fidelity
On the stroke of midnight pass
Like vibrations of a bell
And fashionable madmen raise
Their pedantic boring cry:
Every farthing of the cost,
All the dreaded cards foretell,
Shall be paid, but from this night
Not a whisper, not a thought,
Not a kiss nor look be lost.

Beauty, midnight, vision dies:
Let the winds of dawn that blow
Softly round your dreaming head
Such a day of sweetness show
Eye and knocking heart may bless,
Find the mortal world enough;
Noons of dryness see you fed
By the involuntary powers,
Nights of insult let you pass
Watched by every human love.

We may be moved by this poem simply as a love poem. If we know that Auden was gay, the description of the suffering at the end, from which the speaker wants to protect his lover, takes on a much deeper meaning. And if we know that "Lullaby" is written in trochaic meter and have some awareness of the subversive and revolutionary meanings that have been carried by that metrical tradition, the rhythmic body of the poem can speak to us as eloquently as do its history, its words, and its images.

Anapestic Meter (uu/)

"Questions and Answers," Cirilo F. Bautista (trans. José Edmundo Ocampo Reyes)

Don't you know that a mountain is nothing but smoke?
Don't you know that a thought is nothing but foam?
Don't you know that sackfuls of rice will go bad
when they're hidden deep down in the breast of a poem?

Make a dragon swoop down from a mountain of smoke
that your thoughts made of foam may be put to the test;
make a throne out of rice that's been kept in a nook
that a God may be wrought from the poem in your breast.

This poem, originally written in Tagalog by a Filipino poet, has been trans-lated into anapests to approximate the rhythm of the original. An exhortation for the openness of imagination and of courage, it shows that, like trochees, anapests can have chantlike power. But the effect is more expansive than that of a trochaic chant—more of a sweeping rhythm, like the beating of wings, than like a heartbeat.

The origin of the word anapestic is a Greek word meaning "to strike up," an easy way to remember this pattern which rises at the end of the foot (uu/). When reading or writing anapestic meter, it may be useful to remember that the variations for anapestic meter are similar to those for iambic meter (since both are rising meters).

"I Would Live in Your Love," Sara Teasdale (1911)

I would live in your love as the sea-grasses live in the sea,
Borne up by each wave as it passes, drawn down by each wave that
    recedes;
I would empty my soul of the dreams that have gathered in me,
I would beat with your heart as it beats, I would follow your soul as it
    leads.

In this poem, variations include the cretic (GRAses LIVE) and the bacchius (es DRAWN DOWN), (by EACH WAVE). Anapestic poems frequently use "headless" lines, leaving off an initial unstressed syllable. The two-syllable feet that begin headless anapestic lines are often iambs; here it is a spondee that substitutes for the initial anapest (BORNE UP). Occasionally, anapestic lines also end with an extra syllable, as with the extra-syllable ending in iambic meter.

Like every meter, and every person, anapests have a great range of potential moods. And yet, like every meter, and every person, they have a distinctive flavor all their own as well. There is something deeply familiar about anapests, a quality that can feel gentle and homey, reassuring and even lulling. This is, after all, the meter of *The Cat in the Hat* and "The Night Before Christmas" and of some well-known favorites by "the Fireside poets," a group of five New England poets in the nineteenth century (Whittier, Longfellow, Holmes, Lowell, and Bryant) whose poetry was considered especially good for reading aloud around a fire.

Anapestic meter lends itself to reading aloud at length, particularly to narrative poetry. It engages the forward-stepping pace of the other rising meter, iambic, while also allowing extra space for details. The three syllables in each foot provide the potential for extra relaxation or the opposite, pounding momentum. Read these passages, including passages by two of the Fireside poets *aloud,* either physically aloud or aloud inside your mind, since that is how all metrical poetry is intended to be read. Notice how it feels. Note that in order not to lose pace with the meter, you will have to pause in places like after "climbed" in the first line quoted, after "and" in the third line from the end of the first stanza, and after "on" in the second line from the end.

From "Paul Revere's Ride," Henry Wadsworth Longfellow (1860)

... Then he climbed the tower of the Old North Church,
By the wooden stairs, with stealthy tread,
To the belfry-chamber overhead,
And startled the pigeons from their perch
On the sombre rafters, that round him made
Masses and moving shapes of shade,–
By the trembling ladder, steep and tall,
To the highest window in the wall,
Where he paused to listen and look down
A moment on the roofs of the town
And the moonlight flowing over all.

Beneath, in the churchyard, lay the dead,
In their night-encampment on the hill,
Wrapped in silence so deep and still
That he could hear, like a sentinel's tread,
The watchful night-wind, as it went
Creeping along from tent to tent,
And seeming to whisper, "All is well!"
A moment only he feels the spell
Of the place and the hour, and the secret dread
Of the lonely belfry and the dead . . .

A hurry of hoofs in a village street,
A shape in the moonlight, a bulk in the dark,
And beneath, from the pebbles, in passing, a spark
Struck out by a steed flying fearless and fleet;
That was all! And yet, through the gloom and the light,
The fate of a nation was riding that night.

The last passage quoted, the climax of the poem, demonstrates total command of pacing. Longfellow uses repeated caesuras to break up the lines and
create a momentum that is forced to gather tension to override the pauses.
When the first real pause happens, with the exclamation point, the person
reading aloud experiences a tangible combination of relief and exhilaration.
In the ensuing pause, like a hush, the next line and a half build a sense of extreme seriousness, sobered further by a counterpointing dactylic rhythm:
"fate of a nation was."

With all its potential for narrative and dramatic action, the anapestic meter
can be extremely conversational and natural, especially if there are strong
caesuras in some of the lines. This stanza occurs near the end of a passionate
poem about religious tolerance; it is a moment of lull in the poem's energy.
Read the stanza aloud and notice how many natural opportunities the "light
measure" of anapests provides for your voice to choose to pause, expressing
your individual interpretation while fully respecting the meter.

From "The Quaker Alumni," John Greenleaf Whittier (1860)

Forgive me, dear friends, if my vagrant thoughts seem
Like a school-boy's who idles and plays with his theme.

Forgive the light measure whose changes display
The sunshine and rain of our brief April day.

To read such a skillfully written metrical passage aloud is almost like performing prewritten music on the instrument of your own voice. The last line, in particular, allows your speaking voice to pause expressively for nearly as long as you like after "rain" and after "brief" while still remaining completely within the meter.

Anapestic meter is still being used for serious contemporary subjects, as shown by this excerpt from a recent narrative poem:

From "Mother's Side," Alfred Nicol

But again follows close behind once for some men.
The hope that his sisters invested in him—
like the little warm flame of a whiskey—grew dim,

but was never snuffed out like the promise he made
which he broke every day for as long as he stayed . . .

Here, the use of this traditional meter along with conventional syntax and diction somehow underscores the poem's wan, rueful bitterness about the wasted potential of a life. The conversational tone of anapestic poetry can extend to pathos or to humor as well:

From "The Boys," Oliver Wendell Holmes (1859)

Yes, we're boys,—always playing with tongue or with pen,—
And I sometimes have asked,—Shall we ever be men?
Shall we always be youthful, and laughing, and gay,
Till the last dear companion drops smiling away?

From "A Fable for Critics," James Russell Lowell (1848)

There comes Poe, with his raven, like Barnaby Rudge,
Three-fifths of him genius and two-fifths sheer fudge,
Who talks like a book of iambs and pentameters,
In a way to make people of common-sense damn metres . . .

In the fourth line quoted, Lowell is taking advantage, for humorous purposes, of one of the great potentials of metrical verse: its ability to goad people to stress syllables they wouldn't ordinarily stress.

Anapests' leisurely pacings are wonderful for creating a light, sensual, romantic tone, whether in long lines, as in the poem by Sara Teasdale, or short lines:

From "Maud," Alfred, Lord Tennyson (1855)

She is coming, my own, my sweet;
Were it ever so airy a tread,
My heart would hear her and beat,
Were it earth in an earthy bed;
My dust would hear her and beat,
Had I lain for a century dead,
Would start and tremble under her feet,
And blossom in purple and red.

Because of the short lines, the iambic substitutions feel even more significant in the poem. But whether this passage is considered iambic with anapestic substitutions, or anapestic with iambic substitutions, the anapests are contributing a delicious sense of pausing, of slowness, of space, of readiness for physical and emotional intensity.

The intensely descriptive potential of anapests can be demonstrated by two passages dwelling on the physical detail of death and of sensuality, respectively:

From "The Destruction of Sennacharib," George Gordon, Lord Byron (1815)

And there lay the rider distorted and pale,
With the dew on his brow, and the rust on his mail:
And the tents were all silent, the banners alone,
The lances unlifted, the trumpet unblown.

The repetition of the "un" prefix makes the meter feel completely necessary, and the anapestic pace is solemn, as if a camera were panning slowly over the smallest details of the battlefield. The details and the meter both have a more chaotic, rumpled feeling in this excerpt describing a follower of the wine god Bacchus:

From Atalanta in Calydon, *Algernon Charles Swinburne (1865)*

The ivy falls with the Bacchanal's hair
Over her eyebrows hiding her eyes;
The wild vine slipping down leaves bare
Her bright breast shortening into sighs;
The wild vine slips with the weight of its leaves,
But the berried ivy catches and cleaves
To the limbs that glitter, the feet that scare
The wolf that follows, the fawn that flies.

In addition to the iambic substitutions, the variations include a trochee in the second line and spondees in the fourth and fifth lines. Swinburne manipulates the combination of iambs and anapests to vary the pace and create sensual suspense, at the same time that the imagery and word-music weave their own texture.

The galloping potential of anapests is put to use in this famous riding poem:

From "How They Brought the Good News from Ghent to Aix," Robert Browning (1845)

Not a word to each other; we kept the great pace
Neck by neck, stride by stride, never changing our place;
I turn'd in my saddle and made its girths tight,
Then shorten'd each stirrup, and set the pique right,
Rebuckled the cheek-strap, chain'd slacker the bit . . .

One of the joys of being skilled in meter is the ability to write effective parodies, and this poem is no exception:

"How I brought the good news from Aix to Ghent (or Vice Versa)," R. J. Yeatman and W. C. Sellar" (1933)

I sprang to the rollocks and Jorrocks and me,
And I galloped, you galloped, he galloped, we galloped all three . . .
Not a word to each other; we kept changing place,
Neck to neck, back to front, ear to ear, face to face;

And we yelled once or twice, as we heard a clock chime,
Would you kindly oblige us, *Is that the right time?*

Perhaps because of the energy that rising meter gives to the end of a line, the rising meters—iambs and anapests—lend themselves more easily than trochees or dactyls to the alternation of three- and four-foot lines, called ballad or folk meter (which is in turn, very uncommon in dactyls or trochees):

From "The Hunting of the Snark," Lewis Carroll (1876)

And the Banker, inspired with courage so new
It was matter for general remark,
Rushed madly ahead and was lost to their view
In his zeal to discover the snark.

But while he was seeking with thimbles and care,
A Bandersnatch swiftly drew nigh
And grabbed at the Banker, who shrieked in despair,
For he knew it was useless to fly.

Iambs can slow the tempo of anapestic lines, just as anapests speed up the tempo of an iambic line. The alternation of line length also adds texture to a poem. "The Hunting of the Snark" alternates lines that end in anapests with lines that end in iambs. Since the poem adheres to the syllable count so exactly (there are no other iambs in the poem), those single syllables make a difference: the lines with iambic endings feel considerably shorter, even though the whole poem is in anapestic tetrameter. The most famous poem in anapestic ballad stanza, indeed one of the most famous poems in English, also uses occasional iambs in an anapestic base:

"Annabel Lee," Edgar Allan Poe (1849)

It was many and many a year ago,
In a kingdom by the sea,
That a maiden there lived whom you may know
By the name of Annabel Lee;
And this maiden she lived with no other thought
Than to love and be loved by me.

Here Poe takes full advantage of the light, dreamy potential of anapestic meter, evoking its kinship to the old oral ballads with the "once upon a time" opening, but adding another two lines to the stanzas, perhaps to make us realize we are in the grip of unreality.

For many of the poets quoted in this section, anapestic meter was mostly used as a diversion from other meters, a "light measure" chosen for popular subjects. As a result, much of its potential remains unexplored. To give a taste of the anapest's possible range, here is a passage of political outrage, from the poet who used anapestic meter most consistently, and therefore had the most opportunity to learn to vary it:

From "A Song in Time of Revolution," Algernon Charles Swinburne (1860)

The wind has the sound of a laugh in the clamour of days and of deeds:
The priests are scattered like chaff, and the rulers broken like reeds.

The high-priest sick from qualms, with his raiment bloodily dashed;
The thief with branded palms, and the liar with cheeks abashed.

They are smitten, they tremble greatly, they are pained for their pleasant
    things:
For the house of the priests made stately, and the might in the mouth of
    the kings.

They are grieved and greatly afraid; they are taken, they shall not flee:
For the heart of the nations is made as the strength of the springs of the
    sea. . .

For the breaking of gold in their hair they halt as a man made lame:
They are utterly naked and bare; their mouths are bitter with shame.

Wilt thou judge thy people now, O king that wast found most wise?
Wilt thou lie any more, O thou whose mouth is emptied of lies?

Swinburne uses a number of different devices to change the mood of the meter at various points in the poem. There is the unexpected skipped syllable in the line, "For the breaking of gold in their hair they halt as a man made lame."

There is the alliteration and assonance in the line, "They are grieved and greatly afraid; they are taken, they shall not flee." In the last couplet, there is the staggering of two parallel phrases so they occur at different places in the line.

In "A Song in Time of Revolution," almost all the feet are anapests or iambs. But other triple feet are an excellent way to add texture, variety, and expressiveness to anapestic rhythm. Such modulations are done skillfully in these varied lines from "The Night Before Christmas":

As dry leaves that before the wild hurricane fly,
When they meet with an obstacle mount to the sky.

The moon on the breast of the new-fallen snow
Gave the luster of midday to objects below

"as DRY LEAVES" and "the WILD HUR-" are bacchics. "with an ob-" is called a tribrach, the three-syllable equivalent to a pyrrhic. "FALLen-SNOW" and "GAVE the LUST-" are cretics. These kinds of variations can be as subtle as the common variations in iambic meter. If you read the passage aloud, or aloud to yourself, slowly, you will have a chance to notice how well they work by feeling the difference in your mouth between these syllables and the regular anapestic rhythm. This passage from a contemporary poem shows how complex the variations in a line of anapestic meter can be:

From "Halo in Decline," Indigo Moor

In your death, it appears as by Providence, bold:
all of gold, a thin halo rides high on your cheek
as you float down the Tiber, a glacial sweet shine—
still warm in the current, enough to cause steam
to rise slow in rivulets on Tiber's smooth skin.

The passage is all anapests until the fourth line, which is varied only by an iamb in the first foot. But the last line consists of an iamb, cretic, fourth paean, and bacchic—and yet, in the anapestic context of the poem, it still sounds like an anapestic line.

This poem gathers great expressiveness from an irregular combination of iambs and anapests:

From "Under the Waterfall," Thomas Hardy (1914)

... And when we had drunk from the glass together,
Arched by the oak-copse from the weather,
I held the vessel to rinse in the fall,
Where it slipped, and it sank, and was past recall,
Though we stooped and plumbed the little abyss
With long bared arms. There the glass still is.
And, as said, if I thrust my arm below
Cold water in a basin or bowl, a throe
From the past awakens a sense of that time,
And the glass we used, and the cascade's rhyme.
The basin seems the pool, and its edge
The hard smooth face of the brook-side ledge,
And the leafy pattern of china-ware
The hanging plants that were bathing there ...

The spondee of "bared arms" and the fourth paean of "-er in a bas-" are skillfully expressive variations, both seeming to convey the feeling of cold water on
a bare arm. But perhaps the most surprising variation here is the three iambs in
a row: "The basin seems the pool." If you are reading quickly, it's easy to think
that the second foot is an anapest, "seems the pool." This reading swallows up
the word "seems" entirely, just as the reality of the basin is swallowed up by the
overpowering memory of the two lovers' meeting by the pool. But because the
poem is tetrameter and that would give the line only three feet, we know that
the line really scans as three iambs followed by an anapest. So we need to go
back and read the word "seems" excruciatingly slowly to balance "-in seems"
with the other feet in the poem, enacting in a different way the power of the approaching memory.

An anapestic rhythm infuses this poem:

From "The Lifeguard," James Dickey

In a stable of boats I lie still,
From all sleeping children hidden.
The leap of a fish from its shadow
Makes the whole lake instantly tremble.

With my foot on the water, I feel
The moon outside . . .

I wash the black mud from my hands.
On a light given off by the grave
I kneel in the quick of the moon
At the heart of a distant forest
And hold in my arms a child
Of water, water, water.

The particular dreamy earnestness of tone is hard to imagine without anapestic meter. This free verse, so regular as to feel almost perfectly anapestic in many passages, gives an indication of the wonderful potential of anapests for a contemporary poetry.

Anapests, perhaps because they are a "rising" meter and more similar to iambs than trochees or dactyls, have been used somewhat more often than the falling meters in English-language poetry. But still, it was only in the late nineteenth century that three-syllable feet were fully accepted into poetry in English—a few decades before metrical poetry began to be largely displaced by free verse. Now that we have all meters available to us, to experiment with anapests and find your own vocabulary for the versatile anapestic meter will certainly add to your options as a poet.

Dactylic Meter (/uu)

The word "dactyl" derives from the Greek word for "finger," and a finger provides an easy way to remember this foot whose pattern in the classical system of prosody was a long syllable followed by two short syllables: hold up your index finger and start counting the phalanges from the bottom up. Though your bottom phalange may not really be longer than the top two, you will probably get the analogy. Dactylic meter is my own favorite noniambic meter, the meter that first inspired my interest in noniambic meters when, immersing myself in iambic pentameter passages for my PhD dissertation, I began to find passages of this magnificently fluid meter lurking in iambic and free verse poetry. I found the dactylic meter so gorgeous, and the emotions it seemed to unlock so powerful, that I felt compelled to begin to use it in my own poems.

It is actually surprising that so little dactylic poetry has been published in English, given the importance of this meter to the entire Western tradition of poetry. The **dactylic hexameter,** or line of six dactyls, was the standard epic meter of classical poetry, including Homer's *Odyssey* and *Iliad,* and, following them, Virgil's *Aeneid.* Another central meter was the **elegiac couplet,** consisting of a dactylic hexameter followed by a dactylic pentameter, with spondees allowed to be substituted for the dactyls in certain places. This was a standard mnemonic used by British students studying classical poetry to help them remember the pattern:

> Down in a deep, dark dell sat an old cow munching a beanstalk.
> Out of its mouth came forth yesterday's dinner and tea.

Or, as Ovid put it more succinctly in his *Amores* (1.1.27): "Sex mihi surgat opus numeris, in quinque residat": "Let my work surge in six feet, subside again in five."

Longfellow chose dactylic hexameter for his epic poem of the United States, *Evangeline,* because of the line's epic history, and the dactylic meter gives a strong, rolling quality to Longfellow's story of the exiled woman searching America for her lover. Earlier in this book, you read the opening of *Evangelina.* Here is another passage:

From Evangeline, *Henry Wadsworth Longfellow*

> Far asunder, on separate coasts, the Acadians landed;
> Scattered were they, like flakes of snow when the wind from the northeast
> Strikes aslant through the fogs that darken the Banks of Newfoundland.
> Friendless, homeless, hopeless, they wandered from city to city,
> From the cold lakes of the North to sultry Southern savannas—
> From the bleak shores of the sea to the lands where the Father of Waters
> Seizes the hills in his hands, and drags them down to the ocean,
> Deep in their sands to bury the scattered bones of the mammoth.
> Friends they sought and homes; and many, despairing, heartbroken,
> Asked of the earth but a grave, and no longer a friend nor a fireside.
> Written their history stands on tablets of stone in the churchyards.
> Long among them was seen a maiden who waited and wandered,
> Lowly and meek in spirit, and patiently suffering all things . . .

As if a morning of June, with all its music and sunshine,
Suddenly paused in the sky, and, fading, slowly descended
Into the east again, from whence it late had arisen.
Sometimes she lingered in towns, till, urged by the fever within her,
Urged by a restless longing, the hunger and thirst of the spirit,
She would commence again her endless search and endeavor;
Sometimes in churchyards strayed, and gazed on the crosses and
    tombstones,
Sat by some nameless grave, and thought that perhaps in its bosom
He was already at rest, and she longed to slumber beside him.
Sometimes a rumor, a hearsay, an inarticulate whisper,
Came with its airy hand to point and beckon her forward.
Sometimes she spake with those who had seen her beloved and known
    him,
But it was long ago, in some far-off place or forgotten.
"Gabriel Lajeunesse!" said they; "O, yes! we have seen him.
He was with Basil the blacksmith, and both have gone to the prairies;
Coureurs-des-Bois are they, and famous hunters and trappers,"
"Gabriel Lajeunesse!" said others; "O, yes! we have seen him.
He is a Voyageur in the lowlands of Louisiana."
Then would they say: "Dear child! why dream and wait for him longer?
Are there not other youths as fair as Gabriel? others
Who have hearts as tender and true, and spirits as loyal?
Here is Baptiste Leblanc, the notary's son, who has loved thee
Many a tedious year; come, give him thy hand and be happy!
Thou art too fair to be left to braid St. Catherine's tresses."
Then would Evangeline answer, serenely but sadly—"I cannot!
Whither my heart has gone, there follows my hand, and not elsewhere
For when the heart goes before, like a lamp, and illumines the pathway,
Many things are made clear, that else lie hidden in darkness."

Even the most regular dactylic poetry, of which *Evangeline* is an example, makes frequent use of trochees, often at line endings but throughout the line as well. The trochees add contrast and texture without disrupting the falling rhythm, just as anapests do in an iambic line without disrupting the rising rhythm. The last line of the passage above plays with the expectation of frequent trochees by using the trochaic word "village" directly before a caesura, as part of a dactylic foot. Though the rhythm of the word "village" parallels the final trochee, "farm-ers," the syllable "the" after it adds an almost melancholy fall, reestablishing the dactylic pattern.

Dactyls have a magnificent pull to them, a sway; they come in waves. This passage uses their mystery well. Each line ends with a trochee, making them technically "adonic" lines (see the section on sapphic stanza) but dactylic sounds. Dactyls sound so distinctive that a relatively small but consistent per-centage of them creates a distinct dactylic effect:

"Mushrooms," Sylvia Plath (1957)

Perfectly voiceless,
Widen the crannies,
Shoulder through holes. We

Diet on water

Robert Browning's "The Lost Leader" conveys passionate anger against an-other poet, who has "sold out," in a gathering rush of regular dactyls:

Just for a handful of silver he left us,
    Just for a ribbon to stick in his coat—

While the trochee is by far the most common variation in dactylic meter, another fairly common variation is that dactylic lines sometimes begin with the running start, an "extra-syllable beginning" (structurally analogous to the "ex-tra-syllable ending" that occurs in iambic lines, and, like them, marked in parentheses). The extra-syllable beginning occurs in lines 2, 5, 7, and 10 in this poem about Arachne, a weaver who was turned into a spider by Athena because she boasted that her weaving was better than the goddess's:

"Arachne Gives Thanks to Athena," A. E. Stallings

It is no punishment. They are mistaken—
The brothers, the father. My prayers were answered.
I was all fingertips. Nothing was perfect:
What I had woven, the moths will have eaten;
At the end of my rope was a noose's knot.

Now it's no longer the thing, but the pattern,
And that will endure, even though webs be broken.
I, if not beautiful, am beauty's maker.
Old age cannot rob me, nor cowardly lovers.
The moon once pulled blood from me. Now I pull silver.
Here are the lines I pulled from my own belly—
Hang them with rainbows, ice, dewdrops, darkness.

Some dactylic lines, as does line 5 above, actually begin with two extra unstressed syllables. Some might prefer to scan "At the end of my rope was a noose's knot" as an anapestic line, but since that would make it the only anapestic line in a dactylic poem, the principle of prosodic consistency makes it preferable to scan it with a two-syllable running start and a final foot missing two unstressed syllables:

(u u) l / u u l / u ul / ul / (u u)
At the end of my rope was a noose's knot

Other variations in dactylic lines include the antibacchic (//u) (as in the first foot of line 9 in Stallings's poem), cretic (/u/) (as in the first foot of line 8 in Stallings's poem), first paean (/uuu), and molossus (///) (as in the third foot of the last line of Stallings's poem). As we have seen, a frequent type of "footless" dactylic line, like the footless trochaic line, skips either one or both final unstressed syllables (a line that skips two final unstressed syllables could be called a "double footless line"). Look for the footless lines in the following passage:

From "Goblin Market," Christina Rossetti (1859)

Apples and quinces,
Lemons and oranges,
Plump unpecked cherries,
Melons and raspberries,
Bloom-down-cheeked peaches,
Swart-headed mulberries,
Wild free-born cranberries,
Crab-apples, dewberries,
Pine-apples, blackberries,
Apricots, strawberries;—

There are three footless lines, including those ending with QUINces" and "CHERries." Can you find the third?

The following poem, a paean to marchers for workers' rights, begins in dactylic hexameter, then switches after two stanzas to dactylic pentameter:

"At Last the Women Are Moving," Genevieve Taggard (1935)

Last, walking with stiff legs as if they carried bundles
Came mothers, housewives, old women who knew why they abhorred
    war.
Their clothes bunched about them, they hobbled with anxious steps
To keep with the stride of the marchers, erect bearing wide banners.

Such women looked odd, marching on American asphalt.
Kitchens they knew, sinks, suds, stew-pots and pennies . . .
Dull hurry and worry, clatter, wet hands and backache.
Here they were out in the glare on the militant march.

How did these timid, the slaves of breakfast and supper
Get out in the line, drop for once dish-rag and broom?
Here they are as work-worn as stitchers and fitters.
Mama have you got some grub, now none of their business.

Oh, but those who know in their growing sons and their husbands
How the exhausted body needs sleep, how often needs food,
These, whose business is keeping the body alive,
These are ready, if you talk their language, to strike.

Kitchen is small, the family story is sad.
Out of the musty flats the women come thinking:
Not for me and mine only. For my class I have come
To walk city miles with many, my will in our work.

Like Longfellow, Taggard chose the dactylic hexameter, meter of the great classical epics, to lend heroic dignity to her story. Taggard's dactylic meter is rougher and more awkward than Longfellow's, perhaps in solidarity with the "stiff legs" of the women she writes about. She intersperses many trochees with the dactyls, and she uses running starts ("came," "there," "Oh, but") antibacchics ("clothes bunched a," "stiff legs as," "line, drop for"), cretics ("housewives, old," "bearing wide"), one-syllable feet followed by a rest ("Last," "(e)rect," "once," "odd," "suds"), and first paeans ("Mama have you," "ready, if you"). The dactylic rhythm is powerful, running over these obstacles and rough places, and uniting the poem with great energy. A more measured and metaphysical use of the meter shapes the following poem:

"The Slip," Rachel Hadas

Empty and trembling, haloed by absences,
whooshings, invisible leave-takings, finishes,
images, closure: departures so gracefully
practice their gestures that when they do happen,
dazzled with sunlight, distracted by darkness,
mercifully often we miss the event.
So many hours, days, weeks, years, and decades
spent—no, slathered and lavished and squandered
ardently, avidly gazing at nothing,
pacing the pavement or peering round corners,
setting the table and sniffing the twilight,
sitting and gazing at edges, horizons,
preparing occasions that leave us exhausted,
recovering, staggering back to a climax.
Dramas of use, inanition, repletion!
And there all along, except not there forever,
was the beloved. The foreground? The background?
Thoughtful, impatient, affectionate, angry,
tired, distracted, preoccupied, human,
part of our lives past quotidian limits,
there all the while and yet not there forever.

As with most dactylic poems, the most common substitutions here are trochees. But Hadas uses many different variations to keep this rhythm from being monotonous. She actually substitutes an anapest for a dactyl (when they DO HAPpen); this is a daring move, but she uses performative utterance to get away with it: since the sense demands extreme stress on DO for rhetorical effect anyway, the extreme stress on DO needed to make the reader notice that this really is an anapest in a dactylic context makes total sense. She also uses a spondee

(HOURS, DAYS), a bacchus (WEEKS, YEARS and), an antispast (PEERing ROUND), two amphibrachs in a row (prePARing ocCASions) followed by an entire line of amphibrachs (reCOVering, STAGger ing BACK to a CLIMax). And the metrical climax fully expresses the climax in the poem's meaning; immediately afterward, the poem regains its balance and the last seven lines are completely regular, reminding us that not only the beloved but also the meter were "there all along."

By contrast, the poem below uses completely regular dactylic trimeter without relying on any metrical substitutions except for trochees and footless lines to keep the reader's interest. Instead, the question and answer format provides a dramatic structure of repetition and variation that builds suspense, and the short lines create a sense of movement:

"The Denouement," R. S. Gwynn

Who were those persons who chased us?
They were the last of the others.

Why must we always be running?
We are the last of our own.

Where is the shelter you spoke of?
Between us. All around us.

Shall we be safe until morning?
There is no doorway to enter.

How shall we live in this desert?
Just as we did in the farmlands.

How was it done in the farmlands?
Just as it shall be here.

What is the word for this place?
No one has ever used it.

When shall I hear the word?
Never, until it is spoken.

Who were my father and mother?
Trust me to keep your secret.

What is the mark on your forehead?
What is the mark on your cheek?

Dactylic meter, as a triple, falling meter, is metrically the furthest a poet can move from the double, rising meter of iambic. Perhaps that explains why dactyls seem to carry such surprising and powerful energies. When I began to write in dactyls, I was rewarded immediately by finding a different voice for my poems. That is why I encourage you to explore all the metrical possibilities you can find in your own poems: so you will know how to write all the voices hidden within you.

Mixed Meters

Sometimes you may run across a poem that you know is rising or falling in meter, but the meter is hard to identify as iambs or anapests, or even as trochees or dactyls, since it has about the same amount of double and triple feet. You don't need to choose; these patterns are called mixed meter (the Greek term is *logodaeic*). Often, these poems are easy to read, popular poems, the kind that used to be printed in newspapers back when newspapers printed lots of poetry. They are meant to be read aloud and have an effect similar to accentual poems. Scan the following poem by Georgia Douglas Johnson to notice the anapests and iambs:

Georgia Douglas Johnson, "Your World" (1962)

Your world is as big as you make it
I know, for I used to abide
In the narrowest nest in a corner
My wings pressing close to my side

But I sighted the distant horizon
Where the sky-line encircled the sea
And I throbbed with a burning desire
To travel this immensity.

I battered the cordons around me
And cradled my wings on the breeze
Then soared to the uttermost reaches
with rapture, with power, with ease!

This poem moves fluidly between anapests and iambs; the many extra-syllable endings sometimes give the poem the swing of amphibrachs also. This meter works in quite a different way than the more "literary" poems in this chapter, where a clear base meter persists through various metrical variations and asserts itself again at the end. Johnson's poem is the kind of popular verse that is really meant for the ear, and our ears enjoy the changes of rhythm and tempo, the counterpoint between various triples and a running accentual beat, without needing to focus on the base-meter-and-variation dynamic that is fundamental to the rhythms of most of the other metrical poems we have discussed.

Another kind of mixing of meters is simply to splice together lines of different meters in one poem. This is not done as often as it should be. In the following excerpt, the effect is self-conscious:

From "Mezzo Cammin," Judith Moffett

I mean to mark the Midway Day
With soundings in this verse form. Say,
Muse, how you hate it!
I know your taste for excess. But
These jingly rhymes must undercut,
Counter, deflate it . . .

The short lines consist of a dactyl and a trochee (like the last line of a sapphic stanza), while the longer lines are all iambic tetrameter. The effect is unusual and quite fascinating. In the following poem, a tour de force which imitates the variety of musical instruments, the different meters of each stanza create a palette of different feelings:

From "A Hymn for St. Cecilia's Day," John Dryden (1687)

What passion cannot Music raise and quell?
When Jubal struck the chorded shell,

His listening brethren stood around,
And, wondering, on their faces fell
To worship that celestial sound:
Less than a God they thought there could not dwell
Within the hollow of that shell,
That spoke so sweetly, and so well.
What passion cannot Music raise and quell?

The trumpet's loud clangour
Excites us to arms,
With shrill notes of anger,
And mortal alarms.
The double double double beat
Of the thundering drum
Cries Hark! the foes come;
Charge, charge, 'tis too late to retreat!

The soft complaining flute,
In dying notes, discovers
The woes of hopeless lovers,
Whose dirge is whisper'd by the warbling lute.

Of course, it is not only the meter itself—iambic tetrameters, pentameters, and trimeters, amphibrachic dimeters and trimeters—that creates such palpably different effects, but also Dryden's weaving in of other aspects of the language: word-music, syntax, and syllable weight.

Tips for Writing in Meter

Step 1. Writing Early Drafts
There are two main methods; choose the one that sounds most enjoyable to you.

    Method A: Start by feeling the beat strongly and then open yourself to letting the words come. Do not censor yourself. Relax, or allow the meter itself to relax you. Meter can hypnotize your mind so that you may write things you never intended to say. Dance or chant your words. Write nonsense if it's easier.

Method B: Write what you want to say in prose, free verse, or in a meter that is easy for you. Then choose a meter to translate it into. You might listen for a meter that is beginning to emerge by itself, or simply decide which meter you want to use. As you translate it, read it aloud as you go to make sure you are still on track with the beat.

Whichever method you use, *read aloud* to yourself frequently as you write.

Step 2. Check for Meter

Check for metrical consistency by reading your poem aloud and exaggerating your intended meter. When you find a place where the wrong syllable of a word is emphasized, stop. This is your signal to fix the meter. For example, if you intended to write anapestic meter, read your lines aloud like this:

I am WRITing in ANapests NOW, and you KNOW
that it MAKES things sound STRANGE to do THAT, but don't WORry, just GO on, you KNOW we can SING, happilY

As you are reading and exaggerating, when you get to the word "happilY," your ear will notice that the third syllable sounds unnatural when it is accented. That's a signal that that part of the poem is not following the base meter. Often, a simple change of word order will fix the meter—in this case, "we can HAPpily SING." Until you have the basic pattern down and are quite sure of your ear, it is best to follow the base meter exactly, with no variations at all. (If you are confident you know what you are doing and are ready to try varying the meter on purpose, see step 4.)

Step 3. Check for Language

Check your poem for the following common mistakes and correct them:

- Any unnatural word order (syntax). Example: "my hat so red I put on my head"
- Filler words that don't mean anything. Example: "the sun *so* bright," "when I *did* go outside"

- Archaic or overly literary words that you would never use otherwise, that thought they had a right to sneak in along with the meter. Example: "e'er," "yonder," "lo!"

Step 4. Check for Fluidity

- Once you are sure your meter is right, read your poem aloud and notice places where the rhythm sounds too singsong or mechanical or predictable. Experiment with changing these places. Sometimes a simple word change that doesn't actually change the meter will work. For example, the line "We WALK unDER the SUNny SKY" sounds mechanical, while substituting the word "AMPle" for "SUNny" sounds much more fluid and interesting; although the meter is the same, the consonants and vowels are different, slowing the word in different places and giving the line more rhythmic interest.
- In other cases, you may want to try some of the metrical variations discussed in the chapters that follow. After a little practice, your ear will tell you which variations add fluidity and which ones undermine the meter.
- After adding variations, read your poem aloud again with your meaning or emotional tone in mind, to see if the variation adds meaning to the poem. Be careful that the rhythm works for the mood you are trying to set, not against it.

Step 5. Listen to Your Poem

- Read your poem in a natural voice, with natural intonation, to yourself. Or sing it. See how it sounds. Feel free to dwell on the rhythm, immerse yourself in it. Tinker with it for fun.
- Read it to a friend. Ask your friend to close their eyes and listen not for the meaning of the words, but for the sound. Ask them if they notice any places where the beat sounds off. Ask about boring places, interesting places, and beautiful places.

Step 6. Listen to Your Poem Freshly

Let the poem sit for as long as possible without looking at it, and then read it aloud to yourself one more time.

Amphibrachs, Dipodics, and Hendecasyllabics

The world is so full of a number of things
I'm sure we should all be as happy as kings.

—ROBERT LOUIS STEVENSON

There are numerous other noniambic patterns, and they are all worth writing. Feel free to skip this section if this is your first exposure to this material, but once you have the basics down, you may want to come back to this chapter so you can venture out and try your hand at cretics, amphibrachs, hendeca-syllabics, sapphics (which are discussed in the stanza chapter since they are technically a stanza) and other less common metrical patterns.

Amphibrachs (u/u) make a meter with a distinct and compelling rhythm. The central syllable of each foot is stressed, and the meter is not usually varied. While they may be familiar to you as the meter of many limericks ("There was a young poet from Utah, / who found that she liked writing met-ah"—now you finish the poem!), they have a more dignified history as a staple meter of Russian poetry:

"The White Bird," Anna Akhmatova (1914) (trans. Annie Finch with George Kline)

So worried about me, so jealous, so tender—
As steady as God's sun, as warm as Love's breath—
he wanted no songs of the past I remembered.
He took my white bird, and he put it to death.

At sunset, he found me in my own front room.
"Now love me, and laugh, and write poems," he said.
So I dug a grave in the old alder's gloom,
Behind the round well, for my happy, bright bird.

I promised him I wouldn't cry any more;
The heart in my chest is as heavy as stone,
And everywhere, always, it seems that I hear
The tender, sweet voice of the one who is gone.

It's common in amphibrachs to substitute an iamb or spondee for the final foot (as in the second and fourth lines).

Although amphibrachs are not common in English now outside of limericks, at one time they had great appeal. For proof, here is one of the most popular American poems ever written, sold in numerous editions and memorized
by generations of children:

From "The Old Oaken Bucket," Samuel Woodworth (1817)

How dear to this heart are the scenes of my childhood,
When fond recollection presents them to view!
The orchard, the meadow, the deep-tangled wild-wood,
And every loved spot which my infancy knew!
The wide-spreading pond, and the mill that stood by it,
The bridge, and the rock where the cataract fell,
The cot of my father, the dairy-house nigh it,
And e'en the rude bucket that hung in the well—
The old oaken bucket, the iron-bound bucket,
The moss-covered bucket which hung in the well.

That moss-covered vessel I hailed as a treasure,
For often at noon, when returned from the field,
I found it the source of an exquisite pleasure,
The purest and sweetest that nature can yield.
How ardent I seized it, with hands that were glowing,
And quick to the white-pebbled bottom it fell;
Then soon, with the emblem of truth overflowing,
And dripping with coolness, it rose from the well
The old oaken bucket, the iron-bound bucket,
The moss-covered bucket arose from the well.

How sweet from the green mossy brim to receive it,
As poised on the curb it inclined to my lips!
Not a full blushing goblet could tempt me to leave it,
The brightest that beauty or revelry sips.
And now, far removed from the loved habitation,
The tear of regret will intrusively swell,
As fancy reverts to my father's plantation,
And sighs for the bucket that hangs in the well
The old oaken bucket, the iron-bound bucket,
The moss-covered bucket that hangs in the well!

Amphibrachs are often overlooked when people write about English meter, and you will sometimes see amphibrachic poems classified as anapests with the first syllable missing. But in fact, the two rhythms sound quite distinct. Read aloud two lines of amphibrachs (for example, the lines by Stevenson quoted at the beginning of this section) and two lines of anapests (for example, the lines quoted from "The Boys" by Oliver Wendell Holmes). If you are unsure of the difference, try forcing the lines into each others' meter. If you read the Stevenson lines as if they were exaggerated anapests, pausing a second after each stress, you may feel a little seasick, as if you are swimming against slapping waves: "The WORLD | is so FULL | of a NUM | ber of THINGS." By contrast, if you read them as exaggerated amphibrachs, pausing for a second after each foot, the syntax and phrasing will feel much more natural: "The WORLD is | so FULL of | a NUMber | of THINGS." Similarly, if you read the Holmes lines as exaggerated amphibrachs, it will feel forced, jerky, and constantly interrupted: "we're BOYS al | ways PLAY ing | with TONGUE or | with PEN." But if you read it as exaggerated anapests, it will feel more smooth, as if a wave is cresting at the end of each foot: "we're BOYS | always PLAY | ing with TONGUE | or with PEN." Skillful writers of every meter work with the meter, using phrasing, word stress, and intonation both to reinforce the expected pattern and to add surprise and interest to it. Sometimes when you are reading a passage whose meter you don't recognize, it can feel forced and disconnected, like an academic exercise. But once you grasp the right pattern, if the poet knew what they were doing, everything clicks into place and comes to life. That's when you know you have found the right pattern.

When you are learning to write amphibrachs, as with any meter, it helps to read aloud frequently and make sure that you are paying attention to the foot breaks. Try pausing for a split second between feet to notice how the foot break accentuates your meaning, and to make sure you are using the meter to convey the feeling you want to express. If you get confused, just put the poem away for a while and go do something else. When you return, look at it freshly. If you get really confused, find another poem that uses the meter consistently and regularly to use as a rhythmic model.

Another distinctively energetic metrical pattern is the **dipodic.** The word means "two feet," and dipodic meter literally means a kind of meter where pairs of feet are meant to be heard together. Generally, one of the feet has a stronger stress than the other; an example you might know is the Gilbert and Sullivan song, "I am the very model of a modern major general," or this well-known poem:

From "Casey at the Bat," Ernest Lawrence Thayer (1888)

The Outlook wasn't brilliant for the Mudville nine that day:
The score stood four to two, with but one inning more to play.
And then when Cooney died at first, and Barrows did the same,
A sickly silence fell upon the patrons of the game.

A straggling few got up to go in deep despair. The rest
Clung to that hope which springs eternal in the human breast;
They thought, if only Casey could get but a whack at that—
We'd put up even money, now, with Casey at the bat.

While "Casey at the Bat" is written in rising dipodic meter (alternating strong and weak iambs), the passage below is in falling dipodic meter (alternating strong and weak trochees). But each of them uses the other kind of foot occasionally for variation, as in "Clung to" in the rising poem, or "The servants" in the falling poem.

From "The Galley-Slave," Rudyard Kipling (1886)

Bear witness, once my comrades, what a hard-bit gang were we—
The servants of the sweep-head, but the masters of the sea!
By the hands that drove her forward as she plunged and yawed and
    sheered,
Woman, Man, or God or Devil, was there anything we feared?

Was it storm? Our fathers faced it and a wilder never blew.
Earth that waited for the wreckage watched the galley struggle through.
Burning noon or choking midnight, Sickness, Sorrow, Parting, Death?
Nay, our very babes would mock you had they time for idle breath.

In a famous footnote to an essay about poetry, A. E. Housman said he thought dipodic meter represents the future of poetry, and it does have a compelling sound, with its alternating strong and weak stresses evoking the rhythm of walking. The following example, by Arielle Greenberg, reminds us that metrical poetry does not have to follow syntactical restraints and can explore language in a nonreferential way, as much as free-verse poetry can do. The meter is so strongly established by line 5 that our ear compensates for the missing syllable and replaces it with a long "rest."

"The Meter of the Night Sky," Arielle Greenberg

I wonder what would happen if the K in knife was said,
if part of all the Hs in the book had rubbed away,
changing up the shapes of our ancestor's good white bones.

I wonder who's been sleeping in this bale of hay before,
how many eyes adore me, how many needles here.
I wonder who is bedded, sharp and low, like any twin,
kindled by the flickering camp lantern of my name.

It doesn't happen suddenly, but with a rolling hush:
some blossom, something citric, and oh so cavalier,
moves without me, moves in chorus with the pulse of the night sky.

It's my velvet artwork, making pleasure of a peephole.
Without me, it can wonder every G-note in the scale,
every Aries made of starlight. It's the whirring of my plum.

Hendecasyllabics literally means "eleven syllables." The meter is based on a classical meter and, though rarely used, can be a source of uncommon beauty. If you find you enjoy the sapphic stanza—which some people find so beautiful as to be almost addictive—the hendecasyllabic offers the opportunity to maintain the basic sapphic rhythm for a long period, building up momentum. Hendecasyllabics may look complicated, but really each line is simply a trochaic pentameter with one dactyl in the second foot. As with sapphics, because the meter itself is a distinctive pattern, and not just a base rhythm, this is not a meter that is usually varied or substituted in any way.

From "Hendecasyllabics," Algernon Charles Swinburne (1866)

In the month of the long decline of roses
I, beholding the summer dead before me,
Set my face to the sea and journeyed silent,
Gazing eagerly where above the sea-mark
Flame as fierce as the fervid eyes of lions
Half divided the eyelids of the sunset;
Till I heard as it were a noise of waters

Moving tremulous under feet of angels
Multitudinous, out of all the heavens;
Knew the fluttering wind, the fluttered foliage,
Shaken fitfully, full of sound and shadow;
And saw, trodden upon by noiseless angels,
Long mysterious reaches fed with moonlight,
Sweet sad straits in a soft subsiding channel,
Blown about by the lips of winds I knew not,
Winds not born in the north nor any quarter,
Winds not warm with the south nor any sunshine. . .

A beautiful poem in hendecasyllabics is Frost's "For Once, Then, Something." To emphasize that there is no mood or style or subject that fits with any meter, here is a contemporary poem in hendecasyllabics by four-time National Poetry Slam champion Patricia Smith:

"The Reemergence of the Noose," Patricia Smith

Some lamp sputters its dusty light across a
desk. Some hand, in a fever, works the fraying
brown hemp, twisting and knifing, weaving, tugging
tight this bellowing circle. Randy Travis
sings, moans, radios steamy twangs and hiccups,
blue notes backing the ritual of drooping
loop. Sweat drips in an awkward hallelujah.
God glares down, but the artist doesn't waver—
wrists click rhythm, and rope becomes a path to
what makes saviors; the loop bemoans its need to
squeeze, its craving for the ghost of Negro neck.

Smith writes about composing this poem, "I've been troubled by the proliferation of nooses being discovered lately—hanging from trees on school campuses, looped around the knob of a professor's office door—and I knew a poem was percolating, but I didn't know how or when. After several false starts with the hendecasyllabics (which I can finally spell without looking it up), the structure suggested a mood, and the mood gave the poem permission to exist. It was the perfect form."

If you enjoy exploring new metrical patterns, you may want to investigate the discussion and examples of such meters as the ionics, galliambics, choriambs, Asclepiadean meter, cretics, and dipodics referenced in the bibliography.

Meter and Meaning

In a good poem, rhythmical pattern (and other patterning devices such as rhyme) are not something extra but truly embody and arise from the energies of idea, emotion, and meaning at every point of the poem. We all know this; that is why the following anonymous poem works:

From "Dr. Seuss Tech Support," Anonymous

If a packet hits a pocket on a socket on a port,
And the bus is interrupted as a very last resort,
and the address of the memory makes your floppy disk abort,
then the socket packet pocket has an error to report.

If your cursor finds a menu item followed by a dash,
And the double-clicking icon puts your window in the trash,
and your data is corrupted 'cause the index doesn't hash,
then your situation's hopeless, and your system's gonna crash.

If the label on your cable on the gable at your house,
says the network is connected to the button on your mouse,
But your packets want to tunnel to another protocol,
That's repeatedly rejected by the printer down the hall . . .

The poem is funny because we recognize the goofy "meaning" of the metrical pattern combined with the rhyme, and know that it makes a ridiculous contrast to the technical seriousness of the subject matter. In fact, the metrical pattern and the rhyme are more powerful than the subject matter. They trump the meaning, letting us know the poem is not serious.

The opposite dynamic can also be true; in this largely dactylic free-verse

poem, the meaning is lighthearted enough, but it is lent just a tinge of seriousness and wider implication by a combination of diction, imagery, and especially the dactylic rhythm:

"What Could it Be," Julia Alvarez

Around the kettle of chicken and rice,
the aunts were debating what flavor was missing.
Tía Carmen guessed garlic.
Tía Rosa, some coarsely ground pepper.
Tía Ana, so tidy she wore the apron,
shook her head, plain salt what was needed.
Tía Fofi, afraid to be wrong, echoed salt.
Just a pinch, she apologized, and reached for the shaker.
Tía Gladys said parsley never hurt anything.
Tía Victoria frowned and pronounced,
Tarragon. No one disagreed.

The tarragon dotted the rice in the cauldron.
And now, as if signaled, the spice jars popped open,
unloading their far eastern wonders:
cumin, turmeric, saffron, and endives.
The aunts each put in a shaker of their favorites.
The steam unwrinkled the frowns from their faces.
They cackled like witches, sampled, and nodded.

Around the table the uncles were grunting,
wolfing their food down, gnawing their chicken bones.
And yet the aunts stopped in the middle of swallows,
heads cocked at each other as if they had heard
in some far off room their own baby crying.
It needed a pinch more of . . . saffron? Paprika?
What could it be they had missed putting in?
The uncles ate seconds and rose in a chorus
of chair scrapes and belches,
falling to slumber on living room couches,
empty plates glowed like the eyes of the spellbound.

The language ("wolfing," "gnawing," "spellbound") and some of the dis-tancing, archetypal imagery ("cackled like witches," "rose in a chorus") helps make it seem that more is going on than is being described and dignifies the do-mestic scene with perhaps a slight aura of danger; but without the mysterious undercurrent of the dactylic rhythm tying everything together, much of that strange aura would dissipate.

The association of meter with meaning does not mean that the meaning of any particular meter is fixed; we have seen that various meters can express all kinds of feelings. But it does mean that a good poem is always aware of the ef-fect rhythm is having and works with rhythm rather than trying to ignore it. Like a horse, sometimes meter knows where you want to go better than you do, and it is a good idea to listen to it as much as you can.

QUESTIONS FOR MEDITATION OR DISCUSSION

Try to invent your own meter. What is the experience like?

Robert Creeley wrote, "Form is never more than an extension of content, and content never more than an extension of form." How does this apply to meter? Imagine a line of poetry, and then imagine it being written in a different meter. What if it used exactly the same words, with just a syllable or two added or re-moved? To what extent would it still be the same line?

Do you think that some meters do have their own emotional characteristics, or is meter always flexible? Choose a poem from this chapter with a very distinc-tive mood, such as "The Raven" or Swinburne's "Hendecasyllabics." Try to transfer it to another meter without disturbing the mood. What do you dis-cover?

QUOTES

Since we live in a universe of rhythms, ideas for the meters of poetry might turn up anywhere.
—John Frederick Nims

The meter that's hardest for you is a power source.
—Joshua Davis

I can think of no better training than listening, day by day, for the caesura in a line of dactylic hexameter.
—Louise Bogan

Learning meter will make you a stronger and better poet no matter what you write. Like a dancer who studies ballet you will suddenly have better posture.
—Kazim Ali

I've always been attracted to the spoken word, and that's what starts me on a poem. It always starts with a jingle, and then I fit the poem to it.
—Sandra Cisneros

My ideal reader keeps an eye out for strange metrical fauna such as bacchics and choriambs.
—W. H. Auden

Vary rhythm enough to stir the emotion you want but not so as to lose impetus.
—Basil Bunting

POETRY PRACTICES

Metrical Templates. Copy two trochaic lines, two dactylic lines, two anapestic lines, and two iambic lines from poems in this book. Then write your own eight lines that follow the meter and rhythm of these eight lines exactly.

Metrical Field Trip. Go on a metrical field trip, to the store, a magazine, the movies, your TV set, a prose book, or your friends' or family's conversation. Listen for snatches of metrical language (such as the three dactyls in the beginning of this sentence). Try to find one example from each of the four basic meters. I define a "snatch" as at least three metrical feet in a row.

Metrical Diagnosis. Write four original passages of 10 lines each, in unrhymed trochaic, iambic, anapestic, and dactylic tetrameter. You can write the same passage in four different meters, or write a new passage for each meter. Nonsense or sense is fine. Which meters do you prefer? Which are difficult? Do they bring out different aspects of your poetry, different themes or attitudes? Practice reading and writing the meters you find difficult, until you have facility in all four.

Metrical Translation. Read "Hiawatha," "Iron," or another trochaic poem aloud to yourself until you feel you have entrained your body to the rhythm. Then write at least 20 lines of trochees (be sure to use a trochee in the first foot of each line). Then translate your poem into dactyls or anapests. How does the mood or impact of the poem change?

Blank Noniambic Verse: Completing the Circle. Write a poem of at least 20 lines in whichever of the four basic meters you have not yet written. Take time to read your poems aloud repeatedly and revise each one in accord with its own metrical nature, so that it is fluent, varied in the best way, and takes advantage of the unique expressive capacities of its own meter.

Mix It Up. Explore noniambic variations. Entrain yourself in either anapestic or dactylic meter, by reading until you have the meter firmly in your ear, and then let yourself run with it, writing what sounds good to you. After you have it down, scan it to look for variations. If the meter is too monotonous, make changes to make the rhythm more expressive and interesting. Use the cretic (/u/), bacchic (//u), antibacchic (uu/), and molossus (uuu).

Metrical Explorations. Write at least one original poem, or metrical "translation" of another poem, in one or more of the rarer meters described in this chapter, such as amphibrachs or hendecasyllabics.

PART 2

Form

CHAPTER 6

Paradigms of Rhyme

Since the majority of poetic forms in English are stitched together and shaped through ties of rhyme, it seems appropriate to begin the section on poetic form with a discussion of this important structuring element. True, some poetic forms, such as the pantoum, haiku, and sestina, do not depend on rhyme. But most do. Without it the second half of this book would not exist, since there would be no couplets, quatrains, ghazals, or villanelles, no rhyme royal or rondeau, no blues, no sonnets, and no ballads.

Definitions

Technically, a rhyme is when two words have the same vowel sound in the last stressed syllable as well as the same sounds for everything that follows the last stressed syllable: "fly" and "spy," and also "flying" and "spying."

When marking rhyme patterns, we repeat a lowercase letter to mark rhyming sounds, starting from *a* with each poem, with *x* for unrhymed sounds. Capital letters starting with *A* are used for any words that are repeated exactly.

Rhyme's Roots

Though classical and medieval verse did not rhyme, two factors led rhyme to become firmly established throughout European poetry by the Renaissance. The first was a change in the pronunciation of vowels so that Latin became pronounced as an accented language. Rhyme helps emphasize the patterns of accent, so rhyme and accent usually go together. The second important factor was the influence of the complex and beautiful rhyme patterns of Persian (Iranian) poetry by way of the Moors (Arabs) and then through the Troubadour poets of Provence, in southern France and Spain.

This influence was so prevalent that by 1589, George Puttenham wrote, "All nations now use rhyme." But rhyme in English has remained controversial: poets and critics from Thomas Campion (who called rhyme "vulgar, artificial, easy, rude, barborous, shifting, and fat") to Milton (who said he had freed *Paradise Lost* from "the troublesome and modern bondage of rhyming") to Ezra Pound (who famously called Edgar Allan Poe a "jingle man" because of his intense rhymes) to T. S. Eliot have claimed to find it vulgar and degrading. Still, for hundreds of years rhyme has been so crucial to poetry in English that it is now synonymous with it. Just as, in the eighteenth century, verse was called "numbers," now it is often called "rhyme" and poems are called "rhymes," as in, "Come and listen to my rhymes!"

Here's a story that may help remind us why rhyme persists in spite of it all. Not long ago, the creator of the *Dilbert* cartoons developed a condition called Spasmodic Dysphonia, where the part of the brain that controls speech stops functioning. There is no known cure for the condition. But as he wrote on his blog, "The part of my brain responsible for normal speech was still intact, but for some reason had become disconnected from the neural pathways to my vocal cords. . . . [But then] while helping on a homework assignment, I noticed I could speak perfectly in rhyme:

Jack be nimble, Jack be quick.
Jack jumped over the candlestick.

I repeated it dozens of times, partly because I could. It was effortless, even though it was similar to regular speech. . . . Then something happened.
My brain remapped.
My speech returned.
. . . A few times I felt my voice slipping away, so I repeated the nursery rhyme and tuned it back in. By the following night my voice was almost completely normal.

Amazing and mysterious, and borne out by modern studies showing that rhythmical language is processed in a different part of the brain from prose and normal speech, this story (which presumably involves the accentual meter of the poem as much as the rhyme) reminds us of the power long believed to be held by rhymed words—the reason, for example, that witches' spells always rhyme. Poets who bring rhyme into their poems are harnessing a potentially mighty force.

Kinds of Rhyme

There are many different types of rhyme. They can be classified most clearly by the nature of the rhyme and by its placement in the line. Here is a list of types of rhyme, with discussion at greater length of some of the most important.

Types of Rhyme Classified by Formation

Perfect, exact, true, or pure rhyme: the words begin differently, then have identical stressed vowel sounds, with any other following sounds also being identical: sigh, high, vie, underlie; sowing, flowing, hoeing, ongoing. There are two types of perfect rhyme: rising, single, one-syllable, rising, or masculine rhyme (cat, sat); and falling, double, two-syllable, falling, or feminine rhyme (seven, heaven). Occasionally there are even triple or three-syllable rhymes (visible, risible).

Light rhyme: rhyming a one-syllable with a two-syllable rhyme (arise, prize; falling, ring).

From "Blown Apart by Loss," Rita Dove

Winter came early and still
She frequented the path by the river until . . .

Slant rhyme (also called off-rhyme, half rhyme, near rhyme, imperfect rhyme, and approximate rhyme): rhyme that is not perfect. There are two kinds of slant rhyme: consonant rhyme: the stressed vowel sounds are different, but the consonants or whatever else comes after them is the same:

From "The Calm," John Donne (1597)

earth's hollownesses, which the world's lungs are,
have no more wind than the upper vault of air.

Here are some other examples: come, tomb; taut, knit; nation, attention; gone, moan; heaven, given. The following poem is entirely written with consonant rhyme:

"Futility," Wilfred Owen (1917)

Move him into the sun—
Gently its touch awoke him once,
At home, whispering of fields unsown.
Always it woke him, even in France,
Until this morning and this snow.
If anything might rouse him now
The kind old sun will know.

Think how it wakes the seeds,—
Woke, once, the clays of a cold star.
Are limbs, so dear-achieved, are sides,
Full-nerved,—still warm,—too hard to stir?
Was it for this the clay grew tall?
—O what made fatuous sunbeams toil
To break earth's sleep at all?

Assonant rhyme: the stressed vowel sounds are the same and a consonant that comes after them is different:

When he came to the king's gate,
he sought a drink for Hind Horn's sake.
    —ANONYMOUS BALLAD

From "The Poet Reflects on Her Solitary Fate," Sandra Cisneros

They have left her
To her own device.
Her nightmares and pianos.
She owns a lead pipe.

Emily Dickinson's poems are famous for their consonantal slant rhymes, which sometimes push the rhyme so far that it approaches wrenched rhyme (see below). Note that the rhyme scheme is xaxa, so only the alternating lines rhyme:

Poem 1078, Emily Dickinson (1866)

The Bustle in a House
The Morning after Death
Is solemnest of Industries
Enacted upon Earth—

The Sweeping up the Heart
And putting Love away
We shall not want to use again
Until Eternity.

Slant rhyme, like meter or any other poetic device, has no inherent "meaning" or effect; it can truly be used for a range of purposes. In Dickinson's poems, the use of slant rhyme tends to add a feeling of energy and independence of spirit. In the following contemporary poem, slant rhyme achieves a very different effect, seeming the perfect expression for a mood of jaded, cynical weariness:

"Blues for Dante Alighieri," Kim Addonizio

> . . . without hope we live on in desire. . . .
> *Inferno* IV

Our room was too small, the sheets scratchy and hot—
Our room was a kind of hell, we thought,
and killed a half-liter of Drambuie we'd bought.

We walked over the Arno and back across.
We walked all day, and in the evening, lost,
argued and wandered in circles. At last

we found our hotel. The next day we left for Rome.
We found the Intercontinental, and a church full of bones,
and ate takeout Chinese in our suite, alone.

It wasn't a great journey, only a side trip.
It wasn't love for eternity, or any such crap;
it was just something that happened. . . .

We packed suitcases, returned the rental car.
We packed souvenirs, and repaired to the airport bar
and talked about pornography, and movie stars.

In this passage from the Russian-born poet Joseph Brodsky, both the consonants and the vowels are slightly off.

From "December in Florence," Joseph Brodsky

There are always six bridges spanning the sluggish river.
There are places where lips touched lips for the first time ever,
or pen pressed paper with real fervor.
There are arcades, colonnades, iron idols that blur your lens.
There the streetcar's multitudes, jostling, dense,
speak in the tongue of a man who's departed thence.

As if to underscore the impossibility of exact rhyme, it is not only single consonant sounds that are off-rhymed, but syllables and consonant clusters. The effect is one of poignant dissonance and pain.

Compound rhyme: rhymes two groups of words (of her, love her).
Mosaic rhyme: rhymes one word with a group (justice, trust is). Often this
   kind of rhyme is used for humorous effects, by writers such as Ogden
   Nash and Gilbert and Sullivan, or in this famous limerick by a newspaper editor:

"The Pelican," Dixon Lanier Merritt (1910)

A wonderful bird is the pelican,
His mouth can hold more than his belly can,
He can hold in his beak,
Enough food for a week!
I'm damned if I know how the hell he can!

This poem uses the device more seriously:

From "Churchgoing," Philip Larkin

A serious house on serious earth it is,
In whose blent air all our compulsions meet,
Are recognised, and robed as destinies.
And that much never can be obsolete,
Since someone will forever be surprising
A hunger in himself to be more serious,
And gravitating with it to this ground,
Which, he once heard, was proper to grow wise in,
If only that so many dead lie round.

Larkin saves the only mosaic rhyme till the very end of this seven-stanza poem. It is an impressive rhyme, both because of its difficulty and cleverness, and because of the way the easier words to rhyme come in the second position (see "Advice on Rhyming" at the end of this chapter). When the reader encounters the phrase "grow wise in," it functions as a kind of climax, as the speaker's initial suspicion and cynicism towards the church modulates into reluctant respect.

Rime rich: the rhyme includes the preceding consonants, so the words
sound identical. There are two kinds of rich rhyme:
homographic (words have different meanings but are spelled the same).
Example: "I know you did not mean / that she was acting mean."
homonymic (words look different but sound the same): time, thyme
Identical rhyme: repeating of the exact same word, with same meaning.
Here is an example by the young Yeats:

"He Wishes for the Cloths of Heaven," W. B. Yeats (1899)

Had I the heavens' embroidered cloths,
Enwrought with golden and silver light,
The blue and the dim and the dark cloths
Of night and light and the half-light,
I would spread the cloths under your feet:

But I, being poor, have only my dreams;
I have spread my dreams under your feet;
Tread softly because you tread on my dreams.

Wrenched rhyme: words that depend on exaggerated or distorted pronun-
    ciation or spelling to rhyme: Tulsa, ulcer (Ogden Nash); rhinestones,
    grindstones.
Visual, sight, or eye rhyme: looks but does not sound the same: eight,
    sleight.

Sometimes, eye rhyme can have the effect of slant rhyme even if it is not exact.
This ingenious free verse poem uses a kind of rhyme I have never seen before,
which we might call "anagram rhyme"; it has the effect of an eye rhyme combined with a slant rhyme:

"The Heron," Randall Mann

A pond the color of Oriental teas.
A heron refusing to look anywhere but east.

Mangroves flecked with a fire,
deep-set birches rife

with the wait for night. In stone,
the heron stares: the stoic tones

of the sky a storied procession of palms;
their red-tipped fronds, overhanging lamps.

Water-bird, it has been centuries since I felt
anything for you. You have been left:

look around. Why does the owl
rest on a goddess's shoulder while you wade so low?

Types of Rhyme Classified by Placement

End-rhyme: rhyme at the ends of lines.

Head-rhyme (or initial rhyme): some use this term for alliteration, others
for rhyming initial words.

Internal rhyme: the end of a line rhymes with the center of a line.

There are four types of internal rhyme:

leonine rhyme (or medial rhyme): an internal rhyme directly before the
caesura of the same line. This type of internal rhyme is most common
in popular poems in English, such as this famous poem in trochaic oc-
tometer:

From "The Raven," Edgar Allan Poe (1845)

Once upon a midnight dreary, while I pondered, weak and weary,
Over many a quaint and curious volume of forgotten lore,
While I nodded, nearly napping, suddenly there came a tapping,
As of some one gently rapping, rapping at my chamber door.
"'Tis some visitor," I muttered, "tapping at my chamber door—
Only this, and nothing more."

Ah, distinctly I remember it was in the bleak December,
And each separate dying ember wrought its ghost upon the floor.
Eagerly I wished the morrow;—vainly I had sought to borrow
From my books surcease of sorrow—sorrow for the lost Lenore—
For the rare and radiant maiden whom the angels name Lenore—
Nameless here for evermore.

And the silken sad uncertain rustling of each purple curtain
Thrilled me—filled me with fantastic terrors never felt before;
So that now, to still the beating of my heart, I stood repeating,
"'Tis some visitor entreating entrance at my chamber door—
Some late visitor entreating entrance at my chamber door;—
This it is, and nothing more."

Poe's poem uses internal rhyme to break up the long lines into smaller units, and to emphasize the hypnotic repetitions of the action in the poem's story. These types of internal rhyme are much subtler in their effects:

> Cross-rhyme: the end of the line rhymes with the center of the adjacent line:

> I know there is a summer tree
> beneath the freeing autumn gold

> Interlaced rhyme: the center of the line rhymes with the center of the adjacent line:

> the summer tree lives on beneath
> the living freedom of the gold

> Linked rhyme: the end of a line rhymes with the first syllable of the following line:

> I know there is a summer tree
> beneath the autumn gold

While the various forms of internal rhyme are used most often for decoration in English-language poetry, cross-rhyme is a central element of form in some poetic traditions, including the Celtic. I used it for a poem dedicated to Brigid, the Celtic goddess of healing and poetry, in one of the only contemporary poems written in the ancient Celtic form called the *awdl gwyddyd*, which uses a combination of linked rhyme, internal rhyme, end rhyme, and cross-rhyme:

> *"Brigid," Annie Finch*

> Ring, ring, ring, ring! Hammers fall.
> Your gold will all be beaten
> over sudden flaming fire
> moving from you, the pyre. Sweeten
> your cauldron, until the sun
> runs with one flame through the day
> and the healing water will sing,
> linger on tongues, burn away.

Apocopate rhyme: the last syllable is dropped in one rhyming word: gain, painless.

Enjambed rhyme: the first consonant of the next line completes the end-rhyme:

He arose and I
descended to his side

Rimas dissolutas: a medieval French technique which can be used with any length of line or stanza. The first lines of each stanza rhyme with each other, the second lines of each stanza rhyme with each other, the third lines of each stanza rhyme with each other, etc., as in these stanzas:

From "Black Rook in Rainy Weather," Sylvia Plath

Although, I admit, I desire,
Occasionally, some backtalk
From the mute sky, I can't honestly complain:
A certain minor light may still
Lean incandescent

Out of kitchen table or chair
As if a celestial burning took
Possession of the most obtuse objects now and then—
Thus hallowing an interval
Otherwise inconsequent

A more subtle technique of rhyming than most, here the *rima dissoluta* helps capture the dry alienation of the speaker's mood.

Unpatterned rhyme—random rhymes. These may be as unnatural-seem-ing as John Skelton's famous "Skeltonics," made more overbearing by the short lines, whose style is so distinctive that they have their own nickname:

From "Colin Clout," John Skelton (1521–22)

His head is so fat,
He wotteth never what
Nor whereof he speaketh;
He crieth and he creaketh,
He prieth and he peeketh,
He chides and he chatters,
He prates and he patters,
He clitters and he clatters,
He meddles and he smatters,
He gloses and he flatters;
Or if he speak plain,
Then he lacketh brain,
He is but a fool;
Let him go to school,
On a three footed stool
That he may down sit,
For he lacketh wit;
And if that he hit
The nail on the head
It standeth in no stead.

Or they may be as simple and speechlike in effect as in this poem:

"After Apple Picking," Robert Frost (1914)

My long two-pointed ladder's sticking through a tree
Toward heaven still,
And there's a barrel that I didn't fill
Beside it, and there may be two or three
Apples I didn't pick upon some bough.
But I am done with apple-picking now.
Essence of winter sleep is on the night,
The scent of apples: I am drowsing off.
I cannot rub the strangeness from my sight
I got from looking through a pane of glass

I skimmed this morning from the drinking trough
And held against the world of hoary grass.
It melted, and I let it fall and break.
But I was well
Upon my way to sleep before it fell,
And I could tell
What form my dreaming was about to take.
Magnified apples appear and disappear,
Stem end and blossom end,
And every fleck of russet showing clear.
My instep arch not only keeps the ache,
It keeps the pressure of a ladder-round.
I feel the ladder sway as the boughs bend.
And I keep hearing from the cellar bin
The rumbling sound
Of load on load of apples coming in.
For I have had too much
Of apple-picking: I am overtired
Of the great harvest I myself desired.
There were ten thousand thousand fruit to touch,
Cherish in hand, lift down, and not let fall.
For all
That struck the earth,
No matter if not bruised or spiked with stubble,
Went surely to the cider-apple heap
As of no worth.
One can see what will trouble
This sleep of mine, whatever sleep it is.
Were he not gone,
The woodchuck could say whether it's like his
Long sleep, as I describe its coming on,
Or just some human sleep.

Rhyme: Technically, the repetition of the same vowel sound on a stressed syllable as well as on all the syllables that come after the stressed syllable.

Rhyme and Emphasis

Rhyme emphasizes the rhyming words. This simple effect can be used in numerous ways by skilled poets. In the following poem, rhyme falls on the short, simple word "me":

"She dwelt among the untrodden ways," William Wordsworth (1799)

She dwelt among the untrodden ways
    Beside the springs of Dove,
A Maid whom there were none to praise
    And very few to love:

A violet by a mossy stone
    Half hidden from the eye!
Fair as a star, when only one
    Is shining in the sky.

She lived unknown, and few could know
    When Lucy ceased to be;
But she is in her grave, and, oh,
    The difference to me!

The rhyme on "me" surprisingly—almost shockingly—emphasizes the speaker's aloneness, and the subjective nature of the pain of grieving, at the very moment it introduces the speaker into the poem for the first time.

The emphasis, through rhyming, of strongly contrasting words can strengthen the effects of wit and satire. This is a favorite device of Alexander Pope, as in this couplet:

The hungry judges soon the sentence sign,
and wretches hang that jurymen may dine.

It is the rhyme that highlights the word and the intended effect; if the last line read, "wretches hang for the dinners of jurymen," the cutting sarcasm contrasting the profit of the juries to the fate of the punished poor would be far less effective. Sonia Sanchez explores this device in this stanza from "Song No. 2":

i say, all you young girls molested at ten,
i say, all you young girls giving it up again and again,
i say, all you sisters hanging out in every den
i say, all you sisters needing your own oxygen.

The angry contrast between the meanings of the lines ending in "ten" and oxygen" is heightened, and the irony deepened, because of the repeating of the rhyme sounds in the two words.

Rhyme is also traditionally used in many situations to highlight the endings of final lines, emphasizing a sense of closure. Shakespeare and other writers of blank verse use it to signal the end of an unrhymed passage, as in this passage from *Macbeth:*

From Macbeth, *William Shakespeare (1606)*

. . . Thou sure and firm-set earth,
Hear not my steps, which way they walk, for fear
Thy very stones prate of my whereabout,
And take the present horror from the time,
Which now suits with it. Whiles I threat, he lives:
Words to the heat of deeds too cold breath gives.

A rhymed tercet can add similar closure to a passage in rhymed couplets. And a rhymed couplet is built into the endings of such forms as the English sonnet, a stanza of rhyme royal, or a Spenserian stanza.

Rhyme and Meaning

When you rhyme words, you are linking them in the meaning-dimension as well as in the sound-dimension. If you take a rhymed poem you admire and read only the rhymed words together in a string, you will probably see that they make an intensely linked underpoem, which we experience unconsciously at the same time we are consciously reading the poem as a whole. You can see this in Sonnet 73 (1609), for example, where Shakespeare makes time pass viscerally by rhyming the present-tense verb "hang" with the past-tense verb "sang."

Sonnet 73, William Shakespeare (1609)

That time of year thou mayst in me behold
When yellow leaves, or none, or few, do hang
Upon those boughs which shake against the cold,
Bare ruin'd choirs, where late the sweet birds sang.
In me thou see'st the twilight of such day 5
As after sunset fadeth in the west;
Which by and by black night doth take away,
Death's second self, that seals up all in rest.
In me thou see'st the glowing of such fire,
That on the ashes of his youth doth lie, 10
As the death-bed whereon it must expire
Consum'd with that which it was nourish'd by.
This thou perceiv'st, which makes thy love more strong,
To love that well which thou must leave ere long.

This is the underpoem: "Behold hang cold, sang day west away, rest fire lie expire, nourish'd by strong long." The rhyming words are so vivid that they create
a story parallel to that of the poem as a whole. The same technique has heart-
breaking effects in this brief dramatic monologue:

"Casualty," Langston Hughes

He was a soldier in the army,
But he doesn't walk like one.
He walks like his soldiering
Days are done.

Son! . . . Son!

Hughes is playing off the expected abab rhyme pattern of the ballad stanza. Just
when we think the poem is over because the ballad stanza rhyme is completed,
we are shocked with the clincher, the third rhyme on the same sound, which
turns the entire poem from a general lament into a personal tragedy; the repetition of the word, with its implication that the son is too injured (deaf?) or too
depressed or disoriented to respond, also turns the poem from the third person

to the second person voice. The single word "son" could never have such a powerful effect if the ground hadn't been subtly laid for it by the preceding rhymes. When you write using rhyme, check your underpoem to make sure the rhyming words are intense and effective. Rhyme puts extra focus on words, and this is one way to make sure that your rhyme words are interesting enough to deserve the attention.

The underlying rhyme pattern becomes a surface structure of meaning in the following poem:

"Of Night," Molly Peacock

A city mouse darts from the paws of night.
A body drops from the jaws of night.
A woman denies the laws of night,
Awake and trapped in the was of night.
A young man turns in the gauze of night,
Unravelling the cause of night:
That days extend their claws at night
To re-enact old wars at night,
Though dreams can heal old sores at night
And Spring begins its thaw at night,
While worry bones are gnawed at night.
He sips her through a straw at night.
Verbs whisper in the clause of night.
A finger to her lips, the pause of night.

The internal rhyme creates patterns of meaning in the poem, linking the imagery into a narrative: paws, jaws, laws, was, gauze . . .

Peacock's poem uses monorhyme, the rhyming of many words on a single sound. The same technique, combined with trochees at the beginnings of lines and a powerful rush of images and syntax with no stanza breaks, creates great forward propulsion in this poem:

"Bereft," Robert Frost

Where had I heard this wind before
Change like this to a deeper roar?

What would it take my standing there for,
Holding open a restive door,
Looking down hill to a frothy shore?
Summer was past and day was past.
Somber clouds in the west were massed.
Out in the porch's sagging floor,
leaves got up in a coil and hissed,
Blindly struck at my knee and missed.
Something sinister in the tone
Told me my secret must be known:
Word I was in the house alone
Somehow must have gotten abroad,
Word I was in my life alone,
Word I had no one left but God.

The partly random, hurried-seeming rhyme scheme piles on additional words as if the speaker is too nervous to look back over his shoulder and count them. The syntax adds new information in groups of two or three lines, always changing the pattern so there is no rest or security. The relentlessly monosyllabic rhymes are only altered slightly with the word "alone," which is repeated exactly as if in desperation or resignation.

The following poem uses the same rhyme sound to build an entire poem:

"The Outlier," Paul Muldoon

I

In Armagh or Tyrone
I fell between two stones.

In Armagh or Tyrone
on a morning in June
I fell between two stones.

In Armagh or Tyrone
on a morning in June

in 1951
I fell between two stones.

In Armagh or Tyrone
on a morning in June
in 1951
I fell between two stones
that raised me as their own.

II

I had one eye, just one,
they prised and propped open.

I had one eye, just one,
they prised and propped open
like a Fomorian's.

I had one eye, just one,
they prised and propped open
like a Fomorian's
with a fire-toughened pine.

I had one eye, just one,
they prised and propped open
like a Fomorian's
so all I looked upon
would itself turn to stone.

Because Muldoon's stanza structure (discussed further in chapter 7, "Stan-zas") adds suspense and drama through the addition of new lines, the mono-rhyme seems anything but monotonous; it serves as a counterbalance to the constantly shifting ground of the stanza, even as it adds haunting bleakness to this terrible story of childhood's loss of self.

Of course, rhyme does not have to be so blatant to be effective. In the fol-lowing poem, rhyme works subtly to counterbalance a rhetorical effect:

"The Painted Lady," Margaret Danner

The Painted Lady is a small African
butterfly, gayly toned orchid or peach
that seems as tremulous and delicately sheer

as the objects I treasure, yet, this cosmopolitan
can cross the sea at the icy time of the year
in the trail of the big boats, to France.

Mischance is as wide and somber grey as the lake here
in Chicago. Is there strength enough in my huge
peach paper rose, or lavender sea-laced fan?

Between stanzas 2 and 3, Danner makes a sudden rhetorical leap from the African butterfly's abilities to her own situation (a connection made more meaningful, though no less sudden, by the fact that she often wrote about African American themes). However, the suddenness of that leap is ingeniously counterpointed with the other ways that the stanzas of the poem are woven together: the complex original rhyme scheme, which moves the same three rhyme sounds (including the off-rhyme of "peach" and "year") from stanza to stanza, and the rhyme that links across stanzas, with a particularly powerful internal rhyme just at the moment of the rhetorical leap itself.

Rhyme can also work along with other sound effects to create new effects:

"The Night Piece," Thom Gunn

The fog drifts slowly down the hill,
And as I mount gets thicker still,
Closes me in, makes me its own
Like bedclothes on the paving stone.

Here are the last few streets to climb,
Galleries, run through veins of time,
Almost familiar, where I creep
Toward sleep like fog, through fog like sleep.

Here, as the couplet rhyme scheme begins to "mount," a sort of horror of paralysis mounts with it. When the word "fog" repeats for the second and third time in the last line, it is accompanied by an internal repetition of the rhyme word "sleep," so that, when the expected rhyme comes at the end, it is not just a couplet rhyme anymore but also the near-stupefying completion of a chiasmus (literally, a "crossing"—a rhetorical figure that makes a kind of X by switching the places of repeating words or ideas).

Perhaps the capacity of rhyme to create an unexpected underpoem is the very same reason it can be so disappointing when it doesn't. As Alexander Pope pointed out in his "Essay on Criticism," few things are duller than predictable rhymes:

> While they ring round the same unvary'd Chimes,
> With sure Returns of still expected Rhymes.
> Where-e'er you find the cooling Western Breeze,
> In the next Line, it whispers thro' the Trees;
> If Chrystal Streams with pleasing Murmurs creep,
> The Reader's threaten'd (not in vain) with Sleep.

Sometimes rhyme is mistakenly associated with old-fashioned or conservative poetry; of course there is no necessary connection. This poem by Aaron Shurin uses rhyme-words from Shakespeare's sonnets:

> If the judgment's cruel
> that's a wake-up call: increase
> energy, *attention.* These little pumpkins ornament
> themselves with swells, die
> pushing live volume packed spring-
> form hard as a knock: Decease
> and resist. Content
> surges exactly as memory
> closes its rear-guarding
> eyes
> —the world rushes *in* not *by!* just be
> steady, receptors, measure is fuel:
> whatever moves move with the
> drift which moving never lies.

The 14-line poem uses a distorted sonnet-style rhyme scheme, with the couplet split between the first and third-to-last lines. A paean to the importance of paying attention to the solidity of the present moment without preconceptions, this poem about pumpkin pie, memory, and experience demonstrates that rhyme can help make language fresh and unfamiliar.

Advice on Rhyming

Though rhyme has important effects on structure, emphasis, and meaning, that is not its most important function in a poem. The fundamental reason that rhyme is so prevalent in poetry is that it sounds good; it provides stimulation to the outer or inner ear. Rhyme may sound artificial if you aren't used to it, but after reading poems in rhyme for a while, you will reach a point where you read in a slower fashion, allowing time for the rhymes to surround and surprise you. The repeated use of rhyme also accustoms the reader to the pleasure of like sounds coming together: a reader who expects rhyme to occur on a regular basis begins to desire it, and poetry makes use of this desire to keep the reader involved. A series of rhymed couplets makes use of the recurring desire for rhyme in the first line of each couplet, and the pleasure of satisfied desire in the second line of each couplet. Other, more complex rhyme patterns—moving from the abab to abba stanza, and to such stanzas as rhyme royal and ottava rima—provide increasingly complex forms of pleasure.

It is important to make this movement of desire and satisfaction work on your poem's behalf by keeping an element of unpredictability in your rhyming. Rhymes that are too predictable rob the reader of the sensation of suspense and delay. For example, you can rhyme different parts of speech so the rhyme will have more significance for the reader: "lied" and "pride" is a less predictable and more interesting rhyme than "lied" and "died." An occasional omitted rhyme, or a repeated or extra rhyme when you don't expect it, can provide a useful teasing or surprising effect.

The more natural a rhyme seems, the better; anything forced will distract the reader from the surprise of discovery. The three most common hazards of rhyming all have to do with unnaturalness: trite, overused rhymes, such as "moon" and "June" or "love" and "dove"; the forcing of extra words into a poem only for the rhyme; and unnatural or archaic inversions of speech for the sake of the rhyme.

One easy shortcut to help your rhymes sound more natural is to put the more commonplace word last in the rhyming sequence. A reader will get more satisfaction out of the second of these couplets than the first:

So I could simply be with you,
I found my way to Timbuktoo.

I found my way to Timbuktoo
so I could simply be with you.

Reading the first couplet, the reader may feel that the poet has gone to great lengths to find a word to rhyme with "you." Reading the second couplet, the reader may feel that the poet has cleverly come up with a simple, inevitable, and natural-sounding rhyme for "Timbuktoo." As long as you put the simpler word last, the reader will never know which one you actually thought of first. On the other hand, sometimes the more surprising word is more powerful at the end. Try reversing the second and fourth lines in the last stanza of this poem by Gwendolyn Brooks:

"Beverly Hills, Chicago," Gwendolyn Brooks

The dry brown coughing beneath their feet,
(Only a while, for the handyman is on his way)
These people walk their golden gardens.
We say ourselves fortunate to be driving by today.

That we may look at them, in their gardens where
The summer ripeness rots. But not raggedly.
Even the leaves fall down in lovelier patterns here.
And the refuse, the refuse is a neat brilliancy.

When they flow sweetly into their houses
With softness and slowness touched by that everlasting gold,
We know what they go to. To tea. But that does not mean
They will throw some little black dots into some water
    And add sugar and the juice of the cheapest lemons
    that are sold,

While downstairs that woman's vague phonograph bleats,
"Knock me a kiss."
And the living all to be made again in the sweatingest physical manner
Tomorrow . . . Not that anybody is saying that these people have no
        trouble.
Merely that it is trouble with a gold-flecked beautiful banner.

Nobody is saying that these people do not ultimately cease to be.
And sometimes their passings are even more painful than ours.
It is just that so often they live till their hair is white.
They make excellent corpses, among the expensive flowers . . .

Nobody is furious. Nobody hates these people.
At least, nobody driving by in this car.
It is only natural, however, that it should occur to us
How much more fortunate they are than we are.

It is only natural that we should look and look
At their wood and brick and stone
And think, while a breath of pine blows,
How different these are from our own.

We do not want them to have less.
But it is only natural that we should think we have not enough.
We drive on, we drive on.
When we speak to each other our voices are a little gruff.

Perhaps because the other stanzas do generally follow the principle of ending
on the commonplace word ("sold" instead of "gold," "are" instead of "car,"
"own" instead of "stone"), "gruff" in the last line is rather shocking and effective, and conveys the people's forced resentment as if the rhyme itself were
forced.

    The best advice I've ever heard about how to make rhymes seem natural in-
stead of forced is this, from Richard Wilbur, who got it in turn from Robert
Frost: "Don't rhyme words, rhyme phrases." If you think in terms of entire
phrases, it will be easier for the rhyming words to follow inevitably instead of
needing to be tacked on.

QUESTIONS FOR MEDITATION OR DISCUSSION

Poems throughout this book use rhyme. Look through the other chapters with rhyme in mind. Which four poems in the book do you think use rhyme to the best effect? Why?

Thomas Campion's attack on rhyme, quoted earlier in this chapter, started a notorious debate with Samuel Daniel, which Ben Jonson joined with a lengthy poem called "A Fit of Rime Against Rime":

> He that first invented thee,
> May his joints tormented be,
>   Cramped forever.
> Still may syllables jar with time,
> Still may reason war with rhyme,
>   Resting never.

Centuries later, A. E. Stallings wrote that she was tired of seeing poems lambasted for being "rhyme-driven": "Of course rhyming poetry is rhyme driven. Rhyme is an engine of syntax. If rhyme is in the car I want her stepping on the gas, minding the wheel, eyes on the road, shifting the gears. I don't want her there as mere ornament, nattering on her cell phone, putting her mascara on while gaping in the rear-view mirror." Using poems in this book as examples, do you think that reason is compromised when rhyme is at the wheel? And if so, is that necessarily a bad thing?

What does it mean if rhyme words can convey the entire story of a poem? Do you agree that this happens in Shakespeare's Sonnet 73? I recall poet John Hollander making the same claim about the end words of Robert Frost's sonnet "The Most of It":

> He thought he kept the universe alone;
> For all the voice in answer he could wake
> Was but the mocking echo of his own
> From some tree-hidden cliff across the lake.
> Some morning from the boulder-broken beach
> He would cry out on life, that what it wants

Is not its own love back in copy speech,
But counter-love, original response.
And nothing ever came of what he cried
Unless it was the embodiment that crashed
In the cliff's talus on the other side,
And then in the far-distant water splashed,
But after a time allowed for it to swim,
Instead of proving human when it neared
And someone else additional to him,
As a great buck it powerfully appeared,
Pushing the crumpled water up ahead,
And landed pouring like a waterfall,
And stumbled through the rocks with horny tread,
And forced the underbrush—and that was all.

Do you agree? Try this question on other poems in the book, and with poems of your own.

What do you think the poet means by the word "rhyme" in the phrase "hope and history rhyme" in the last line of the poem below? Do you think the rhyming of hope and history is an accurate metaphor for justice?

History says, Don't hope
On this side of the grave.
But then, once in a lifetime
The longed-for tidal wave
Of justice can rise up
And hope and history rhyme.
    —SEAMUS HEANEY

QUOTES

The popularitie of Rime creates as many Poets as a hot summer flies.
    —Thomas Campion

Rhyme is the fittest harmonie of words that comportes with our Language.
    —Samuel Daniel

I put a premium on rhymes—how could I
    Not living the times of the Supa
Emcees where styles are def, lyrics fly,
      Tight the way our minds move over
      Beats and grooves.
   —Major Jackson

I wish to write such rhymes as shall not suggest a restraint, but contrariwise the wildest freedom.
   —Ralph Waldo Emerson

Interviewer: "Mr. Frost, how do you get your ideas for poems?"
Robert Frost: "By searching for rhyme-words."

In small towns, where one must spend close daily life with unchosen fellows, the major use of speech is to accommodate. A small-town reader-writer has an island of use-vocabulary, set in a vast sea of recognition vocabulary, which using rhyme forces him to embark upon. Words that he loves, but that do not readily come to mind for use, are found by rowing out after rhyme. Free verse, which draws from the island of speech, does not force this quest.
   —Mona Van Duyn

The profit of rhyme is that it drops seeds of a sweeter and more luxuriant rhyme, and of uniformity that it conveys itself into its own roots in the ground out of sight.
   —Walt Whitman

Rhyme becomes necessary in poetry as rhythm weakens.
   —Louise Bogan

Rhyme has been said to contain in itself a constant appeal to Memory and Hope.
   —Arthur Hallam

For slant-rhyme, I find that if I listen for the "weight" of the vowels, then balance vowel sounds of equivalent "weights," the poem . . . feels satisfying.
   —Marilyn Nelson

Excessive devotion to rhyme has thickened the modern ear. Shifting away from rhyme might be a liberation of rhyme . . . freed from its exacting task . . . it could be applied with greater effect where most needed.
   —T. S. Eliot

I'm always inadvertently using rhyme. I don't ever try; it comes out naturally. My ear has been tuned.
   —Sandra Cisneros

Rhyme has the great advantage of infuriating the simple people who naively think there is something under the sun more important than a convention. They have an innocent belief that an idea may be "deeper," more durable than any convention. This is not the least of the charms of rhyme, nor thereby does it caress the ear less sweetly.
   —Paul Valéry

Never too late to rhyme!
   —Robert Creeley (unpublished letter to Chris Stroffolino)

POETRY PRACTICES

(Group) Sound Volleyball. Everyone sit in a circle. One person throws in a word to start (any word will do). The person to your left (or right) answers with a word that rhymes, off-rhymes, alliterates, or has assonance with the first. The idea is to keep the words going around the circle as long as possible. It's up to your group whether you allow people to repeat words or not. The response should be immediate. Keep going until one person is left, or until you get sick of it. Example: first/thirst/thrust/trust/tryst/cyst/crypt/crap/flap/flip/hip/chip/chirp/burp/bread/head et cetera.

Four Objects, Sixteen Lines. Pick four objects in the room. For each object, write a four-line stanza in abab rhyme that ends with the name of the object.

Beginning the End. Choose a rhymed poem you enjoy and write a poem using the same end-words in the same order.

Crazy Rhyme Quilt. Write a poem that uses at least eight of the kinds of rhyme discussed in this chapter. Optional: trade these poems with a partner, and see if you can recognize all the kinds of rhyme in each other's poems.

Invent an original rhyme scheme.

> "Word-music" means all the patterns made by the sounds of consonants and vowels together: assonance (repeated vowel sounds), consonance (repeated consonant sounds), alliteration (a special term for consonance or assonance at the beginnings of words), and rhyme (a combination of assonance and consonance in a stressed syllable at the end of a word).

CHAPTER 7

Stanzas: A Poem's Breathing Rooms

Poetic form, like rhythm, is at once physical and anything but physical. It is impossible to revise a poem's structure, its shape, without restructuring its meaning, too. And often, by shaping a poem's physical identity, we free the poem to teach us what we didn't know we needed to know about its deeper levels. So be patient with a poem's overall form and shape, just as you have learned to be with its rhythms and lines. While meter is about structuring the poetic line, poetic form is about structuring the poem as a whole. The basic unit of form is the **stanza,** and most poetic forms either consist of—or, like the sonnet, evolved from—stanzas.

The stanza determines how a poem can take a breath, step back and look at itself, hear itself speak. If a student of mine is completely stuck working on a poem and asks for my opinion on what to do next, more often than not they will show me a single block of text. Having learned in my own experience that often the first step toward finding the final shape of a poem I'm revising is to divide it into stanzas, I frequently advise them to break it into units that will reflect the different movements and parts of the poem. After a poem is separated into independent parts, it's much easier to discover its underlying structure and to experiment with different kinds of logical, narrative, or emotional order.

Sometimes these divisions are a temporary part of the revision process, but often they enhance the final version of the poem as well. As a reader, I find that stanzas make it easier for me to approach and fully enjoy a poem. Stanzas guide me through light and shadow, rhythms of words and silences, spaces where I can stop and think without interrupting the poem. The word "stanza" comes from the Italian word for "room" (as if a poem were a house or other building). I also like to think of stanza breaks as veins or channels that bring air and light into a poem and allow us to better experience the terrain.

The Stanza in Free Verse and Shaped Poems

Stanzas work best if the breaks between them are taken seriously: honored, re-spected, used consciously to strengthen the transitions and meanings of a poem. It's hard to find a good poem that doesn't follow this principle. For example:

"London," William Blake (1794)

> I wandered through each chartered street,
> Near where the chartered Thames does flow,
> And mark in every face I meet,
> Marks of weakness, marks of woe.
>
> In every cry of every man,
> In every infant's cry of fear,
> In every voice, in every ban,
> The mind-forged manacles I hear:
>
> How the chimney-sweeper's cry
> Every blackening church appals,
> And the hapless soldier's sigh
> Runs in blood down palace-walls.
>
> But most, through midnight streets I hear
> How the youthful harlot's curse
> Blasts the new-born infant's tear,
> And blights with plagues the marriage-hearse.

Each stanza makes its own logical unit (and each stanza is also one complete sentence). Like paragraphs in a clearly written piece of prose, each stanza has a clear and separate focus and could be paraphrased independently of the others. The first sets the scene; the second moves from sight to sound and further clarifies the problem; the third focuses on the exploited child and the man sacrificed to violence; and the last brings in the prevailing problem of prostitu-tion and associated disease. Try reading the poem without stanza breaks:

> I wandered through each chartered street,
> Near where the chartered Thames does flow,

And mark in every face I meet,
Marks of weakness, marks of woe.
In every cry of every man,
In every infant's cry of fear,
In every voice, in every ban,
The mind-forged manacles I hear:
How the chimney-sweeper's cry
Every blackening church appals,
And the hapless soldier's sigh
Runs in blood down palace-walls.
But most, through midnight streets I hear
How the youthful harlot's curse
Blasts the new-born infant's tear,
And blights with plagues the marriage-hearse.

Does it help you appreciate even more how essential the stanzas are to the impact of this poem? (For the opposite effect, try reading Robert Frost's "Bereft" [in chapter 6] with a stanza break after each sentence, and notice how much the power of its forward rush is diminished.)

As in everything else involving writing poetry, of course, the choices in how to use stanzas are infinite even within their limitations. Between the ongoing narrative of a poem like *Beowulf* (originally written without any line breaks at all, let alone stanza breaks) and Blake's "London" lies a continuum of ways to use the stanza. For example, if the separate stanza technique is your basic approach, then diverging from it with an occasional enjambment across stanzas will be experienced by the reader as a powerful change—especially without punctuation, as in this poem, where it happens twice:

"*To Earthward,*" Robert Frost (1923)

Love at the lips was touch
As sweet as I could bear;
And once that seemed too much;
I lived on air

That crossed me from sweet things,
The flow of—was it musk

From hidden grapevine springs
Down hill at dusk?

I had the swirl and ache
From sprays of honeysuckle
That when they're gathered shake
Dew on the knuckle.

I craved strong sweets, but those
Seemed strong when I was young;
The petal of the rose
It was that stung.

Now no joy but lacks salt
That is not dashed with pain
And weariness and fault;
I crave the stain

Of tears, the aftermark
Of almost too much love,
The sweet of bitter bark
And burning clove.

When stiff and sore and scarred
I take away my hand
From leaning on it hard
In grass and sand,

The hurt is not enough:
I long for weight and strength
To feel the earth as rough
To all my length.

A poem's stanzas are a powerful part of its first impression, so it is worth choosing them carefully. If your poem is in unrhymed free verse, you can decide stanza breaks purely on the basis of the poem's meaning:

"Last Apple," Malka Heifetz Tussman (trans. Marcia Falk)

"I am like the last apple
that falls from the tree
and no one picks up."

I kneel to the fragrance
of the last apple
and I pick it up.

In my hands—the tree,
in my hands—the leaf,
in my hands—the blossom,
and in my hands—the earth
that kisses the apple
that no-one picks up.

"Last Apple" uses the stanza breaks organically to reflect the poem's logical parts. An alternative approach is to use stanzas to counterpoint the poem's logic. This free-verse poem breaks stanzas to keep momentum going, to build surprise, to move energy through the poem:

From "June 2," Cole Swensen

Rain falls.
It's June.
I'm dressed in red.
I'm falling.

I'm walking down a stair. It's not brick red, like the roofs, but brazened

Open as if onto
the body room after room

Meet me
by the unused stair

that opens onto the river; you open the door and there, on the water
I was raised to a pious life

and cannot live here.

In **shaped poetry** (sometimes called "visual poetry," or *carmina figurata*), the shape of a stanza is a visual aspect of the poem's art, and a key to the poem's meaning. The earliest shaped poems we know were by ancient Greek poets, who called them *technopaegnia*. These could be extremely clever; for example, the fourth-century B.C. poet Simias of Rhodes wrote "The Egg," a poem shaped like an egg which had to be read alternately from the top and bottom, ending at the center, as if the egg were being eaten. During the Renaissance, this idea was revived by Europeans along with so much else from classical culture, and over a hundred shaped poems were written. Here is perhaps the best known:

From "Easter-Wings," George Herbert (1633)

LORD, who createdst man in wealth and store,
   Though foolishly he lost the same,
     Decaying more and more,
       Till he became
        Most poor:
        With thee
       O let me rise
     As larks, harmoniously,
   And sing this day thy victories:
Then shall the fall further the flight in me.

My tender age in sorrow did beginne:
   And still with sicknesses and shame
     Thou didst so punish sinne,
       That I became
        Most thinne.
        With thee
       Let me combine,

And feel this day thy victorie,
    For, if I imp my wing on thine,
Affliction shall advance the flight in me.

In the most skillful shaped poems, such as this one, the words don't simply fill up a shape; they do so in such a way that each word falls in a place that makes visual sense. With the invention of the typewriter in the twentieth century, shaped poetry gained a new potential for accuracy, and of course the computer, allowing infinite worry-free rearranging, has made it more popular still. Today shaped poetry is a thriving genre, and the visual qualities of print are used regularly to deepen a poem's impact, as in this poem by one of the most imaginative shape poets:

"Bleeding," May Swenson

Stop bleeding   said the knife
I would if I   could said the cut.
Stop bleeding   you make me messy with the blood.
I'm sorry   said the cut.
Stop or I will   sink in farther said the knife.
Don't said the   cut.
The knife did   not say it couldn't help it but it sank in farther.
If only you   didn't bleed said the knife I wouldn't have to do this.
I know said   the cut I bleed too easily I hate that I can't
help it I   wish I were a knife like you and didn't have to bleed.
Meanwhile   stop bleeding will you said the knife.
Yes you   are a mess and sinking in deeper said the cut I will
have to   stop.
Have you   stopped by now said the knife.
I've almost   stopped I think.
Why must you   bleed in the first place said the knife.
For the reason   maybe that you must do what you
must do said   the cut.
I can't stand   bleeding said the knife and sank in farther.

I hate it too   said the cut I know it isn't you it's me
you're lucky to   be a knife you ought to be glad about that.
Too many cuts   around said the knife they're messy I don't know
how they stand   themselves.
They don't said   the cut.
You're bleeding   again.
No I've stopped   said the cut see you are coming out now the
blood is drying   it will rub off you'll be shiny again and clean.
If only cuts   wouldn't bleed so much said the knife coming out a little.
But then knives   might become dull said the cut.
Aren't you bleeding   a little said the knife.
I hope not said the   cut.
I feel you are just   a little.
Maybe just a little   but I can stop now.
I feel a little   wetness still said the knife sinking in
a little but then   coming out a little.
Just a little maybe   just enough said the cut.
That's enough now   stop now do you feel better now said the knife.
I feel I have to   bleed to feel I think said the cut.
I don't I don't have   to feel said the knife drying now becoming shiny.

The jagged cut does more than illustrate the meaning of the poem; it illumi-
nates it. The very fact that the shape is a nonverbal device underscores that the
unhealthy aspect of the relationship between knife and cut (the way they need
and encourage each other) is inescapable just *because* it is unacknowledged, unspoken.

Shaped poetry (along with **concrete poetry,** which uses typography and
other effects to make the words of a poem works of visual art in themselves) reminds us of the centrality of visual experience to reading poetry. Though visual
power is part of the impact of all stanzas, shaped or concrete poetry is the exception; most stanzas are centrally concerned with the musical aspects of poetry. What follows are descriptions of important traditional stanzas, along with
a few of my own favorites.

Two- and Three-Line Stanzas

Any two-line stanza is called a **couplet.** By far the most common and well known of couplets is the iambic pentameter rhymed couplet, named the **heroic couplet.** During the eighteenth century, the heroic couplet was considered the perfect poetic form, and it is remarkably capable of capturing thought in a memorable way, as in these couplets:

> *From "Essay on Man," Alexander Pope (1744)*

> God loves from whole to parts: but human soul
> Must rise from individual to the whole.
> Self-love but serves the virtuous mind to wake,
> As the small pebble stirs the peaceful lake;
> The centre mov'd, a circle straight succeeds,
> Another still, and still another spreads;
> Friends, parent, neighbour, first it will embrace;
> His country next; and next all human race;
> Wide and more wide, th' o'erflowings of the mind
> Take ev'ry creature in of ev'ry kind:
> Earth smiles around, with boundless bounty blest,
> And Heav'n beholds its image in his breast.

Heroic couplets are usually printed together, not separated by spaces. However, since they tend to fall into a series of self-contained units and sometimes memorable units, usually ending with a period or comma, it also makes sense to consider them as separate stanzas. And the same criteria of cohesion and integrity apply to them as apply to separate stanzas. Some of these couplets about poetry, excerpted from various places in another long poem by Pope, are likely to be familiar to you:

> *From "Essay on Criticism," Alexander Pope (1711)*

> A little Learning is a dang'rous Thing;
> Drink deep, or taste not the Pierian Spring:

Words are like Leaves; and where they most abound,
Much Fruit of Sense beneath is rarely found.

True Wit is Nature to Advantage drest,
What oft was Thought, but ne'er so well Exprest

Nay, fly to Altars; there they'll talk you dead;
For Fools rush in where Angels fear to tread.

In Poets as true Genius is but rare,
True Taste as seldom is the Critick's Share.

True Ease in Writing comes from Art, not Chance,
As those move easiest who have learn'd to dance.

Good-Nature and Good-Sense must ever join;
To err is Human; to Forgive, Divine.

Skilled writers of heroic couplets tend to link the pairs of lines together by other means in addition to rhyme. Common techniques include **parallelism** (lines echoing each others' grammatical structure) or a **chiasmus** (x-shaped grammatical structure). In the fifth couplet above, Pope uses a chiasmus to cement the lines together: "Poets" in the first half of the first line corresponds to "Critick's" in the second half of the second line, while "true Genius" in the second half of the first line corresponds grammatically with "true Taste" in the first half of the second line. In the unforgettably gruesome couplets below, Margaret Cavendish uses a chiasmus in the next-to-last couplet, and grammatical parallelism in the second couplet:

"Nature's Cook," Margaret Cavendish (1653)

DEATH is the *Cook* of *Nature;* and we find
Meat drest severall waies to please her *Mind.*
Some *Meates shee* rosts with *Feavers, burning hot,*
And some *shee* boiles with *Dropsies* in a *Pot.*
Some for *Gelly* consuming by degrees,
And some with *Ulcers,* Gravie out to squeese.
Some *Flesh* as *Sage she* stuffs with *Gouts,* and *Paines,*

Others for tender *Meat* hangs up in *Chaines.*
Some in the *Sea she pickles* up to keep,
Others, as *Brawne* is sous'd, those in *Wine steep.*
Some with the *Pox,* chops *Flesh,* and *Bones* so small,
Of which *She* makes a *French Fricasse* withall.
Some on *Gridirons* of *Calenture* is broyl'd,
And some is trodden on, and so quite spoyl'd.
But those are *bak'd,* when smother'd they do dye,
By *Hectick Feavers* some *Meat* She doth *fry.*
In *Sweat* sometimes *she stues* with *savoury smell,*
A *Hodge-Podge* of *Diseases* tasteth well.
Braines drest with *Apoplexy* to *Natures* wish,
Or swimmes with *Sauce* of *Megrimes* in a *Dish.*
And *Tongues* she dries with *Smoak* from *Stomack's* ill,
Which as the second *Course* she sends up still.
Then *Death* cuts *Throats,* for *Blood-puddings* to make,
And puts them in the *Guts,* which *Collicks* rack.
Some hunted are by *Death,* for *Deere* that's red.
Or *Stal-fed Oxen,* knocked on the *Head.*
Some for *Bacon* by *Death* are *Sing'd,* or *scal'd,*
Then powdered up with *Flegme,* and *Rhume* that's salt.

The balance and control that heroic couplets convey can work beautifully not only for uplifting and improving subjects but also for satire, or to create contrasts with chaotic or gruesome subject matter, as Cavendish shows.

A three-line stanza is called a **tercet** no matter what rhyme pattern it has. With all lines rhyming, it is called a **triplet:**

From "A Vision of Poets," Elizabeth Barrett Browning (1844)

He hears a silent gliding coil.
The snakes strain hard against the soil,
His foot slips in their slimy oil,

And toads seem crawling on his hand,
And clinging bats but dimly scanned
Full in his face their wings expand.

Our ears seem used to hearing two rhyming lines; adding a third in a row, as Browning does here to create an intense gothic effect, can feel like an exaggeration. That may be why the best-known three-line stanza is **terza rima,** which never juxtaposes the rhyming lines.

Terza rima is a leapfrogging stanza of interweaving rhymes. Each new stanza takes the rhyme from the middle line of the last stanza, repeats it as the first and last line, and adds a new rhyme in the middle line: aba bcb cdc ded efe fgf, and so on. Because the terza rima pattern is self-generating with its ongoing momentum, and is always refreshed by the addition of the new rhyme, it has a lot of stamina. So it was an inspired choice for Dante's ambitious three-volume medieval epic poem, the *Divine Comedy.* Here is the famous opening of the first book of the poem in the original Italian and in English:

From The Inferno, *Dante Alighieri (1321)* (TRANS. MICHAEL PALMA)

Nel mezzo del cammin di nostra vita
mi ritrovai per una selva oscura
ché la diritta via era smarrita.

Ahi quanto a dir qual era è cosa dura
esta selva selvaggia e aspra e forte
che nel pensier rinova la paura!

Tant'è amara che poco è più morte;
ma per trattar del ben ch'i' vi trovai,
dirò de l'altre cose ch'i' v'ho scorte.

Io non so ben ridir com'i' v'intrai,
tant'era pien di sonno a quel punto
che la verace via abbandonai.

Midway through the journey of our life, I found
myself in a dark wood, for I had strayed
from the straight pathway to this tangled ground.

How hard it is to tell of, overlaid
with harsh and savage growth, so wild and raw
the thought of it still makes me feel afraid.

Death scarce could be more bitter. But to draw
the lessons of the good that came my way,
I will describe the other things I saw.

Terza rima can also create impetus and passion in shorter lyric poems. Here is the first section of one of the most famous terza rima poems:

From "Ode to the West Wind," Percy Bysshe Shelley (1819)

O wild West Wind, thou breath of Autumn's being,
Thou from whose unseen presence the leaves dead
Are driven, like ghosts from an enchanter fleeing,

Yellow, and black, and pale, and hectic red,
Pestilence-stricken multitudes:—O thou
Who chariotest to their dark wintry bed

The wingèd seeds, where they lie cold and low,
Each like a corpse within its grave, until
Thine azure sister of the Spring shall blow

Her clarion o'er the dreaming earth, and fill
(Driving sweet buds like flocks to feed in air)
With living hues and odours plain and hill;

Wild Spirit, which art moving everywhere;
Destroyer and Preserver; hear, O hear!

Shelley uses a couplet to signal the end of the passage, creating the effect of a sonnet.

Terza rima can be varied by following its constraints less exactly, as Derek Walcott does in his epic poem *Omeros* and in this poem:

From "The Bounty," Derek Walcott

The mango trees serenely rust when they are in flower,
nobody knows the name for that voluble cedar
whose bell-flowers fall, the pomme-arac purples its floor.

The blue hills in late afternoon always look sadder.
The country night waiting to come in outside the door;
the firefly keeps striking matches, and the hillside fumes

with a bluish signal of charcoal, then the smoke burns
into a larger question, one that forms and unforms,
then loses itself in a cloud, till the question returns.

Walcott generally follows the pattern of having the middle line of a stanza pick up a rhyme from the preceding stanza, but the first and last lines of the stanza only tend to rhyme in alternate stanzas. The effect can be disconcerting on the level of the stanza, but the sense of terza rima is maintained throughout the poem.

Couplet: two-line stanza
Tercet: three-line stanza
Quatrain: four-line stanza
Cinquain: five-line stanza
Decima: ten-line stanza

Four-Line Stanzas

Just as rooms have four walls, four lines is by far the most common length for a poetic stanza. There are a surprising number of ways to organize these four lines. **Dickinson stanza** (also called **ballad stanza, hymn stanza,** or **folk stanza**) is a four-line stanza whose second and fourth lines always rhyme, but first and third lines may not: abab or xaxa. In poetry, this stanza is excellent for telling long stories (see chapter 10 on the ballad). It usually has a 4-3-4-3 movement (sometimes 4-4-4-4), in iambic or accentual meter. The pattern of 4-3-4-3 feet or accents is the most common meter in English besides iambic pentameter; you have probably heard it hundreds of times in folk songs, hymns, country music songs, advertisements, TV show theme songs, or nursery rhymes like this nonsense rhyme:

"Three Children," Mother Goose (1719)

Three children sliding on the ice
Upon a summer's day,
As it fell out, they all fell in,
The rest they ran away.

Now had these children been at home,
Or sliding on dry ground,
Ten thousand pounds to one penny
They had not all been drowned.

You parents all that children have,
And you that have got none,
If you would have them safe abroad,
Pray keep them safe at home.

The alternating rhymes give the listener a clear sense of the movement of the poem, counteract monotony, and make it clear where one stanza ends and the next begins—especially useful if you are going to make the kind of associative leaps that are common to ballads. The same kind of effect happens here in a more serious poem:

From "As I Walked Out One Evening," W. H. Auden (1942)

As I walked out one evening,
Walking down Bristol Street,
The crowds upon the pavement
Were fields of harvest wheat.

And down by the brimming river
I heard a lover sing
Under an arch of the railway:
"Love has no ending . . .["]

But all the clocks in the city
Began to whirr and chime:
"O let not Time deceive you,
You cannot conquer Time . . .

"In headaches and in worry
Vaguely life leaks away,
And Time will have his fancy
To-morrow or to-day. . .

"The glacier knocks in the cupboard,
The desert sighs in the bed,
And the crack in the tea-cup opens
A lane to the land of the dead. . . .

"O stand, stand at the window
As the tears scald and start;
You shall love your crooked neighbour
With your crooked heart."

It was late, late in the evening,
The lovers they were gone;
The clocks had ceased their chiming,
And the deep river ran on.

Auden's poem gains much of its uncanny impact from the echoes of folk poetry that are strengthened by his choice of stanza. A famous poem by Countee Cullen uses the same associations to underscore its point:

"Incident," Countee Cullen (1925)

Once riding in old Baltimore,
Heart-filled, head-filled with glee,
I saw a Baltimorean
Keep looking straight at me.

Now I was eight and very small,
And he was no whit bigger,

And so I smiled, but he poked out
His tongue, and called me, "Nigger."

I saw the whole of Baltimore
From May until December;
Of all the things that happened there
That's all that I remember.

The singsong familiarity of the verse form makes the shock at the end of the second stanza feel that much more visceral; the reader's feeling of being punched in the stomach is similar to what we imagine the speaker might have felt. In the same stanza, Cullen exploits, by contradicting it, the principle that the second rhyme sound should be more familiar than the first; the second rhyme is emphasized with a rather nightmarish inevitability that goes along with the rhythmic lulling.

Another four-line stanza pattern rhymes aabb. This stanza is a particular challenge to pull off; the danger is that it will seem to split into two couplets. In this extremely well-known poem, Byron varies the devices that tie the stanzas together to keep them fresh:

From "The Destruction of Sennacherib," George Gordon, Lord Byron (1815)

Like the leaves of the forest when Summer is green,
That host with their banners at sunset were seen;
Like the leaves of the forest when Autumn hath blown,
That host on the morrow lay withered and strown.

For the Angel of Death spread his wings on the blast,
And breathed in the face of the foe as he passed;
And the eyes of the sleepers waxed deadly and chill,
And their hearts but once heaved, and for ever grew still!

And there lay the steed with his nostril all wide,
But through it there rolled not the breath of his pride;
And the foam of his gasping lay white on the turf,
And cold as the spray of the rock-beating surf.

And there lay the rider distorted and pale,
With the dew on his brow, and the rust on his mail;
And the tents were all silent, the banners alone,
The lances unlifted, the trumpet unblown.

The first stanza quoted uses suspense; the second uses a surprisingly unparallel parallelism ("Angel of death," "eyes of the sleepers"); the third uses a single intense image; the last uses a contrast between a closeup and a broad view of the battlefield. Each of these stanzas creates a different kind of link to tie the poem together across its center "seam."

One especially memorable four-line stanza is the **"In Memoriam" stanza,** named after Alfred, Lord Tennyson's celebrated long elegy for Arthur Hallam. The stanza rhymes abba, and the fourth line, coming so far after its rhyme-mate, has a haunting, lost quality. It is rare for a stanza to be named after a single poem, but Tennyson's tour de force draws on that lost quality so well that it is easy to see why the name has stuck. Once, the best friend of one of the students in a class I was teaching had died suddenly. That day we read the entire poem aloud, each of us reading a stanza until we had gone around the class several times and finished the poem. It was a moving experience, not only because the poem focuses on the incomprehensibility of early death, but also because the structure of the stanzas, each of which ends on a kind of waiting note, linked all of us who read together as if in a chain.

From "In Memoriam," Alfred, Lord Tennyson (1850)

Oh, yet we trust that somehow good
        Will be the final end of ill,
        To pangs of nature, sins of will,
Defects of doubt, and taints of blood;

That nothing walks with aimless feet;
        That not one life shall be destroy'd,
        Or cast as rubbish to the void,
When God hath made the pile complete;

That not a worm is cloven in vain;
        That not a moth with vain desire

Is shrivell'd in a fruitless fire,
Or but subserves another's gain.

Behold, we know not anything;
  I can but trust that good shall fall
  At last—far off—at last, to all,
And every winter change to spring.

So runs my dream; but what am I?
  An infant crying in the night;
  An infant crying for the light,
And with no language but a cry.

Here is a more recent poem using the same stanza. Written in 1959 about the danger of nuclear war in the aftermath of Hiroshima, today it resonates equally well as a poem about global climate change:

"Advice to a Prophet," Richard Wilbur

When you come, as you soon must, to the streets of our city,
Mad-eyed from stating the obvious,
Not proclaiming our fall but begging us
In God's name to have self-pity,

Spare us all word of the weapons, their force and range,
The long numbers that rocket the mind;
Our slow, unreckoning hearts will be left behind,
Unable to fear what is too strange.

Nor shall you scare us with talk of the death of the race.
How should we dream of this place without us?—
The sun mere fire, the leaves untroubled about us,
A stone look on the stone's face?

Speak of the world's own change. Though we cannot conceive
Of an undreamt thing, we know to our cost
How the dreamt cloud crumbles, the vines are blackened by frost,
How the view alters. We could believe,

If you told us so, that the white-tailed deer will slip
Into perfect shade, grown perfectly shy,
The lark avoid the reaches of our eye,
The jack-pine lose its knuckled grip

On the cold ledge, and every torrent burn
As Xanthus once, its gliding trout
Stunned in a twinkling. What should we be without
The dolphin's arc, the dove's return,

These things in which we have seen ourselves and spoken?
Ask us, prophet, how we shall call
Our natures forth when that live tongue is all
Dispelled, that glass obscured or broken

In which we have said the rose of our love and the clean
Horse of our courage, in which beheld
The singing locust of the soul unshelled,
And all we mean or wish to mean.

Ask us, ask us whether with the worldless rose
Our hearts shall fail us; come demanding
Whether there shall be lofty or long standing
When the bronze annals of the oak-tree close.

Wilbur is a learned and conscious poet; it seems likely that he was using the
"In Memoriam" rhyme scheme purposely for this poem about loss. Since
Wilbur's lines vary in length, there is not such a clear sense of anticipation and
delay as there is at the end of each stanza of the Tennyson. The more casual,
prosaic tone of the longer lines also mutes the effect, but it remains as a sobering undercurrent.

Another haunting four-line stanza form is the unique **sapphic stanza,**
whose invention is credited to the great ancient Greek poet Sappho. This stanza
is one of very few that always has a particular, exact metrical pattern:

Trochee-trochee-dactyl-trochee-trochee
Trochee-trochee-dactyl-trochee-trochee

Trochee-trochee-dactyl-trochee-trochee
Dactyl-trochee

"Moon and Stars," Sappho (trans. John Myers O'Hara) (1910)

When the moon at full on the sill of heaven
Lights her beacon, flooding the earth with silver,
All the shining stars that about her cluster
Hide their fair faces;

So when Anactoria's beauty dazzles
Sight of mine, grown dim with the joy it gives me,
Gorgo, Atthis, Gyrinno, all the others
Fade from my vision.

If you failed to stress the word "when" in the first line, no doubt you had to read it again until you did so. Here is a contemporary metrical translation of another Sappho poem:

Sappho, "Household of the Muses" (trans. Annie Finch)

It is not appropriate, in a household
Given to the Muses. Those lamentations
Do not belong here.

Again, unlike with other metrical patterns in this book so far, which can be changed through substitutions or expressive variation without destroying the basic meter, this particular pattern of trochees and dactyls *is* the definition of a sapphic stanza. Because the stanza is defined by its exact pattern of metrical feet, if it were altered through variation, it would probably not be "read" as a sapphic stanza by readers. This is why poets who use sapphic stanzas do not usually alter their meter for expressive purposes.

Often, when a new poetic form is first used, poets are self-conscious about writing in such an unusual form—and the self-consciousness shows itself, very literally, in allusions to the form and its history. Because Sappho is known as a great love poet, it is no coincidence that Swinburne, the decadent late-nine-teenth-century poet who was one of the first to appreciate the sapphic stanza's unique appeal for poetry in English, dedicated his only sapphic stanzas to Aphrodite, the goddess of love.

"Hymn to Aphrodite," Algernon Charles Swinburne (1868)

All the night sleep came not upon my eyelids,
Shed not dew, nor shook nor unclosed a feather,
Yet with lips shut close and with eyes of iron
Stood and beheld me.

Then to me so lying awake a vision
Came without sleep over the seas and touched me,
Softly touched mine eyelids and lips; and I too,
Full of the vision,

Saw the white implacable Aphrodite,
Saw the hair unbound and the feet unsandalled
Shine as fire of sunset on western waters;
Saw the reluctant

Feet, the straining plumes of the doves that drew her,
Looking always, looking with necks reverted,
Back to Lesbos, back to the hills whereunder
Shone Mitylene;

Heard the flying feet of the Loves behind her
Make a sudden thunder upon the waters,
As the thunder flung from the strong unclosing
Wings of a great wind.

Here is a more contemporary version of the stanza, with just a few variations from the meter:

"Effort at Speech," William Meredith
For Muriel Rukeyser

Climbing the stairway gray with urban midnight,
Cheerful, venial, ruminating pleasure,

Darkness takes me, an arm around my throat and
Give me your wallet.

Fearing cowardice more than other terrors,
Angry I wrestle with my unseen partner,
Caught in a ritual not of our making,
panting like spaniels.

Bold with adrenaline, mindless, shaking,
God damn it, no! I rasp at him behind me,
Wrenching the leather from his grasp. It
breaks like a wishbone,

So that departing (routed by my shouting,
not by my strength or inadvertent courage)
Half the papers lending me a name are
gone with him nameless.

Only now turning, I see a tall boy running,
Fifteen, sixteen, dressed thinly for the weather.
Reaching the streetlight he turns a brown face briefly
phrased like a question.

I like a questioner watch him turn the corner
Taking the answer with him, or his half of it.
Loneliness, not a sensible emotion,
breathes hard on the stairway.

Walking homeward I fraternize with shadows,
Zigzagging with them where they flee the streetlights,
Asking for trouble, asking for the message
trouble had sent me.

All fall down has been scribbled on the street in
Garbage and excrement: so much for the vision
Others taunt me with, my untimely humor,
so much for cheerfulness.

Next time don't wrangle, give the boy the money,
Call across chasms what the world you know is.
Luckless and lied to, how can a child master
human decorum?

Next time a switchblade, somewhere he is thinking,
I should have killed him and took the lousy wallet.
Reading my cards he feels a surge of anger
blind as my shame.

Error from Babel mutters in the places,
Cities apart, where now we word our failures:
Hatred and guilt have left us without language
that might have led to discourse.

We use the word "lesbian" today because Sappho, author of great love poems to women, lived on the island of Lesbos. So the sapphic stanza has naturally been felt an appropriate form for lesbian love poetry:

From "Dusk: July," Marilyn Hacker

I would love my love, but my love is elsewhere.
I would take a walk with her in the evening's
Milky pearl. I'd sleep with my arms around her
Confident body,

Arms and legs asprawl like an adolescent.
We're not adolescents. Our friends are dying
And between us nothing at all is settled
Except our loving.

The beautiful, captivating last line of the sapphic stanza is perhaps its most compelling charm. This shorter last line, consisting of one dactyl and one trochee, is called an **adonic,** named after a poem written in that stanza to mourn the death of the goddess Venus's beautiful young lover, Adonis. Recently, I told a poet-friend that the sapphic strikes me as an erotic stanza, even aside from its history. Challenged to explain why, I told her that it has to do with the tension of opposites: the single dactylic foot hidden inside the trochaic lines, building momentum there until, in the adonic, it emerges into a pairing, a balance, with a single trochee. As this tension and resolution between trochee and dactyl recurs in each stanza, the adonic takes on more and more potential power. A good adonic is hard to forget. If you listen for adonics, you will hear them everywhere: "Tell me you love me"; "Here, let me help you"; "How could you do that?"; "Look, I'm your mother!"; "Wow, I'm exhausted."

A more complicated four-line classical stanza that is still used, though less frequently than the sapphic, is the **alcaic stanza,** attributed to the poet Alcaeus. The first two lines are the same: / / u / / / u u / u / (first and second feet may be changed to amphibrachs [u/u], and the last foot to a pyrrhic [uu]). The third line is / / u / / / u / / (any or all of the feet may be changed—the first and third to amphibrachs [u / u] and the second to /u/). The fourth line is / uu / uu / / (last foot may be changed to a trochee [/u]). Here are some examples:

From "Psalm 120," Mary Sidney (ca. 1590)

Too long, alas, too long have I dwelled here
With friendly peaces furious enemies:
Who when to peace I seeke to call them,
Faster I find to the warre they arm them.

From "Evening," William Blake

Now, while the west-wind slumbereth on the lake,
Silently dost thou with delicate shimmer
O'erbloom the frowning front of awful
Night to a glance of unearthly silver.

From "The Garden at Dawn," Robin Skelton

My morning mind is clouded and blurred with dream.
Dream holds the one great key to the shining whole
We share with whirlpools, gods, and children
Aware realities move like music.

From "Going Back to the River," Marilyn Hacker

Life's not forever, love is precarious.
Wherever I live, let me come home to you
As you are, as I am, where you
Meet me and walk with me to the river.

It is such a subtle meter that it may be hard to hear the pattern, and yet even so, a shimmering complexity keeps moving in rhythm directly under the surface of the poem.

Longer Stanzas

There are no well-known five-line stanzas, though of course poets have invented them for particular poems. Here is one poem that uses a simple five-line stanza rhymed ababa:

"Home is So Sad," Philip Larkin

Home is so sad. It stays as it was left,
Shaped to the comfort of the last to go
As if to win them back. Instead, bereft
Of anyone to please, it withers so,
Having no heart to put aside the theft

And turn again to what it started as,
A joyous shot at how things ought to be,
Long fallen wide. You can see how it was:
Look at the pictures and the cutlery.
The music in the piano stool. That vase.

Typical of Larkin's great formal virtuosity, this poem makes good use of the rather forlorn potential of the "extra" last line in this stanza, which lingers on, unwanted and unsure, after the usual, and probably expected, abab quatrain has finished.

During the Tudor and Stuart periods, arguably the most inventive and exciting time for poetry in English, a six-line stanza, made of a quatrain followed by a couplet, was common:

From "Venus and Adonis," William Shakespeare (1593)

He burns with bashful shame: she with her tears
Doth quench the maiden burning of his cheeks;
Then with her windy sighs and golden hairs
To fan and blow them dry again she seeks:
He saith she is immodest, blames her 'miss;
What follows more she murders with a kiss.

Even as an empty eagle, sharp by fast,
Tires with her beak on feathers, flesh and bone,
Shaking her wings, devouring all in haste,
Till either gorge be stuff'd or prey be gone;
Even so she kissed his brow, his cheek, his chin,
And where she ends she doth anew begin.

This adaptable stanza was used both for very short lyrics of two or three stanzas, and for long narratives such as this 1,194-line poem. The constant restarting, summing up, and restarting again of the action creates an interesting motion through a poem. This stanza is thought to have influenced the development of the English sonnet form.

Closely related to the six-line stanza is the seven-line stanza used by the colonial poet Anne Bradstreet for her "Contemplations." Bradstreet used the stanza ababccc, each stanza ending in a hexameter, to recreate the meandering paths of spiritual reflection:

From "Contemplations" (1678)

Then higher on the glistening Sun I gazed,
Whose beams was shaded by the leavie tree;
The more I looked, the more I grew amazed,
And softly said, "What's glorly like to thee?"
Soul of this world, this universe's Eye,
No wonder some made thee a diety;
Had I not known better, alas, the same had I.

Of the longer stanzas, **rhyme royal** is one of the most well known and versatile. A seven-line stanza rhyming ababbcc, it can be used for long narrative poems and also serves well for short lyrics. Traditionally, it is in iambic pentameter, but it doesn't need to be. Rhyme royal is also called "Troilus stanza" because Chaucer first used it in English, for his beautiful long narrative poem *Troilus and Criseyde:*

From Troilus and Criseyde, *Geoffrey Chaucer (ca. 1386)*

Out of these blake wawes for to sayle,
O wind, O wind, the weder ginneth clere;
For in this see the boot hath swich travayle,
Of my conning, that unnethe I it stere:
This see clepe I the tempestous matere
Of desespeyr that Troilus was inne:
But now of hope the calendes biginne.

The name "rhyme royal" relates to the fact that this stanza was traditional in ceremonies honoring royalty. Two notable long contemporary poems in rhyme royal are Sonia Sanchez's elegy for her brother, and Major Jackson's long tour de force dedicated to Gwendolyn Brooks:

From *"Letter to Brooks," Major Jackson*

12.
What fevered my wrist was this: you could
    Have amicably thanked me for the ride,
Extending your elbow-length glove, you could
    Have disappeared in that opulent façade,
    Instead you asked if I'd read alongside
That night. I left and bought a pad from Kmart
Then wrote all the poems I knew by heart,

13.
Which numbered two,—one of those, a haiku.
    The evening thickens dense as trees
Except the feel of reading on stage with you.

Truth be told, I've come to believe such deeds
Define as much the black tradition and seed
The garden Clarence Major speaks. If it thrives,
Scores bend on hand and knee keeping it alive.

Here, the metrically irregular lines and occasional slant rhymes create a tension with the regularity of the form.

The eight-lined stanza called **ottava rima,** rhymed ababab cc, is only one line longer than rhyme royal, but that one line makes all the difference. It gives the stanza enough space to change direction and bring in a variety of moods. The third repetition of each a and b rhyming word also allows the stanza to gather more force, which gives additional energy to the couplet when it finally happens. Originally Italian, the stanza was tried by several poets in English, including those early experimenters with the sonnet, Wyatt and Sidney. But it was during the Romantic period that *Don Juan,* Byron's satirical narrative poem about a man who can't resist women, established ottava rima as an important stanza in English. Byron's extremely popular poem endowed this stanza with a reputation for wit and satire and a declamatory and public, rather than privately musing, tone:

From Don Juan, *George Gordon, Lord Byron (1819)*

My poem's epic and is meant to be
Divided in twelve books, each book containing,
With love and war, a heavy gale at sea,
A list of ships, and captains, and kings reigning,
New characters; the episodes are three.
A panoramic view of hell's in training,
After the style of Virgil and of Homer,
So that my name of epic's no misnomer.

All these things will be specified in time
With strict regard to Aristotle's rules,
The vade mecum of the true sublime,
Which makes so many poets and some fools.
Prose poets like blank verse, I'm fond of rhyme.
Good workmen never quarrel with their tools.

I've got new mythological machinery,
And very handsome supernatural scenery.

There's only one slight difference between
Me and my epic brethren gone before,
And here the advantage is my own, I ween,
(Not that I have not several merits more,
But this will more peculiarly be seen);
They so embellish, that 'tis quite a bore
Their labyrinth of fables to thread through,
Whereas this story's actually true.

The next poet to be known for his use of ottava rima, William Butler Yeats, built on the Byronic tradition but gave the stanza his own stamp, infusing it with his distinctive tone of meditative high seriousness:

From "Among School Children," W. B. Yeats (1928)

Labour is blossoming or dancing where
The body is not bruised to pleasure soul.
Nor beauty born out of its own despair,
Nor blear-eyed wisdom out of midnight oil.
O chestnut-tree, great-rooted blossomer,
Are you the leaf, the blossom or the bole?
O body swayed to music, O brightening glance,
How can we know the dancer from the dance?

Stanzas longer than eight lines are unusual, but one incomparable nine-line stanza will always hold a special place in poetry in English: the **Spenserian stanza.** Devised by Spenser for use in his magnificent, fanciful epic poem in honor of Queen Elizabeth, the *Faerie Queene,* it is a nine-line stanza with a unique interlocking rhyme scheme (ababbcbcc) and a very beautiful extra-long last line (six feet long, called an "alexandrine"). Though few poets have tried it—Keats's "Eve of St. Agnes" is a famous exception—it is worth trying. When I have written Spenserian stanzas, I've found myself caught up in passages of intricate description, but the stanza also lends itself to drama, as in this passage describing the warlike Britomart, a legendary soldier who here stands for the military strength of England and of Queen Elizabeth I:

From The Faerie Queene, *Edmund Spenser (1590)*

Wherewith enrag'd she fiercely at them flew,
And with her flaming sword about her layd,
That none of them foule mischiefe could eschew,
But with her dreadfull strokes were all dismayd:
Here, there, and euery where about her swayd
Her wrathfull steele, that none mote it abide;
And eke the *Redcrosse* knight gaue her good aid,
Ay ioyning foot to foot, and side to side,
That in short space their foes they haue quite terrifide.

Tho whenas all were put to shamefull flight,
The noble *Britomartis* her arayd,
And her bright armes about her body dight:
For nothing would she lenger there be stayd,
Where so loose life, and so vngentle trade
Was vsd of Knights and Ladies seeming gent:
So earely ere the grosse Earthes gryesy shade
Was all disperst out of the firmament,
They tooke their steeds, & forth upon their iourney went.

These adjacent stanzas from Keats's poem make use of both the potential for drama and for description:

From "The Eve of St. Agnes," *John Keats (1819)*

Out went the taper as she hurried in;
Its little smoke, in pallid moonshine, died:
She clos'd the door, she panted, all akin
To spirits of the air, and visions wide:
No uttered syllable, or, woe betide!
But to her heart, her heart was voluble,

Paining with eloquence her balmy side;
As though a tongueless nightingale should swell
Her throat in vain, and die, heart-stifled, in her dell.

A casement high and triple-arch'd there was,
All garlanded with carven imag'ries
Of fruits, and flowers, and bunches of knot-grass,
And diamonded with panes of quaint device,
Innumerable of stains and splendid dyes,
As are the tiger-moth's deep-damask'd wings;
And in the midst, 'mong thousand heraldries,
And twilight saints, and dim emblazonings,
A shielded scutcheon blush'd with blood of queens and kings.

A shorter stanza might easily be thrown off balance by the longer line at the end, but Spenser's genius was to balance the long line and the long stanza, a symmetry that his great admirer Keats found a perfect frame for his own skill at intricate description.

When Keats died of consumption at the age of 25, two years after writing this famously lush poem, his close friend Percy Bysshe Shelley added to the significance of the Spenserian stanza by choosing it for his elegy on Keats, "Adonais." The elegy is 495 lines long and offers plenty of time for Shelley's metaphysical meditations:

From "Adonais: An Elegy on the Death of John Keats,"
Percy Bysshe Shelley (1821)

He is made one with Nature: there is heard
His voice in all her music, from the moan
Of thunder, to the song of night's sweet bird;
He is a presence to be felt and known
In darkness and in light, from herb and stone,
Spreading itself where'er that Power may move
Which has withdrawn his being to its own;
Which wields the world with never-wearied love,
Sustains it from beneath, and kindles it above.

He is a portion of the loveliness
Which once he made more lovely: he doth bear
His part, while the one Spirit's plastic stress
Sweeps through the dull dense world, compelling there,
All new successions to the forms they wear;
Torturing th' unwilling dross that checks its flight
To its own likeness, as each mass may bear;
And bursting in its beauty and its might
From trees and beasts and men into the Heaven's light.

The splendours of the firmament of time
May be eclips'd, but are extinguish'd not;
Like stars to their appointed height they climb
And death is a low mist which cannot blot
The brightness it may veil. When lofty thought
Lifts a young heart above its mortal lair,
And love and life contend in it for what,
Shall be its earthly doom, the dead live there
And move like winds of light on dark and stormy air.

It is hard to imagine such ample musings taking place in a more confined space such as rhyme royal or ottava rima. But then, the wonderful thing about a stanza is that once it has been used for a certain kind of poem, it comes to seem as if it has always been that way.

The last stanza we will discuss is a 10-line stanza, the **decima.** The decima is of Hispanic origin and dates back to the fifteenth century. It has been used only rarely in English so far, though it has recently been rediscovered by contemporary Hispanic poets including Pat Mora and Cynthia Gutierrez. There are numerous variations of rhyme scheme, but the stanza always has 10 lines. While Mora uses an unrhymed stanza, the most common rhyme scheme is probably abbaaccddc:

"Decima," George Santayana

Silent daisies out of reach,
Maidens of the starry grass,

Gazing on me as I pass
With a look too wise for speech,
Teach me resignation—teach
Patience to the barren clod,
As, above your happier sod,
Bending to the wind's caress,
You—unplucked, alas!—no less
Sweetly manifest the god.

Santayana, perhaps the first poet to bring this stanza into English, was known for his philosophical meditations. Here, he uses a short line to meditate on the timeless lesson of a simple theme.

The Dynamic Stanza

While most common stanzas can be classified by length, as they are here, it is important to realize that length is not the defining characteristic of a stanza. What really holds a stanza together is the energetic connection among its own lines, and between it and other stanzas in the poem. A case in point is Paul Muldoon's poem "The Outlier" in chapter 6, in which each stanza adds a new line. This form, so appropriate for the poem with its echoes of childhood poems that keep adding parts, such as "The Farmer in the Dell," reminds us that a strong poem makes its form for its own purposes. The following poem, from a young poet's first book, builds stanzas based on the numbers in the Fibonacci sequence:

"Light Warning," Emily Galvin

No.

Wait

for it.

You know how

The air feels after everything

Has been carried out, doors and windows closed?

Deep wintertime—I felt the cold coming through the glass, the old blade
loose

In my left hand. Late at night I used to sit against the window at the far
end of my bed

And hope like hell that something would break through. The intimacy of
drywall, cold air leaking through. I watched the glass sink through
itself inside the window-frame. Sore ribs. I kept on staring through,

As if only waiting. Wheels in the ditch. Body on the wall. Red sky all night
that time of year. Where I live now, it never gets that cold.
Sometimes, though, when the fires get close enough to let a little ash
into the air, I think of windowpanes, and sparks fly out my mouth.

This is an idea that could easily have fallen flat, but in this case, there is an electric engagement with the form that builds a kind of tensile connection within
and between the stanzas. A workable stanza is always dynamic. As you choose
or devise a stanza for your poem, make sure that you feel the quickening of interest that assures you that this stanza is, indeed, alive for you for the duration
of this poem.

Whether you write in free verse or form, your poetry will benefit if you become comfortable with writing stanzas of different lengths. You will find that a
poem that doesn't work at all in a long stanza can come to life if you put it into
a short stanza, and vice versa. Since stanzas frame the entire context of a poem,
a strong vocabulary of stanzas is one of the most useful tools a poet can have.

QUESTIONS FOR MEDITATION OR DISCUSSION

What does a room mean to you? In your notebook, freewrite a description of a
room where you would like to be. How big would it be? How wide? How tall?
Would it be rectangular or circular or something else? What would the walls be
like? Then imagine a poetic stanza that feels the same way. It could be an existing stanza or one you invent yourself. How do you think that stanza functions
like a room? Does the metaphor tell you anything more about how poetry
works?

T. S. Eliot wrote, "The bad poet is usually unconscious where he [*sic*] ought to be conscious, and conscious where he ought to be unconscious." Where do you think a poet should be conscious, and where unconscious? Is the stanza a place for consciousness or unconsciousness?

QUOTES

Without form, how could words bear the weight of emotions?
    —Maya Sharma

To see the world for what it is, one needs the line, and later the larger field of the stanza or whatever you care to call it.
    —Charles Simic

I don't feel that writing in traditional forms is giving up power, going over to the enemy. The word belongs to no one, the houses built of words belong to no one. We have to take them back from those who think they own them.
    —Julia Alvarez

POETRY PRACTICES

Group (Readabout). Choose a long poem in stanzas and read it aloud, each person taking one stanza. It's fine to repeat the poem a few times. This is a good way to get a sense of the movement of a particular stanza shape.

Stanza Sampler. Take one of your unrhymed poems and break it up into at least four different lengths of stanza. You might try it in couplets, tercets, quatrains, seven-line stanzas, and irregular-length stanzas. Notice the differences it makes to the poem. Are you inspired to make different kinds of revisions for the different poems?

Follow That Tune. Write a poem to be sung to the tune of the *Gilligan's Island* theme song, your favorite country song, or another ballad stanza tune that you know well.

Meditation Rooms. Many stanza forms, including, in this chapter, rhyme royal, ottava rima, the Spenserian stanza, and the decima, have been used for meditative poetry: poetry that meditates on philosophical themes. Choose one of these stanzas and write a poem musing on a theme. Give yourself plenty of room.

Cutting Up Free Verse. Take a free verse poem you want to revise and cut it up with scissors into stanzas or, if you don't have stanzas, into units that seem to belong together. Rearrange the stanzas various ways. When you have something you like, tape it together.

Train of Quatrains. For this exercise, you can use an existing poem of your own in quatrains, or write a new poem in quatrains, or use someone else's poem in quatrains. Whichever you choose, revise at least three stanzas of the poem into three different quatrain rhyme patterns: abab, aabb, and abba. You will need to alter the grammar and the rest of the lines in each stanza somewhat to make it flow smoothly. How does the reorganization of the rhyme pattern affect the poem?

Weaving a Story. Write a narrative poem in terza rima. Optional: base it on an incident from Dante's *Divine Comedy;* on a dream; or on a vision of the afterlife. Or try writing a narrative in Spenserian stanzas, rhyme royal, or ottava rima. You can start a new narrative, or add some stanzas onto an existing narrative poem such as *The Faerie Queene* or *Don Juan.*

Stanza Essences. Write a new poem in three different ways: one version in heroic couplets, one in sapphics or alcaics, and one in rhyme royal.

CHAPTER 8

Worth Repeating: Forms Based on Repetition

You know I'm drifting and I'm drifting just like a ship out on the sea.
Well, I'm drifting and I'm drifting like a ship out on the sea.
Well, you know I ain't got nobody in this world to care for me.

The second line of the blues poem above may look as if it doesn't add anything important, but try reading the stanza without it. Then read the full stanza again. Try to describe what the repeated line adds to the poem.

Is it something about rhythm, pacing? Is it something that happens in your body as you wait for the line to finish? Is it a change in mood or tone of voice? Whatever the repeated line adds, we feel it in our heartbeats, our breathing, the tensing of our muscles. The physicality of poetry is its most untranslatable and unique characteristic, and repeating poems are structured to glory in this physicality.

While all poems have some elements of repetition—rhymes, sounds, rhythms, stanzas, images, even the fact of line breaks (even images and metaphors are based on kinds of repetition) the special kinds of poems in this chapter are structured on repeating phrases or refrains. Numerous poetic patterns from numerous cultures are based on this kind of blatant repetition. Like the blues, repeating structures were often originally songs or oral poems; they are "lyric" poems in the truest sense of the word. The structures of repeating poems provide templates for passion, awe, melancholy, delight, anger, and other emotional experience, reminding us that all emotions, however profound or transcendent, are experienced in our bodies, and connecting us, through our bodies, with the eternal cycles of time.

One of the most simple, powerful literary techniques, the repetition of the beginning words or phrases of lines, or of clauses, is called **anaphora.** It dates back at least to the Hebrew of the Old Testament:

From "Song of Solomon" (ca. 965 B.C.), King James Bible (1611)

His head is as the most fine gold, his locks are bushy, and black as a raven.
His eyes are as the eyes of doves by the rivers of waters, washed with milk,
    and fitly set.
His cheeks are as a bed of spices, as sweet flowers: his lips like lilies,
    dropping sweet smelling myrrh.
His hands are as gold rings set with the beryl: his belly is as bright ivory
    overlaid with sapphires.
His legs are as pillars of marble, set upon sockets of fine gold: his
    countenance is as Lebanon, excellent as the cedars.
His mouth is most sweet: yea, he is altogether lovely. This is my beloved,
    and this is my friend, O daughters of Jerusalem.

The repetition of the word "his," combined with the repeating grammatical structure, creates the simplest kind of anaphora. A more obvious use of anaphora occurs in the work of Walt Whitman, who was directly influenced by the King James Bible. Whitman is the poet who is best known for using anaphora in English. Here it lends an incantatory impact to the opening of one of his most moving poems:

From "Out of the Cradle, Endlessly Rocking," Walt Whitman (1859)

Out of the cradle endlessly rocking,
Out of the mocking-bird's throat, the musical shuttle,
Out of the Ninth-month midnight,
Over the sterile sands and the fields beyond, where the child leaving his
    bed wander'd alone, bare headed, barefoot,
Down from the shower'd halo,
Up from the mystic play of shadows twining and twisting as if they were
    alive,
Out from the patches of briers and blackberries,
From the memories of the bird that chanted to me,
From your memories sad brother—from the fitful risings and fallings I
    heard,
From under that yellow half-moon late-risen, and swollen as if with tears,
From those beginning notes of yearning and love there in the transparent
    mist,

From the thousand responses of my heart never to cease,
From the myriad thence-arous'd words,
From the word stronger and more delicious than any,
From such as now they start the scene revisiting,
As a flock, twittering, rising, or overhead passing,
Borne hither, ere all eludes me, hurriedly,
A man, yet by these tears a little boy again,
Throwing myself on the sand, confronting the waves,
I, chanter of pains and joys, uniter of here and hereafter,
Taking all hints to use them, but swiftly leaping beyond them,
A reminiscence sing.

Anaphora is a decorative technique, not a structural one: it can't be predicted like the rhyme scheme of a sonnet. Like all decorative techniques in poetry, it requires a sure instinct and a light touch to avoid deadening the effect by becoming too predictable. Here, Whitman uses it beautifully, modulating from the repetitions of "out" to "from" with a transition as subtle as a skilled painter blending colors. Here is the end of a poem by a young contemporary poet using anaphora for more startling effects:

From "O Great Slacker," Olena Kalytiak Davis

... becaUSE after a while Sorrow is a tasty Meat
beCAUSE we can't see ourselves Gnawing, Chewing
BEcause there is nothing New and nothing not New, Known
beCause we like to call ourselves WE and stand Together
beCaUse that allows ME to separate out from this sown this mown this
      cowering Crowd
and say onto you: i am your Remembrancer, your Requiter
i am Loud in your Sickness
you are Gnashing my Teeth
in Vain

The repeating words function as placeholders and time-markers. Combined with Davis's unorthodox use of capitalization, syntax, and diction, they give a ritualistic quality to the poem, perhaps partially in echo of another heavily anaphoric and idiocynsncratic poem written centuries earlier, Christopher Smart's *Jubilate Agno*:

From Jubilate Agno, *Christopher Smart (1760)*

For I will consider my Cat Jeoffry.
For he is the servant of the Living God, duly and daily serving him.
For at the first glance of the glory of God in the East he worships in his
     way.
For in this is done by wreathing his body seven times round with elegant
     quickness.
For then he leaps up to catch the musk, which is the blessing of God upon
     his prayer.
For he rolls upon prank to work it in.
For having done duty and received blessing he begins to consider
     himself.
For this he performs in ten degrees.
For first he looks upon his forepaws to see if they are clean.
For secondly he kicks up behind to clear away there.
For thirdly he works it upon stretch with the forepaws extended.
For fourthly he sharpens his paws by wood.
For fifthly he washes himself.
For sixthly he rolls upon wash.
For seventhly he fleas himself, that he may not be interrupted upon the
     beat.
For eighthly he rubs himself against a post.
For ninthly he looks up for his instructions.
For tenthly he goes in quest of food.
For having consider'd God and himself he will consider his neighbour.
For if he meets another cat he will kiss her in kindness.
For when he takes his prey he plays with it to give it a chance.
For one mouse in seven escapes by his dallying.
For when his day's work is done his business more properly begins.
For he keeps the Lord's watch in the night against the adversary.
For he counteracts the powers of darkness by his electrical skin and
     glaring eyes.
For he counteracts the Devil, who is death, by brisking about the life.
For in his morning orisons he loves the sun and the sun loves him.
For he is of the tribe of Tiger.
For the Cherub Cat is a term of the Angel Tiger.

For he has the subtlety and hissing of a serpent, which in goodness he
   suppresses.
For he will not do destruction if he is well-fed, neither will he spit without
   provocation.
For he purrs in thankfulness, when God tells him he's a good Cat.
For he is an instrument for the children to learn benevolence upon.
For every house is incomplete without him, and a blessing is lacking in the
   spirit...
For the Lord commanded Moses concerning the cats at the departure of
   the Children of Israel from Egypt.
For every family had one cat at least in the bag.
For the English Cats are the best in Europe.
For he is the cleanest in the use of his forepaws of any quadruped.
For the dexterity of his defence is an instance of the love of God to him
   exceedingly.
For he is the quickest to his mark of any creature.
For he is tenacious of his point.
For he is a mixture of gravity and waggery.
For he knows that God is his Saviour.
For there is nothing sweeter than his peace when at rest.
For there is nothing brisker than his life when in motion.
For he is of the Lord's poor and so indeed is he called by benevolence
   perpetually—Poor Jeoffry! poor Jeoffry! the rat has bit thy throat.
For I bless the name of the Lord Jesus that Jeoffry is better.
For the divine spirit comes about his body to sustain it in complete cat.
For his tongue is exceeding pure so that it has in purity what it wants in
   music.
For he is docile and can learn certain things.
For he can set up with gravity which is patience upon approbation.
For he can fetch and carry, which is patience in employment.
For he can jump over a stick which is patience upon proof positive.
For he can spraggle upon waggle at the word of command.
For he can jump from an eminence into his master's bosom.
For he can catch the cork and toss it again.
For he is hated by the hypocrite and miser.
For the former is afraid of detection.
For the latter refuses the charge.

For he camels his back to bear the first notion of business.
For he is good to think on, if a man would express himself neatly.
For he made a great figure in Egypt for his signal services.
For he killed the Ichneumon-rat very pernicious by land.
For his ears are so acute that they sting again.
For from this proceeds the passing quickness of his attention.
For by stroking of him I have found out electricity.
For I perceived God's light about him both wax and fire.
For the Electrical fire is the spiritual substance, which God sends from
        heaven to sustain the bodies both of man and beast.
For God has blessed him in the variety of his movements.
For, tho he cannot fly, he is an excellent clamberer.
For his motions upon the face of the earth are more than any other
        quadruped.
For he can tread to all the measures upon the music.
For he can swim for life.
For he can creep.

In the poem below, the repetitions are more formally structured and predictable. They create a sense of import and solemnity, perhaps evoking the kind
of Native American ritual traditions about which Harjo often writes:

"Ah, Ah," Joy Harjo

for Lurline McGregor

Ah, ah cries the crow arching toward the heavy sky over the marina.
Lands on the crown of the palm tree.

Ah, ah slaps the urgent cove of ocean swimming through the slips.
We carry canoes to the edge of the salt.

Ah, ah groans the crew with the weight, the winds cutting skin.
We claim our seats. Pelicans perch in the draft for fish.

Ah, ah beats our lungs and we are racing into the waves.
Though there are worlds below us and above us, we are straight ahead.

Ah, ah tattoos the engines of your plane against the sky—away from these
waters.
Each paddle stroke follows the curve from reach to loss.

Ah, ah calls the sun from a fishing boat with a pale, yellow sail. We fly by
on our return, over the net of eternity thrown out for stars.

Ah, ah scrapes the hull of my soul. Ah, ah.

From the first line, with its unexpected period after "marina," it is clear that repetition will be given priority over idiomatic usage in this poem. The exactness
of the repetition of the words "ah, ah" has the force of a traditional chant. Such
consistent poetic decisions set an appropriately serious stage for the introduction of the phrase "hull of my soul" in the last line, which otherwise might have
seemed too intense for the poem.

The following poem also uses repetition in a formal manner, as if the repeated phrases are patiently building a strong, steady place to structure an intense emotional experience:

"Looking at Each Other," Muriel Rukeyser (1913)

Yes, we were looking at each other
Yes, we knew each other very well
Yes, we had made love with each other many times
Yes, we had heard music together
Yes, we had gone to the sea together
Yes, we had cooked and eaten together
Yes, we had laughed often day and night
Yes, we fought violence and knew violence
Yes, we hated the inner and outer oppression
Yes, that day we were looking at each other
Yes, we saw the sunlight pouring down
Yes, the corner of the table was between us
Yes, bread and flowers were on the table
Yes, our eyes saw each other's eyes
Yes, our mouths saw each other's mouth
Yes, our breasts saw each other's breasts
Yes, our bodies entire saw each other

Yes, it was beginning in each
Yes, it threw waves across our lives
Yes, the pulses were becoming very strong
Yes, the beating became very delicate
Yes, the calling the arousal
Yes, the arriving the coming
Yes, there it was for both entire
Yes, we were looking at each other

The word "yes" is used so naturally as part of each clause that it is only as the end of the poem approaches that one realizes the people in the poem are also saying "yes" to each other's love. In order for that meaning of the word "yes" to emerge, a reader has to move outside the formal structure of the poem, which makes us realize how much we have been contained inside the immediacy of the described experience. "Looking at Each Other" is based on syntactical repetition (repeating a sentence structure). Rukeyser establishes the pattern of syntactical repetition just enough with the repeating word "we" so that we can recognize it beginning to break down as the lovers' passion starts to break through. In the box you will find examples of more formal structures of repetition, developed by rhetoricians in Classical times to make their writing more powerful.

Some classical rhetorical strategies involving repetition:

Anaphora:
Repetition of the same word at the beginning of successive lines or clauses
See poem by Oleana Kalytiak Davis, this chapter.

Epistrophe
The opposite of anaphora: repetition of the same word at the ends of successive clauses

Symploce: combination of anaphora and epistrophe

The yellow fog that rubs its back upon the window-panes,
The yellow smoke that rubs its muzzle on the window-panes
T. S. Eliot, "The Love Song of J. Alfred Prufrock," 1917

Anadiplosis:
Repetition of the last word of one clause at the beginning of the following clause:

> Here is no question of whiteness,
> white as white can be, with a purple mole
> at the center of each flower.
> Each flower is a hand's span . . .
>   William Carlos Williams, "Queen Anne's Lace," 1921

Polyptoton
Words are repeated as different parts of speech, or as different forms of the same word-stem.

> Thou, whose shadow shadows doth make bright—
> How would thy shadow's form form happy show . . .
>   Shakespeare, Sonnet 43

Also see the use of the words "losing," "lost," and "loss" at the end of Elizabeth Bishop's "One Art" in the section on the villanelle.

Antanaclasis
Repetition of a word with a different meaning (pun)

> If we don't hang together, we'll hang separately (Benjamin Franklin).

Epizeuxis:
Emphatic repetition of a word with no other words between:

> Who lit cigarettes in boxcars boxcars boxcars racketing through snow
> toward lonesome farms in grandfather night (Allen Ginsberg, *Howl*)

The powerful and pleasurable technique of repetition is central to the very nature of poetry. So it is not surprising that poets over the centuries, and all over the world, have developed poetic forms, simple and elaborate, that structure and channel repeating patterns of poetic lines: forms like the African American blues, the Malaysian pantoum, the French villanelle, sestina, roundel, and triolet, the Italian canzone, and the Indian and Middle Eastern ghazal. To write a poem in one of these repeating forms requires, and helps develop, skills that are important to your writing of poetry generally. To make the repeating lines of a villanelle work effectively, for example, you will need to learn how to use restraint effectively, including the creation of suspense, the management of pacing, and great sensitivity to timing and context. You will also learn a kind of ingenuity: how to do a lot with a little, how to achieve effects with very few additional words, how to achieve subtle differences of tone through placement of the repeating words. And these kinds of skills are key to any poem.

We will now explore some of the best-known and most-loved of these repeating forms. As you learn to write these kinds of poems, keep in mind that though repeating structures can help make poems memorable, moving, and fun to read, there is a danger of monotony. To guard against this danger, keep three principles in mind when writing a repeating poem: 1. A line that will occur twice should be at least twice as good as a regular line. 2. Reading aloud as you revise (always, of course, but especially with repeating poems) will help ensure that you are building dramatic tension as the poem goes on. 3. Shifts in context can keep refrains fresh; usually, refrains work best when they have a different emotional connotation—or even a different meaning—each time they occur.

The Blues

The **blues poem,** a uniquely American poetic form, is based on the pattern of lyrics of blues songs that African American musicians developed in the South after the Civil War, drawing from West African work songs with a call-and-response pattern. For decades an oral tradition, the blues were popularized and recorded by musicians such as Robert Johnson and W. C. Handy in the early twentieth century. Ever since Countee Cullen and Langston Hughes wrote the first blues poems during the Harlem Renaissance, this classic song form has inspired African American poets, and more recently poets of other races.

Hughes's early "The Weary Blues" embeds actual blues lyrics into a different stanza structure:

"The Weary Blues," Langston Hughes (1923)

Droning a drowsy syncopated tune,
Rocking back and forth to a mellow croon,
  I heard a Negro play.
Down on Lenox Avenue the other night
By the pale dull pallor of an old gas light
  He did a lazy sway . . .
  He did a lazy sway . . .
To the tune o' those Weary Blues.
With his ebony hands on each ivory key
He made that poor piano moan with melody.
  O Blues!
Swaying to and fro on his rickety stool
He played that sad raggy tune like a musical fool.
  Sweet Blues!
Coming from a black man's soul.
  O Blues!
In a deep song voice with a melancholy tone
I heard that Negro sing, that old piano moan—
  "Ain't got nobody in all this world,
  Ain't got nobody but ma self.
  I's gwine to quit ma frownin'
  And put ma troubles on the shelf."
Thump, thump, thump, went his foot on the floor.
He played a few chords then he sang some more—
  "I got the Weary Blues
  And I can't be satisfied.
  Got the Weary Blues
  And can't be satisfied—
  I ain't happy no mo'
  And I wish that I had died."
And far into the night he crooned that tune.
The stars went out and so did the moon.

The singer stopped playing and went to bed
While the Weary Blues echoed through his head.
He slept like a rock or a man that's dead.

The simplicity of the poem's structure creates a dignified, archaic setting for the deep traditions it evokes, and for the ambiguity of the emotions at the end. Later poets began the tradition of copying the actual structure of blues lyrics. The blues traditionally sing of problems, hardships, "the blues"—but these "literary" blues poems have sung the range of emotions from humor, such as Raymond Patterson's "Computer Blues," which includes the lines, "Hey, you blowed the fuse, / ain't no computer built /that can stand the blues" to righteous anger, as in Sanchez's poem "Song No. 2" below.

The structure of blues is simple. The first line is repeated, sometimes with a slight change, and the stanza ends with a rhyming third line. Since the repeating lines happen right after each other, it is a special challenge to make each line sound fresh, or freshly motivated. In Leadbelly's song "Good Morning Blues," the repetition adds suspense that increases the humor of the final line:

Good mornin' blues, blues, how do you do?
Good mornin' blues, blues, how do you do?
I'm doin' all right, good mornin', how are you?

Like many poems based on song forms, blues poems often complicate the original form by adding new subtleties appropriate to the page. Written blues can add new lines, change the repeating line, or take away the rhyme from the basic pattern.

The most important aspects of writing blues are to keep the imagery vivid, the language direct, and the emotion true. Singing as you go is probably a good idea; if you can't sing it, maybe you don't feel it. Here is Sonia Sanchez's "Song No. 2":

i say. all you young girls waiting to live
i say. I say i say all you young girls waiting to live
i say. all you sisters takin yo pill
i say. all you sisters thinkin you won't, but you will

don't let them kill you with their stare
don't let them closet you with no air
don't let them feed you sex piece-meal
don't let them offer you any old deal.

i say. step back sisters. We're rising from the dead
i say. step back johnnies. we're dancing on our heads
i say. step back man. no mo hangin by a thread
i say. step back world. can't let it all go unsaid.

i say. all you young girls molested at ten
i say. all you young girls giving it up again and again
i say. all you sisters hanging out in every den
i say. all you sisters needing your own oxygen.

don't let them trap you with your coke
don't let them treat you like one fat joke
don't let them bleed you till you broke
don't let them blind you in masculine smoke.

i say. step back sisters. we're rising from the dead
i say. step back johnnies. we're dancing on our heads
i say. step back man. no mo hanging by a thread.
i say. step back world. can't let it all go unsaid.

When writing a poem in blues form, it's important to listen for the differences between your repeating lines, and to bear in mind the emotional weight of the blues tradition. Once when I asked Sanchez to talk about the blues, she made a remark that shows how much the blues is a physically felt poetic form for her: "When I have been expansive and sassy and wanted to flaunt it and to come off the edge of the paper, I have dealt with the blues, sung the blues, lived the blues, tasted the blues—I have made the blues, I've been the blues."

The blues form is so versatile that it has influenced much contemporary poetry and is beginning to develop its own characteristic variations. This blues poem by Natasha Tretheway combines the blues with the couplet of a sonnet at the end:

"Graveyard Blues," Natasha Trethewey

It rained the whole time we were laying her down;
Rained from church to grave when we put her down.
The suck of mud at our feet was a hollow sound.

When the preacher called out I held up my hand;
When he called for a witness I raised my hand—
Death stops the body's work; the soul's a journeyman.

The sun came out when I turned to walk away,
Glared down on me as I turned and walked away—
My back to my mother, leaving her where she lay.

The road going home was pocked with holes,
The home-going road's always full of holes;
Though we slow down, time's wheel still rolls.

I wander now among names of the dead:
My mother's name, stone pillow for my head.

As A. E. Stallings points out about this poem, "The concluding couplet thus does double duty, for it is at the same time a blues tercet missing its final line; the poem ends in an absence, in inconsolable silence."

The Villanelle

Like the blues, the **villanelle** is based on a pattern of repeating lines, and like the blues, it was invented to be heard. This captivating form is based on a traditional dance and accompanying song sung by farmworkers (the name comes from the Italian word *villano*, meaning peasant). In the sixteenth century the villanelle stanza arrived in France, where it was used for poems of any length. Later, English poets standardized the 19-line version that is familiar to us today.

A good villanelle is like a good romantic relationship. It is structured by two lines that are dying to get together; there is a period of suspense before they do get together; and in the meantime, a changing context provides a series of new discoveries about the lines each time they appear. Good villanelles in English are rare, but they are worth the effort because, when they work, they are unforgettable.

The form of a villanelle keeps the two repeating lines close but apart through seven stanzas of mounting tension until, in the last two lines of the poem, they join. The key to a good villanelle is to come up with two lines that are genuinely attracted to each other but also completely independent of each other, so that their final coupling will feel both inevitable and surprising:

> I wake to sleep, and take my waking slow.
> I learn by going where I have to go
> —FROM "THE WAKING," Theodore Roethke (1953)

Or,

> Do not go gentle into that good night.
> Rage, rage against the dying of the light.
> —FROM "DO NOT GO GENTLE INTO THAT GOOD NIGHT,"
>   Dylan Thomas (1951)

Or,

> the art of losing is not too hard to master,
> though it may look like (*Write* it!) like disaster
> —FROM "ONE ART," Elizabeth Bishop (1976)

Here is the way this particular magic happens: a villanelle is built of five stanzas of three lines each and a sixth, four-line stanza. The first and third lines of the first stanza take turns being repeated as the last lines of the other three-line stanzas. It's like making a braid with three strands: you alternate one line from the top, one line from the bottom, until you have used them each three times, and then you end with both of them together.

Every line ends in one of two rhyme sounds, which are marked a and b in the poem below. As discussed in the rhyme chapter, the standard way to show repeating lines in a rhymed poem is to capitalize the letters and number them. In the poem below, A1 and A2 are the two repeating lines. It's more complicated to describe than it is to show, so take a look at the poem below. Successful villanelles often deal, as does this one, with obsessive or haunting subject matter:

"The House on the Hill," Edwin Arlington Robinson (1894)

They are all gone away,	A1
The House is shut and still,	b
There is nothing more to say.	A2
Through broken walls and gray	a
The winds blow bleak and shrill:	b
They are all gone away.	A1
Nor is there one to-day	a
To speak them good or ill:	b
There is nothing more to say.	A2
Why is it then we stray	a
Around the sunken sill?	b
They are all gone away,	A1
And our poor fancy-play	a
For them is wasted skill:	b
There is nothing more to say.	A2
There is ruin and decay	a
In the House on the Hill:	b
They are all gone away,	A1
There is nothing more to say.	A2

Don't forget to make sure that all the middle lines rhyme with each other. It's easy to overlook this step in the excitement of figuring out how to make your repeating lines (the technical term is **repetends**) sound natural.

Though Robinson's villanelle is very successful at using end-stopped lines (sentences that end with the end of the line), many of the best villanelles use enjambment to incorporate the repetends in a more natural-sounding way:

"Milk the Mouse," Michael Ryan

He'll pinch my pinky until the mouse starts squeaking.
The floor lamp casts a halo around his big, stuffed chair.
Be strong Be tough! It is my father speaking.

I'm four or five. Was he already drinking?
With its tip and knuckle between his thumb and finger,
he'll pinch my pinky until the mouse starts squeaking

Stop, Daddy, stop (it was more like screeching)
and kneels down before him on the hardwood floor.
Be strong Be tough! It is my father speaking.
What happened to him that he'd do such a thing?
It's only a game, he's doing me a favor
to pinch my pinky until the mouse starts squeaking

because the world will run over a weakling
and we must crush the mouse or be crushed later.
Be strong Be tough! It is my father speaking.

To himself, of course, to the boy inside him weeping,
not to me. But how can I not go when he calls me over
to pinch my pinky until the mouse starts squeaking
Be strong Be tough? It is my father speaking.

Though Ryan alters punctuation and changes the meaning of the repeating lines significantly through context, the discomfiting strength of this villanelle is enhanced by the exactness with which he repeats the actual words of those lines. As with all repeating poetic forms, how much liberty to take with the form is purely a matter of personal style. This famous villanelle takes some liberties:

"One Art," Elizabeth Bishop (1976)

The art of losing isn't hard to master;
so many things seem filled with the intent
to be lost that their loss is no disaster.

Lose something every day. Accept the fluster
of lost door keys, the hour badly spent.
The art of losing isn't hard to master.

Then practice losing farther, losing faster:
places, and names, and where it was you meant
to travel. None of these will bring disaster.

I lost my mother's watch. And look! my last, or
next-to-last, of three loved houses went.
The art of losing isn't hard to master.

I lost two cities, lovely ones. And, vaster,
some realms I owned, two rivers, a continent.
I miss them, but it wasn't a disaster.

—Even losing you (the joking voice, a gesture
I love) I shan't have lied. It's evident
the art of losing's not too hard to master
though it may look like (*Write* it!) like disaster.

With characteristic ingenuity, Bishop chooses to alter the line about "disaster" quite a bit but to keep the other line almost unchanged, like a sort of anchor that makes the changes to the other line more unnerving by contrast. This strategy goes well with the restrained and somewhat ironic tone of her villanelle. At the other end of the spectrum is an equally famous villanelle that uses the form without any changes at all, this time in order to create a rhapsodic sense of certainty.

"Do Not Go Gentle into That Good Night," Dylan Thomas (1951)

Do not go gentle into that good night,
Old age should burn and rave at close of day;
Rage, rage against the dying of the light.

Though wise men at their end know dark is right,
Because their words had forked no lightning they
Do not go gentle into that good night.

Good men, the last wave by, crying how bright
Their frail deeds might have danced in a green bay,
Rage, rage against the dying of the light.

Wild men who caught and sang the sun in flight,
And learn, too late, they grieved it on its way,
Do not go gentle into that good night.

Grave men, near death, who see with blinding sight
Blind eyes could blaze like meteors and be gay,
Rage, rage against the dying of the light.

And you, my father, there on the sad height,
Curse, bless, me now with your fierce tears, I pray.
Do not go gentle into that good night.
Rage, rage against the dying of the light.

Written when Thomas's father was dying, this poem seems to hold on to the exactness of the form as a way of both resisting the knowledge of change and marshaling more energy to address it.

Generally speaking, the lines may have greater impact if they are repeated without changing, and one change can have great impact (as does the change in the last line of "One Art") if it is the only big change in the poem. To have the most options and the most potential power in your villanelle, my advice is to do your best to write your villanelle perfectly with no changes to the repeating lines, and then change them later if you think it will improve the poem. That way, if you decide to vary the repetends, you'll be confident you are doing it for the good of your poem rather than out of laziness.

While the villanelle form has not been changed and varied as much as the sonnet—probably because it hasn't been around in English nearly as long—there are still plenty of examples of creative variations on the form. Here is one with very short lines:

"Contagion," Mendi Obadike

Hearing her cry
from the hallway,

I don't know why

another eye
opens in me.
Hearing her cry—

selfishly, I
try to close it.
I don't know why.

Something inside
burns and chokes my
hearing. Her cry.

I break and hide
from everything.
I don't know. Why?

I don't know why
I can't stomach
hearing her cry.
I don't know why.

While Obadike has omitted the rhyming of the middle lines in each stanza and used vowel rhyme for some of the first lines, she employs the repetends very strictly, with no variations at all except in punctuation. This combination works well with such short lines; to follow the entire rhyme scheme exactly in such a small space might have been overwhelming, but the exact repetition of the repetends carries a sense of the full rigor of the form.

The Sestina and Canzone

The **sestina** and **canzone** were invented by the troubadours, under the poetic influence of Persian (Iranian) poetry by way of Spain. In fact, the sestina, **ballade, kyrielle, rondeau,** canzone, and **triolet** are just a few among the hundreds of poetic forms invented by the troubadours, those ingenious poets of certain regions of France in the twelfth and thirteenth centuries. Both men and women were troubadours, and their main subject was love; these poets felt it was an insult to one's beloved not to invent a brand-new poetic form for your love poem.

The sestina, like the villanelle, has the virtue of a certain simplicity, which may explain why these two forms have become especially popular in English-language verse. A sestina repeats end-words (sometimes called **teleutons,** from the Greek word *telos,* meaning end), not entire lines. It consists of six six-line stanzas and a three-line stanza. The six stanzas repeat the same end-words in a set pattern. The pattern may look confusing at first, but you make the same motions each time as you move from one stanza to the next: like braiding hair, you take the outside strands first, first the bottom and then the top, using the previous stanza's last word, first word, next to last word, second word, and so on in that order until all six words have been used. If you do this, you will end up with this pattern (keeping the original stanza's number for each word): first stanza 123456, second stanza 615243, third 364125, fourth 532614, fifth 451362, sixth 246531. For closure, there is a three-line stanza (called an *envoi* or *tornada*) that includes all six words: 5, 3, 1 as end words, and 2, 4, 6 in the beginnings or middles of the lines. (The double sestina does the same thing over again with the same six words, for a total of 12 six-line stanzas and an envoi.)

Poets began to use the sestina in English during the Renaissance, generally as something of a curiosity. Here are two stanzas of Sidney's double sestina, a conversation about unrequited love between two shepherd-boys:

From "Ye Gote-heard Gods," Sir Philip Sidney (1590)

Strephon:
You Gote-heard Gods, that loue the grassie mountaines,
You Nimphes that haunt the springs in pleasant vallies,
You Satyrs ioyde with free and quiet forests,
Vouchsafe your silent eares to playning musique,
Which to my woes giues still an early morning;
And drawes the dolor on till wery euening.

Klaius:
Mercurie, foregoer to the euening,
heauenlie huntresse of the sauage mountaines,
louelie starre, entitled of the morning,

While that my voice doth fill these wofull vallies,
Vouchsafe your silent eares to plaining musique,
Which oft hath Echo tir'd in secrete forrests . . .

The rhythm of the end-stopped lines, the chorus of different shepherds' voices, and the mythological theme lend a charming and unique ritualistic effect to this poem, establishing an evocative ancestry for the sestina in English.

Though structurally rather easy to write (and thus one of the most common formal poetry assignments in beginning poetry workshops), the sestina is difficult to write successfully. It tends to sag in the middle, so it can be helpful to consider planting a deliberate surprise there. And of course, the end words are crucial. As poet Jim Cummins has remarked, "Two teleutons die, and the air goes out of the ball; the game is over." It can make a sestina more lively to use one or two words that can take on multiple meanings or act as different parts of speech, as with the word "long" in the following sestina, but don't overdo this tactic or your readers will get dizzy.

From "Sestina of the Tramp-Royal," Rudyard Kipling (1896)

But, Gawd, what things are they I 'aven't done?
I've turned my 'and to most, an' turned it good,
In various situations round the world
For 'im that doth not work must surely die;
But that's no reason man should labour all
'Is life on one same shift—life's none so long.

Therefore, from job to job I've moved along.
Pay couldn't 'old me when my time was done,
For something in my 'ead upset it all,
Till I 'ad dropped whatever 'twas for good,
An', out at sea, be'eld the dock-lights die,
An' met my mate—the wind that tramps the world!

It's like a book, I think, this bloomin' world,
Which you can read and care for just so long,
But presently you feel that you will die
Unless you get the page you're readi'n' done,

An' turn another—likely not so good;
But what you're after is to turn 'em all.

There is nothing quite like the feeling of inhabiting the world of a sestina, where the end-words you created yourself become so familiar that they begin to feel oddly natural each time you encounter them again. Ezra Pound evoked this strange energy when he called the sestina "a thin sheet of flame folding and in-folding upon itself." Pound's "Sestina: Altaforte" was one of the first powerful modern examples of the form, and it was only with the twentieth century's tolerance for strangeness and defamiliarization that the sestina really began to come into its own and establish a tradition among poets in English. The repetition in a sestina such as Elizabeth Bishop's famous "Sestina," which uses the teleutons "house," "grandmother," "child," "stove," "almanac," and "tears," can lead a reader into a dream world of compulsions and inevitabilities:

"Sestina," Elizabeth Bishop (1965)

September rain falls on the house.
In the failing light, the old grandmother
sits in the kitchen with the child
beside the Little Marvel Stove,
reading the jokes from the almanac,
laughing and talking to hide her tears.

She thinks that her equinoctial tears
and the rain that beats on the roof of the house
were both foretold by the almanac,
but only known to a grandmother.
The iron kettle sings on the stove.
She cuts some bread and says to the child,

It's time for tea now; but the child
is watching the teakettle's small hard tears
dance like mad on the hot black stove,
the way the rain must dance on the house.
Tidying up, the old grandmother
hangs up the clever almanac

on its string. Birdlike, the almanac
hovers half open above the child,
hovers above the old grandmother
and her teacup full of dark brown tears.
She shivers and says she thinks the house
feels chilly, and puts more wood in the stove.

It was to be, says the Marvel Stove.
I know what I know, says the almanac.
With crayons the child draws a rigid house
and a winding pathway. Then the child
puts in a man with buttons like tears
and shows it proudly to the grandmother.

But secretly, while the grandmother
busies herself about the stove,
the little moons fall down like tears
from between the pages of the almanac
into the flower bed the child
has carefully placed in the front of the house.

Time to plant tears, says the almanac.
The grandmother sings to the marvelous stove
and the child draws another inscrutable house.

Bishop's sestina is something of a tour de force; she forgoes the usual tricks of making a word "go farther" by using it in several senses, and she also violates the typical rule of varying parts of speech in the teleutons. They are all nouns, and yet the poem maintains interest and energy.

In a letter to Marianne Moore about another of her sestinas, "A Miracle for Breakfast," Bishop wrote an observation about the issue of end words: "It seems to me that there are two ways possible for a sestina—one is to use unusual words as a termination, in which case they would have to be used differently as often as possible. . . .That would make a very highly seasoned kind of poem. And the other way is to use as colorless words as possible—like Sydney [Sir Philip Sidney], so that it becomes less of a trick and more of a natural theme and variations. I guess I have tried to do both at once."

Another significant twentieth-century sestina uses the self-contained world of the form to cast a different kind of spell, an agonized and reverent response to the Holocaust. Serving in the army in World War II, Anthony Hecht helped liberate a concentration camp, about which he has written, "the place, the suffering, the prisoners' accounts were beyond comprehension. For years afterward I would wake up shrieking." This poem is about a child killed by the Nazis:

"The Book of Yolek," Anthony Hecht

> *Wir Haben ein Gesetz,*
> *Und nach dem Gesetz soll er sterben.**

The dowsed coals fume and hiss after your meal
Of grilled brook trout, and you saunter off for a walk
Down the fern trail. It doesn't matter where to,
Just so you're weeks and worlds away from home,
And among midsummer hills have set up camp
In the deep bronze glories of declining day.

You remember, peacefully, an earlier day
In childhood, remember a quite specific meal:
A corn roast and bonfire in summer camp.
That summer you got lost on a Nature Walk;
More than you dared admit, you thought of home:
No one else knows where the mind wanders to.

The fifth of August, 1942.
It was the morning and very hot. It was the day
They came at dawn with rifles to The Home
For Jewish Children, cutting short the meal
Of bread and soup, lining them up to walk
In close formation off to a special camp.

How often you have thought about that camp,
As though in some strange way you were driven to,
And about the children, and how they were made to walk,
Yolek who had bad lungs, who wasn't a day

Over five years old, commanded to leave his meal
And shamble between armed guards to his long home.

We're approaching August again. It will drive home
The regulation torments of that camp
Yolek was sent to, his small, unfinished meal,
The electric fences, the numeral tattoo,
The quite extraordinary heat of the day
They all were forced to take that terrible walk.

Whether on a silent, solitary walk
Or among crowds, far off or safe at home,
You will remember, helplessly, that day,
And the smell of smoke, and the loudspeakers of the camp.
Wherever you are, Yolek will be there, too.
His unuttered name will interrupt your meal.

Prepare to receive him in your home some day.
Though they killed him in the camp they sent him to,
He will walk in as you're sitting down to a meal.

* We have a law, and according to the law he must die.

The forgotten child, abominably killed, is forever memorialized in these stanzas, even if you don't notice the special secret the poem holds. Jeff Balch has recently pointed out that "The Book of Yolek" contains a hidden acrostic, in the style of Jewish liturgical poems of remembrance. Look at the last letters of each of the teleutons. P implies the letter *peh*, which appears in the upper right corner of traditional Jewish gravestones and stands for the word meaning "here."

If Bishop's and Hecht's poems take advantage of the strangeness a sestina can impart, the following poem revels in its potential for realism. The poet zeroes in on the biggest challenge of the form, the repeating of the same words through the potentially sagging middle, and turns it to her dramatic advantage:

"Untoward Occurrence at an Embassy Poetry Reading," Marilyn Hacker

Thank you. Thank you very much. I'm pleased
to be here tonight. I seldom read

to such a varied audience. My poetry
is what it is. Graves, yes, said love, death
and the changing of the seasons
were the unique, the primordial subjects.

I'd like to talk about that. One subjects
oneself to art, not necessarily pleased
to be a colander for myths. It seasons
one to certain subjects. Not all. You can read
or formulate philosophies; your death
is still the kernel of your dawn sweats. Poetry

is interesting to people who write poetry.
Others are involved with other subjects.
Does the Ambassador consider death
on the same scale as you, Corporal? Please
stay seated. I've outreached myself. I read
your discomfort. But tonight the seasons

change. I've watched you, in town for the season,
nod to each other, nod to poetry
represented by me, and my colleagues, who read
to good assemblies; good citizens, good subjects
for gossip. You're the audience. Am I pleased
to frighten you? Yes and no. It scares me to death

to stand up here and talk about real death
while our green guerrillas hurry up the seasons.
They have disarmed the guards by now, I'm pleased
to say. The doors are locked. Great poetry
is not so histrionic, but our subjects
choose us, not otherwise. I will not read

manifestos. Tomorrow, foreigners will read
rumors in newspapers. . . . Oh, sir, your death
would be a tiresome journalistic subject,
so stay still till we're done. This is our season.

The building is surrounded. No more poetry
tonight. We are discussing, you'll be pleased

to know, the terms of your release. Please read
these leaflets. Not poetry. You're bored to death
with politics but that's the season's subject.

Because of the predictability of the end words, the sestina can lend itself well to humor. John Ashbery's "Farm Implements and Rutabagas in a Landscape" presents a surreal picnic where Popeye, Bluto, Wimpy, and Olive Oyl trade non sequiturs in a bizarre setting. Oulipo poet Harry Matthews's "Histoire" treats the teleutons as a kind of ad lib game, forcing terms like "fascism," "sexism," "racism" and "Marxism" to act as food items, places, and parts of the body with very amusing results. Even Bishop's "Sestina" has a whimsical quality.

Generally, you will have the most success with a sestina if you choose at least half concrete nouns; in most poems, abstract words can get extremely dull when they are repeated so often. Earle Birney's sestina based on the words "isthmus," "iguanas," "earthquake," "women," "hotsprings," and "Diaz" is quite a mouthful. Of course, words that are extremely interesting can call a lot of attention to themselves when they are repeated so often. As for the common question of whether it's legitimate to change the end-words by pluralizing or other small alterations: whether to do so is, as we have seen, a matter of personal style. As with the villanelle, my advice would be to stay as close to the pattern as possible before deciding to make any change. The best alterations are the result of aesthetic choice, not evidence of the lack of patience to follow the pattern exactly!

The following sestina is from a young adult novel by Helen Frost, written entirely in sestinas and sonnets:

"my choice . . . KATIE," Helen Frost

I sleep in my sleeping bag in a room
with a lock in the basement of the place
on Jackson Street. And I feel safe.
If Keesha wants to talk to me, she knocks
first, and if I want to let her in, I do.
If I don't, I don't. It's my choice.

There's not too much I really have a choice
about. Mom would say I chose to leave my room
at home, but that's not something anyone would do
without a real good reason. There's no place
for me there since she got married. Like, one time, I knocked
her husband's trophy off his gun safe,

and he twisted my arm—hard. I never feel safe
when he's around. I finally asked my mom to make a choice:
him or me. She went, *Oh, Katie, he'll be fine.* Then she knocked
on our wooden table. I blew up. I stormed out of the room
and started thinking hard. In the first place,
I know he won't be *fine.* I didn't tell her what he tries to do

to me when she works late. In a way, I want to, but even if I do,
she won't believe me. She thinks we're safe
in that so-called nice neighborhood. *Finally, Katie, a place
of our own.* And since she took a vow, she thinks she has no choice
but to see her marriage through. No room
for me, no vow to protect *me* if he comes knocking

on my door late at night. He knocks
and then walks in when I don't answer. Or even when I do
answer: *Stay out! This is my room
and you can't come in!* I could never be safe
there, with him in the house. So, sure, I made a choice.
I left home and found my way to this place,

where I've been these past two weeks. And I found a place
to work, thirty hours a week. Today Mom knocked
on the door here. She wanted to talk. I told her, *You made your choice;
I made mine.* She wondered what she could do
to get me to come home. But when I said, *It's not safe
for me as long as he's there,* she left the room.

My choice is to be safe.
This room is dark and musty, but it's one place
I do know I can answer *no* when someone knocks.

The variations, such as "knock," "knocked," and "knocking," suit the informal tone of this poem; but so much variation would ruin the intense power of some other sestinas. Whatever you do, be consistent; if you are going to change one word in your sestina, it's best to change several, so it will look like a deliberate decision and not an oversight. If you are consistent, you can make just about any variation. I've even heard of a sestina that uses the repeating words at the beginnings of the lines instead of the end. Another modification is rhyme; here are two stanzas of a rhymed sestina:

From "Sestina," Algernon Charles Swinburne (1872)

Yet the soul woke not, sleeping by the way,
. . . Watched as a nursling of the large-eyed night,
And sought no strength nor knowledge of the day,
. . . Nor closer touch conclusive of delight,
Nor mightier joy nor truer than dreamers may,
. . . Nor more of song than they, nor more of light.

For who sleeps once and sees the secret light
. . . Whereby sleep shows the soul a fairer way
Between the rise and rest of day and night,
. . . Shall care no more to fare as all men may,
But be his place of pain or of delight,
. . . There shall he dwell, beholding night as day.

I will close with a few words about the canzone. This form is similar to the sestina, but almost twice as long, one reason it is rarely used. The five teleutons appear in this order (each line represents one 12-line stanza):

ABAACAADDAEE
EAEEBEECCEDD
DEDDADDBBDCC
CDCCECCAACCB
BCBBDBBEEBAA
ABCDE

Probably the most accomplished recent canzone in English is the following elegy:

"Lenox Hill," Agha Shahid Ali

*(In Lenox Hill Hospital, after surgery, my mother said the sirens sounded like
the elephants of Mihiragula when his men drove them off cliffs in the Pir
Panjal Range.)*

The Hun so loved the cry, one falling elephant's,
he wished to hear it again. At dawn, my mother
heard, in her hospital-dream of elephants,
sirens wail through Manhattan like elephants
forced off Pir Panjal's rock cliffs in Kashmir:
the soldiers, so ruled, had rushed the elephant,
The greatest of all footprints is the elephant's,
said the Buddha. But not lifted from the universe,
those prints vanished forever into the universe,
though nomads still break news of those elephants
as if it were just yesterday the air spread the dye
("War's annals will fade into night / Ere their story die"),

the punishing khaki whereby the world sees us die
out, mourning you, O massacred elephants!
Months later, in Amherst, she dreamt: She was, with diamonds, being stoned to death. I prayed: If she must die,
let it only be some dream. But there were times, Mother,
while you slept, that I prayed, "Saints, let her die."
Not, I swear to you, that I wished you to die
but to save you as you were, young, in song in Kashmir,
and I, one festival, crowned Krishna by you, Kashmir
listening to my flute. You never let gods die.
Thus I swear, here and now, not to forgive the universe
that would let me get used to a universe

without you. She, she alone, was the universe
as she earned, like a galaxy, her right not to die,
defying the Merciful of the Universe,
Master of Disease, "in the circle of her traverse"
of drug-bound time. And where was the god of elephants,

plump with Fate, when tusk to tusk, the universe,
dyed green, became ivory? Then let the universe,
like Paradise, be considered a tomb. Mother,
they asked me, So how's the writing? I answered My mother
is my poem. What did they expect? For no verse
sufficed except the promise, fading, of Kashmir
and the cries that reached you from the cliffs of Kashmir

(across fifteen centuries) in the hospital. Kashmir,
she's dying! How her breathing drowns out the universe
as she sleeps in Amherst. Windows open on Kashmir:
There, the fragile wood-shrines—so far away—of Kashmir!
O Destroyer, let her return there, if just to die.
Save the right she gave its earth to cover her, Kashmir
has no rights. When the windows close on Kashmir,
I see the blizzard-fall of ghost-elephants.
I hold back—she couldn't bear it—one elephant's
story: his return (in a country far from Kashmir)
to the jungle where each year, on the day his mother
died, he touches with his trunk the bones of his mother.

"As you sit here by me, you're just like my mother,"
she tells me. I imagine her: a bride in Kashmir,
she's watching, at the Regal, her first film with Father.
If only I could gather you in my arms, Mother,
I'd save you—now my daughter—from God. The universe
opens its ledger. I write: How helpless was God's mother!
Each page is turned to enter grief's accounts. Mother,
I see a hand. Tell me it's not God's. Let it die.
I see it. It's filling with diamonds. Please let it die.
Are you somewhere alive, Mother?
Do you hear what I once held back: in one elephant's
cry, by his mother's bones, the cries of those elephants

that stunned the abyss? Ivory blots out the elephants.
I enter this: The Belovéd leaves one behind to die.
For compared to my grief for you, what are those of Kashmir,

and what (I close the ledger) are griefs of the universe
when I remember you—beyond all accounting—O my mother?

The Rondeau, Triolet, Kyrielle, and Tritina

Three shorter forms that also use intense repetition are the rondeau, triolet, and **tritina.** Though the enterprising Sir Thomas Wyatt wrote several rondeaux during the Renaissance, the rondeau and triolet forms really gained their place in English in the late nineteenth century. The tritina was invented in the twentieth century by Marie Ponsot, perhaps as a version of the sestina. The rondeau may be the most versatile of the three, the triolet the most memorable, and the tritina the most haunting. The rondeau's 13 lines use only two rhymes plus a *rentrement* (a partial-line repetition, made of the first word or few words of line 1), in this pattern:

(R)a
a
b
b
a

a
a
b
R

a
a
b
b
a
R

When it was reintroduced centuries later, the rondeau was used mostly for very light verse, as is evident from this first stanza:

From "The Same Imitated," Austin Dobson (1877)

YOU bid me try, *blue-eyes,* to write
A Rondeau. What!—forthwith?—tonight?
Reflect. Some skill I have, 'tis true;
But thirteen lines!—and rimed on two!
"Refrain" as well. Ah, Hapless plight!

Like Hughes, whose "The Weary Blues" may be the first blues poem written in English, Dobson is extremely self-conscious about writing in a new form. This is common with any form new to a poet; you may have written a sonnet about writing a sonnet yourself, or seen a poem like this by a fellow poet new to a form. Twenty years after Dobson's version, the rondeau was so established that not only was it not necessary to be self-conscious; it was possible for Paul Laurence Dunbar to use the form in a dense, wry, agonized, and multilayered way in his signature poem:

"We Wear the Mask," Paul Laurence Dunbar (1896)

We wear the mask that grins and lies,
It hides our cheeks and shades our eyes—
This debt we pay to human guile;
With torn and bleeding hearts we smile
And mouth with myriad subtleties,

Why should the world be over-wise,
In counting all our tears and sighs?
Nay, let them only see us, while
We wear the mask.

We smile, but oh great Christ, our cries
To Thee from tortured souls arise.
We sing, but oh the clay is vile
Beneath our feet, and long the mile,
But let the world dream otherwise,
We wear the mask!

Dunbar is normally known for more lighthearted poems about the African American experience. As happens surprisingly often with poets, his most famous poem is uncharacteristic of his normal style. Perhaps the extreme constraints of the rondeau, by contrast with his usual looser and more popular ballad style, distracted and freed him to express a more painfully honest level of emotion.

This contemporary rondeau by the formally virtuosic Marilyn Hacker, embedded into a longer poem, also explores painful emotion:

From "Love, Death, and the Changing of the Seasons," Marilyn Hacker

Why did Ray leave her pipe tobacco here
in the fridge? Iva asks me while we're
rummaging for mustard and soy sauce
to mix with wine and baste the lamb. "Because
cold keeps it fresh." That isn't what she means,

we both know. I've explained, there were no scenes
or fights, really. We needed time to clear
the air, and think. What she was asking, was,
"Why did Ray leave

her stuff if she's not coming back?" She leans
to extremes, as I might well. String beans
to be sauteed with garlic, then I'll toss
the salad; then we'll eat (Like menopause
it comes in flashes, more or less severe:
why did you leave?)

In the rondeau redouble, repetitions haunt even more, with the form ABAB babA abaB babA' abaB' babaR (the capital letters indicate the repetition of whole lines, and R, the *rentrement,* does not have to rhyme with anything). The kyrielle, a simple form rhyming aabB so the last line of every stanza is a refrain, has been used for religious verses; Thomas Campion's refrain is "O God, be merciful to me."

Like the rondeau, the triolet lends itself well, though not exclusively, to light or semilight verse:

"Triolet," G. K. Chesterton

I wish I were a jelly fish
That cannot fall downstairs:
Of all the things I wish to wish
I wish I were a jelly fish
That hasn't any cares,
And doesn't even have to wish
"I wish I were a jelly fish
That cannot fall downstairs."

Here is one of the best-known recent triolets:

"Triolet on a Line Apocryphally Attributed to Martin Luther," A. E. Stallings

Why should the Devil get all the good tunes,
The booze and the neon and Saturday night,
The swaying in darkness, the lovers like spoons?
Why should the Devil get all the good tunes?
Does he hum them to while away sad afternoons
And the long, lonesome Sundays? Or sing them for spite?
Why should the Devil get all the good tunes,
The booze and the neon and Saturday night?

The amphibrachic swing of the meter, combined with the ironic tone and theme, create a bittersweet quality that brings out hidden depths in a form which has often been thought of as suited only for trifles.

A related, almost brand-new form is the tritina. Each of the tritina's three three-line stanzas ends with the same three words, but in a different order. The poem concludes with a line containing all the end words:

"Roundstone Cove," Marie Ponsot

The wind rises. The sea snarls in the fog
far from the attentive beaches of childhood—
no picnic, no striped chairs, no sand, no sun.

Here even by day cliffs obstruct the sun;
moonlight miles out mocks this abyss of fog.
I walk big-bellied, lost in motherhood,

hunched in a shell of coat, a blindered hood.
Alone a long time, I remember sun—
poor magic effort to undo the fog.

Fog hoods me. But the hood of fog is sun.

The Paradelle

The most amusing, and most recently invented, repeating form in the French tradition is the paradelle, which appeared in the 1980s when poet Billy Collins published a bizarre poem called "Paradelle for Susan" that began with this stanza:

I remember the quick, nervous bird of your love.
I remember the quick, nervous bird of your love.
Always perched on the highest, thinnest branch.
Always perched on the highest, thinnest branch.
Thinnest love, remember the quick branch.
Always nervous, I perched on your highest bird the.

Accompanying the poem was a footnote explaining that the paradelle was an obscure form invented by the medieval French troubadours, akin to the villanelle and sestina. Many people took this footnote as truth. However, when you look carefully at a paradelle, you realize that it is impossible that it could have been invented by the troubadours. The reason is that it's just about impossible to write a poem that makes sense in this form, and the troubadours always made sense. In fact, the paradelle is the perfect postmodern form, at once a historical parody and a challenge to engage in exploratory writing. The paradelle also seems to have been influenced by the blues, marking it as a distinctively American form and giving it an odd familiarity for all its strangeness. This fact may also account for its popularity, which has certainly surprised its inventor.

To write a paradelle, you write a line and repeat it; write another line and repeat it; and then end the stanza with two lines that include all the words from those two lines and no other words. You repeat this for three stanzas. The fourth stanza is the climax of the poem; it includes all the words from the entire poem and no other words.

It can seem impossible to do this and have the poem make (logical) sense. I couldn't imagine how anyone could approach the paradelle other than impressionistically until I encountered Henry Taylor's paradelle, which is the closest I've seen to one that does make sense. As I learned from him later, his secret was to write the last two lines of each stanza first:

"Paradelle: Nocturne de la Ville," Henry Taylor

>   Somewhat behind, rather than
>   After, Villiers de l'Isle-Adam

An empty chair inhabits a troubled dream.
An empty chair inhabits a troubled dream.
Hoisted to light from wells of unknown depth,
Hoisted to light from wells of unknown depth.
Hoisted from an unknown chair to dreams of light,
A troubled depth inhabits empty wells.

The lamp says he feels it's slow use his way.
The lamp says he feels it's slow use his way.
"Around the street here I'm no drunk prisoner.
Around the street here I'm no drunk prisoner."
The drunk feels his slow way around the street lamp.
"It's no use," he says. "I'm a prisoner here."

Leaves fall from trees, moths fly to city lights.
Leaves fall from trees, moths fly to city lights.
On thin ice skaters flash across the dark.
On thin ice skaters flash across the dark.
Ice leaves the city to flash on fall trees;
Thin skaters fly from moths across dark lights.

It's fall. The city around feels slow to light.
No thin trees fly, flash a chair from ice;
A hoisted lamp lights moths. Across the street
From here an empty drunk leaves skaters troubled;
His unknown prisoner inhabits depths of dream.
"I'm on the way to use dark wells," he says.

Now there is a whole anthology of paradelles available. It includes other examples of paradelles that do make sense, and that seem to have lost their self-consciousness about being a new form. It is interesting to consider whether the paradelle could ever become so established that it would no longer be considered to have a necessarily playful aspect.

The Ghazal

The **ghazal,** an ancient Arabic form from the seventh century, has been wildly popular in Persia, India, and elsewhere for centuries. Like the pantoum, the ghazal was radically simplified when it first came to America in the 1970s; the first contemporary American "ghazals" were simply poems in two-line free-verse stanzas. The most devoted practitioner of the form in this manifestation is Robert Bly, who has published three volumes of ghazals. Bly seems most interested in how the juxtapositions of the ghazal can urge us into spiritual and social awareness:

"Call and Answer," Robert Bly

Tell me why it is we don't lift our voices these days
And cry over what is happening. Have you noticed
The plans are made for Iraq and the ice cap is melting?

I say to myself: "Go on, cry. What's the sense
Of being an adult and having no voice? Cry out!
See who will answer! This is Call and Answer!"

We will have to call especially loud to reach
Our angels, who are hard of hearing; they are hiding
In the jugs of silence filled during our wars.

Have we agreed to so many wars that we can't
Escape from silence? If we don't lift our voices, we allow
Others (who are ourselves) to rob the house.

How come we've listened to the great criers—Neruda,
Akhmatova, Thoreau, Frederick Douglas—and now
We're silent as sparrows in the little bushes?

Some masters say our life lasts only seven days.
Where are we in the week? Is it Thursday yet?
Hurry, cry now! Soon Sunday night will come.

In recent years, the ghazal in English has developed a closer formal relation to its actual roots thanks to the work of the poet Agha Shahid Ali. During his tragically brief life, the delightful and charismatic Ali educated a generation of poets in the traditional requirements and beauties of the ghazal.
As a result, we now know much more about the complexities of the form in
its original incarnations.

The ghazal uses repetition in a daring and interactive way. Each stanza is a
self-contained couplet. The second line of each stanza ends with a rhyme word
(the *quafia*) followed by a repeating phrase (the *radif*). In Tamam Khan's
"Ghazal About Marakesh," for example, two-line stanzas end with the phrases
"hued in Marakesh," "allude in Marakesh," and "interlude in Marakesh." It is
customary for a poet to embed their own name in the ghazal's last stanza.

Traditionally, and nowadays as well, the ghazal is sung by poets who have
the status of rock stars, to an audience that chants back the refrain at the end of
each stanza (the rhyme word is the clue that the refrain is coming). The subjects
of the stanzas can range from philosophy to history to love to politics; each
stanza can be completely self-contained in meaning, with only the form and the
repeating words linking the stanzas together. The excitement and pleasure of
the ghazal lies in the metaphysical capaciousness of the form and the poet's and
reader's pleasure in its ingenuity and linguistic challenges.

Obviously, when you are writing a ghazal the choice of the radif will be your
most important decision. The choice of the rhyme sound for the quafia is almost as important; be sure you choose a sound that has plenty of interesting
rhymes, since you may be having so much fun you will find it hard to stop
adding couplets to your ghazal, and you won't want to run out. I always re-

member Agha Shahid Ali's valuable piece of advice: use a rhyming dictionary to find very fresh, unusual rhyming words for the quafia.

"Ghazal of the Lagoon," John Drury

Morning, on the promenade, there's a break in the light
rain here in the serene republic. I take in the light.

Every walker gets lucky at this gaming table,
where the gondoliers, like croupiers, rake in the light.

Through the glare of a restaurant's window, I see
fish glinting, like spear points that shake in the light.

I could sit on the edge and get wet forever,
all to consider a speed boat's wake in the light.

Furnaces burn. We sweat until we shine, fired up
by the wavy vases glassblowers make in the light.

Row me out, friars, in your *sandolo* on the waves
that glitter like ducats, for God's sake, in the light.

The harshness of the repeating "-ake" sound gives Drury's poem additional interest, and perhaps adds to the impression of sharply shimmering water. The same sound has a very different feeling in another ghazal, where it acquires a melancholy, depressive force through being repeated exactly, a few syllables after the rhyming sound. Khalvati uses her name in the last couplet, as tradition dictates.

"Ghazal," Mimi Khalvati

When you wake to jitters every day, it's heartache.
Ignore it, explore it, either way, it's heartache.

Youth's a map you can never refold,
from Yokohama to Hudson Bay, it's heartache.

The moon in a swoon, you're in his arms,
the fandango starts, the palm trees sway, it's heartache.

Oh love, love, who are centuries old.
It's not time or absence I can't weigh, it's heartache.

Heartache with women, heartache with men.
Call myself straight or call myself gay, it's heartache.

Stop at the wayside, name each flower,
the loveliness that will always stay: it's heartache.

Wherever I am, I'm elsewhere too
in a cloud you'd think, but isn't, grey. It's heartache.

Why do nightingales sing in the dark?
What the eye can't see, the soul will say, it's heartache.

Who would dare to call their pain despair?
As long as faith holds true, men can pray, it's heartache.

Let the Sufi meaning of my name,
"a quiet retreat," heal as it may its heartache.

Pantoum

The **pantoum** form known in English is a simplified version of a traditional
Malaysian form. Because of the ingenuity and profound simplicity of its structural principle—the same principle as leapfrog—the pantoum is perhaps one of
the easiest repeating forms to write successfully in English. Like sewing, like
weaving, like day and night, the pantoum gains power through repeated alterna-
tions: the first and third lines in the first stanza become the second and fourth
lines in the next stanza, then the first and third lines of the second stanza become
the second and fourth lines in the third stanza, and so on for as long as you want
your poem to last. The last stanza usually repeats lines 1 and 3 of the first stanza
but in reverse order, making a perfectly closed circle. Sometimes the stanzas can

rhyme, as they do in the original Malaysian form and in Nellie Wong's "Grandmother's Pantoum" below, but they don't have to rhyme, and some poets even use the form with only end words repeated instead of entire lines.

Vince Gotera advises his poetry students to choose a subject for the pantoum that they feel obsessive about, so that the repetitions will seem more natural. He says, "The pantoum can give the poet a formula in which things can be said again and again credibly and plausibly. In addition, I am attracted to the pantoum because it is originally a Malay form; I am a Filipino American and thus part of a people descended from Malays. The pantoum, to me, is a way of coming home." One of Gotera's pantoums, "Chain Letter Pantoum," is on the obsessive subject of chain letters. Anne Waldman's "Baby's Pantoum" uses the form to show the diffuse, perpetually present-time perspective of a newborn. The form can create a dizzying spiral effect that lends itself to almost any lyrical, passionate theme; I've seen good pantoums about subjects from dancing to thunderstorms. On the other hand, in the words of poet Stephen Cramer, "If you're writing a pantoum and not paying strong enough attention to the line, you can feel like you're walking the wrong way on a conveyor belt."

At its best, like all repeating forms, the pantoum repeats lines in such a way that they sound new each time they occur. In "Grandmother's Song," for example, first the grandmothers are blinded by the sun's rays, then those looking at the bracelets and rings are blinded.

"Grandmother's Song," Nellie Wong

Grandmothers sing their song
Blinded by the sun's rays
Grandchildren for whom they long
For pomelo-golden days

Blinded by the sun's rays
Gold bracelets, opal rings
For pomelo-golden days
Tiny fingers, ancient things

Gold bracelets, opal rings
Sprinkled with Peking dust
Tiny fingers, ancient things
So young they'll never rust

Sprinkled with Peking dust
To dance in fields of mud
So young they'll never rust
Proud as if of royal blood

To dance in fields of mud
Or peel shrimp for pennies a day
Proud as if of royal blood
Coins and jade to put away

Or peel shrimp for pennies a day
Seaweed washes up the shore
Coins and jade to put away
A camphor chest is home no more

Seaweed washes up the shore
Bound feet struggle to loosen free
A camphor chest is home no more
A foreign tongue is learned at three

Bound feet struggle to loosen free
Grandchildren for whom they long
A foreign tongue is learned at three
Grandmothers sing their song

The cycling, recurring shape of the pantoum seems a perfect choice for this poem about the cycles of generations, the persistence of the present within the past, and the recurring pull of tradition on a child.

The pantoum is used in a very different and equally effective way in the following poem:

From "A Date With Robbe-Grillet," Elaine Equi

What I remember didn't happen.
Birds stuttering.
Torches huddled together.
The café empty, with no place to sit.

Birds stuttering.
On our ride in the country
the café empty, with no place to sit.
Your hair was like a doll's . . .

By using lines very similar to each other ("birds stuttering" and "birds strutted," for example), varying line-lengths, and striking a delicate balance of syntax and imagery between lulling coherence and jarring incoherence, Equi intensifies the disorienting quality of the pantoum's repetitions and creates a dreamworld where it's hard to see the forest for the trees. Her use of the pantoum is suited to a poem devoted to Robbe-Grillet, whose novels and films dissolve time and character with dreamlike and compelling repetitions.

The following pantoum uses the same disorienting quality to delve, through circumlocutions and repetition, into a painful subject.

"The Mountain Is Holding Out," Paul Muldoon

The mountain is holding out
for news from the sea
and the raid on the redoubt.
The plain won't level with me

for news from the sea
is harder and harder to find.
The plain won't level with me
now it's non-aligned

and harder and harder to find.
The forest won't fill me in
now it, too, is non-aligned
and its patience wearing thin.

The forest won't fill me in
nor the lake confess
to its patience wearing thin.
I'd no more try to second guess

why the lake would confess

to its regard for its own sheen,
no more try to second guess
why the river won't come clean

on its regard for its own sheen
than why you and I've faced off across a ditch.
For the river not coming clean
is only one of the issues on which

you and I've faced off across a ditch
and the raid on the redoubt
only one of the issues on which
the mountain is holding out.

By reserving the crucial mention of "you and I" until late in the poem, the poem creates the effect of holding out. As the repeating phrases circle around to the beginning again just after this moment, the frustrating sense of defensiveness is complete, self-enclosed like the small military fortification known as a "redoubt."

Refrain in Free Verse and Form

Like the chorus of a song, a **refrain** links together different parts of a poem by repeating the same words over and over between them. Refrains are part of the structure of many poetic forms, including the rondeau, ballade, and triolet, and some ballads. But refrains can be added to any poem, to bring in beauty and variety and a kind of resonance. This is as true of poems in free verse as of poems in meter. Lucia Trent's "Breed, Women, Breed" uses a regular refrain at the beginning of each free verse stanza:

"Breed, Women, Breed," Lucia Trent (1929)

Breed, little mothers,
With tired backs and tired hands,
Breed for the owners of mills and the owners of mines,
Breed a race of danger-haunted men,
A race of toiling, sweating, miserable men,

Breed, little mothers,
Breed for the owners of mills and the owners of mines,
Breed, breed, breed!

Breed, little mothers,
With the sunken eyes and the sagging cheeks,
Breed for the bankers, the crafty and terrible masters of men,
Breed a race of machines,
A race of anemic, round-shouldered, subway-herded machines!

Breed, little mothers,
With a faith patient and stupid as cattle,
Breed for the war lords,
Offer your woman flesh for incredible torment,
Wrack your frail bodies with the pangs of birth
For the war lords who slaughter your sons!

Breed, little mothers,
Breed for the owners of mills and the owners of mines,
Breed for the bankers, the crafty and terrible masters of men,
Breed for the war lords, the devouring war lords,
Breed, women, breed!

Jane Kenyon's best-known poem, "Otherwise," uses a more irregular refrain, the phrase "It might have been otherwise," repeated after various sentences describing her activities during one day. The refrain gives a dignity and importance to the mundane activities she describes:

"Otherwise," Jane Kenyon

I got out of bed
on two strong legs.
It might have been
otherwise. I ate
cereal, sweet
milk, ripe, flawless
peach. It might

have been otherwise.
I took the dog uphill
to the birch wood.
All morning I did
the work I love.

At noon I lay down
with my mate. It might
have been otherwise.
We ate dinner together
at a table with silver
candlesticks. It might
have been otherwise.
I slept in a bed
in a room with paintings
on the walls, and
planned another day
just like this day.
But one day, I know,
it will be otherwise.

Refrains in free verse, as in the Trent and Kenyon poems, often tie together a variety of aspects of the poem. In formal verse, on the other hand, a refrain can add a paradoxical element of difference. This can be most evident in a poem in strict form, where the content is controlled:

From "A Boy's Will," Henry Wadsworth Longfellow (1858)

Often I think of the beautiful town
That is seated by the sea;
Often in thought go up and down
The pleasant streets of that dear old town,
And my youth comes back to me.
And a verse of a Lapland song
Is haunting my memory still:
"A boy's will is the wind's will,
And the thoughts of youth are long, long thoughts."

I can see the shadowy lines of its trees,
And catch, in sudden gleams,
The sheen of the far-surrounding seas,
And islands that were the Hesperides
Of all my boyish dreams.
And the burden of that old song,
It murmurs and whispers still:
"A boy's will is the wind's will,
And the thoughts of youth are long, long thoughts."

I remember the black wharves and the ships,
And the sea-tides tossing free;
And Spanish sailors with bearded lips,
And the beauty and mystery of the ships,
And the magic of the sea.
And the voice of that wayward song
Is singing and saying still:
"A boy's will is the wind's will,
And the thoughts of youth are long, long thoughts."

I remember the bulwarks by the shore,
And the fort upon the hill;
The sunrise gun, with its hollow roar,
The drum-beat repeated o'er and o'er,
And the bugle wild and shrill.
And the music of that old song
Throbs in my memory still:
"A boy's will is the wind's will,
And the thoughts of youth are long, long thoughts."

I remember the sea-fight far away,
How it thundered o'er the tide!
And the dead captains, as they lay
In their graves, o'erlooking the tranquil bay
Where they in battle died.
And the sound of that mournful song
Goes through me with a thrill:

"A boy's will is the wind's will,
And the thoughts of youth are long, long thoughts"...

I once read this poem to an audience, at Longfellow's two-hundredth birth-day party in the museum that was his childhood home. Since it is a poem of 10 stanzas with a long refrain, I was anxious the refrain might be tedious for the listeners, but that was not at all the case; in every stanza, the refrain conveyed a different mood and called for a different kind of delivery. If you try reading this excerpt from it aloud, you may have the same experience. Edgar Allen Poe, in his discussion of the composition of "The Raven" in the questions at the end of this chapter, that the same refrain, if skillfully handled, can have many different meanings in different contexts.

Sometimes the words of a refrain are varied for a specific effect. For exam-ple, Thom Gunn's "Carnal Knowledge," a poem about making love with a woman even though they both know he is gay, ends every stanza until the last one with the alternating refrains, "I know you know I know you know I know" and "You know I know you know I know you know." In the last of the six stan-zas, as the speaker grows impatient with the pretense and tells the woman to leave, the refrain sheds its layers of complexity, and the last stanza ends simply, "I know you know." The change is effective precisely because of the conscien-tiousness with which the refrains have been repeated up until that point.

QUESTIONS FOR MEDITATION OR DISCUSSION

How do you feel about the kinds of extreme constraints that the forms intro-duced in this chapter impose on a poem? How do they change the experience of writing a poem at each stage: inspiration, initial writing, revision, comple-tion? Are there certain themes that feel right to address in repeating forms?

One of the most common points made by the 60 contributors to the anthology *A Formal Feeling Comes: Poems in Form by Contemporary Women*, including Ju-dith Barrington and Honor Moore, whose remarks are excerpted below, was that strict form helped them express painful feelings and describe painful ex-periences they had not been able to address before in poetry. Does this surprise you? Have other kinds of formal shapes (besides the poetic) ever been helpful to you after painful experiences?

What have the poems in this chapter gained by the use of repetition? What have they lost?

It is a truism that subtlety is the key to using a repeating form successfully. The following poem, a tour-de-force written by the anagrammatic alter ego of form guru Lewis Turco, takes on this assumption head-on:

"Sestina," Wesli Court

It drives you crazy to write a sestina.
First off, in order to write a sestina
you need six end-words that don't shout, "Sestina!"
One should hide the fact that it's a sestina
you're writing. I mean, why holler "Sestina!"
if you don't have to? Why give the sestina

game away right away? For a sestina
needs to be a subtle thing. A sestina
should lead readers away from the sestina,
make them think, "This is no kind of sestina,
it's a sixteener, maybe, no sestina
sustaining itself on sestets. Sestina

indeed! I don't believe it. A sestina
doesn't announce itself, "I'm a sestina,
no less! I live on end-words, a sestina
to end sestinas! I'm a sustainer
of sounds, echoes of a choral Sistiner
bouncing off Michaelangelo sixteen or

so ways from Rome to Nome." A fine sestina
that would be. Thirty-nine lines of sestina
mumbling into the reader's ear, "Sestina,
sestina, sestina." Who could sustain a
poem like that for so long? A sestina
ought perhaps to read more like a sonetto

rispetto than like what it is. Sestina
end-words are *teleutons*, and a sestina
should tell you tons about what a sestina
is all about. Certainly, a sestina
is about disguise, subtlety, sestina
reticence, reluctance to be sestina-

like. Rather, it ought to be a soul-stainer,
nuanced, a mind-mellower. A sestina
ought not to be the thing, just the sustainer
of thingness in the memory. Sestina
is teleutonals, not end-words. Sestina
is an earful of sense, not a sestina

ending in a coda that says *sestina,*
 repeating end-words, *sestina, sestina,*
sestina, and a final time, *sestina!*

What is the serious point of this poem? Do you find it convincing?

Assuming you've written at least one of the forms covered in this chapter, how
was the experience different for you than writing other kinds of poems in free
verse or form? How did you approach the challenge of creating a sense of
movement or plot? How different do your repeating lines or phrases feel from
each other? Do you feel that the poem is still in your own "voice" or does the
form seem to have taken over?

QUOTES

It was only after the University, when I started reading traditional narratives
and listening to oral technique, that it began to click in my mind that I had been
doing the same thing unconsciously and that other Native writers had been doing it too. . . . It has given my work more validity, to know that I am using an ancient technique. But I try not to overdo it. I use repetition just enough to create
a nice tension. The skill comes in recognizing when not to overdo it.
    —Lenore Keeshig-Tobias

I make reference to Keats, Donne, and Shakespeare every time I write a sonnet, but the blues is a homegrown form with a rich history that is equally alive to me. If I bow to Keats and Wang Wei, I must also bow to Langston Hughes. To be true to the selves that I am, I must keep my muse versatile and diverse.
   —Marilyn Chin

One of the striking things about the blues tradition is the way the instrument becomes that other, alternative voice . . . the realm of conventionally articulate speech is not sufficient for saying what needs to be said. We are often making that same assertion in poetry.
   —Nathaniel Mackey

[The sestina's] restraint became the walls of the room, the recurrence of end words a verbal equivalent for the relentlessness of the molester's intentions. Embraced in its sure architecture, the violated child, silent for thirty years, is free to tell her story.
   —Honor Moore

A few years ago, I wrote a sequence of six villanelles dealing with my mother's death by drowning. I do not think I could have written that particular piece without a strict form . . . I also think that the villanelle itself was important to the subject—I couldn't have used just any tight form. I had always thought that the shape of the villanelle, with its repeating lines that come together at the end, suggested both tides and circles.
   —Judith Barrington

There are so many sounds! A poem having one rhyme?
A good life with a sad, minor crime at the end.

Each new couplet's a different ascent: no great peak
but a low hill quite easy to climb at the end . . .
   —John Hollander, "Ghazal"

In carefully thinking over all the usual artistic effects—or more properly *points,* in the theatrical sense—I did not fail to perceive immediately that no one had been so universally employed as that of the *refrain.* The universality of its employment sufficed to assure me of its intrinsic value, and spared me the necessity

of submitting it to analysis. I considered it, however, with regard to its suscepti-
bility of improvement, and soon saw it to be in a primitive condition. As commonly used, the refrain, or burden, not only is limited to lyric verse, but depends
for its impression upon the force of monotone—both in sound and thought. The
pleasure is deduced solely from the sense of identity—of repetition. I resolved to
diversify, and so heighten the effect, by adhering in general to the monotone of
sound, while I continually varied that of thought: that is to say, I determined to
produce continuously novel effects, by the variation of the *application* of the refrain—the refrain itself remaining, for the most part, unvaried.

—Edgar Allan Poe, on the composition of "The Raven"

POETRY PRACTICES

Learning to Repeat. Write a poem in any of the forms in this section.

Repeat Translation. Write the same poem five times, in all the five forms covered in this chapter, so you will see what each shape can do with the same impetus and theme.

Blues Riff. Listen to some classic blues songs. Then write a poem in blues
stanza using one of the lines from a song combined with lines of your own.

Ghazal Performance. Write a ghazal. Perform it to a group of people in the
traditional manner, with the audience reciting the *radif.*

Dramatic Sestina. Write a sestina addressed to an audience, based on the
model of "Untoward Occurrence at an Embassy Poetry Reading." Pay extra attention to the middle, so it doesn't sag.

Villanelle Permutations. Write a villanelle with no variation in the repetends
(check to see how much use you've made of enjambment, and whether you've
varied the meanings of the repeating lines through context). Save this version
as Version 1. Then alter it to vary only the first repetend, first slightly (save as
Version 2) and then more dramatically (Version 3). Then vary only the second
repetend, first slightly (Version 4), then dramatically (Version 5). Compare
your five versions. Which is the stronger poem?

Pioneer Repetition. Write a poem in a repeating form that has rarely been
used, such as the elegantly simple **quatern.** The quatern is a poem of 16 lines, in
any meter, divided into four stanzas. The same line appears as the first line of

the first stanza, the second line of the second stanza, the third line of the third stanza, and the last line of the poem.

Nonce Repetition. Invent your own form making use of repeating lines or refrains.

Rhetorical Quilt. Write a poem using four or more of the rhetorical figures that involve repetition.

CHAPTER 9

Chaos in Fourteen Lines: The Sonnet

Sociologists have discovered a surprising fact. When a group of people are in an unfenced space, no matter how large, they gravitate toward the outskirts and leave the middle empty. On the other hand, in a fenced space, they will spread out and enjoy the use of the whole area. Maybe this truth helps explain the charm of courtyards, and the fact that the word "paradise" meant, originally, "a walled enclosure." It may also help explain the lasting appeal of the **sonnet,** the form that Rita Dove has called a "little world."

Did I say lasting appeal? Doesn't everyone know that the sonnet should be dead by now? As the poet Tim Yu put it in his blog, " The real issue, to my mind, in using a form like the sonnet is *belatedness.*" Doesn't it go without saying that the sonnet is a form too late for itself, too old-fashioned to really exist? Somehow, though, the sonnet has not cooperated with the reports of its death. People keep writing them. This chapter will explore why, and how, and along the way, investigate a new model of how poetry works through time that might modify somewhat the twentieth-century doctrine of poetic "progress."

"A sonnet is a moment's monument, / memorial to one dead deathless hour," wrote Dante Gabriel Rossetti in one of the most famous sonnets on the sonnet (as you might expect, no other form has inspired nearly as many tributes to itself). Rossetti expresses one of the most useful powers of the sonnet: the ability to keep a moment, to hold a feeling or experience and turn it around in the light of our awareness until many facets are evident. This multifaceted quality gives the sonnet a paradoxical feeling of freedom and expanse within confines:

"Nuns Fret Not," William Wordsworth (1807)

Nuns fret not at their convents' narrow room;
And hermits are contented with their cells;

And students with their pensive citadels;
Maids at the wheel, the weaver at his loom,
Sit blithe and happy; bees that soar for bloom,
High as the highest Peak of Furness-fells,
Will murmur by the hour in foxglove bells:
In truth the prison, into which we doom
Ourselves, no prison is: and hence for me,
In sundry moods, 'twas pastime to be bound
Within the Sonnet's scanty plot of ground;
Pleased if some Souls (for such there needs must be)
Who have felt the weight of too much liberty,
should find brief solace there, as I have found.

This sonnet is in iambic pentameter, as are all the sonnets in this chapter unless specified otherwise. Wordsworth uses both the meter and the form with grace to illustrate the paradox of what Emerson called the "restraints that make us free." I recently saw the deep, embracing blossoms of purple foxgloves for the first time in a friend's garden; I now understand even better the sensual pleasure, wonder, and calmness that Wordsworth, who wrote 500 sonnets, was describing here. For me also, the feeling of starting a sonnet can carry a sense of mingled freedom, comfort and curious excitement that is different from starting any other kind of poem.

The quality of exploring all facets of a subject does not mean sonnets are always calm; it also means they are able to carry the full force of a lyric outburst with complete conviction. Claude McKay's sonnet "If We Must Die," written in 1919 in response to a wave of white attacks on African Americans, is such a sonnet. This poem's urgency carried so clearly that it was recited decades later by Winston Churchill to exhort Britain to fight the Nazis, and entered into the U.S. *Congressional Record:*

"If We Must Die," Claude McKay (1919)

If we must die—let it not be like hogs
Hunted and penned in an inglorious spot,
While round us bark the mad and hungry dogs,
Making their mock at our accursed lot.
If we must die—oh, let us nobly die,

So that our precious blood may not be shed
In vain; then even the monsters we defy
Shall be constrained to honor us though dead!
Oh, Kinsmen! We must meet the common foe;
Though far outnumbered, let us show us brave,
And for their thousand blows deal one deathblow!
What though before us lies the open grave?
Like men we'll face the murderous, cowardly pack,
Pressed to the wall, dying, but fighting back!

While the sentiments are powerful, the imagery strong, and the art skillful, I don't think these qualities account fully for the impact that McKay's sonnet had on so many people. Though all these aspects play a part in the poem's effect, I give the most credit to how well McKay understood and worked with the sonnet form itself. The first two quatrains have a somber tone, a heaviness emphasized by the repeating phrase "if we must die," with its sonorous spondee. But at the beginning of line 9, with the phrase "Oh, Kinsmen!," McKay's sonnet seems to stop, take a deep breath, and regather its energies for a big push to the finish.

The ninth line of either the Italian or the English sonnet form is called the **volta,** the Italian word for "turn." At this point, the sonnet form is designed to change from one idea, tone, or approach in the octave to a different idea, tone, or approach in the sestet. And, just as the secret of success in poetry may be to make full use of what you find most unique and distinctive about poetry, the secret to success with any poetic form may be making full use of whatever is most unique and distinctive about the form. Skillful sonnets usually take good advantage of the volta, the most unique and distinctive aspect of a sonnet.

In McKay's volta, many factors, including syntax, meter, trope, word-music, and connotation as well as meaning, conspire to make the turn as effective as it is. Let's start with the word "must," for example. If you read aloud the lines containing this word at the beginnings of the first two quatrains, you will hear something between resigned bitterness and sad determination conveyed by the spondaic stress on the first "must," and a firmer, mounting determination in the second "must." But after the volta, the same word has changed its intensity entirely, the spondee conveying an unstoppable force that floods over the expected unstressed syllable in irresistible exhortation.

Word-music plays a part as well, as the three "m"s in "men," "must," and "meet" gather together to surpass and overwhelm the previous "m"s in "making their mock" and "monsters." It is also significant that one of these "m" sounds happens in the syllable "men," contrasting "men" with the simile of "hogs" that opened the poem, and setting the stage for the transformation that will happen by the end of the poem, where the African American prisoners will have become "men" while their oppressors still remain a "pack" of dogs. The phrase "Oh, Kinsmen!" right at the volta is the heart of the sonnet not only because it brings in the word "men," but also because it does so through the word "kinsmen," emphasizing that it is only in their sense of brotherhood that the prisoners will find the strength they need to prevail.

When you read the poem aloud, you may notice that your energy level and pulse rate rise after line 9. I think the most significant reason for this change is metrical. With the word "kinsmen," the poem begins to take on a more trochaic feel. The caesura after "kinsmen" sets the stage for the rest of the line to sound strongly trochaic: "We must meet the common foe" sounds exactly like a footless trochaic line, and phrases such as "far outnumbered" continue the powerful rocking trochaic rhythm, in contrast to the doggedly iambic feeling of the octave, where the only trochaic words ("hunted" and "making") are dutifully combined to their traditional and most impotent place in the first foot of the line. The trochaic undercurrent of this poem is no surprise in the context of African American poetics; as discussed previously , the trochaic meter has been used by African American poets as a powerful alternative to iambic meter in such poems as Cullen's "Heritage" and Brooks's *The Anniad.*

It's hard to imagine "If We Must Die" in another kind of poetic form—a ballad, or quatrains, or free verse. Who would have thought the sonnet, known so well as the vehicle for plaintive or poignant poems of love, would also prove the perfect vehicle for McKay's revolutionary call: at once big and loose enough for the pacing and circling of authentic power, and small and structured enough for the channeling and building of directed force? How can a poetic form be so versatile? We might as well ask, though, how can a human voice be so versatile? Something in the shape of the sonnet seems so well suited to convey human feeling that it can feel almost like a throat, a hand, a voice—and yes, also like a stanza or room that is especially well proportioned to suit the human form.

And, as it turns out, there is truth behind this idea of the connection between the sonnet and the human body. Almost all traditionally formed sonnets have 14 lines and consist of an **octave** (8 lines) and a **sestet** (6 lines) with the significant shift in emphasis of the volta between them. The critic Paul Oppenheimer has observed that since the last two lines of a sonnet are often separated off from the rest in a couplet or an implied couplet that closes the poem, the proportions of the form are 6:8:12. And this proportion, in fact, represents the special mathematical ratio which the Greeks called the Golden Mean.

Quatrain: a group of four lines linked by rhyme

Octave: First eight lines of a sonnet

Sestet: last six lines of a sonnet

Volta: the "turn" after line 8 of a sonnet, often signaled by a word such as "but" or "yet," where the poem takes on a new perspective or attitude

The Golden Mean: the ratio in which the distance of the two extremes from the middle number is the same fraction of their own quantity (b a over a = c b over c)

Italian sonnet: Sonnet rhyming abbaabbacdecde (Italian sestet) or cdc-cdcd (Sicilian sestet)

English sonnet: Sonnet rhyming ababcdcdefefgg

A ratio found throughout nature, the Golden Mean is apparent in the proportions by which flower petals grow, twigs sprout from stems, and the shapes of snowflakes crystallize. It is also a ratio evident in the proportions of the human body. Oppenheimer feels that this compelling ratio is one of the reasons for the sonnet's lasting power, which has brought it into numerous languages and made it part of the vocabulary of virtually every major poet in Italian, German, French, Spanish, and English over seven centuries.

In fact, the sonnet is the ultimate stanza, an enclosed place of words alive with currents of energy and places to rest. It has provided a place for some of the most intense and memorable lines in English-language poetry to come into being: How do I love thee? Let me count the ways . . . Getting and spending, we lay waste our powers . . . That time of year thou mayst in me behold . . . Euclid alone has looked on Beauty bare . . . Oh mother, mother, where is happiness . . . one day

I wrote her name upon the strand . . . A sudden blow, the great wings beating still . . . When I have fears that I may cease to be . . . Fool, said my muse to me, look in thy heart and write.

The Italian and English Sonnet

The **Italian** or **Petrarchan** sonnet is the strictest form, with only two rhyming sounds in the octave and three in the sestet. This economy of rhyme sounds can bring great beauty, so the form sounds like the inhale and exhale of a breath. This two-part structure lends power to the volta, which we have seen can structure the thought process in ways from the obvious ("In truth, the prison . . .") to the more subtle:

"Unholy Sonnet," Mark Jarman

After the praying, after the hymn-singing,
After the sermon's trenchant commentary
On the world's ills, which make ours secondary,
After communion, after the hand wringing,
And after peace descends upon us, bringing
Our eyes up to regard the sanctuary
And how the light swords through it, and how, scary
In their sheer numbers, motes of dust ride, clinging-
There is, as doctors say about some pain,
Discomfort knowing that despite your prayers,
Your listening and rejoicing, your small part
In this communal stab at coming clean,
There is one stubborn remnant of your cares
Intact. There is still murder in your heart.

This poem, where the worshiper tries to integrate repressed feelings into a pious character, serves as a good illustration for Oppenheimer's idea of the sonnet as the container for the personality's complexity (see below). The smooth and almost imperceptible transition of the volta perhaps underscores the difficulty the speaker has at first in consciously accepting the hidden thoughts.

This caustic narrative sonnet uses the volta to create a change of scene:

Sonnet 115, John Berryman (1947)

All we were going strong last night this time,
the mosts were flying & the frozen daiquiris
were downing, supine on the floor lay Lise
listening to Schubert grievous & sublime,
my head was frantic with a following rime:
it was a good evening, and evening to please,
I kissed her in the kitchen—ecstasies—
among so much good we tamped down the crime.

The weather's changing. This morning was cold,
as I made for the grove, without expectation,
some hundred Sonnets in my pocket, old,
to read her if she came. Presently the sun
yellowed the pines & my lady came not
in blue jeans & a sweater. I sat down & wrote.

Edna St. Vincent Millay, one of the most noted writers of sonnets in the twentieth century and called by Edmund Wilson the successor to Shakespeare, frequently favored the Italian form. Some say the Italian form is harder to write in English than the English form, since it needs more rhymes for each sound; but in Millay's hands the rhymes rarely sound forced. Here is her contribution to the genre of the sonnet about writing a sonnet:

"I will put Chaos into fourteen lines," Edna St. Vincent Millay (1941)

I will put Chaos into fourteen lines
And keep him there; and let him thence escape
If he be lucky; let him twist, and ape
Flood, fire, and demon—his adroit designs
Will strain to nothing in the strict confines
Of this sweet Order, where, in pious rape,
I hold his essence and amorphous shape,
Till he with Order mingles and combines.
Past are the hours, the years, of our duress,
His arrogance, our awful servitude:
I have him. He is nothing more nor less

Than something simple yet not understood;
I shall not even force him to confess;
Or answer. I will only make him good.

The Italian sonnet's lack of a closing couplet and greater balance between octave and sestet doesn't mean it can't be used to great rhetorical force. The combination of energy and containment, development and resting, that structures "If We Must Die" is part of the quality that helped make Emma Lazarus's sonnet for the Statue of Liberty so durable and beloved:

"The New Colossus," Emma Lazarus (1883)

Not like the brazen giant of Greek fame
With conquering limbs astride from land to land;
Here at our sea-washed, sunset gates shall stand
A mighty woman with a torch, whose flame
Is the imprisoned lightning, and her name
Mother of Exiles. From her beacon-hand
Glows world-wide welcome; her mild eyes command
The air-bridged harbor that twin cities frame,
"Keep, ancient lands, your storied pomp!" cries she
With silent lips. "Give me your tired, your poor,
Your huddled masses yearning to breathe free,
The wretched refuse of your teeming shore,
Send these, the homeless, tempest-tost to me,
I lift my lamp beside the golden door!"

While the first line and a half after the volta is somewhat thrown away, Lazarus more than makes up for it in the last four lines of the sestet, which can stand as a quatrain on their own, and which carry in four lines all the accumulated force that McKay disperses throughout his sestet. So, while "The New Colossus" may not fully embody the potential of the sonnet as a sonnet, it is still a reflection of the rhetorical power of the form.

The **English** or **Shakespearean** sonnet, adapted from the Petrarchan model by Sir Henry Howard, Earl of Surrey, and Sir Thomas Wyatt, and perfected by Shakespeare, has a more logically complex shape than the Italian, with a pattern of 4-4-4-2 lines:

Sonnet 12, William Shakespeare (1609)

When I do count the clock that tells the time,
And see the brave day sunk in hideous night;
When I behold the violet past prime,
And sable curls all silvered o'er with white;
When lofty trees I see barren of leaves,
Which erst from heat did canopy the herd
And summer's green all girded up in sheaves
Borne on the bier with white and bristly beard:
Then of thy beauty do I question make
That thou among the wastes of time must go,
Since sweets and beauties do themselves forsake,
And die as fast as they see others grow;
And nothing 'gainst Time's scythe can make defence
Save breed to brave him, when he takes thee hence.

Like Mckay's English sonnet, this one uses the first quatrain to establish an idea and the second to build on it in a different but related way. Where as McKay's volta introduced a new emotional tone, in this sonnet, as in most of Shakespeare's line 9, the volta brings in a new idea or logical approach: the idea of the lover—and a new attitude of questioning insecurity. The final couplet, like the final couplet of "If We Must Die," sums up the problem and offers a solution—in this case to produce "breed," creative or actual progeny.

The English sonnet's closing couplet, and the great logical potential of its structure, doesn't mean it can't be used for a poem with a delicate balance between octave and sestet. This remarkable sonnet about balance has always seemed to me not only like a love poem but also like a tribute to the sonnet form itself:

"The Silken Tent," Robert Frost (1942)

She is as in a field of a silken tent
At midday when a sunny summer breeze
Has dried the dew and all its ropes relent,
So that in guys it gently sways at ease,
And its supporting central cedar pole,
That is its pinnacle to heavenward

And signifies the sureness of the soul,
Seems to owe naught to any single cord,
But strictly held by none, is loosely bound
By countless silken ties of love and thought
To every thing on earth the compass round,
And only by one's going slightly taut
In the capriciousness of summer air
Is of the slightest bondage made aware.

There is a very unusual secret in this sonnet. Read it through carefully and see if you can find what it is (hint: it has something to do with punctuation).

Whether in the Italian or English form, the sonnet allows for dialectical opposition, tension and resolution within one stanza; it can unite opposing attitudes within one identity. Paul Oppenheimer makes a convincing argument that because the sonnet allowed room to struggle with oneself, it marks not only the beginning of modern poetry but the beginning of the modern idea of our "self" as having a complex internal life. If this is so, then the sonnet form is likely to continue to be useful at least as long as we encourage such feelings of interiority; and the current resurgence of sonnets suggests that the form can help express the decentered contemporary "self" as well.

Writing Sonnets

Louise Bogan, a famously careful poet, only allowed herself to write one sonnet, which she called "Single Sonnet":

"Single Sonnet," Louise Bogan (1937)

Now, you great stanza, you heroic mould,
Bend to my will, for I must give you love:
The weight in the heart that breathes, but cannot move,
Which to endure flesh only makes so bold.

Take up, take up, as it were lead or gold
The burden; test the dreadful mass thereof.
No stone, slate, metal under or above
Earth, is so ponderous, so dull, so cold.

Too long as ocean bed bears up the ocean,
As earth's core bears the earth, have I borne this;
Too long have lovers, bending to their kiss,
Felt bitter force cohering without motion.

Staunch meter, great song, it is yours, at length,
To prove how stronger you are than my strength.

With all the intimidating drama and power that this form has inspired, embodied by Bogan in images of heavy ancient minerals, it can take some daring to attempt one of your own. Some poets are awed at the thought of trying to join the company of the fabulous sonnets they have read. Others feel anger and hatred at a poetic shape they equate with constraint and tradition. And perhaps others are threatened by the very power that Oppenheimer describes, the power to create a sense of internal "self" from two opposing forces.

However, not every poem in the sonnet form is centered on the conventional idea of the self or its moods. Claude McKay's sonnet, for example, takes on a public and very external voice; John Berryman's is a narrative; and the following sonnet is a kind of charm, impersonal in voice though deeply felt. (Please note that it is not iambic pentameter, unlike the other sonnets discussed so far.)

"Tiger Drinking at Forest Pool," Ruth Padel

Water, moonlight, danger, dream.
Bronze urn, angled on a tree root: one
Slash of light, then gone. A red moon
Seen through clouds, or almost seen.
Treasure found but lost, flirting between
The worlds of lost and found. An unjust law
Repealed, a wish come true, a lifelong
Sadness healed. Haven, in the mind,
To anyone hurt by littleness. A prayer
For the moment, saved; treachery forgiven.
Flame of the crackle-glaze tangle, amber
Reflected in grey milk-jade. An old song
Remembered, long debt paid.
A painting on silk, which may fade.

This more recent sonnet, while unyieldingly classical in form, communicates a disjunctive, postmodern sense of (un)self:

"Sonnet," Karen Volkman

Say sad. Say sun's a semblance of a bled
blanched intransigence, collecting rue
in ray-stains. Smirching pages. Takes its cue
from sateless stamens, flanging. Florid head

got no worries, waitless. Say you do. Say
photosynthesis. Light, water, airy bread.
What eats its source, its orbit? Something bad:
some plural petal that will not root or ray.

Sow stray. Salt night for saving, dreaming clay
for heap, for hefting. Originary ash
for stall and stilling. Say it *will*, it said.

Corolla corona, bliss-bane—delay
surge and sediment. Say instrument and gash
and ruminant remnant. Rex the ruse. Be dead.

In fact, the sonnet form is extremely versatile, which is probably the real secret of its longevity. When you write one, you may be surprised. Once you get the hang of it, the pleasure of freedom within confines can become intoxicating, and can draw depths out of your poetry that you didn't know existed. In the effort to make your sonnet work right, because of its many constraints, you may need to revise more courageously than you have ever revised before and may find new images, themes, and rhymes being summoned to enrich your poems. But be prepared for the first few sonnets to be throwaways, especially if you haven't written one before. As a young poet, Ezra Pound wrote a sonnet every day for a year. I doubt that he kept many of them.

Sonnets have most often been written in iambic pentameter, but it is the rhyme scheme that defines a sonnet; there can be sonnets in any meter or in free verse. Mona van Duyn's "Sonnet for Minimalists" is in iambic dimeter. Ruth Padel's sonnet, above, opens in trochees and wavers between iambic pentameter and tetrameter lines; while heavily rhythmical, it is so irregular that it should probably be called free verse. June Jordan's "Something Like a Sonnet for Phillis Miracle Wheatley," in honor of the eighteenth-century poet who was brought to the United States as a slave, is written in dactylic meter:

"Something Like a Sonnet for Phillis Miracle Wheatley," June Jordan

Girl from the realm of birds florid and fleet
flying full feather in far or near weather
Who fell to a dollar lust coffled like meat
Captured by avarice and hate spit together
Trembling asthmatic alone on the slave block
built by a savagery travelling by carriage
viewed like a species of flaw in the livestock
A child without safety of mother or marriage

Chosen by whimsy but born to surprise
They taught you to read but you learned how to write
Begging the universe into your eyes:
They dressed you in light but you dreamed with the night.
From Africa singing of justice and grace,
Your early verse sweetens the fame of our Racc.

When writing a sonnet, I tend to stop frequently and "listen" internally for what should come next, with the form as a guide. I try not to write down anything unless it comes from an internal voice, because I know that with a sonnet the original shape will probably stick around a long time as I revise (unlike with other poems, where I tend to switch the order of stanzas). Once the rhyme words are in place I keep them in their original spots as much as possible, revising around them but keeping them as a scaffolding. One point to keep in mind is that the sonnet form is so embedded in the subliminal memories of English speakers that sometimes, a poem wants to be a sonnet without our conscious knowledge. If you keep this option in mind, it may help you to finish a poem more easily than you expected.

Like many powerful things, a sonnet is a two-edged sword. It can work for you if you understand its strengths, but against you if you treat them too lightly or ignore their power. The main thing to remember is to be sensitive to the divisions of the quatrains and the volta: make sure each quatrain has its own idea, and that the powerful transition of the volta corresponds with a transition in your mood or meaning.

Sonnets and Sequences

The most common mistake I see in beginning sonnets is that the poet tries to squeeze too much into the poem: too many thoughts, too many images, too many characters, too many plots. It is as if a sonnet's unique structure, with its two symmetrical yet asymmetrical parts and the torque-like energy that both blends and opposes them with each other, has its own size and weight which must be taken into account. Although of course there are always exceptions, at first it is a good idea to assume that you can't fit the same number of different things into a sonnet that you might expect to fit into, say, a fourteen-line poem in free verse. The very aspect of the sonnet that gives it its extra purport, its momentum and influence, means that it can become too easily crowded and confused, with the subject matter distracting from and obfuscating the form, rather than making good use of the form. It's better to keep it simple, to focus on one idea or aspect of an idea for each sonnet. Rossetti called the poem "a moment's monument" for good reason.

What should you do if you have already written one of these jam-packed sonnets? Consider unfolding it into a **sequence** of two or three or six sonnets, or more, each sonnet treating one aspect of your story or idea. You will be better able to develop your poems with vivid imagery if you allow plenty of space to stretch out in each sonnet-room. From their very beginning, sonnets have been composed in long sequences, from Petrarch and Shakespeare themselves (the sonnet sequences that earned the names Petrarchan and Shakespearean for the Italian and English sonnets were 227 sonnets long and 154 sonnets long, respectively) up through Elizabeth Barrett Browning's sequence of 44 *Sonnets from the Portuguese* (of which her famous "How do I love thee? Let me count the ways" is only the best known), to later narratives-in-sonnets such as George Meredith's *Modern Love* and Edna St. Vincent Millay's *Fatal Interview.*

If this idea appeals to you, one particular kind of sonnet sequence you might enjoy trying is a **crown of sonnets,** a sequence in which the last line of each sonnet doubles as the first line of the next. A recent example is Marilyn Nelson's "A Wreath for Emmett Till." When the crown is complete, you will have seven sonnets (unless you want to write a double crown, which is twice as long). The last sonnet takes the last line of sonnet six as its first line, and the first line of the first sonnet as its last line. While your crown may look like a circle, the best crowns, like all the best sonnet sequences, work more like a spiral than a circle, taking the reader through a sequence of different and deepening aspects of the central concern, rather than circling through the same places. Generally, to avoid monotony you will want to aim for a lot of variety in sound and meaning among the repeating lines that link together your crown, just as it is generally best to aim for variety in the rhyme sounds within each sonnet.

Reclaiming the Sonnet

Some contemporary poets trying to write sonnets find themselves oppressed, not only by the form's traditional creation of a certain kind of self, but also by the stereotype that a sonnet sequence is written by a man about a voiceless woman. In this case, you might reflect that, almost as soon as that custom started, women were overturning it. For example, the sixteenth-century French poet Louise Labe wrote a wonderful book of sonnets on male beauty and her own passion; her sonnet on impotence is a classic, as is her best-known poem, "Kiss Me Again":

Sonnet 18, Louise Labé (1555) (trans. Annie Finch)

Kiss me again, rekiss me, and then kiss
me again, with your richest, most succulent
kiss; then adore me with another kiss, meant
to steam out fourfold the very hottest hiss
from my love-hot coals. Do I hear you moaning? This
is my plan to soothe you: ten more kisses, sent
just for your pleasure. Then, both sweetly bent
on love, we'll enter joy through doubleness,
and we'll each have two loving lives to tend:
one in our single self, one in our friend.
I'll tell you something honest now, my Love:
it's very bad for me to live apart.
There's no way I can have a happy heart
without some place outside myself to move.

Written before Shakespeare's sonnets, this sonnet sequence brings a female voice into the love-sonnet tradition from the beginning. The tradition can remain a hard one to enter, especially if you are conscious of its history, its power, and the intimidating genius of some of the poets who have used it before. Many contemporary poets are irresistibly attracted to the sonnet, but at the same time feel a strong need to distance themselves from it lest they be overwhelmed by the form. They have created this distance in three main ways: through subject matter, through form, and through syntax.

Among contemporary poets in the United States, gay poets have been particularly interested in working within the long tradition of the love sonnet, perhaps because their subject matter inherently provides a position of distance. Marilyn Hacker's very fine crown of sonnets "Eight Days in April" celebrates love between women. The line of accomplished gay male sonnetteers stretches back from the contemporary poet Rafael Campo through Owen Dodson:

"Midnight Bell," Owen Dodson (1947)

This cannot be the hour for oral speech:
Words vying with the wind, with private sounds
Of other lovers striving on the beach,
With waves: the sand sniffers, the hounds.
No, this is quiet in between the long
Sentences, the lengths of speech at will.
Let the eyes remember, the ears catch the songs
We sing deep in the bone, in the still
Unoutward parts, that have their resurrection
In themselves. Cancel the mouth of poetry and prose;
Be eager now to seek the dark confection
In the flesh and feed until desire goes,
Until we sleep, until we cannot tell
Why midnight walked and did not ring her bell.

The traditional sonnet remains an excellent place to contest, undermine and reconfigure romantic stereotypes. Poets have also innovated by introducing subject matter earlier thought inappropriate for sonnets. John Donne's sonnets on religion were revolutionary in the seventeenth century:

"Batter My Heart," John Donne (1633)

Batter my heart, three person'd God; for, you
As yet but knocke, breathe, shine, and seeke to mend;
That I may rise, and stand, o'erthrow mee, and bend
Your force, to breake, blowe, burn and make me new.
I, like an usurpt towne, to another due,
Labour to'admit you, but Oh, to no end,
Reason your viceroy in mee, mee should defend,
But is captiv'd, and proves weake or untrue.
Yet dearely I love you, and would be loved faine,
But am betroth'd unto your enemie:
Divorce mee, untie, or breake that knot againe;
Take mee to you, imprison mee, for I
Except you'enthrall mee, never shall be free,
Nor ever chast, except you ravish mee.

In the early nineteenth century, Wordsworth's introduction of topical and political subject matter also broke taboos. It may be hard to imagine many subjects outside of gay love that would be considered subversive for a sonnet now; perhaps that is why, until recently, contemporary heterosexual American poets have been tending to distance themselves from the sonnet's form instead of from its themes.

Variations and Deformations of the Sonnet

Never static, the form of the sonnet has mutated numerous times since its invention by a lawyer in twelfth-century Italy, based on an old folk song stanza. Milton and Spenser each invented new sonnets that are named after them, and Shakespeare and Petrarch each built such durable versions of the form in their respective languages that the two major forms of sonnet took their names.

Until the twentieth century, the major variations in the sonnet were "formal" variations that preserved the basic qualities of the form. The **Miltonic sonnet** is a Petrarchan sonnet without the volta. The **Spenserian sonnet** has an innovative overlapping rhyme scheme but still keeps the couplet separate:

Some variations on the sonnet:

Caudated (tail) sonnet: a sonnet of any type, followed by an extra couplet
(or sometimes an extra trimeter, followed by a heroic couplet, followed by a trimeter rhymed with the first, followed by another heroic
couplet). For examples, see Milton's "On the New Forcers of Conscience" and Hopkins's "Tom's Garland."

Chained or linked sonnet: each line starts with last word of previous line

Continuous or reiterating sonnet: uses only one or two rhymes in the entire sonnet

Crown of sonnets: a sequence of sonnets, each of which begins with the
last line of the previous sonnet

Curtal sonnet: a shortened sonnet, a form invented by Gerard Manley Hopkins

French sonnet: starts like the Italian sonnet, then adds a couplet at the
volta, followed by an alternating quatrain: abbaabbaccdede

Heroic sonnet: an 18-line sonnet. English version: add a fourth quatrain,
before the couplet. Italian version: two "heroic octaves" of abababcc
plus a couplet

Interwoven sonnet: includes both medial and end rhyme

Miltonic sonnet: an Italian sonnet with no break in sense at the volta, creating a gradual culmination of the idea

Retrograde sonnet: reads the same backward as forward

Sonnet sequence: a group of sonnets on the same theme (most sonnets in
Rennaissance were written in long sequences of up to 50 sonnets)

ababbcbccdcdee. Gerard Manly Hopkins's **curtal sonnet** uses the same proportions but makes them smaller, so instead of 8 and 6 lines, the two parts are 6 and
4½ lines in length:

"Pied Beauty," Gerard Manly Hopkins (1877)

Glory be to God for dappled things
For skies of couple color as a brindled cow;
For rosemoles all in stipple upon trout that swim
Fresh firecoal chestnut falls; finches' wings;

Landscape plotted and pieced
Fold, fallow and trim.
Glory be to God for dappled things
All things counter, original, spare, strange;
Whatever is fickle, freckled (who knows how?)
With swift, slow; sweet, sour; adazzle, dim
He fathers forth whose beauty is past change;
Praise him.

Gwendolyn Brooks's mid-twentieth-century experiment maintained the sonnet's formal structure, but changed the feeling of the form:

"the sonnet-ballad," Gwendolyn Brooks (1949)

Oh mother, mother, where is happiness?
They took my lover's tallness off to war,
Left me lamenting. Now I cannot guess
What I can use an empty heart-cup for.
He won't be coming back here any more.
Some day the war will end, but, oh, I knew
When he went walking grandly out that door
That my sweet love would have to be untrue.
Would have to be untrue. Would have to court
Coquettish death, whose impudent and strange
Possessive arms and beauty (of a sort)
Can make a hard man hesitate—and change.
And he will be the one to stammer, "Yes."
Oh mother, mother, where is happiness?

While Brooks maintains the form of an English sonnet, the dialogue, the directly emotional voice of the girl, the simple and universal narrative, and the repetition of the first line, like a refrain, add the immediacy and narrative urgency of a ballad.

When I was in my twenties, partly out of poetic curiosity, partly for feminist reasons, and partly out of a desire to help reestablish form with a difference in the postmodern age, I set out to invent my own sonnet. Based on many such experiments, here are my personal minimum criteria for a variation to feel closely related enough to the sonnet so that I still feel the connection to the form's roots: the poem keeps some kind of consistent meter, though not necessarily iambic pentameter; the poem's length and proportions, like the sonnet's, feel similar to the palm of my hand; the poem has some kind of meaning-dynamic between different parts, analogous to the volta; and every line in the poem has at least one rhyming partner, to keep the vital propulsive force of the form. Nearly twenty years later, I was finally given the form of my sonnet by a figure from a dream. It's a much more radical departure than I could have imagined in my twenties: a nine-line poem in dactylic tetrameter with the form abcbcbaca, which I call the "nonnet." It's taken me yet another decade of organic, tentative, tactful experiment, pushing at my own boundaries, to begin to feel familiar with writing nonnets, and I am just beginning to suspect that my form may be workable and useful. If it turns out that it is, my variation would be honored to be in the company of numerous others, famous and obscure, from all centuries.

Contemporary formal variations of the sonnet include such permutations as unrhymed metrical sonnets of 14 lines with a volta; rhymed nonmetrical (free verse) sonnets; sonnets that are metrically variable (avoiding a consistent meter); and sonnets of various lengths (including 16, 18, and 12 lines) that keep rhyme and meter. When the influential poet Robert Lowell published three books of unrhymed sonnets in the 1960s and 1970s, most were dense iambic pentameter:

"History," Robert Lowell

History has to live with what was here,
clutching and close to fumbling all we had—
it is so dull and gruesome how we die,
unlike writing, life never finishes.
Abel was finished; death is not remote,
a flash-in-the-pan electrifies the skeptic,
his cows crowding like skulls against high-voltage wire,
his baby crying all night like a new machine.
As in our Bibles, white-faced, predatory,
the beautiful, mist-drunken hunter's moon ascends—
a child could give it a face: two holes, two holes,
my eyes, my mouth, between them a skull's no-nose—

O there's a terrifying innocence in my face
drenched with the silver salvage of the mornfrost.

Lowell's unrhymed sonnet follows strictly the rhetorical shape of the English
sonnet, with each quatrain having its own subject, a dramatic change of mood
at the volta, and a concluding couplet that steps back from the poem to take a
wider view.

Informal sonnet variations (or "deformations," as Michael Boughn has pro-
posed calling them in recognition of their subversive attitude toward the form)
jettison meter as well, basically keeping nothing but the name "sonnet," though
they may be 14 lines and/or may have a volta. The most central writers of this
kind of sonnet are Ted Berrigan and Bernadette Mayer. Here is a poem from
Berrigan's first book, *Sonnets* (1964), for which he took fragments of poems
written earlier and collaged them into an approximate sonnet shape:

In Joe Brainard's collage its white arrow
he is not in it, the hungry dead doctor.
Or Marilyn Monroe, her white teeth white—
I am truly horribly upset because Marilyn
and ate King Korn popcorn," he wrote in his
of glass in Joe Brainard's collage
Doctor, but they say "I LOVE YOU"
and the sonnet is not dead.
takes the eyes away from the gray words,
Diary. The black heart beside the fifteen pieces
Monroe died, so I went to a matinee B-movie
washed by Joe's throbbing hands. "Today
What is in it is sixteen ripped pictures
does not point to William Carlos Williams.

While there is no regular meter or rhyme, the poem has 14 lines and,
significantly, the line "and the sonnet is not dead" is not only in regular meter
(trochaic tetrameter, or headless iambic tetrameter, depending how much one
privileges the iambic meter), but appears resoundingly at the end of the octave,
constituting a volta. This tradition of playful or subversive deformation of the
form has continued, largely through the influence of Mayer's book *Sonnets,*
consisting of free-verse poems of different lengths that usually preserve a volta

or turn about halfway through. Some more recent examples that preserve only one formal aspect of the traditional sonnet are Lee Ann Brown's "Quantum Sonnet," consisting of disjointed phrases of free verse rhymed according to the Shakespearean pattern, and Terrance Hayes's poem "Sonnet," consisting of the same iambic pentameter line ("We sliced the watermelon into smiles") repeated 14 times. Other deformations take the form more loosely still, sometimes treating it as a conceptual framework only. Jen Bervin's book *Nets,* for example, uses tracing paper to cross out certain words in sonnets by Shakespeare to create a palimpsest series of "sonnets." A remarkable range of other experiments with the idea and the body of the sonnet are collected in the British anthology *The Reality Street Book of Sonnets.*

Poet David Cappella has applied the terms "endoskeleton" and "exoskeleton" to the two basic approaches to varying the sonnet. I find Cappella's categories extremely useful because they are descriptive rather than judging in one direction or the other. As he has explained, "Some sonnets use the sonnet form as an endoskeleton—those are the poems that are actually written according to the sonnet form. But my poems use the form as an exoskeleton. I think of the sonnet form as a hard skeleton that exists outside and beyond my poems. My poems assume that the sonnet exoskeleton exists and play off of it, inhabit it, even though they are not structured internally according to the form."

One of the most interesting aspects of the sonnet's recent history, however, is that there seems to be a trend now away from informal deformations or exoskeletons, and back, as if in backlash, to the strictest and most conservative form of the sonnet, as in the case of Karen Volkman, whose sonnet appears earlier in this chapter. Volkman's collection of extremely experimental iambic pentameter sonnets does not experiment at all with the most traditional aspects of the form—not even with meter. Such poets are radically questioning the hundred-year-old idea that form is old-fashioned and free verse is new.

The sonnet has already risen from the dead once. It suffered over a hundred years of silence during the reign of the heroic couplet. Only a short few decades before the sonnets of Wordsworth and Keats, Samuel Johnson wrote in his authoritative *Dictionary,* "[The sonnet] is not very suited to the English Language, and has not been used by anyone of eminence since Milton"—thus giving eternal hope to any poet who feels drawn to an unpopular form or style of writing.

Now, the sonnet may be rising from the dead again. Could it be that further great changes for the sonnet are in store? Or could be that Western poetry is finally building a sustainable tradition, a vocabulary of kinds of formal and free poetry that will last, as the ghazal has lasted for millennia in India and the Arabic world? The very familiarity of the sonnet expands a poet's possibilities for working with and changing it, and when you begin to explore this stubbornly persisting form, you may find that its apparently confining poetic structure is, in fact, one of the most accommodating.

QUESTIONS FOR MEDITATION OR DISCUSSION

Look through the sonnets in this chapter and elsewhere in the book. Notice the many different ways that the volta structures the thought processes of these sonnets. What general trends and categories of volta do you see?

Read as many English and Italian sonnets as you can find, in this book and elsewhere. Looking at theme, mood, and movement, how would you characterize the differences between the traditions of these two central forms of the sonnet?

Keats invented the form for this sonnet in an attempt to improve on the English and Italian sonnet forms. How is his form different from the others? Do you think it succeeds as a new sonnet form? Why or why not? You may need to write at least one to understand how it works.

"If By Dull Rhymes Our English Must Be Chain'd," John Keats (1848)

If by dull rhymes our English must be chain'd
And, like Andromeda, the sonnet sweet
Fetter'd, in spite of pained loveliness;
Let us find out, if we must be constrain'd,
Sandals more interwoven and complete
To fit the naked foot of Poesy;
Let us inspect the lyre and weigh the stress
Of every chord and see what may be gain'd
By ear industrious and attention meet:
Misers of sound and syllable, no less
Than Midas of his coinage, let us be
Jealous of dead leaves in the bay wreath crown;
So if we may not let the Muse be free,
She will be bound with garlands of her own.

William Carlos Williams, a founder of twentieth-century free verse, wrote, "You cannot write a sonnet without making gestures of loyalty to the court of Elizabeth I." What do you think of this statement?

QUOTES

I feel the initial choice, the conscious choice, of one verse form over another is not always the choice to match the feeling, but rather a choice to contain, to control, to otherwise make the feeling safe to explore . . . the verse form almost becomes the arms of comfort in which to express the enormity of emotion.
   —Molly Peacock

There's the sonnet shape, fair enough, but it's not just a matter of rhyming the eight lines and the other six; they happen to be set on top of one another like two boxes, but they're more like a torso and pelvis.
   —Seamus Heaney

I am a poet who has from the very beginning written in free verse, but there have been times in my life when I have retreated to form. When I have had to deal with formal pain, I have retreated to the sonnet.
   —Sonia Sanchez

I like the sonnet form because it gives you the chance to develop some thought, and then come to a conclusion. It's all totally false—that's not how you really think, but in a way, it is how you think, so that's why sonnets are interesting. Sonnets pretend to reflect the way you think. That's always been my theory. . . . A good way to write a sonnet is to walk fourteen blocks. Write one line for each block . . . You can do it easily in a city, because there are all these words around.
   —Bernadette Mayer

POETRY PRACTICES

(Group) Bouts-Rime. This is a traditional poetry game. Agree on a set of end words (you can borrow them from an existing sonnet if you like). Each person will write a sonnet using the same end words.

(Group) Group Sonnet. Agree on a meter, rhyme scheme, and number of lines for your sonnet. Mark a piece of paper with one letter of the rhyme scheme ac-

companied by a number (a-1 for the first a-rhyme, etc.) on each line. Pass the paper around a group of 14 people, or the right size group so there is one person per line. As soon as one person writes a line marked by a 1, they write the letter and *only* the rhyme sound (not the word) on the board. For example, if you have line a-1 and you end it with "boat," you would write "a = ote" to signify the sound *only* without giving away your word. Each person writes one line with the agreed-on meter and rhyme and folds the paper so the next person can't see the previous line, then passes it along. Option: the first person can leave a grammatical clue (verb, plural noun, etc.) for the next line. Share the finished product.

Basic Sonnet Exericise. Write an English sonnet or an Italian sonnet. Optional: recast the sonnet in the other form. How does this change the poem?

Sonnet Sprints. Write three English or Italian sonnets, as quickly as you like. Then choose one of them to work on slowly. Feel free to steal from the others.

(Advanced Exercise) Garlands of Your Own. Invent a sonnet form of your own. I would suggest that if you want your form perceptibly to evoke the sonnet tradition, and the harmonious and concentrated power that distinguishes that tradition, you follow or at least recognize these guidelines:

a. Use meter—any meter, as long as you keep to the same meter throughout.

b. Keep the length at 14 lines, or within one or two lines of it.

c. If you invent a new rhyme scheme, make sure that it is a symmetrical one: each word should rhyme with something, with no loose ends.

d. Either use a volta, or otherwise keep in mind an energy pattern like the in-and-out breath of the Italian sonnet, or the logical argument of the English sonnet.

CHAPTER 10

Deep Story: The Ballad

When you choose to write a **ballad,** you are hooking into one of the oldest living forms of poetry in English, a form that is almost purely narrative and yet carries strong dramatic and lyric intensity. You may find that your poems gain depth and power by the mere fact of participating in such a mysterious, sometimes funny, sometimes violent, sometimes heart-wrenching tradition—a tradition that preserved for centuries, alongside the traditions of written poetry, the influences and moods of the vibrant oral culture that once permeated English-language poetry.

Ballads are story-poems (or, more accurately, song-poems, since this kind of poem was traditionally sung) that focus on crucial moments of action, with little interpretation or introspection. The doggedly "anonymous" nature of the ballads, their focus on love and gore, and the fact that the scholars who collected and published them in the eighteenth and nineteenth centuries—Bishop Percy, Walter Scott, and James Francis Child—traced most of them to women, during the same period that Grimm and Anderson were collecting fairy tales from the illiterate women who had them passed them down through generations, have led to the speculation that the ballads were largely the work of female poets. And at this point it does seem likely that, to quote Virginia Woolf, "Anonymous was a woman." While we may never know for sure, perhaps this association of the ballad with a marginal counterculture has to do with the fact that some of the twentieth-century and contemporary poets who have done the most brilliant work with the form have been women or African American poets.

The ballad is one of the most ancient, flexible, and enduring kinds of narrative poems. Traditionally, the action in a ballad is compressed and can span great leaps in time, in part because the action—passion, murder, betrayal—is attention-getting even from a distance. But to counterbalance this large scale, ballads traditionally also focus in on a few small details—the eels that Lord

Randal ate for lunch, the shoe in the rubble of the bombed Birmingham church—that add memorability and telegraph the strength of their emotion. A refrain frequently holds the ballad together and adds continuity and drama; since ballads, like sonnets, have a history in musical performance, the refrain also makes them work better as songs. Some scholars believe that, traditionally, a lead singer sang the narrative lines and a chorus sang the refrains.

Folklorists who record material from oral culture use the term "type" for the basic skeleton of a common story or song, and "variants" for the different versions developed by various performers. Traditional ballads exist in multiple variants, altered over time by many singers; for example, the well-known ballad "Lord Randal," about a young man poisoned by his sweetheart, is one of 15 variants of the same basic story and format collected by Child. Several of these variants are addressed to "Lord Randal," but others use "Lord Donald," "King Henry," "Billy," or other names. In the "Billy" variant, the young man is poisoned by his grandmother instead of his sweetheart. Child prefaces the ballad with the list of people from whom he had collected this version: "Note: a. Communicated by Mrs. L. F. Wesseihoeft, of Boston, as sung to her when a child by her grandmother, Elizabeth Foster, born in Maine, who appears to have learned the ballad of her mother about 1800. b. By a daughter of Elizabeth Foster, as learned about 1820. c. By Miss Ellen Marston of New Bedford, as learned from her mother, born 1778. ? d. By Mrs. Cushing, of Cambridge, Mass., as learned in 1838 from a schoolmate, who is thought to have derived it from an old nurse. e. By Mrs. Augustus Lowell, of Boston. f. By Mrs. Edward Atkinson, of Boston, learned of Mrs. A. Lowell, in girlhood. g. By Mrs. A. Lowell, as derived from a friend.":

"Tiranti, My Son" (Child Ballad #12, Variant I), Anonymous (eighteenth century)

"O WHERE have you been, Tiranti, my son?
O where have you been, my sweet little one?"
"I have been to my grandmother's; mother make my bed soon,
For I'm sick to my heart, and I'm faint to lie down."

"What did you have for your supper, Tiranti, my son?
What did you have for your supper, my sweet little one?"
"I had eels fried in butter; mother, make my bed soon,
For I'm sick to my heart, and I'm faint to lie down."

"Where did the eels come from, Tiranti, my son?
Where did the eels come from, my sweet little one?"
"From the corner of the haystack; mother, make my bed soon,
For I'm sick to my heart, and I'm faint to lie down."

"What color were the eels, Tiranti, my son?
What color were the eels, my sweet little one?"
"They were streaked and striped; mother, make my bed soon,
For I'm sick to my heart, and I'm faint to lie down."

"What'll you give to your father, Tiranti, my son,
What'll you give to your father, my sweet little one?"
"All my gold and my silver; mother, make my bed soon,
For I'm sick to my heart, and I'm faint to lie down."

"What'll you give to your mother, Tiranti, my son?
What'll you give to your mother, my sweet little one?"
"A coach and six horses; mother, make my bed soon,
For I'm sick to my heart, and I'm faint to lie down."

"What'll you give to your grandmother, Tiranti, my son?
What'll you give to your grandmother, my sweet little one?"
"A halter to hang her; mother, make my bed soon,
For I'm sick to my heart, and I'm faint to lie down."

"Where'll you have your bed made, Tiranti, my son?
Where'll you have your bed made, my sweet little one?"
"In the corner of the churchyard; mother, make my bed soon,
For I'm sick to my heart, and I'm faint to lie down."

Like a strictly observed meter that conveys strong feeling when the poet alters it slightly (think of Millay's "Love is Not All"), the restricted form of the ballad can convey great emotion when the personal is finally allowed to seep through the objective outlines of the story and the relentless repetition of the refrain. When Tiranti answers, "a halter to hang her, mother," those words can convey as much emotion as many a long lyric poem. In the ballad "Clerk Saunders," Lady Margaret spends the night with her lover Saunders, only to have her

brothers discover them and murder her lover. It is hard to imagine a more piti-
ful cry than her plea at his grave:

> Is there any room at your head, Saunders?
> Is there any room at your feet?
> Or any room at your side, Saunders,
> Where fain, fain I would sleep?

Ballads are usually written in a four-line stanza, called the "folk stanza" or
"ballad stanza," in which at least the second and fourth lines rhyme. The unrhymed first and third lines typically add action and new information, while
the rhymed lines build emotion through sound and repetition. The first and
third lines of a stanza have four beats, and the second and fourth typically have
three, resulting in a pattern of 4-3-4-3 beats per line. There has been much discussion over whether ballad meter is an accentual or an accentual-syllabic meter; the best explanation seems to be that it is a dipodic meter (see chapter 5),
with stronger stresses on the first and third syllables, and weaker stresses on the
second and fourth. Because of the dipodic pattern, it can sound as if there is an
omitted unstressed syllable (sometimes called "a metrical rest") at the end of
lines 2 and 4. This American version of an old Scottish ballad uses the standard
4-3-4-3 stanza:

> *"The Willow Tree," Anonymous (American version, collected*
> *eighteenth century)*

> There was a youth, a cruel youth,
> Who lived beside the sea,
> Six little maidens he drowned there
> By the lonely willow tree.

> As he walked o'er with Sally Brown,
> As he walked o'er with she,
> And evil thought came to him there,
> By the lonely willow tree.

> O turn you back to the water's side,
> And face the willow tree,

Six little maidens I've drowned here,
And you the seventh shall be.

Take off, take off, your golden crown,
Take off your gown, cried he.
For though I am going to murder you
I would not spoil your finery.

Oh, turn around, you false young man,
Oh turn around, cried she,
For 'tis not meet that such a youth
A naked woman should you see.

He turned around, that false young man,
And faced the willow tree,
And seizing him boldly in both her arms,
She threw him into the sea.

Lie there, lie there, you false young man,
Lie there, lie there, cried she,
Six little maidens you've drowned here,
Now keep them company!

He sank beneath the icy waves,
He sank down into the sea,
And no living thing wept a tear for him,
Save the lonely willow tree.

If you are writing a ballad and want to get the hang of this form, try singing your poem to the tune of "Amazing Grace," "The Yellow Rose of Texas," or the *Gilligan's Island* theme song. The tunes of many of Bob Dylan's songs would also work. Folk meter or ballad meter is also the meter of hymns and country music, and some children's songs. By singing, you'll probably be able to tell quite easily whether your poem is in the right rhythm.

While the 4-3-4-3 form is the most typical kind of ballad and the easiest to use, there are many versions of the stanza. One common variation is the 4-4-4-4 pattern of "Tiranti, My Son." Any narrative poem in quatrains with a refrain, especially one with gory or creepy subject matter, is likely to be classified as a ballad. The remarkable overlooked poet Helen Adam, known for her association with poets such as Robert Duncan during the San Francisco Renaissance of the 1960s, was born in Scotland at a time when the ballad tradition was still a living oral tradition. She absorbed the ballad thoroughly, and used numerous variations of it in crafting uniquely uncanny poems. In this one, the dipodic swing of the meter is almost dizzying:

"I Love My Love," Helen Adam (1960)

In the dark of the moon the hair rules.—Robert Duncan

There was a man who married a maid. She laughed as he led her home.
The living fleece of her long bright hair she combed with a golden comb.
He led her home through his barley fields, where the saffron poppies grew.
She combed, and whispered, "I love my love." Her voice like a plaintive
    coo.
Ha! Ha!
Her voice like a plaintive coo.

He lived alone with his chosen bride. At first their life was sweet.
Sweet was the touch of her playful hair binding his hands and feet.
When first she murmured adoring words, her words did not appall.
"I love my love with a Capital A. To my love I give my All.
Ah! Ha!
To my love I give my All."

She circled him with the secret web she wove as her strong hair grew.
Like a golden spider she wove and sang, "My love is tender and true."
She combed her hair with a golden comb, and shackled him to a tree.
She shackled him fast to the Tree of Life. "My love I'll never set free.
No. No.
My love I'll never set free."

Whenever he broke her golden bonds he was held with bonds of gold.
"Oh! cannot a man escape from love, from Love's hot smothering hold?"
He roared with fury. He broke her bonds. He ran in the light of the sun.

Her soft hair rippled and trapped his feet, as fast as his feet could run,
Ha! Ha!
As fast as his feet could run.

He dug a grave, and he dug it wide. He strangled her in her sleep.
He strangled his love with a strand of hair, and then he buried her deep.
He buried her deep when the sun was hid by a purple thunder cloud.
Her helpless hair sprawled over the corpse in a pale resplendent shroud.
Ha! Ha!
A pale resplendent shroud.

Morning and night of thunder rain, and then it came to pass
That the hair sprang up through the earth of the grave, and it grew like
     golden grass.
It grew and glittered along her grave alive in the light of the sun.
Every hair had a plaintive voice, the voice of his lovely one.

"I love my love with a capital T. My love is Tender and True.
I'll love my love in the barley fields when the thunder cloud is blue.
My body crumbles beneath the ground but the hairs of my head will grow.
I'll love my love with the hairs of my head. I'll never, never let go.
Ha! Ha!
I'll never, never let go."

The hair sang soft, and the hair sang high, singing of loves that drown,
Till he took his scythe by the light of the moon, and he scythed that
     singing hair down.
Every hair laughed a lilting laugh, and shrilled as his scythe swept
     through.
"I love my love with a capital T. My love is Tender and True.
Ha! Ha!
Tender, Tender, and True."

All through the night he wept and prayed, but before the first bird woke
Around the house in the barley fields blew the hair like billowing smoke.
Her hair blew over the barley fields where the slothful poppies gape.
All day long all its voices cooed, "My love can never escape,

No, No!
My love can never escape."

"Be still, be still, you devilish hair. Glide back to the grave and sleep.
Glide back to the grave and wrap her bones down where I buried her
        deep.
I am the man who escaped from love, though love was my fate and
        doom.
Can no man ever escape from love who breaks from a woman's womb?"

Over his house, when the sun stood high, her hair was a dazzling storm,
Rolling, lashing o'er walls and roof, heavy, and soft, and warm.
It thumped on the roof, it hissed and glowed over every window pane.
The smell of the hair was in the house. It smelled like a lion's mane,
Ha! Ha!
It smelled like a lion's mane.

Three times round the bed of their love, and his heart lurched with
        despair.
In through the keyhole, elvish bright, came creeping a single hair.
Softly, softly, it stroked his lips, on his eyelids traced a sign.
"I love my love with a capital Z. I mark him Zero and mine.
Ha! Ha!
I mark him Zero and mine."

The hair rushed in. He struggled and tore, but wherever he tore a tress,
"I love my love with a capital Z," sang the hair of the sorceress.
It swarmed upon him, it swaddled him fast, it muffled his every groan.
Like a golden monster it seized his flesh, and then it sought the bone,
Ha! Ha!
And then it sought the bone.

It smothered his flesh and sought the bones. Until his bones were bare
There was no sound but the joyful hiss of the sweet insatiable hair.
"I love my love," it laughed as it ran back to the grave, its home.
Then the living fleece of her long bright hair, she combed with a golden
        comb.

Because the ballad tradition is so familiar, so engrained in our literature, it is easy to play off of it for various effects, as Langston Hughes does in "Madam and the Census Man." Hughes uses a short-lined version of the ballad form, as Adam used a long-lined version:

"Madam and the Census Man," Langston Hughes (1949)

The census man,
The day he came round,
Wanted my name
To put it down.

I said, JOHNSON,
ALBERTA K.
But he hated to write
The K that way.

He said, What
Does K stand for?
I said, K—
And nothing more.

He said, I'm gonna put it
K—A—Y.
I said, If you do,
You lie.

My mother christened me
ALBERTA K.
You leave my name
Just that way!

He said, Mrs.,
(With a snort)
Just a K
Makes your name too short.

I said, I don't
Give a damn!
Leave me and my name
Just like I am!

Furthermore, rub out
That MRS., too—
I'll have you know
I'm *Madam* to you!

As it gently mocks Madam K, this poem connects to the tradition of comic ballads, which often take place in domestic settings and pit a woman against a man. On another level, the ancient form elevates Madam K's dignity, giving her resistance to being disrespected the dramatic poetic form of a historic event. Speaking in the form strengthened by the tradition of centuries of anonymous ballad-makers before her, she gains authority and authenticity.

As long as ballads have been composed (I don't say "written," because of the oral roots of the form), some of them have told stories of historical and political events. This tradition works well for more serious contemporary ballads, from Robert Pinsky's "The Shirt" to Dudley Randall's "The Ballad of Birmingham." Although "The Ballad of Birmingham" involves dialogue, the frame of the poem is narrative. It is composed in four "balances," a common structure of pairs of stanzas that correspond to or answer each other:

"Ballad of Birmingham: On the Bombing of a Church in Alabama, 1963,"
Dudley Randall (1969)

"Mother, dear, may I go downtown
Instead of out to play,
And march the streets of Birmingham
In a Freedom March today?"

"No, baby, no, you may not go
For the dogs are fierce and wild;
And clubs and hoses, guns and jails
Aren't good for a little child."

"But, mother, I won't be alone.
Other children will go with me,
And march the streets of Birmingham
To make our country free."

"No, baby, no, you may not go
For I fear those guns will fire.
But you may go to church instead
And sing in the children's choir."

She has combed and brushed her night-dark hair,
And bathed rose petal sweet,
And drawn white gloves on her small brown hands,
And white shoes on her feet.

The mother smiled to know her child
Was in the sacred place,
But that smile was the last smile
To come upon her face.

For when she heard the explosion,
Her eyes grew wet and wild.
She raced through the streets of Birmingham
Calling for her child.

She clawed through bits of glass and brick,
Then lifted out a shoe.
"O, here's the shoe my baby wore,
But, baby, where are you?"

If your ballad feels awkward or the language unnatural, don't give up right away. It takes a little practice to be able to use the stanza naturally. Because a ballad's lines are so short and the audience's attention needs to be riveted to the plot, it is even more important to keep your language conversational. The main things to avoid, as with all metered poetry, are unnatural word order and extra "filler" words. A light touch is key to a good ballad. If you find yourself struggling with a stanza, rather than trying to force it, consider letting it go and starting that stanza again from scratch.

Child wrote that "the true popular ballads are the spontaneous products of nature." While this remark does not do justice to the artistry of those who composed them, it is true that the most effective ballads do have a quality of inevitableness and ease. One tactic that may help you achieve a more natural effect is to tap literally into the form's oral roots. Try singing your stanzas, instead of writing them down, as you compose them. If you find yourself repeating a lot, you will have learned firsthand the source of one of the form's conventions. William Motherwell, an early collector of Scottish ballads, described in 1827 how the "uniformity of phraseology . . . not only assisted the memory in an eminent degree, but served as a kind of groundwork, on which the poem could be raised. . . . Indeed the original production of these common-places betokens no slender ingenuity on the part of these song inditers." The technique of using repeating phrases to compose poetry orally is also, of course, key to the epic tradition.

Poets since the eighteenth century have been writing "literary" poems that, like "The Ballad of Birmingham," take advantage of the evocative power of ballad tradition. Some well-known examples from the Romantic period are Keats's "La Belle Dame Sans Merci" and Coleridge's long "Rime of the Ancient Mariner." An excerpt from Coleridge's poem shows that it has many differences from the traditional ballad, and yet it evokes them to good advantage:

From "The Rime of the Ancient Mariner," Samuel Taylor Coleridge (1798)

I look'd upon the rotting sea,
And drew my eyes away;
I look'd upon the rotting deck,
And there the dead men lay.

I looked to heaven, and tried to pray;
But or ever a prayer had gusht,
A wicked whisper came, and made
My heart as dry as dust.

I closed my lids, and kept them close,
And the balls like pulses beat;
For the sky and the sea, and the sea and the sky
Lay like a load on my weary eye,
And the dead were at my feet.

But the curse liveth for him in the eye of the dead men.

The cold sweat melted from their limbs,
Nor rot nor reek did they:
The look with which they look'd on me
Had never pass'd away.

An orphan's curse would drag to hell
A spirit from on high;
But oh! more horrible than that
Is the curse in a dead man's eye!
Seven days, seven nights, I saw that curse,
And yet I could not die.

The action moves much, much more slowly than the action of a traditional ballad, and repetition is not used as a consistent part of the poem's structure but only occasionally, for effect, as in the last stanza quoted; Coleridge also adds sophisticated structural variations such as the italicized refrain and the six-line stanza. Still, it is probable that this poem's distinct links to the ballad tradition are a major factor in its lasting appeal.

The opening of the following poem also uses echoes of traditional ballads, but in a sophisticated literary way:

From "The Burglar of Babylon," Elizabeth Bishop (1965)

On the fair green hills of Rio
There grows a fearful stain:
The poor who come to Rio
And can't go home again.

On the hills a million people,
A million sparrows, nest,
Like a confused migration
That's had to light and rest,

Building its nests, or houses,
Out of nothing at all, or air.

You'd think a breath would end them,
They perch so lightly there.

But they cling and spread like lichen,
And the people come and come.
There's one hill called the Chicken,
And one called Catacomb;

There's the hill of Kerosene,
And the hill of Skeleton,
The hill of Astonishment,
And the hill of Babylon.

The formulaic opening "fair green hills," and the repetition of the names of the hills, give the poem the quality of an authentic tale. The poem goes on to tell the story of Micucu, who was "a burglar and killer /An enemy of society." Micucu goes to his aunt who tells him to hide in the hills:

Below him was the ocean.
It reached far up the sky,
Flat as a wall, and on it
Were freighters passing by,

Or climbing the wall, and climbing
Till each looked like a fly,
And then fell over and vanished;
And he knew he was going to die.

He could hear the goats baa-baa-ing.
He could hear the babies cry;
Fluttering kites strained upward;
And he knew he was going to die.

Micucu is killed, and the long poem ends with another poignant repetition:

On the fair green hills of Rio
There grows a fearful stain:

The poor who come to Rio
And can't go home again.

There's the hill of Kerosene,
And the hill of the Skeleton,
The hill of Astonishment,
And the hill of Babylon.

Like Bishop's poem, contemporary poet Lee Ann Brown's "The Ballad of Susan Smith" makes use of the uncanny familiarity and ancient power of the ballad form. To tell the story of the white woman who killed her children in 1999 and blamed an imaginary black man for the crime, Brown uses a pattern of 4-4-4-4 accents and faithfully follows a repeating refrain just as in a ballad written centuries ago.

From "Ballad of Susan Smith," Lee Ann Brown

I put my car into reverse
  On a lee and lonely
This will be my Babies' hearse
  Down by the green lake side-ee-o

I am a daughter of the Mills
  On a lee and lonely
Young I am but doomed to kill
  Down by the green lake side-ee-o . . .

The action in all these ballads shifts focus from the long term—the Civil Rights movement, a pattern of six murders, Susan Smith's lying legal strategy—to the small, precise detail: the exact words someone said, the golden crown, the bloody hands, the fluttering kite, the baby shoes. Such details lend the stories their vividness.

QUESTIONS FOR MEDITATION OR DISCUSSION

Imagine taking one of the most traumatic or difficult events in your memory—either a personal tragedy or a community tragedy—and turning it into a ballad. If you don't like the idea, why not? Does it feel too public, or too simple, or too disrespectful? If you do like the idea, why? Do you feel relief? Amusement? Exhilaration? A sense of connection? What do you imagine it was like to live in the kind of community that routinely turned difficult or tragic stories into ballads?

Arguably, popular songs have taken some of the place of ballads in our culture today, putting difficult events into artistic form. One example is the song "Abraham, Martin, and John," popular in the wake of the assassinations of John F. Kennedy and Martin Luther King. I remember listening to this song as a very young teenager and finding it a cathartic experience. My son may feel the same way about a contemporary song, "September Sky," written after the September 11, 2001, attack on New York. Can you think of other songs that have the same effect?

Sing one or more ballads, either traditional or contemporary. Try solo singing and group singing with the group singing the refrains. How does this change your experience of the poems?

Psychologists and historians (most notably the philosopher of history Hayden White) claim that the act of telling a story about a difficult event is an important way for a person or a culture to come to terms with it. Is this true in your experience? Can you think of times when you were bursting to tell a story about something that had happened to you? What do those stories have in common? Would any of them be an appropriate story for a ballad, or does a ballad lend itself to a different kind of story? Do you think that rhyme and meter are more suitable for certain kinds of stories, and prose for other stories?

QUOTES

I'm no singing it exactly the way my mother sang it and I'm no singing the way that my uncle taught it to me. Because I have taken it played with the words and put my own identity into it.
    —Sheila Stewart, ballad singer

What I do remember is the way he sang it, standing easily and using not much more than a speaking rather than a singing voice. . . . Far from intruding itself, his personality vanished altogether; there was only a voice rhythmically telling a story to a tune.
    —Willa Muir

The diction of a ballad may be conversational but the rhythm is not.
   —Susan Tichy

POETRY PRACTICES

Ballad Comparison. Here is one of the six Scottish versions, collected by Child, of the ballad that became "The Willow Tree" in the United States (printed in this chapter). Compare the two versions; notice how the story both changes and stays the same.

"Lady Isabel and the Elf-Knight" (Child Ballad #4), Version D, Anonymous (eighteenth century)

O heard ye of a bloody knight,
Lived in the south country?
For he has betrayed eight ladies fair
And drowned them in the sea.

Then next he went to May Collin,
She was her father's heir,
The greatest beauty in the land,
I solemnly declare.

"I am a knight of wealth and might,
Of townlands twenty-three;
And you'll be lady of them all,
If you will go with me."

"Excuse me, then, Sir John," she says;
"To wed I am too young;
Without I have my parents' leae,
With you I dare na gang."

"Your parents' leave you soon shall have,
In that they will agree;
For I have made a solemn vow
This night you'll go with me."

From below his arm he pulled a charm,
And stuck it in her sleeve,
And he has made her go with him,
Without her parents' leave.

Of gold and silver she has got
With her twelve hundred pound,
And the swiftest steed her father had
She has taen to ride upon.

So privily they went along,
They made no stop or stay,
Till they came to the fatal place
That they call Bunion Bay.

It being in a lonely place,
And no house there was night,
The fatal rocks were long and step,
And none could hear her cry.

"Light down," he said, "fair May Collin,
Light down and speak with me,
For here I've drowned eight ladies fair,
And the ninth one you shall be."

"Is this your bowers and lofty towers,
So beautiful and gay?
Or is it for my gold," she said,
"You take my life away?"

"Strip off," he says, "thy jewels fine,
So costly and so brave
For they are too costly and too fine
To throw in the sea wave."

"Take all I have my life to save,
O good Sir John, I pray;

Let it ne'er be said you killed a maid
Upon her wedding day."

"Strip off," he says, "thy Holland smock,
That's bordered with the lawn,
For it's too costly and too finde
To rot in the sea sand."

"O turn about, Sir John," she said,
"Your back about to me,
For it never was comely for a man
A naked woman to see."

But as she turned him round about,
She threw him in the sea,
Saying, "Lie you there, you false Sir John,
Where you thought to lay me.

"O lie you there, you traitor false,
Where you thought to lay me,
For though you stripped me to the skin,
Your clothes you've got with thee."

Her jewels fine she did put on,
So costly, rich and brave,
And then with speed she mounts his steed,
So well she did behave.

That lady fair being void of fear,
Her steed being swift and free,
And she has reached her father's gate
Before the clock struck three.

Then first she called the stable groom,
He was her waiting man;
Soon as he heard his lady's voice
He stood with cap in hand.

"Where have you been, fair May Collin?
Who owns this dapple grey?"
"It is found one," she replied,
"That I got on the way."

Then out bespoke the wily parrot
Unto fair May Collin:
"What have you done with false Sir John,
that went with you yestreen?"

"O hold your tongue, my pretty parrot,
And talk no more to me,
And where you had a meal a day
O now you shall have three."

Then up bespoke her father dear.
From his chamber where he lay:
"What aileth thee, my pretty Poll,
That you chat so long or day?"

"The cat she came to my cage-door,
The thief I could not see,
And I called to fair May Collin,
To take the cat from me."

Then first she told her father dear
The deed that she had done,
And next she told her mother dear
Concerning false Sir John.

"If this be true, fair May Collin,
That you have told to me,
Before I either eat or drink
This false Sir John I'll see."

Away they went with one consent,
At dawning of the day,

Until they came to Carline Sands,
And there his body lay.

His body tall, by that great fall,
By the waves tossed to and fro,
The diamond ring that he had on
Was broke in pieces two.

And they have taken up his corpse
To yonder pleasant green,
And there they have buried false Sir John
For fear he should be seen.

Now that you know how different two versions of the same ballad can be from each other, write your own version of one of Child's ballads, of another ballad in this chapter, or of a ballad written by another student. Keep a few key elements, but make lots of significant changes in the poem to suit your own politics, gender, class, personal history, or other agenda (thanks to Susan Tichy for this assignment).

A Ballad for Now. Write a ballad on a political, social, or environmental theme.

Tabloid Ballad. Write a ballad based on a wild story from a tabloid newspaper (thanks to R. S. Gwynn for this assignment).

Personal Ballad. Write a ballad based on a story that happened to a friend or family member.

Ballad of a Secret. Write a ballad based on a secret (thanks to Susan Tichy for this assignment).

CHAPTER 11

Procedural Poetry

This last chapter deals with some forms that are "out of the box" of the common view of poetic form and provide a different kind of formal poetic experience for the writer and/or reader. Some people would not call many procedural, found, or genre poems formal poems at all, because their form may be hidden, or may depend on a relationship with another text that may or may not be present. I include them because it seems to me that the creative direction, the structuring activity, and above all the repetition involved in these kinds of poem are more akin to the impulse underlying other kinds of formal poetry than they are different.

Procedural and Nonce Poems

Procedural poetry is a type of exploratory poetry; as such, it does not see itself as committed to language's common conventions of syntax and referentiality. If words don't seem to make sense or mean anything, that is not necessarily a problem in exploratory poetry; on the contrary, that may make it easier to appreciate the many possibilities of meaning in the poem. It may seem odd that poets who grant themselves such extreme freedom where language's meaning is concerned are sometimes enthusiastic about embracing formal limitations. But it seems that certain poets' pleasure in the challenge of formal constraints is not bounded by aesthetic schools. Desire for constraint is exactly the point of similarity they share with other formal poets.

Exploratory poetry, with roots in surrealism and modernist experiments, takes playing with language seriously. Procedural poems are poems that rely on chance operations and—often random—limits and rules to open language to the personal unconscious or even, some feel, to the collective unconscious we all share. In Tristan Tzara's classic procedure "Hat," a poet throws words from a source text (a poem, a newspaper article, the first chapter of a novel) into a hat and picks them out at random to generate a new text. In Antonin Artaud's group game of "Exquisite Corpse," each person writes a line, then passes the poem to the next person, folding the page down to cover what they wrote. After everyone has written a line, someone reads the text aloud. The game can be played with chance slightly diminished by choosing a topic, a first or last word for each line, or a word that must be used, or it can be played with greater constraints. I've played it with my students to create a perfectly formed sonnet; everyone agrees to follow the same meter, and each person shares the rhyme sound of their last word with the person who needs to rhyme with it. The results are quite amazing, since the regular form makes the chance logic stand out in even sharper contrast. Here is the poet Marilyn Hacker describing a similar experiment:

> Tom Disch and I wrote collaborative Shakespearean sonnets: except for the couplet, with the ABAB structure, you'd be rhyming with yourself—I'd do the "A" lines, and he the "B"s. But you'd never have seen the actual line which preceded yours: Tom would tell me "I wrote a line ending with a preposition indicating direction"—or I'd say "I concluded with a plural noun—give it a verb." For the couplet, whoever wrote its first line gave the other the rhyme-sound: "off," "ite," whatever—as well as the syntactical requirement. Without having seen each other's lines, we came up with a sonnet that concluded: "The road reels by in millions of white flashes / like checks from out of state that no one cashes." A classic American couplet, I would say.

More recent poets have developed such procedures in various directions, including "S + 7," an amusing game in which you choose a source poem and substitute for each important word in the poem a word of the same part of speech chosen from seven words away in either direction in the dictionary. The result can be a bizarre parody, as when x and x turned Maya Angelou's poem written for Bill Clinton's inauguration, "On the Pulse of the Morning," into an S + 7 poem called "On the Pumice of Morons." A looser procedure of substitution creates an oddly un/familiar revealing version of a Shakespeare sonnet by Harryette Mullen:

From "Dim Lady," Harryette Mullen

My honeybunch's peepers are nothing like neon. Today's special at Red
Lobster is redder than her kisser. If Liquid paper is white, her racks
are institutional beige . . .

While "Hat" might not involve enough types of repetition or constraint for the
results to be considered a poetic form, the rules of S + 7 are, it seems to me,
inarguably formal as far as the writer is concerned; a poet looking for the appropriate word to substitute is experiencing decidedly formal challenges and
pleasures, similar to those a poet experiences looking for the word to satisfy the
third *b* rhyme in an Italian sonnet. On the other hand, the reader confronted
with an S + 7 poem may not have a formal reading experience at all, compared
with the reader of the sonnet, unless the reader happens to know both the procedure by which the poem was written and the source text.

The Oulipo poets, a group of French exploratory poets who reveled in poetic formal limitations as generative devices, developed this law: "A text written
according to a constraint describes the constraint." The reader's awareness of
the form is irrelevant. This is what legendary experimental formalist poet Jackson MacLow meant when he wrote (in an unpublished email to poet Jena Osman): "One thing I've noted . . . is that you and others seem to conflate verse
forms with methods—that the latter are thought of as instances of the former.
One can make either formal poems or nonformal (e.g., so-called free verse) by
any writingway." MacLow seems to be implying that, by calling poetry formal
just because it is produced by a formal procedure, we obliterate the difference
between verse that seems formal to the reader and verse that doesn't.

On the other hand, there are many procedural poems that are similar to
typical formal poems in the sense that the reader as well as the writer can perceive what is happening formally. These would include poems by Joan Retallack, an ingenious procedural poet whose book *Afterimages* consists of blocks
of text on which she tossed a paper clip, repeating the words and letters that had
been encircled by the paper clip at the bottom of each page. Retallack's poem
"AID/I/SAPPEARANCE, an elegy for a friend who died of AIDS, uses an
equally clear formal device that many readers find very moving. The poem is
based in part on a found text from the essay "The Atomic Theory and the Fundamental Principles underlying the Description of Nature" by physicist Niels
Bohr, in *The Philosophical Writings of Niels Bohr*.

A I D /I/ S A P P E A R A N C E
for Stefan Fitterman

1. in contrast with the demand of continuity in the customary description
2. of nature the indivisibility of the quantum of action requires an essential
3. element of discontinuity especially apparent through the discussion of the
4. nature of light she said it's so odd to be dying and laughed still it's early
5. late the beauty of nature as the moon waxes turns to terror when it wanes
6. or during eclipse or when changing seasons change making certain things
7. disappear and there is no place to stand on and strangely we're glad

A I D S
for tefn Fttermn
1. n contrt wth the emn of contnuty n the cutomry ecrpton
2. of nture the nvblty of the quntum of cton requre n eentl
3. element of contnuty epeclly pprent through the cuon of the
4. nture of lght he t o o t be yng n lughe tll t erly
5. lte the beuty of nture the moon wxe turn to terror when t wne
6. or urng eclpe or when chngng eon chnge mkng certn thng
7. pper n there no plce to tn on n trngely we're gl

B H J C E R T
fo fn Fmn
1. n on w mn of onnuy n uomy pon
2. of nu nvly of qunum of on qu n nl
3. lmn of onnuy plly ppn oug uon of
4. nu of lg o o yng n lug ll ly
5. l uy of nu moon wx un o o wn wn
6. o ung lp o wn ngng on ng mkng n ng
7. pp n no pl o n on n ngly w gl

F G K Q U

o n mn

1. no n w m no on ny no my pon
2. o n nvly o nm o on n nl
3. lm no onny plly pp no on o
4. no l o o yn nl ll ly
5. l y o n moon wx no own wn
6. o n l pow n n no n n mn n n
7. pp n no pl o no n n nly w l

L P V

o n mn

1. no n w m no on ny no my on
2. o n ny o nm o on n n
3. m no onny y no on o
4. no o o y n n y
5. y o n moon wx no own wn
6. o now n n no n n mn n n
7. n no o no n n n y w

M O W

n

1. n n n n n y n y n
2. n n y n n n n
3. n n n y y n n
4. n y n n y
5. y n n x n n n
6. n n n n n n n n
7. n n n n n n y

N X

1. y y
2. y
3. y y
4. y y
5. y
6.
7. y

Y

1.
2.
3.
4.
5.
6.
7.

Retallack writes, "The disappearance moves through the letters of the alphabet (and the source text) in this way: Beginning with letters A I D S, it spreads to adjoining letters B H J C E R T, to F G K Q U, to L P V, to M O W, to N X, to Y." Of course, what this means is that after enough letters of the alphabet disappear, the only letters left are *o* and *y*. Finally these expressions of sadness disappear as well.

Many procedural forms look very similar to traditional forms, such as the chant or sestina (a sestina by Oulipo poet Harry Matthews is discussed in the chapter on Repeating Forms). Others have forms that are easily perceived:

"Call Me Ishmael," Jackson MacLow

Circulation. And long long
Mind every
Interest Some how mind and every long

Coffin about little little
Money especially
I shore, having money about especially little

Cato a little little
Me extreme
I sail have me an extreme little

Cherish and left, left,
Myself extremest
It see hypos myself and extremest left,

City a land. Land.
Mouth; east,
Is spleen, hand mouth; an east, land.

A kind of super-acrostic, this clever poem consists a ritual spelling out of the famous opening sentence of Melville's *Moby Dick* that enacts itself in each stanza without ever speaking itself. The decision to use one word to stand for each letter, and to maintain those words within each stanza but to change them from stanza to stanza, makes the poem into a series of unique permutations that may be seen as a comment on the way our identity is constantly constructed anew.

Some procedural poets' work is faithful to the computer-generated or pulled-out-of-a-hat gifts of chance or the collective unconscious; others use these procedures as the starting point for a poem and might take it a long way from where it began. This poem is from a long series of poems in the same invented form:

From "Isotopes," Dan Zimmerman

W	A	V	E
O	B	I	T
M	O	O	R
B	A	L	E

I owe, to a verbal mob,
a Babel movie or two
above a limbo tower
or below a movie bat.
I've a bramble to woo,
a bamboo tower, live
owl tier above a mob,
brow to a limbo eave.
move a wit, able boor,
rove a loom, bait a web:
we roil above a tomb;
we brim a love taboo.
be a boa, violet worm:
I leave a bomb or two.

Each line of the poem uses each letter of the wordsquare once. The result is a poem incorporating an uncanny overlap of sounds and feelings, a deep exploration of one corner of the language.

The reader is also well aware of the constraint operating in Christian Bök's tour de force of prose poetry, *Eunoia,* which (influenced by Georges Perec's classic avant-garde text written without the letter *e*) has a chapter for each vowel in the alphabet that includes *only* that vowel. Here are the openings of two chapters:

CHAPTER I for Dick Higgins

Writing is inhibiting. Sighing, I sit, scribbling in ink
this pidgin script. I sing with nihilistic witticism,
disciplining signs with trifling gimmicks—impish
hijinks which highlight stick sigils. Isn't it glib?
Isn't it chic? I fit chil writing shtick which might instill priggish misgiv-
ings in critics blind with hindsight. I dismiss nit-
picking criticism which flirts with philistinism. I
bitch; I kibitz—griping whilst criticizing dimwits,
sniping whilst indicting nitwits, dismissing simplis-
tic thinking, in which phillipic wit is still illicit.

CHAPTER O for Yoko Ono

Loops on bold fonts now form lots of words for books.
Books form cocoons of comfort—tombs to hold book-
worms. Profs from Oxford show frosh who do post-
docs how to gloss works of Wordsworth. Dons who
work for proctors or provosts do not fob off school to
work in crosswords, nor do dons go off to dorm
rooms to loll on cots. Dongs go crosstown to look for
bookshops known to stock lots of topnotch goods:
cookbooks, workbooks—room on room of how-to
books for jocks (how to jog, how to box), books on
pro sports, golf or polo. Old colophons . . .

344 A POET'S EAR

Clearly there is great skill and ingenuity at work here, not to mention patience. (In his essay "How to Write Euonia," Bök lists as step 5, "Work on these stories everyday for seven years. Work only at night between the hours of 11:00 P.M and 5:00 A.M . . .")

Yet still, as Jena Osman explains, procedural poems "seem to diminish or completely eliminate authorial intention . . . [in the] belief that systems of 'constraint' . . . reveal something in language that our conventional usages might occlude." In this way, procedural poets have something in common with formalist poets generally: any poet who writes in "traditional" form would probably agree that one of the main appeals of writing in form is that something larger, or smaller, than your own individual voice is given a part in the poem's composition. Poets who write in form have all had experiences when the need to find a word that rhymes or fits a certain metrical pattern reveals an unexpected possibility that seems to come from outside our usual way of thinking.

Actually, many of the forms invented by exploratory poets—from the Oulipo poets to Jackson MacLow—are surprisingly close in structure to traditional forms. Or maybe not so surprisingly. After all, as revolutionary as the philosophy and attitudes of procedural poetry may be, all poets are basically limited to working with the same languages, the same words and sounds, the same mathematical possibilities of arrangement, and the same brain structures and body rhythms. While coediting *An Exaltation of Forms*, a book devoted to the variety of poetic forms, I conducted an active search among exploratory poets for innovative kinds of poetic forms. After several years of inquiries, most of what emerged involved innovative compositional methods rather than innovative kinds of form, seeming to indicate there really may be a limited number of basic ways of arranging words into poems.

Exploratory poems, with their unique ability to force writers and readers to focus on painful and alienating aspects of contemporary language, or on new ways of understanding poetry, have a strongly democratic, even revolutionary role to play. They can make us aware of oppressive language and stiflingly habitual thought patterns. If you are feeling stuck in a formal rut, inventing your own procedural technique or using one pioneered by an exploratory poet can show you a new way to relate to the formal potential of poetry. Exploratory poets tend to be passionate about poetry's potential to open people's minds to new ways of thinking; their emphasis on the importance of creative freedom has been both influential and salutary.

Many exploratory poems, such as Retallack's AIDS elegy, are written in nonce forms. A nonce form is simply a form that you, the poet, invent for a particular poem—"for the nonce," meaning, "for now"—and don't use again. Nonce forms don't have to be exploratory; they can be as simple as inventing a stanza form that rhymes in a certain pattern, or uses a certain order of line lengths. Sometimes a nonce form can arise while you are in the process of working on a poem, and sometimes you can think it out ahead of time. Inventing your own form can be one of the most empowering and liberating activities for a poet who is just beginning to learn forms. Sonia Sanchez told me that she always asks her students to invent a nonce form, since it is the best way for them to feel as if the tools of poetic form are truly *theirs.*

Don't worry too much about pure originality in your nonce form. As discussed above, there are really only a limited number of formal materials available: meter, line length, rhyme, stanza length, refrain, and various other kinds of repetition. But the combinations of these elements with each other and with words are infinite. Concentrate on using the materials to create the effect you want, as if you were a painter working with different colors, or an architect using design elements to create a building.

I often find it helpful to think metaphorically when creating a nonce form for a particular poem. If I want the poem to be upbeat, I might think metaphorically and choose the rising and expansive rhythm of anapests (which are of course not always in reality upbeat in mood). If the theme of a poem reminds me in some metaphorical way of baskets or weaving, I might think of using terza rima, which interweaves stanzas, overlapping different threads somewhat like a basket. This kind of metaphorical form can be evident on the surface—like the shape of the wreath commemorating the murdered teenager in Marilyn Nelson's crown of sonnets "A Wreath for Emmett Till"—or it can remain a secret, unspoken aspect of the poem, like the hidden name of Yolek in Anthony Hecht's sestina.

Some nonce forms are conceived with the poem; others develop during the process of rewriting, sometimes after multiple revisions. Either way, nonce forms can be so engrossing to work on that it is easy to forget they don't have an existence independent of you. Since, in this book, you have already learned a wide basic vocabulary of formal tools and strategies, you are in a good position to put the needs of a particular poem first as you create a nonce form.

Found and Genre Poems

A found poem is any poem that is made up of language found elsewhere. It can be language from a lecture, from overheard speech, from a classic or contemporary book, from a catalog, a medical textbook, a law brief, a child's story, a political speech, a newspaper, a sermon, etc., etc. Much found poetry is not formal; two of the most well-known examples floating around the Internet are free verse poems made up of excerpts from speeches by, respectively, President George W. Bush and Secretary of Defense Donald Rumsfeld.

However, much found poetry does turn out to be formal (structured by repetition) because the very act of finding the language either borrows or imposes a form. An example of a borrowed form is Charles Bernstein's poem consisting of a list of names of businesses taken from the yellow pages that all begin with the word "Bob's" ("Bob's Body Shop," "Bob's Car Wash," etc.). An example of a poet imposing a form is Jen Bervin, who, following the procedure that poet Ronald Johnson did earlier with Milton's *Paradise Lost,* creatively erases most of Shakespeare's sonnets. Bervin's book *Nets* prints the sonnets in white ink; on a transparent oversheet, certain words she has chosen to catch in her nets are printed in black. Here is Shakespeare's Sonnet 15, with her version of it:

> When I consider every thing that grows
> Holds in perfection but a little moment,
> That this huge stage presenteth nought but shows
> Whereon the stars in secret influence comment;
> When I perceive that men as plants increase,
> Cheered and check'd even by the self-same sky,
> Vaunt in their youthful sap, at height decrease,
> And wear their brave state out of memory;
> Then the conceit of this inconstant stay
> Sets you most rich in youth before my sight,
> Where wasteful Time debateth with Decay,
> To change your day of youth to sullied night;
> And all in war with Time for love of you,
> As he takes from you, I engraft you new.

On the transparent oversheet, over the white text of the sonnet, appears an evocative minimalist poem that captures, as do many of the nets, some essence of the original:

Sonnet 15

the stars

the selfsame sky

for love of you

Because of the consistency with which Bervin repeats her procedure, I think of *Nets* as essentially a book of formal poetry. Whether or not her nets would stand on their own without Shakespeare is a moot point; they are perpetually wedded to the original sonnets, and if they borrow some of their formality from that fact, they are entitled to it by virtue of the marriage.

Found poems can be extremely fun to write. For one thing, they get you in the habit of thinking creatively during every moment of your daily life. Every license plate, construction sign, notice board, bit of graffiti, or other piece of language you pass during your day is a potential poem. After doing some found poetry exercises, you are likely to find that your mind is buzzing and the world seems packed with poetry. To discover or create a formal design as part of your found poems can add another layer of creative pleasure for you and your readers.

A more active way to create a found poem is to write an echo poem, built by a procedure akin to the Oulipo game S + 7, but with more freedom in the choice of words:

"Pledge: 1," Michael Magee

I plug elegance
two thief rag
off-Dionysus tastes of America
in tune theory public
four widgets hands
one day shun

on dirge odd
ring the busy bell
with lip hurting
and just this
for all

This poem is part of a series of 16 poems, all echoing the pledge in different ways. Like so many of the procedural forms that "operate" on language, the poem is both funny and somber, a chance to spoof and mock and take off on serious language that, at its most successful, also offers a serious critique of that language.

A more tangential relation to found language appears in the popular type of poem that I have called a genre poem. These poems borrow a form, and often a style, a tone, a physical layout, and even particular words and phrases, from a nonliterary genre, or kind, of language. Examples would be poems that look and act like letters, recipes, newspaper articles, wedding invitations, *TV Guide* reviews, catalogs, and so on. Genre poems are sometimes thought of as forms, and writing them can feel as if one is writing a form, because of the element of copying. However, while a genre may involve formal elements (for example, the listing of ingredients in a recipe), there is always much more to a successful genre poem than simply the structural repetition of form. Here is one, from a book of poems about the life of Sylvia Plath:

"Wedding Invitation III," Cathy Bowman

Mr. and Mrs. Naked and Bald
have the wind sneer of announcing
the opaque belly-scale
of their daughter
Dark Flesh, Dark Pairing
to
Easter Egg, the Ill-Starved Thing
on Sunday, the fish-tail of September
The Suck of the Sea, New Jersey

Here, while the stanza form does have some visual formal elements, it is mostly the replication of the tone, syntax, and vocabulary that create the relationship between this genre poem and the original model. The same would be true of most genre poems.

QUESTIONS FOR MEDITATION AND DISCUSSION

Prominent Language poet Charles Bernstein, in "Against National Poetry Month as Such," writes, "Promoting poetry as if it were an 'easy listening' station just reinforces the idea that poetry is culturally irrelevant . . . I want a poetry that's bad for you." No wonder exploratory poetry is one of the more controversial topics in poetry today. Does it arouse strong feelings in you? Why? How important is "making sense" to you as a poet and as a reader?

Imagine that you find a piece of amazing, poetic writing in a manual on how to assemble a kite. If you copy it and print it out with your name on it, does it become one of your poems? What if you break it up into free-verse lines? What if you change the language slightly and turn it into metrical lines?

QUOTES

There is no "direct treatment" of the thing possible, except the "things" of language.
   —Bruce Andrews

Language is one of the principal forms our curiosity takes. It makes us restless. . . . Language itself is never in a state of rest.
   —Lyn Hejinian

POETRY PRACTICES

1. Write a poem according to the procedure "S + 7."
2. Write a poem according to one of the other procedures illustrated here.
3. Invent a nonce form and write a poem in it.
4. Write a found poem or a genre poem.
5. "Bernstein's and Mayer's Experiments." Try a few of the poetic "experiments" below, adapted from a list developed by Charles Bernstein and Bernadette Mayer. You may want to use them to write a poem, to stimulate the idea for a poem or a line, or simply to practice loosening up your lin-

guistic imagination. Let the experiment take you wherever it will; don't worry if the poem (if you end up with one) is exploratory or more conventional.

- Acrostic chance: Pick a book at random and use the title as an acrostic key phrase. For each letter of the key phrase, go to the page number in the book that corresponds ($a = 1$, $z = 26$) and copy as the first line of poem from the first word that begins with that letter to end of line or sentence. Continue through all key letters, leaving stanza breaks to mark each new key word.
- Find and replace: Systematically replace one word in a poem with another word or string of words. Perform this operation serially with the same poem, increasing the number of words in the replace string.
- Alphabet poems: Make up a poem of 26 words so that each word begins with the next letter of the alphabet. Write another alphabet poem but scramble the letter order.
- Alliteration (assonance): Write a poem in which all the words in each line begin with the same letter.
- Doubling: Starting with one sentence, write a series of paragraphs each doubling the number of sentences in the previous paragraph and including all the words used previously (cf. Ron Silliman's "Ketjak").
- Group sonnet: 14 people each write one 10-word line (or alternate measure) on an index card. Order to suit.
- Write a poem with each line filling in the blanks of "I used to be . . . but now I am . . ." (I used to write poems, but now I just do experiments; I used to make sense, but now I just make poems).
- Counting: Write poems that conform to various numeric patterns for number of words in a line or sentence, number of lines in a stanza or paragraph, number of stanzas or paragraphs in a work. Alternately, count letters or syllables. Use complex numeric series or simpler fixed-number patterns.
- Write a poem consisting only of prepositions, then of prepositions and one other part of speech.
- Write a series of eight-word lines consisting of one each of each part of speech.
- Write poems consisting of one-word lines; write poems consisting of two-word lines; write poems consisting of three-word lines.

Afterword: Form and Inspiration

Far from being something separate from creativity, the work of poetic craft, if done in a skilled and attentive way, can interact with your unconscious mind and bring you back full circle into the realm of inspiration. Some poets find that they feel less alone when writing in form. It can seem as if another creator is in the poem with you, adding a complex depth of playfulness, history, or wisdom. Form can bring us closer to poets of the past with whom we feel a kinship, or closer to our readers, or to ourselves and our own inspiration.

After all, repetition is one of the oldest and most universal cultural strategies on the planet. Long before writing, the tools of poetic form were developed in every tribal society. Poetic repetition not only makes a poem easy to remember; it can lull the logical part of the brain to hypnotize a listener. And in an age of reading, meter remains a tool for conveying the most particular and subtle shades of feeling, emotion held and expressed physically without words. Skill in meter promises something that can't be achieved in any other written way: the ability to convey exactly the sounds of words and lines, to create intonations that readers will hear in their minds across cultures and centuries.

Now that you have read this book and attained an understanding of poetic form in English, you might use the knowledge in a number of ways. You could tuck it in the back of your mind and let it help you become a more appreciative reader of poems in form; you could draw on it for new poems and new approaches to revision; or you could follow it on a journey toward ever more kinds of poem-making. However you use your skill, I hope it will bring you joy, as you enter into a more attentive and active dance with poetry's multiplicity of rhythms.

A Poet's Bookshelf on Form: For Further Reading

General Reference

Brogan, T. V. F. *Princeton Encyclopedia of Poetry and Poetics*
Drury, John. *A Poet's Dictionary*
Kinzie, Mary. *A Poet's Guide to Poetry*
Padgett, Ron. *Teachers and Writers Collaborative Book of Forms*

Form Handbooks and Introductions

Boland, Eavan, and Mark Strand. *The Making of a Poem*
Deutsch, Babette. *Poetry Handbook*
Fry, Stephen. *The Ode Less-Travelled*
Fussell, Paul. *Poetic Meter and Poetic Form*
Oliver, Mary. *Rules of the Dance: A Handbook for Writing and Reading Metrical Verse*
Turco, Lewis. *The New Book of Forms*
Williams, Miller. *Patterns of Poetry*

Demonstrations of Forms

Blaser, Robin. *The Shapes of Our Singing*
Hollander, John. *Rhyme's Reason*

Contemporary Formal Poetry Anthologies

Dacey, Philip, and David Jauss, eds. *Strong Measures*
Finch, Annie, ed. *A Formal Feeling Comes*
Jarman, Mark, and David Mason, eds. *Rebel Angels*
Richman, Robert, ed. *The Direction of Poetry*

Accent

Attridge, Derek. *The Rhythms of English Verse*
Berry, Francis. *Poetry and the Physical Voice*
Carper, Thomas. *Meter and Meaning: An Introduction to Rhythm in Poetry*

Prosody (Theory and History)

Attridge, Derek. *Poetic Rhythm: An Introduction*
Baker, David, ed. *Meter in English: A Symposium*
Gross, Harvey. *The Sound of Poetry*
MacAuley, James. *Versification*
Nabokov, Vladimir. *Notes on Prosody*
O'Donnell, Brendan. *The Passion of Meter: A Study of Wordsworth's Metrical Art*
Saintsbury, George. *A History of English Prosody from the 12th Century to the Present Day*

Meter and Form (General Writing Guides)

Baer, William. *Writing Metrical Poetry: Contemporary Lessons for Mastering Traditional Forms*
Finch, Annie, and Kathrine Varnes. *An Exaltation of Forms: Contemporary Poets Celebrate the Diversity of Their Art*
Fry, Stephen. *The Ode Less-Travelled*
Hollander, John. *Rhyme's Reason*
Oliver, Mary. *Rules for the Dance: A Handbook for Writing and Reading Metrical Verse*
Pinsky, Robert. *The Sounds of Poetry; a Brief Guide*
Shapiro, Karl, and Robert Beum. *A Prosody Handbook*
Turco, Lewis. *The New Book of Forms*
Williams, Miller. *Patterns of Poetry*

Meter and Form (The Metrical Palette)

Finch, Annie. "Metrical Subversions: Prosody, Poetry and My Affair With the Amphibrach." *The Body of Poetry*
Hornsby, Roger. *Reading Latin Poetry*
Nims, John Frederick. "Maverick Meters." In Finch and Varnes, *An Exaltation of Forms: Contemporary Poets Celebrate the Diversity of Their Art*
Skelton, Robin. *The Shapes of Our Singing: A Comprehensive Guide to Verse Forms and Metres from Around the World*

Meter and Form (Iambic Pentameter)

Shaw, Robert B. *Blank Verse: A Guide to its History and Use*
Steele, Timothy. *All the Fun's In How You Say a Thing*

Shaped Poetry

Higgins, Dick. *Pattern Poetry: Guide to an Unknown Literature*

Rhyme

Corn, Alfred. *The Poem's Heartbeat*
Espy, Willard. *Words to Rhyme With*
Jones, John. *Pope's Couplet Art*
Jonson, Ben. "A Fit of Rhyme Against Rhyme." In *The Works of Ben Jonson*
The Oxford Rhyming Dictionary
Piper, William Bowman. *The Heroic Couplet*
Wimsatt, W. K. *The Verbal Icon: Studies in the Meaning of Poetry*

Free Verse

Beyers, Chris. *A History of Free Verse*
Dobyns, Stephen. *Best Words, Best Order*
Fenellosa, Ernest, edited by Ezra Pound. *The Chinese Written Character as a Medium for Poetry*
Hartman, Charles O. *Free Verse: An Essay on Prosody*
Justice, Donald. "The Free-Verse Line in Stevens." In *Oblivion: On Writers & Writing*
Lake, Paul. "Verse That Print Bred." In Finch, *After New Formalism*
Longenbach, James. *The Art of the Poetic Line*
Perloff, Marjorie. "After Free Verse: The New Non-linear Poetries." In Bernstein, *Close Listening*
Scully, James. *Line Break*

Repeating Forms

Ali, Agha Shahid. *Ravishing DisUnities: Real Ghazals in English*
Cummins, James. *The Perry Mason Sestinas*
Frost, Helen. *Keesha's House: A Novel in Verse*
Welford, Theresa. *The Paradelle: An Anthology*

Sonnet

Colie, Rosemary. *The Resources of Kind: Genre Theory in the Renaissance*
Doczi, Georgi. *The Power of Limits*
Hilson, Jeff, ed. *The Reality Street Book of Sonnets* (experimental sonnets)
Levin, Phillis, ed. *The Penguin Book of the Sonnet*
Oppenheimer, Paul. *The Origin of the Sonnet*

Ballad

Fowler, David. *A Literary History of the Popular Ballad*

Exploratory Forms

Dworkin, Craig. *Reading the Illegible*
Hinton, Laura, and Cynthia Hogue. *We Who Love to Be Astonished*
Hoover, Paul. *Postmodern American Poetry*
Kuszai, Joel, ed. *Poetics@*
Perelman, Bob. *The Marginalization of Poetry*
Silliman, Ron. *In the American Tree*
Sloan, Mary Margaret. *Innovative Poetry by Women*

Poetics of Formalism

Caplan, David. *Questions of Possibility: Contemporary Poetry and Poetic Form*
Cushman, Steven. *Fictions of Form in American Poetry*
Finch, Annie. *The Body of Poetry*
Finch, Annie, ed. *After New Formalism*
Finch, Annie, and Susan Schultz, eds. *Multiformalisms*
Gwynn, R. S., ed. *The New Expansive Poetry*
McDowell, Robert, ed. *Poetry After Modernism*
Walzer, Kevin. *Expansive Poetics*

Note: Because website URLs change often and can be found through search engines, this book does not include information on website resources. However, comprehensive, up-to-date links to formal poetry resources may be found at the author's website.

Appendix: Scansions

This section includes representative excerpts from poems in regular meter, and longer excerpts from poems with more irregular meters. There are also links to on-line scansion resources at the author's website, www.anniefinch.com. If you get really stuck, you may email the author with scansion questions through the website's contact page.

Chapter 11: Accent

"Jeans," Roseanne Roseannadanna (Gilda Radner)

′   ′   ′   ′

Jeans jeans the magical pants   (seven syllables)

the more they itch the more you dance   (eight syllables)

the more you dance the more people watch   (nine syllables)

to see how you scratch that itch in your crotch.   (ten syllables)

"The Seafarer" (ninth century)

maeg ic be me sylfum   soðgied wrecan

siþas secgan   hu ic geswincdagum

earfoðwile   oft þrowade

bitre breostceare   gebidan hæbbe

gecunnad in ceole   cearselda fela

From "The Seafarer" (A.D. 950) (trans. Annie Finch)

I keep the track   of a song true of me,

to tell of trials,   struggling times,

hard days,   how I endured.

I have carried   bitter cares,

had on ships   a house of cares;

From "Respiration," Mos Def

This ain't no time where the usual is suitable

Tonight alive, let's describe the inscrutable

The indisputable, we New York the narcotic

Strength in metal and fiber optics

where mercenaries is paid to trade hot stock tips

for profits, thirsty criminals take pockets

"The Moose," Elizabeth Bishop
For Grace Bulmer Bowers

From narrow provinces

of fish and bread and tea,

home of the long tides

where the bay leaves the sea

twice a day and takes

the herrings long rides,

where if the river

enters or retreats

in a wall of brown foam

depends on if it meets

the bay coming in,

the bay not at home . . .

"Famine," Landis Everson

In the middle of the night at least twenty deer

Came out upon my pillow to graze,

Gazing down at me with sad, round eyes,

ˊ   ˊ   ˊ   ˊ
Their pointed hooves quilting my pillow.

ˊ   ˊ   ˊ   ˊ
And I thrashed gently in sleeplessness,

ˊ   ˊ   ˊ   ˊ
Moving not to disturb them, wondering

ˊ   ˊ   ˊ   ˊ
At the famine this year that forces so many

ˊ   ˊ   ˊ   ˊ
To roam to poor, unfamiliar pastures.

ˊ   ˊ   ˊ   ˊ
The moon through the window throws cold light

ˊ   ˊ   ˊ   ˊ
Upon their curved backs, making a forest

ˊ   ˊ   ˊ   ˊ
Of crossed antler shadows on sheets

ˊ   ˊ   ˊ   ˊ
That until now have been flawless and starved.

From "The Girlfriends," Elizabeth Woody

ˊ   ＼ ˊ   ˊ   ˊ
Filled with old lovers, in the clutch of the chair,

ˊ   ˊ   ˊ   ˊ
you are a bloom of uncombed hair.

Scanning Exercises

From "Easter 1916," W. B. Yeats (1919)

ˊ   ˊ   ˊ
Hearts with one purpose alone

ˊ   ˊ   ˊ
Through summer and winter seem

ˊ   ˊ   ˊ
Enchanted to a stone

＇　　　＇　　＇
To trouble the living stream.

＇　　　＇　　　　＇
The horse that comes from the road,

＇　　　＇　　＇
The rider, the birds that range

＇　　＇　　　＇
From cloud to tumbling cloud,

＇　　＇　　　＇
Minute by minute they change;

＇　　＇　　　　＇
A shadow of cloud on the stream

＇　　＇　　＇
Changes minute by minute;

＇　　﹨　＇　　　＇
A horse-hoof slides on the brim,

＇　　＇　＇
And a horse plashes within it;

＇　　　＇　　＇
The long-legged moor-hens dive,

＇　　＇　　﹨　＇
And hens to moor-cocks call;

＇　　＇　　＇
Minute by minute they live:

＇　　　＇　　＇
The stone's in the midst of all.

"From a Railway Carriage," Robert Louis Stevenson (1913)

＇　　　＇　＇　　　＇
Faster than fairies, faster than witches,

＇　　　＇　＇　　　＇
Bridges and houses, hedges and ditches;

＇　　＇　　＇　　＇
And charging along like troops in a battle

＇　　　　＇　　　＇　　＇
All through the meadows the horses and cattle:

All of the sights of the hill and the plain

Fly as thick as driving rain;

And ever again, in the wink of an eye,

Painted stations whistle by.

Here is a child who clambers and scrambles,

All by himself and gathering brambles;

Here is a tramp who stands and gazes;

And here is the green for stringing the daisies!

Here is a cart runaway in the road

Lumping along with man and load;

And here is a mill, and there is a river:

Each a glimpse and gone forever!

If wishes were horses, beggars would ride.

If turnips were watches, I would wear one by my side.

And if "ifs" and "ands" were pots and pans,

There'd be no work for tinkers!

Chapter 12: Meter

From "Sir Gawain and the Green Knight," The Gawain Poet
fourteenth century)

4-beat accentual meter

From Þe lorde ful lowde with lote and laȝter myry,

When he seȝe Sir Gawayn, with solace he spekez;

Þe goude ladyez were geten, and gedered þe meyny,

He schewez hem þe scheldez, and schapes hem þe tale

From "Sir Gawain and the Green Knight" (trans. Marie Borroff)

4-beat accentual meter

The lord laughed aloud, with many a light word.

When he greeted Sir Gawain—with good cheer he speaks.

They fetch the fair dames and the folk of the house;

He brings forth the brawn, and begins the tale

Of the great length and girth, the grim rage as well,

Of the battle of the boar they beset in the wood.

From "The Wife of Bath's Tale," Geoffrey Chaucer (ca. 1390)

iambic pentameter

˘   ′ | ˘   ′ | ˘ ′ | ˘   ′ | ˘ ′ | (˘)
My fifthe housbonde, God his soule blesse,

˘   ′ | ˘ ′ | ˘ ′ | ˘   ′| ˘ ′| (˘)
Which that I took for love and no richesse,

˘   ′ | ˘   ′ | ˘ ′ | ˘   ′|˘ ′
He somtyme was a clerk of Oxenford,

˘ ′ | ˘   ′ | ˘   ′ | ˘ ′ | ˘ ′
And hadde left scole, and wente at hom to bord

˘   ′ | ˘ ′ | ′ ˘ | ˘ ′|˘ ′
With my gossib, dwellynge in oure toun,

From "The Wife of Bath's Tale" (trans. Sinan Kökbugur)

Iambic pentameter

˘   ′ | ˘ ′ | ˘   ′ | ˘ ′| ˘ ′
My fifth husband, may God his spirit bless!

˘ ′| ˘   ′| ˘ ′ | ˘   ′ | ′   ˘
Whom I took all for love, and not riches,

˘   ′ | ˘   ′ | ˘ ′| ˘ ′| ′ ˘
Had been sometime a student at Oxford,

˘ ′ | ˘   ′ | ˘ ′ | ˘   ′ | ˘ ′
And had left school and had come home to board

˘ ′ | ˘   ′ | ˘   ′ | ˘ ′| ˘   ′
With my best gossip, dwelling in our town,

′   ′ | ˘ ′ | ˘   ′ | ˘ ′|˘ ′
God save her soul! Her name was Alison.

˘   ′ | ˘   ′ | ˘ ′ | ˘   ′|˘ ′
She knew my heart and all my privity

′ ˘ | ˘ ′ | ˘ ′|˘ ′ | ′ | ′
Better than did our parish priest, s'help me!

From *Hiawatha,* Henry Wadsworth Longfellow (1855)

Trochaic tetrameter

ˊ ˘| ˊ ˘ | ˊ ˘ | ˊ ˘
Ye who love the haunts of Nature,

ˊ ˘ | ˊ ˘ | ˊ ˘| ˊ ˘
Love the sunshine of the meadow,

ˊ ˘ | ˊ ˘ | ˊ ˘| ˊ ˘
Love the shadow of the forest,

ˊ ˘ | ˊ ˘| ˊ ˘ | ˊ   ˘
Love the wind among the branches,

ˊ ˘| ˊ ˊ ˘| ˘ ˘ | ˊ   ˘
And the rain-shower and the snow-storm,

ˊ ˘ | ˊ ˘ |˘ ˊ | ˊ ˘
And the rushing of great rivers

ˊ   ˘ | ˊ ˘| ˊ ˘ | ˊ   ˘
Through their palisades of pine-trees,

ˊ ˘ | ˊ ˘| ˊ ˘ | ˊ   ˘
And the thunder in the mountains

. . .

From "To My Dearest and Loving Husband," Anne Bradstreet (1678)

˘ ˊ|˘ ˊ | ˘   ˊ | ˘ ˊ | ˘ ˊ
If ever two were one, then surely we.

˘ ˊ| ˘ ˊ | ˘ ˊ | ˘ ˊ | ˘   ˊ
If ever man were loved by wife, then thee;

˘ ˊ| ˘ ˊ | ˘   ˊ|˘ ˊ|˘ ˊ
If ever wife was happy in a man,

˘ ˊ | ˘ ˊ| ˘ ˊ | ˘ ˊ|˘ ˊ
Compare with me ye women if you can.

˘ ˊ |˘ ˊ | ˘   ˊ | ˘ ˊ |˘ ˊ
I prize thy love more than whole mines of gold . . .

˘   ′ | ˘ ˘ ′ | ˘   ′ |˘ ′ | ˘ ′
The heavens reward thee manifold, I pray.

˘   ′ | ˘ ′ | ˘ ′ | ˘   ′| ˘ ′ | ˘
Then while we live, in love let's so persever,

˘   ′ | ˘ ′ | ˘   ′ | ˘   ′ | ˘   ′|˘
That when we live no more we may live ever.

From "The Night Before Christmas," Henry Livingston Jr. (ca. 1822)

˘ ˘ ′ | ˘ ˘   ′ | ˘ ˘ ′ | ˘   ˘   ′
Twas the night before Christmas, and all through the house,

˘ ˘ ′| ˘   ˘   ′|˘   ˘ ′|˘ ˘ ′
not a creature was stirring, not even a mouse.

˘   ′ |˘   ˘   ′ |˘ ˘ ′ |˘   ˘   ′
The stockings were hung by the chimney with care,

˘ ′ |˘ ˘ ′ |˘ ˘ ′ | ′ ˘   ′
in hopes that St. Nicholas soon would be there.

˘   ′|˘   ˘   ′ |˘ ˘   ′ |˘   ˘ ′
The children were nestled all snug in their beds,

˘   ′|˘ ˘   ′|˘ ′   ′ |˘ ˘   ′
while visions of sugarplums danced in their heads,

˘   ˘ ′ |˘ ˘   ′ |˘   ˘ ′|˘ ˘ ′
and mamma in her 'kerchief, and I in my cap,

˘ ′ |˘ ˘   ′ |˘ ˘ ′ | ′ ˘   ′
had just settled down for a long winter's nap,

˘   ′ |˘ ˘ ′ |˘ ˘ ′ | ′   ˘ ′|˘
when out on the lawn there arose such a clatter . . .

From *Evangeline, Henry Wadsworth Longfellow (1850)*

′ ˘ ˘ | ′ ˘   ˘ |′ ˘   ˘ | ′   ˘ ˘ | ′   ˘   ˘ | ′ ˘
This is the forest primeval. The murmuring pines and the hemlocks,

′ ˘   ˘ | ′   ˘ ˘|′ ˘ | ′   ˘ ˘ ˘|′   ˘ ˘ | ′˘
Bearded with moss, and in garments green, indistinct in the twilight,

′   ˘ | ′˘ ˘|′   ˘ | ′ ˘|′ ˘   ˘| ′˘
Stand like Druids of eld, with voices sad and prophetic,

＇　˘　|　＇　˘　|　＇　　˘　|　＇　　˘　|　＇　˘　˘　|　＇　˘
Stand like harpers hoar, with beards that rest on their bosoms.

＇　　˘　˘|　＇˘|　＇　˘　　˘　|　＇　　＼　|　＇　˘　˘　|　＇　˘
Loud from its rocky caverns, the deep-voiced neighboring ocean

＇　　˘　˘|　＇　˘　　˘|　＇　˘　˘　|　＇　˘　　˘　|　＇　˘　˘|　＇　˘
Speaks, and in accents disconsolate answers the wail of the forest.

＇　˘　˘　|　＇　˘　˘|　＇　˘　˘|　＇　　˘　˘　|　＇　　˘　˘|　＇　˘
This is the forest primeval; but where are the hearts that beneath it

＇　　˘　˘　|　＇　　˘　　˘|　＇　˘　˘　|　＇　˘　˘　|　＇　˘　˘|
Leaped like the roe, when he hears in the woodland the voice of the

　　＇　˘
huntsman?

＇　˘　˘　|　＇　　＼　|　＇　˘　˘|　＇　˘　˘|＇˘˘|　＇　˘
Where is the thatch-roofed village, the home of Acadian farmers?

＇　˘　|　＇　＼　˘|　＇　˘　|　＇　˘　˘|　＇　˘　˘　|　＇　　＼
Men whose lives glided on like rivers that water the woodlands,

"Hound Pastoral," Lisa Jarnot

˘　　˘　＇　|˘　˘　＇
Of the hay in the barn

˘　　˘　　＇　　|˘　˘　＇
and the hound in the field

˘　˘　＇　|˘　˘　＇　|˘　˘
of the bay in the sound, of the

(˘˘)　＇　|　˘　˘　＇　|˘　˘　＇
sound of the hound in the field

From "Parable," Allison Joseph

＇　˘|　＇　˘|　＇　˘|　＇　˘
Sweep the walk and cook the dinner,

＇　˘|　＇　˘|　＇　＼　|　＇　˘
have his babies but stay thinner.

ˊ　　˘| ˊ　　˘ | ˊ　　˘　| ˊ　　˘
Raise his children, feed them knowledge,

ˊ　　˘| ˊ　　　˘ | ˊ　　˘ | ˊ˘
clean the house with spit and polish.

ˊ　　˘ | ˊ˘ | ˊ　　˘ | ˊ　˘
Wipe their noses, scrub their fingers,

ˊ　˘ | ˊ　　˘| ˊ　　˘ | ˊ　˘
do their laundry, tweeze their splinters,

ˊ　˘ | ˊ˘˘ | ˊ　˘ | ˊ　˘
buy the groceries, sew on patches,

ˊ　　˘ | ˊ　　ˋ | ˊ　˘| ˊ　˘
while your hair falls out in thatches.

"Nineveh Fallen," Rachel Loden
Kuyunjik, palace mound

ˊ˘˘ | ˊ˘　ˋ
Nineveh fallen. My

ˊ　˘　˘| ˊ˘˘
Ghostly battalion

ˊ˘　ˋ | ˊ˘ˋ
Silver-bell ankle rings

ˊ˘˘| ˊ˘˘
Tatterdemalion

ˊ˘˘ | ˊ˘˘ | ˊ (˘˘)
Babylon Cadillac. Black

ˊ˘ | ˊ˘˘
Candle guttering . . .

Chapter 13: The Many Voices of Iambic Meter

"Approaching a Significant Birthday, He Peruses
The Norton Anthology of Poetry," R. S. Gwynn

˘ ´| ˘ ´ | ˘ ´ | ˘ ´ | ˘ ´
All human things are subject to decay.

´ ˘ | ˘ ´| ˘ ´ | ˘ ´ | ˘ ´
Beauty is momentary in the mind.

˘ ´ | ˘ ´ | ˘ ´ | ˘ ´ | ˘ ´
The curfew tolls the knell of parting day.

˘ ´ | ˘ ´ | ˘ ´ | ˘ ´ | ˘ ´
If Winter comes, can Spring be far behind?

˘ ´ | ˘ ´ ´| ˘ ´ | ˘ ´ | ˘ ´
Forlorn! the very word is like a bell . . .

"Ulysses," Alfred Lord Tennyson (1842)

˘ ´|˘ ´ | ˘ ´ ‖ ˋ | ˘ ´ |˘ ´
It little profits that an idle king,

˘ ´ | ´ ´ ‖ ˘ ´ | ˘ ´ | ˘ ´
By this still hearth, among these barren crags,

´ ˘ | ˘ ´|˘ ´ ‖˘ ´ | ˘ ´
Match'd with an aged wife, I mete and dole

˘ ´| ˘ ´ ‖´ ˘|˘ ´ | ˘ ´
Unequal laws unto a savage race,

˘ ´ | ˘ ´ | ˘ ´ ‖˘ ´ | ´ ´
That hoard, and sleep, and feed, and know not me.

˘ ´ | ˘ ´ | ˘ ´|˘ ‖´|˘ ´
I cannot rest from travel; I will drink

´ ˘ | ˘ ´ ‖ ˋ ´ |˘ ´ | ˘ ´
Life to the lees. All times I have enjoy'd

´ ˘ | ˘ ´| ˘ ´ | ˘ ´‖´ | ˘ ´
Greatly, have suffer'd greatly, both with those

˘ ´ | ˋ ‖ ˘ |˘ ´ ‖˘ ´ | ˘ ´
That loved me, and alone; on shore, and when

˘ ´ | ˘ ´ ‖ ˘ ´|˘ ´|˘ ´
Thro' scudding drifts the rainy Hyades

´ ˘ | ´   ´ ‖˘ ´ | ˘ ´ | ˘ ´
Vext the dim sea. I am become a name;

˘   ´| ˘   ´ | ˘ ‖ ´ | ˘ ´ | ˘   ´
For always roaming with a hungry heart

´   ˘ |˘ ´ | ˘   ´   ‖   ´ ˘ | ˘   ´
Much have I seen and known,—cities of men

˘   ´ | ˘ ‖ ´ | ˘   ‖ ´ | ˘ ‖ ´ | ˘ ´
And manners, climates, councils, governments,

˘ ´ | ˘   ´ ‖ ˘   ´ | ˘   ˘ | ´   ´
Myself not least, but honor'd of them all,—

˘   ´ ‖ ˘ ´ | ˘   ´ |˘ ´ | ˘   ´
And drunk delight of battle with my peers,

´   ˘| ˘   ´ |˘   ´ ‖ ˘ ´ | ˘   ´
Far on the ringing plains of windy Troy.

˘ ´ | ˘ ´ ‖˘ ´ | ˘ ´| ´   ´
I am a part of all that I have met;

˘ ´ | ˘ ´ |˘ ˘ ‖´ | ˘   ´ | ´   ´
Yet all experience is an arch wherethro'

´   ˘ | ˘ ´ | ˘   ´ ‖ ˘   ´ | ˘   ´
Gleams that untravell'd world whose margin fades

˘ ´|˘ ´ | ˘   ´ |˘‖ ´ | ˘   ´
For ever and for ever when I move.

˘   ´ | ˘ ´| ˘ ´   ‖ ˘ ´ | ˘ ´
How dull it is to pause, to make an end,

˘ ´ | ˘ ´ | ˘ ‖ ´ | ˘ ´   ´ | ˘ ´
To rust unburnish'd, not to shine in use!

From "Breaking Old Grounds," by Charles Martin

˘ ´ |˘ ´ | ˘ ´ | ˘ ´| ˘   ´
It really seems to want to be our friend,

˘ ´| ˘   ˋ |˘   ´ | ˘   ´ | ˘ ´
Returning, is it, out of sympathy

˘   ´ | ˘ ´ | ˘   ´ |˘˘   ´ | ˘   ´
Or just to see how everything will end?

´   ˘ | ˘ ´ |˘   ´ | ˘   ´ | ˘ ´
Waiting, in either case, for one like me

˘   ˘ ´ | ˘   ´| ˘ ´|˘ ´ | ˘   ´
To show up some morning at the backyard fence.

"I Shall Go Back," Edna St. Vincent Millay (1923)

˘ ´ | ˘ ´ | ˘ ´ | ˘ ˘ | ´ ´
I shall go back again to the bleak shore,

˘ ´ | ˘ ´| ˘ ´ | ˘ ´| ˘ ´
And build a little shanty on the sand

˘ ´ |˘ ´ | ˘ ˘ | ˘ ´ | ˘ ´
In such a way that the extremest band

˘ ´ | ˘ ´| ´ ´| ˘ ´ | ˘ ´
Of brittle seaweed will escape my door

´ ˘ |˘ ´ | ˘ ´ | ˘ ´ |˘ ´
But by a yard or two. And nevermore

´ ˘| ˘ ´ | ˘ ´ | ´ ˘ | ˘ ´
Shall I return to take you by the hand.

˘ ´ | ˘ ´ |˘ ´ |˘ ´| ˘ ´
I shall be gone to what I understand,

˘ ´| ˘ ˘ ´ |˘ ´|˘ ´ | ˘ ´
And happier than I ever was before.

˘ ´ | ˘ ´ | ˘ ´|˘ ´| ´ ´
The love that stood a moment in your eyes,

˘ ´ | ˘ ´ |˘ ´| ˘ ´ | ˘ ´
The words that lay a moment on your tongue,

˘ ´ | ˘ ´ | ˘ ´|˘ ´| ˘ ´
Are one with all that in a moment dies,

˘ ´|˘ ´| ˘ ´ | ˘ ´|˘ ´
A little undersaid and oversung.

˘ ´| ` ´ | ˘ ´|˘ ´ | ˘ ´
But I shall find the sullen rocks and skies

˘ ´ | ˘ ´ | ˘ ´ | ˘ ´|˘ ´
Unchang'd from what they were when I was young.

"The Illiterate," William Meredith (1958)

´ ˘ | ` ´ | ˘ ´|˘ ´ |˘ ´
Touching your goodness, I am like a man

˘ ´ |˘ ´|˘ ´|˘ ´|˘ ´
Who turns a letter over in his hand.

˘ ´ | ` ´ | ˘ ´|˘ ´| ˘ ´
And you might think this was because the hand

˘　　′|˘　′|˘　′　|　′　　˘|˘　　′
Was unfamiliar but, truth is, the man

˘　　′|˘　　′|˘　′|˘　　˘　　′|˘′
Has never had a letter from anyone;

˘　　′　|˘　˘　′　|˘　′　|˘　　′|˘　　′
And now he is both afraid of what it means

˘　˘　′　|˘　′　|˘　′|˘　′|˘　　′
And ashamed because he has no other means

˘　′　|˘　　′|˘　′　|˘　˘　′|˘　　′
To find out what it says than to ask someone.

˘　′|˘　　′　|˘　　′|˘　′　|˘　′
His uncle could have left the farm to him,

˘　˘　′|˘　　′|˘　′|˘　′|˘　　′
Or his parents died before he sent them word,

˘　˘　′　|＼　′　|˘　′|˘　′|˘　′
Or the dark girl changed and want him for beloved.

˘　′　|˘　′|˘　′　|˘　′|˘　′　(')
Afraid and letter-proud, he keeps it with him.

＼　′　|＼　′|˘　′|˘　′|˘　′
What would you call his feeling for the words

˘　′　|˘　′|˘　′|˘　　˘　|˘　′
That keep him rich and orphaned and beloved?

Trochees as Variations

From "Among School Children," W. B. Yeats (1928)

′　˘　|˘　′|˘　′　|˘　′|˘　　′
Labour is blossoming or dancing where

˘　′|˘　′|＼　′　|′　˘　′|˘　′
The body is not bruised to pleasure soul,

˘　′|˘　′|′　˘|˘　′　|˘　′
Nor beauty born out of its own despair.

From "I Wandered Lonely as a Cloud," William Wordsworth (1804)

˘ ´ | ˘   ´ | ˘ ´ | ˘   ´
I wandered lonely as a cloud

  ˘   ´ | ˘ ´ | ˘ ´ | ˘   ´
That floats on high o'er vales and hills,

    ˘   ´ | ˘ ´ | ˘ ´ | ˘   ´
When all at once I saw a cloud,

˘   ´ | ˘ ´ | ˘   ´ | ˘ ´
A host of golden daffodils,

  ˘ ´ | ˘ ´ | ˘ ´ | ˘   ´
Beside the lake, beneath the trees,

  ´   ˘ ˘ | ˘   ´ | ˘ ˘| ˘   ´
Fluttering and dancing in the breeze.

Spondees and Pyrrhics as Variations

  ´   ´ | ´   ´ | ˘ ˘|˘ ´ | ´   ´
Do not go gentle into that good night,

  ´   ´ |˘ ´ | ˘ ´|˘ ˘ | ˘   ´
Rage, rage against the dying of the light.

  ´   ˘|˘ ´ | ´ ´   ˘ |˘ ´ | ˘   ´
How many dawns, chill from his rippling rest

˘   ´ |´   ´ | ˘ ´ | ˘ ´|˘ ´
The seagull's wings shall dip and pivot him,

  ´   ˘ | ´   ´ | ˘ ´ |˘   ´ |˘ ´
Shedding white rings of tumult, building high

  ´ ˘ | ˘   ´ | ´   ´ |˘ ´|˘ ´
Over the chained bay waters Liberty—

˘ ´ | ˘   ´|˘ ´ | ˘   ˘ | ´   ´
I summon up remembrance of things past

  ˘   ´ | ˘   ´ |˘   ´ |˘´ | ´ ´
And beauty making beautiful old rhyme

˘   ´ | ´ ´|˘ ˘ |˘ ´ | ´   ´
If this be error and upon me proved

˘   ´|˘ ´ | ´   ´ | ˘   ´|˘ ´
That I in your sweet thought would be forgot

From "Some Girls," Suzanne Doyle
for Andrea Vargas

˘ ′ |˘ ′|˘   ˘ | ′   ′ |˘ ′
The risk is moral death each time we act,

˘ ′|˘   ′ |˘   ′|˘   ′|˘   ′
And every act is whittled by the blade

˘ ′ |˘ ˘| ′   ′   ′ |˘   ′|˘ ′
Of history, pared down to brutal fact . . .

′   ˘|˘ ′|˘ ˘   ′ |˘   ′ |˘ ′ ′
We are a different kind of tough; we hawk

˘ ′|˘ ′ |˘ ˘ ′ | ′   ′ |˘ ′ |˘ ′
Our epic violence in bleak bars, in bed, in art.

˘   ′ |˘ ˘ |′   ′   ′ |˘   ′ |˘ ′
We crept in the tall grass and slept till noon

˘ ˘ | ′   ′ |˘ ′ ′ |˘   ′ |˘   ′
With his damned hoobla-hoobla-hoobla-how

′   ˘|˘ ′ | ′   ′ |˘ ′ |˘ ′
There is a wide, wide wonder in it all

′ ˘ |˘   ′|˘ ˘ | ′   ′ | ′   ′
Slowly the poison the whole blood stream fills

From "Essay on Criticism," Alexander Pope (1711)

˘   ′ | ′   ′ |˘ ′ |˘   ′ |˘   ′
But when loud surges lash the sounding shore,

˘   ′ | ′   ′ | ′ ˘ ′ |˘   ′|˘   ′
The hoarse, rough verse should like the torrent roar;

˘   ′|˘ ′ | ′   ′ | ′ ′   ′ |˘   ′
When Ajax strives some rock's vast weight to throw,

˘ ′ | ′   ′|˘   ˘ |˘   ′ | ′   ′
The line too labors, and the words move slow;

˘ ′ | ˘   ′ |˘   ′|˘|˘   ′ |˘   ′
Not so, when swift Camilla scours the plain,

˘   ′ |˘   ˘ ′ |˘   ′ |˘   ′ |˘ ′ |˘   ′
Flies o'er the unbending corn, and skims along the main.

Headless and Extra-syllable Lines

From "Those Winter Sundays, " Robert Hayden

(˘) ′ | ˘   ′ | ˘   ′|˘   ′ | ˘   ′ (˘)
Sundays too my father got up early

From "Prologue" to The Canterbury Tales, Geoffrey Chaucer

(˘)   ′ | ˘   ′|˘   ′ | ˘   ′|˘   ′(˘)
When that Aprille with his showres soote

From *Hamlet,* William Shakespeare (1602)

˘   ′ |˘   ′ |˘   ′ || ˋ ˘|˘   ′   (˘)
To be, or not to be: that is the question:

′   ˘ | ˘   ′ |˘   ˘|˘   ′ | ˘ ′ (˘)
Whether 'tis nobler in the mind to suffer

˘   ′ | ˘   ′| ˘   ˘ | ˋ ′|˘   ′ |(˘)
The slings and arrows of outrageous fortune,

˘ ˘ | ′   ′ | ˘ ′ |˘ ′|˘   ′   (˘)
Or to take arms against a sea of troubles,

˘   ′ | ˘ ′|˘   ′ | ˋ ||˘   ′ |˘   ′
And by opposing end them? To die: to sleep;

˘   ′ ||˘   ˘|˘   ′ | ˘   ′|˘   ′
No more; and by a sleep to say we end

˘   ′ | ˋ   ˘ |˘   ′ |˘   ′|˘ ˘   ′
The heart-ache and the thousand natural shocks

˘   ′ |˘   ′ |˘ ||′|˘   ′ | ˘   ′|(˘)
That flesh is heir to, 'tis a consummation

˘ ′ |˘ ˘|ˋ   ′ | ˘ ′ | ˘ ′
Devoutly to be wish'd. To die, to sleep;

˘   ′ | ˘   ′ | ˘   ′ | ˘ ′ | ˘ ′
To sleep: perchance to dream: ay, there's the rub;

˘ ˘ | ˋ   ′ | ˘ ′ | ˘   ′ | ˋ   ′
For in that sleep of death what dreams may come

˘   ′ | ˘   ′ |˘   ′ | ˘   ′ |˘ ′
When we have shuffled off this mortal coil,

˰   ˊ |˯   ˊ | ˰   ˊ |˯   ˊ
Must give us pause: there's the respect

˯   ˊ | ˯ ˌ|˯ ˯|˯ ˌ| ˊ   ˊ
That makes calamity of so long life;

˯   ˊ | ˯   ˊ | ˯   ˊ | ˯   ˊ |˯ ˊ
For who would bear the whips and scorns of time,

˯ ˯ ˊ |˯   ˊ | ˯   ˊ | ˰   ˊ |˯ ˊ
The oppressor's wrong, the proud man's contumely,

˯   ˊ |˯   ˯|˰   ˊ |˯   ˊ |˯ ˯
The pangs of despised love, the law's delay,

˯ ˊ |˯ ˊ |˯ ˊ|˯   ˊ |˯   ˊ
The insolence of office and the spurns

˯   ˊ|˯   ˊ|˯ ˯|˯ ˯   ˊ |˯ ˊ
That patient merit of the unworthy takes,

˯   ˊ |˯ ˊ | ˰   ˊ |˯ ˊ|˯ ˊ
When he himself might his quietus make

˯ ˯ | ˊ   ˊ |˯   ˊ | ˯   ˊ |˯ ˊ
With a bare bodkin? who would fardels bear,

˯   ˊ | ˯   ˊ |ˊ ˯ |˯ ˌ|˯ ˊ
To grunt and sweat under a weary life,

˯   ˊ |˯   ˊ |˯ ˊ | ˯ ˌ|˯ ˊ
But that the dread of something after death,

˯   ˊ | ˯ ˌ|˯   ˊ |˯ ˊ | ˰   ˊ
The undiscover'd country from whose bourn

˯   ˊ|˯ ˯| ˯ ˊ   ‖ ˊ ˯ |˯ ˊ
No traveller returns, puzzles the will

˯   ˊ |˯ ˌ|˯   ˊ | ˰   ˊ|˯ ˊ
And makes us rather bear those ills we have

˯ ˊ|˯ ˌ|˯   ˊ |˰   ˊ |˯ ˊ
Than fly to others that we know not of?

˯   ˊ | ˯   ˊ |ˊ   ˊ |˯ ˯|˯ ˊ
Thus conscience does make cowards of us all;

˯   ˊ |˯ ˌ|˯   ˊ |˯   ˊ |˯ ˊ (˯)
And thus the native hue of resolution

˯   ˊ |˯   ˊ |˯   ˯ |ˊ   ˊ |˯ ˊ
Is sicklied o'er with the pale cast of thought,

Sonnet 30, Edna St. Vincent Millay (1931)

´ ˘| ˘ ´ |˘ ˘|˘   ´ |˘   ´
Love is not all: it is not meat nor drink

˘   ´ |˘   ´ |˘   ´ |˘ ´ | ˘ ´
Nor slumber nor a roof against the rain;

˘   ´ |˘   ´ |˘   ´ |˘   ´ | ˘ ´
Nor yet a floating spar to men that sink

˘   ´ | ˘ ´ | ˘   ´ |˘ ´ |˘ ´
And rise and sink and rise and sink again;

´   ´ | ˘ ´ |˘   ´ |˘   ´ |˘   ´
Love can not fill the thickened lung with breath,

˘   ´ | ˘ ´ | ˘ ´|˘   ´|˘   ´
Nor clean the blood, nor set the fractured bone;

˘   ´ |˘ ˘ ´ |˘ ´|˘   ´ | ˘ ´
Yet many a man is making friends with death

˘ ˘ ´|˘ ´ | ˘ ´ |˘ ´ |˘ ´
Even as I speak, for lack of love alone.

˘ ´ | ˘ ´ | ˘ ´|˘ ´|˘ ˘   ´
It well may be that in a difficult hour,

´   ´ |˘ ´ |˘   ´ | ˘ ˘|˘ ´
Pinned down by pain and moaning for release,

˘ ´ | ˘ ´ | ˘ ´|˘´|˘   ´(˘)
Or nagged by want past resolution's power,

˘ ´ | ˘ ´|˘ ˘ ´ | ˘ ´ |˘ ´
I might be driven to sell your love for peace,

˘ ´ |˘ ´|˘ ˘ ´| ˘ ´ |˘ ´
Or trade the memory of this night for food.

˘ ´ | ´ ´ |˘ ´| ˘ ´ |˘ ´
It well may be. I do not think I would.

"Chosen," Marilyn Nelson

˘ ´ | ´ ˘ |˘ ´ | ˘ ´ |˘ ´
Diverne wanted to die, that August night.

˘ ´ | ´ ´|˘ ´ |˘ ´ |˘ ´
His face hung over hers, a sweating moon.

˘   ´ |˘ ´ |˘ ´ | ´ ˘|˘ ´
She wished so hard, she killed part of her heart.

˘   ′ | ˘   ′ | ˘   ′ | ˘ ′| ˘   ′
If she had died, her one begotten son,

˘   ′ | ˘   ′ | ˘   ′| ˘   ′ | ˋ   ′
her life's one light, would never have been born.

′   ′ | ˘   ′ | ˘   ′ | ˘ ′| ˘   ′
Pomp Atwood might have been another man:

′   ˘ |˘ ′| ˘ ′ | ˘ ′ | ˘ ′
born with a single race, another name.

˘ ′ | ˘   ′ | ˘   ′ | ˘ ′ | ˘   ′
Diverne might not have known the starburst joy

˘ ′ | ˘   ′ | ˘ ˋ | ˘ ′ | ˘ ′
her son would give her. And the man who came

′ ˘ |˘ ′ | ˋ   ′ ′ |˘ ′ |˘ ′
out of a twelve-room house and ran to her

′   ′ |˘ ′| ′ ′ ′ | ˘ ′ |˘ ′
close shack across three yards that night, to leap

′ ˘ |˘ ′ | ˋ   ′ |˘ ′ | ˘ ′
onto her cornshuck pallet. Pomp was their

′ ˘ | ˘ ′| ˘ ˋ | ˘ ′|˘ ′
share of the future. And it wasn't rape.

˘   ′ |˘ ˋ | ′ ′ |˘ ′ | ˘ ′
In spite of her raw terror. And his whip.

From "Birches," Robert Frost (1915)

˘ ′| ˋ ′ |˘ ′ |˘ ′ | ˘ ′
When I see birches bend to left and right

˘   ′ |˘ ′ |˘   ′ |˘ ′ |˘ ′
Across the lines of straighter darker trees,

˘ ′ |˘ ′ | ˋ   ′ |˘   ′ |˘ ′
I like to think some boy's been swinging them.

˘   ′ |˘ ′ |˘ ′ | ˘ ′ | ˘ ′
But swinging doesn't bend them down to stay

˘ ′ | ′   ′| ′ ˘ |˘   ′ | ˘ ′ | (˘)
As ice-storms do. Often you must have seen them

＇　˘ ｜ ˘　＇ ｜˘　＇｜˘　＇ ｜˘　＇ (˘)
Loaded with ice a sunny winter morning

＇˘ ｜˘ ＇　｜ ˘　＇　｜˘ ＇｜ ˘　＇
After a rain. They click upon themselves

˘　˘ ｜　＇　＇｜˘　＇ ｜ ＼　＇｜ ˘　＇ (˘)
As the breeze rises, and turn many-colored

˘　˘ ｜＇　＇　｜˘　＇｜˘　＇ ｜˘　＇ (˘)
As the stir cracks and crazes their enamel.

＇　˘ ｜＇　＇　｜＇　＼ ｜＇　＇｜˘　＇
Soon the sun's warmth makes them shed crystal shells

＇　˘ ˘　｜ ˘　＇｜˘ ＇｜˘　＇｜˘　＇ (＇)
Shattering and avalanching on the snow-crust—

＼　＇　｜˘　＇｜˘　＇｜˘　＇｜˘ ＇
Such heaps of broken glass to sweep away

＼　＇ ｜˘　＇｜˘　＇｜˘ ＇｜˘ ˘　＇ (˘)
You'd think the inner dome of heaven had fallen.

˘　˘　＇　｜˘ ˘　＇｜˘　＇ ｜˘＇｜˘　＇
They are dragged to the withered bracken by the load

˘　＇｜˘　＇ ｜˘ ＇　｜ ˘　＇　｜˘ ˘　＇
And they seem not to break; though once they are bowed

˘ ＇ ｜˘　＇ ｜˘　＇｜˘ ＇ ｜˘ ＇
So low for long they never right themselves:

˘　＇｜＼　＇ ｜＇　＇ ｜˘ ＇｜˘　＇
You may see their trunks arching in the woods

＼　＇｜˘ ˘　＇｜˘　＇ ＇ ｜˘ ˘　＇
Years afterwards, trailing their leaves on the ground ..

Expressive Variation and Keeping Your Balance

"Batter My Heart," John Donne (1610)

＇　˘｜˘　＇ ｜＇　＇ ｜˘　＇ ｜˘ ＇
Batter my heart, three-person'd God, for you

˘ ＇｜ ˘　＇ ｜＇　＇ ｜˘　＇ ｜˘ ＇
As yet but knock, breathe, shine, and seek to mend;

˘ ＇｜＼　＇ ｜˘　＇ ｜˘ ＇｜＼ ˘　＇
That I may rise and stand, o'erthrow me, and bend

＼　＇ ｜˘　＇ ｜＇　＇ ｜˘　＇ ｜˘ ＇
Your force to break, blow, burn, and make me new.

ˋ ˊ |ˇ ˊ|ˇ   ˊ |ˇ ˇ ˊ|ˇ   ˊ
I, like an usurp'd town to'another due,

ˊ ˇ |ˇ ˇ ˊ |ˋ   ˊ |ˇ ˊ |ˇ   ˊ
Labor to'admit you, but oh, to no end;

ˊ ˇ | ˇ   ˊ |ˋ ˇ ˇ | ˊ   ˋ |ˇ ˊ
Reason, your viceroy in me, me should defend,

ˇ ˊ| ˇ   ˊ |ˇ   ˊ | ˋ ˇ |ˇ   ˊ
But is captiv'd, and proves weak or untrue.

ˇ   ˊ |ˇ ˇ ˊ | ˋ   ˇ   ˊ |ˇ ˊ |ˇ ˊ
Yet dearly I love you, and would be lov'd fain,

ˇ   ˊ | ˇ   ˊ | ˊ ˇ|ˇ   ˊ|ˇ ˊ
But am betroth'd unto your enemy;

ˇ ˊ | ˇ   ˇ ˊ |ˇ   ˊ | ˇ   ˊ | ˇ ˊ
Divorce me, untie or break that knot again,

ˊ   ˇ |ˇ ˊ | ˇ   ˊ|ˇ   ˊ | ˇ ˊ
Take me to you, imprison me, for I,

ˇ ˊ | ˇ ˇ   ˊ |ˋ   ˊ|ˇ   ˊ |ˇ   ˊ
Except you'enthrall me, never shall be free,

ˇ   ˊ|ˇ   ˊ | ˇ ˊ |ˋ   ˊ|ˇ   ˊ
Nor ever chaste, except you ravish me.

Sonnet 116, William Shakespeare (1609)

ˊ ˇ | ˊ ˇ|ˇ   ˊ |ˇ   ˇ | ˊ   ˊ
Let me not to the marriage of true minds

ˇ ˊ |ˇ ˊ |ˇ ˇ | ˊ ˋ |ˊ ˊ
Admit impediments. Love is not love

ˇ   ˊ| ˇ   ˊ |ˇ ˊ|ˇ ˊ|ˇ   ˊ
Which alters when it alteration finds,

ˇ   ˊ | ˇ   ˋ | ˇ ˊ |ˇ ˊ|ˇ ˊ
Or bends with the remover to remove:

ˇ ˊ |ˇ ˋ |ˇ ˊ|ˇ ˊ|ˇ   ˊ
O no! it is an ever-fixed mark

ˇ   ˊ |ˇ   ˊ |ˇ   ˋ |ˇ ˊ|ˇ   ˊ (ˇ)
That looks on tempests and is never shaken;

ˇ ˇ|ˇ   ˊ |ˇ ˊ|ˇ   ˊ | ˇ ˇ   ˊ
It is the star to every wandering bark,

˘　　ʹ　　|　˘　　ʹ　　|　˘　ʹ　|　˘　　ʹ　　|　˘　ʹ　(˘)
Whose worth's unknown, although his height be taken.

ʹ　　ˎ　|　ʹ　　　ʹ　|　˘　　ʹ|˘　ʹ　|　˘　　　ʹ
Love's not Time's fool, though rosy lips and cheeks

˘　ʹ　|　˘　　ʹ　|˘　　ʹ　|˘　　ʹ　|　˘　　　ʹ
Within his bending sickle's compass come:

ʹ　　ʹ|˘　　ʹ　|　˘　˘　|　ʹ　　　ʹ　|　˘　　　ʹ
Love alters not with his brief hours and weeks,

˘　　ʹ　　|˘　ʹ　|ˎ　˘|˘　˘　|˘　　ʹ　|　˘　　ʹ
But bears it out even to the edge of doom.

˘　　ʹ|　˘　ʹ|˘　　˘　|˘　ʹ|ˎ　　ʹ
If this be error and upon me proved

ˎ　ʹ|˘　　ʹ　|　˘　ʹ|ʹ　ʹ|˘　ʹ
I never writ, nor no man ever loved.

Iambic Dimeter, Trimeter, Tetrameter, and Fourteeners

From "Open House," Theodore Roethke (1941)

˘　　ʹ|˘　ʹ　|˘　ʹ
My secrets cry aloud.

˘　ʹ　|　˘　ʹ　|　˘　ʹ
I have no need for tongue.

˘　　ʹ　|　ˎ　ʹ|˘　ʹ
My heart keeps open house,

˘　　ʹ　|˘　ʹ　|˘　ʹ
My doors are widely swung.

"I Had a Dove," John Keats

˘　ʹ|˘　ʹ　|˘　˘　　ʹ　|　ˎ　　ʹ
I had a dove and the sweet dove died;

˘　ʹ|　ʹ　　ʹ　　　ʹ　　|˘　ʹ　|˘　ʹ|(˘)
And I have thought it died of grieving:

˘　　ʹ　|　˘　˘　ʹ　|　˘　˘　ʹ　|　˘　　ʹ
O, what could it grieve for? Its feet were tied,

˘　˘　ʹ|˘　ʹ　|　˘　˘　ʹ　|　ˎ　　ʹ　|(˘)
With a silken thread of my own hand's weaving;

(˘) ´ | ` ˘ ´ | ` ´ | ˘ ˘ ´
Sweet little red feet! why should you die—

(˘) ´ | ´ ˘ ´ |˘ ´ | ´ ´
Why should you leave me, sweet bird! why?

˘ ´ |˘ ´ |˘ ˘ ´ |˘ ´
You liv'd alone in the forest-tree,

(˘) ´ | ` ˘ ´ | ˘ ˘ ´ | ` ˘ ´
Why, pretty thing! would you not live with me?

˘ ´ | ˘ ´ | ˘ ´ | ˘ ´ ´
I kiss'd you oft and gave you white peas;

(˘) ´ | ˘ ` ´ |˘ ˘ ´ |˘ ´ ´
Why not live sweetly, as in the green trees?

"My Papa's Waltz," Theodore Roethke (1942)

˘ ´| ˘ ´ | ˘ ´
The whiskey on your breath

˘ ´ | ˘ ´ | ` ´ (˘)
Could make a small boy dizzy;

˘ ´| ˘ ´ | ˘ ´
But I hung on like death:

˘ ´ |˘ ˘ | ˘ ´(˘)
Such waltzing was not easy . . .

From "Under the Rose," Christina Rossetti (1866)

˘ ´ | ˘ ´ |˘ ´
I think my mind is fixed

˘ ´ | ` ˘ | ´ ´
On one point and made up:

˘ ˘ ´ |˘ ´ |˘ ´
To accept my lot unmixed;

´ ˘| ˘ ´ | ˘ ´
Never to drug the cup . . .

"Justice," Langston Hughes (c. 1931)

˘   ´   ˘ |˘ ˘   ´ | ´   ˘
That Justice is a blind goddess

˘ ˘   ´ |˘   ´ |˘   ´ |˘   ´
Is a thing to which we black are wise:

˘   ´ |˘   ´ |´   ´ |˘ ˘   ´
Her bandage hides two festering sores

˘   ´ | ˘   ´ | ˘   ´
That once perhaps were eyes.

"Love (III)," George Herbert (1633)

´   ´ | ˋ   ´|˘   ´ |˘   ´ | ˘   ´
Love bade me welcome; yet my soul drew back,

´ ˘ |˘   ´ | ˘   ´
Guilty of dust and sin.

˘   ´ | ´   ´ |˘   ´|˘   ´ | ´   ´
But quick-eyed Love, observing me grow slack

˘   ´| ˘   ´ |˘   ´
From my first entrance in,

´   ´ |˘ ´| ˋ   ´ |˘   ´ |˘   ´
Drew nearer to me, sweetly questioning

˘ ´| ´   ˋ |˘   ´
If I lacked anything...

From "Metamorphoses," Ovid, trans. Arthur Golding (1567)

˘   ´|˘ ´| ˘   ´ | ˘   ´ |˘   ´ |˘   ´|˘   ´
Howebeit he that did pursue of both the swifter went,

˘   ´ |˘ ´|˘   ´ |˘   ´ | ´   ˘ ´|˘   ´| ˋ   ´
As furthred by the feathred wings that Cupid had him lent,

˘   ´ |˘   ´ |˘   ´|´   ˋ   ´ |˘   ´ |˘   ´|˘   ´
So that he would not let hir rest, but preased at hir heele

˘   ´ |˘   ´ |˘   ´ |´ ˘ ´ |˘   ´ |˘   ´ |˘   ´
So neere that through hir scattred haire she might his breathing feele...

˘   ´|˘ ˘   ´|˘   ´|˘   ´ |˘   ´ ´|˘   ´ |˘   ´
This piteous prayer scarsly sed: hir sinewes waxed starke,

˘   ´ |˘   ´|˘ ´ |˘   ´ |˘   ´ |˘   ´ |˘   ´
And therewithall about hir breast did grow a tender barke.

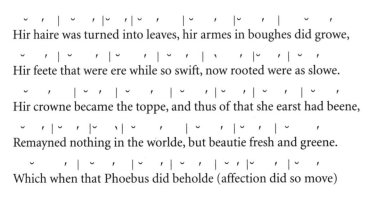

Hir haire was turned into leaves, hir armes in boughes did growe,

Hir feete that were ere while so swift, now rooted were as slowe.

Hir crowne became the toppe, and thus of that she earst had beene,

Remayned nothing in the worlde, but beautie fresh and greene.

Which when that Phoebus did beholde (affection did so move)

Note: At this time in the history of the language, "remained" was pronounced with three syllables.

Chapter 14 : The Metrical Palette

"Metrical Feet: A Lesson for a Boy" (1803)

Trochee trips from long to short.

From long to long in solemn sort,

Slow Spondee stalks, strong foot!, yet ill-able.

Ever to keep up with Dactyl's trisyllable.

Iambics march from short to long,.

With a leap and a bound the swift Anapests throng.

Trochaic Meter (/ u)

Double, double, toil and trouble,

Fire burn, and cauldron bubble . . .

Eye of newt, and toe of frog,

′ ˘ | ′ , ˘ | ′   ˘ | ′ (˘)
Wool of bat, and tongue of dog,

′ ˘ | ′   ˘ | ′   ˎ | ′ (˘)
Adder's fork, and blind-worm's sting,

′ ˘ | ′   ˘ | ′ ˘ | ′ (˘)
Lizard's leg, and howlet's wing,

′ ˘| ′   ˘ | ′ ˘ ˘ | ′ ˘
For a charm of powerful trouble,

′ ˘| ′   ˎ | ′ ˘ | ′ ˘
Like a hell-broth boil and bubble.

"Tyger ! Tyger !" William Blake (1794)

′ ˘ | ′ ˘ | ′ ˘ | ′ (˘)
Tyger! Tyger! burning bright

′ ˘ | ′ ˘ |′ ˘ | ′ (˘)
In the forests of the night,

′ ˘| ′ ˘ | ′   ˘ | ′ (˘)
What immortal hand or eye

(˘) | ′   ˘ | ′ ˘ |′   ˘ |′ (˘)
Could frame thy fearful symmetry?

′   ˎ | ′ ˘ | ′   ˘ | ′ (˘)
In what distant deeps or skies

′   ˘ | ′ ˘|ˎ ˎ | ′ (˘)
Burnt the fire of thine eyes?

′   ˘ | ′   ˎ | ′ ˘| ′ (˘)
On what wings dare he aspire?

′ ˘ | ′   ˎ | ′   ˘ |′ ˘
What the hand dare seize the fire?

From *The Song of Hiawatha*, Henry Wadsworth Longfellow (1860)

′ ˘ | ′   ˘ | ′   ˘ | ′   ˘
By the shores of Gitche Gumee,

′ ˘ | ′ ˘ | ′ ˯ | ′   ˘
By the shining Big-Sea-Water,

′   ˘ | ′   ˘ | ′   ˯ | ′   ˘
Stood the wigwam of Nokomis,

′   ˘ | ′ ˘ | ′   ′ | ′   ˘
Daughter of the Moon, Nokomis.

′   ˘ | ′   ˘ | ′   ˘ | ′ ˘
Dark behind it rose the forest,

′   ˘ | ′   ˘ | ′   ˘ | ′   ˯
Rose the black and gloomy pine-trees,

′   ˘ | ′   ˘ | ′   ˘ | ′   ˘
Rose the firs with cones upon them;

′   ˘ | ′ ˘ | ′   ˘ | ′   ˘
Bright before it beat the water.

′   ˘ | ′   ˘ | ′ ˘ | ′ ˘
Beat the clear and sunny water,

′   ˘ | ′ ˘ | ′   ˯ | ′   ˘
Beat the shining Big-Sea-Water.

From "Iron," Sarah Josepha Hale (1823)

′ ˘ | ′   ˘ | ′ ˘ | ′   ˘
...Then a voice, from out the mountains,

′ ˘ | ′   ′ | ′   ˘ | ′   (˘)
As an earthquake shook the ground,

˘   ′ | ′ ˘ | ′   ˘ | ′   ˘
And like frightened fawns the fountains,

′ ˘ | ′ ˘ | ′ ˘ | ′   (˘)
Leaping, fled before the sound;

˯   ˘ | ′ ˘ | ′   ′ | ′ ˘
And the Anak oaks bowed lowly,

′ ˘ ˘ | ′ ˘ | ′   ˘ | ′. (˘)
Quivering, aspen-like, with fear-

´   ˘ | ´   ˘ | ´   ` | ´   ˘
While the deep response came slowly,

´ ˘ | ´   ˘ | ´   ` | ´
Or it must have crushed mine ear!

From *The Anniad*, Gwendolyn Brooks (1949)

´   ˘ | ´   ˘ | ´ ˘| ´ (˘)
Think of sweet and chocolate,

´   ˘ | ´ ˘ | ´ ˘ | ´   (˘)
Left to folly or to fate,

´   ˘ | ´   ˘ | ´   ˘ |´ (˘)
Whom the higher gods forgot,

´   ˘ | ´ ˘ | ´   ˘ | ´ (˘)
Whom the lower gods berate;

´ ˘ |´   ˘ | ´   ˘ |´ (˘)
Physical and underfed

´ ˘ ˘ |´   ˘ | ´   ˘ | ´ (˘)
Fancying on the featherbed

´   ˘ | ´ ˘ | ´   ˘| ´ (˘)
What was never and is not . . .

"Lullaby," W. H. Auden (1940)

´   ˘ | ´ ˘ | ´   ˘ | ´ (˘)
Lay your sleeping head, my love,

´ ˘ | ´ ` | ´   ˘ | ´ (˘)
Human on my faithless arm;

´   ˘ |´ ˘ | ´   ˘|´ (˘)
Time and fevers burn away

´   ˘|´ ˘ ˘ | ´ ˘ | ´   (˘)
Individual beauty from

´   ˘ | ´ ˘ |´ ˘ | ´ (˘)
Thoughtful children, and the grave

´   ˘ | ´ ˘| ´   ˘|´ (˘)
Proves the child ephemeral:

(˘)|´ ˘| ´   ˏ | ´   ˘|´ (˘)
But in my arms till break of day

´ ˘ |´ ˘ | ´ ˘ |´ (˘)
Let the living creature lie,

´ ˘ |´ ˘ |´ ˘|´ (˘)
Mortal, guilty, but to me

ˏ ˘ |´ ˘ |´   ˘|(´)
The entirely beautiful.

Anapestic Meter (˘˘)

"I Would Live in Your Love," Sara Teasdale (1911)

˘ ˘   ´ |˘ ˘   ´ |˘ ˘ ´ | ˏ ˘ ´ |˘ ˘ ´
I would live in your love as the sea-grasses live in the sea,

´   ´ |˘ ˘   ´ |˘˘ ´ |˘ ˏ   ´ |˘ ´   ´
Borne up by each wave as it passes, drawn down by each wave

˘ ˘ ´
that recedes;

˘ ˘   ´ |˘ ˘ ´ |˘ ˘   ´ | ˏ ˘ ´ |˘ ˘ ´
I would empty my soul of the dreams that have gathered in me,

˘ ˘   ´ |˘   ˘   ´ |˘˘ ´ |˘ ˘   ´|˘   ˘   ´ |
I would beat with your heart as it beats, I would follow your soul

˘ ˘ ´
as it leads.

From "Paul Revere's Ride," Henry Wadsworth Longfellow (1860)

˘ ˘ ´ |˘ ´ |˘ ˘ ´ | ˏ   ´
. . . Then he climbed the tower of the Old North Church,

˘ ˘   ´ |˘ ´ | ˘ ´ |˘ ´
By the wooden stairs, with stealthy tread,

˘ ˘ ´ |˘ ´ | ˘ ´|˘ ´
To the belfry chamber overhead,

˘   ´ |˘ ˘ ´|˘   ´ | ˘ ´
And startled the pigeons from their perch

On the sombre rafters, that round him made

Masses and moving shapes of shade,—

By the trembling ladder, steep and tall,

To the highest window in the wall,

Where he paused to listen and look down

A moment on the roofs of the town

And the moonlight flowing over all.

From "A Fable for Critics," James Russell Lowell (1848)

There comes Poe, with his raven, like Barnaby Rudge,

Three-fifths of him genius and two-fifths sheer fudge,

Who talks like a book of iambs and pentameters,

In a way to make people of common-sense damn metres . . .

From "Maud," Alfred, Lord Tennyson (1855)

She is coming, my own, my sweet;

Were it ever so airy a tread,

My heart would hear her and beat . . .

˘   ′ | ˘   ′ |˘   ′ |˘   ˘   ′
Would start and tremble under her feet,

˘   ′ | ˘   ˘   ′ |˘   ˘   ′
And blossom in purple and red.

From "The Destruction of Sennacharib," Lord Byron (1815)

˘   ′ | �’   ˘   ′|˘   ˘   ′ |˘   ˘   ′
And there lay the rider distorted and pale,

˘   ˘   ′ | ˘   ˘   ′ | ˘   ˘   ′ | ˘   ˘   ′
With the dew on his brow, and the rust on his mail:

˘   ˘   ′ | ˘   ˘   ′ |˘   ˘   ′ | ˘   ˘ ′
And the tents were all silent, the banners alone,

˘   ′ |˘   ˘ ′ |˘   ˘   ′ | ˘   ˘   ′
The lances unlifted, the trumpet unblown.

From *Atalanta in Calydon,* Algernon Charles Swinburne (1865)

˘   ′|˘ ′ | ˘   ˘   ′ | ˘   ˘   ′
The ivy falls with the Bacchanal's hair

′ ˘| ˘   ′| ′   ′|˘   ˘   ′
Over her eyebrows hiding her eyes;

˘   ′ | ′   ′| ˘   ˎ | ′   ′
The wild vine slipping down leaves bare

˘   ′ | ˎ   ′ |˘ ˘ ′ |˘ ′
Her bright breast shortening into sighs;

˘   ′ | ′   ′ | ˘   ˘   ′ |˘ ˘ ′
The wild vine slips with the weight of its leaves,

˘   ˘   ′ | ˘   ′|˘ ′ |˘   ˘   ′
But the berried ivy catches and cleaves

˘   ˘   ′ | ˘   ′|˘   ˘   ′ | ˘   ′
To the limbs that glitter, the feet that scare

˘   ′ | ˘   ′|˘   ˘   ′ | ˘   ′
The wolf that follows, the fawn that flies.

From Robert Browning, "How They Brought the Good News
from Ghent to Aix" (1845)

```
˘    ′  | ˘  ˘   ′ | ˘   ˘   ′ | ˘   ˘   ′
```
I sprang to the stirrup, and Joris, and he;

```
˘  ′ | ˘        ′      ′ | ˘      ˘   ′ | ˘    ˘     ′
```
I gallop'd, Dirck gallop'd, we gallop'd all three;

```
       ˋ      ′    |   ˋ   ˘  ′   | ˘ ˘  ′ | ˋ   ˘   ′
```
"Good speed!" cried the watch, as the gate-bolts undrew;

```
      ˋ     ′ | ˘    ˘   ′ | ˘ ˘  ′ | ˘ ˘      ′
```
"Speed!" echoed the wall to us galloping through;

```
  ˘  ′  | ˋ   ˘   ′ | ˘    ˘   ′  | ˋ    ˘   ′
```
Behind shut the postern, the lights sank to rest,

```
   ˘  ′ | ˘ ˘    ′ | ˋ    ˘    ′ | ˘    ˘  ′
```
And into the midnight we gallop'd abreast.


```
   ˘  ˘   ′  | ˘  ˘    ′ | ˘  ˘   ′ | ˘    ′    ′
```
Not a word to each other; we kept the great pace

```
  ˋ   ˘    ′  | ˋ     ˘   ′   | ˘ ˘   ′ | ˘    ˘    ′
```
Neck by neck, stride by stride, never changing our place

From "The Hunting of the Snark," Lewis Carroll (1876)

```
   ˘  ˘   ′ | ˘  ˘  ′ | ˘   ˘   ′ | ˘    ˘   ′
```
And the Banker, inspired with courage so new

```
˘  ˘   ′ | ˘   ˘   ′ | ˘    ˘   ′
```
It was matter for general remark,

```
   ˋ       ′ | ˘ ˘ ′ | ˘   ˘   ′ | ˘    ˘    ′
```
Rushed madly ahead and was lost to their view

```
˘  ˘   ′ | ˘  ˘   ′ | ˘   ˘    ′
```
In his zeal to discover the snark.

"Annabel Lee," Edgar Allan Poe (1849)

```
˘  ˘    ′ | ˘  ˘    ′ | ˘˘  ′ | ˘ ′
```
It was many and many a year ago,

```
˘ ˘ ′  | ˘    ′ | ˘  ′
```
In a kingdom by the sea,

```
   ˘ ˘   ′ | ˘   ˘   ′ | ˘   ′ | ˘   ′
```
That a maiden there lived whom you may know

˘ ˘ ′ | ˘ ′ | ˘ ˘ ′
By the name of Annabel Lee;

˘ ˘ ′ |˘ ˘   ′ | ˘   ′|˘ ˘   ′
And this maiden she lived with no other thought

˘ ˘ ′ | ˘ ˘ ′ | ˘ ′
Than to love and be loved by me.

From "A Song in Time of Revolution," Algernon Charles Swinburne (1860)

˘ ′ | ˘ ˘ ′ |˘ ˘ ′ | ˘ ˘ ′ | ˘ ˘ ′ | ˘ ˘ ′
The wind has the sound of a laugh in the clamour of days and of deeds:

˘ ′ | ˘ ′ |˘ ˘   ′ | ˘ ˘   ′|˘ ′ |˘ ˘ ′
The priests are scattered like chaff, and the rulers broken like reeds.

˘ ′ | ˘ ′ | ˘   ′ | ˘ ˘ ′ |˘ ′ |˘ ˘ ′
The high-priest sick from qualms, with his raiment bloodily dashed;

˘   ′ | ˘ ′ |˘ ′ | ˘ ˘ ′|˘ ˘   ′ | ˘ ′
The thief with branded palms, and the liar with cheeks abashed.

˘ ˘ ′|˘ ˘   ′ |˘ ′ |˘ ˘ ˘ ′ | ˘ ˘
They are smitten, they tremble greatly, they are pained for their

′ | ˘   ′
pleasant things:

˘ ˘ ′ | ˘ ˘ ′ | ˘ ′ ′ |˘ ˘ ˘ ′ | ˘ ˘ ′ |
For the house of the priests made stately, and the might in the mouth

˘ ˘ ′
of the kings.

˘ ˘ ′ | ˘ ′ |˘ ˘ ′ | ˘ ˘ ′|˘ ˘ ′ | ′ ′
They are grieved and greatly afraid; they are taken, they shall not flee:

˘ ˘ ′ | ˘ ˘ ′|˘ ˘ ′ | ˘ ˘ ′ | ˘ ˘ ′ |
For the heart of the nations is made as the strength of the springs

˘ ˘ ′
of the sea,. . .

˘ ˘ ´ | ˘ ˘ ´ | ˘ ˘ ´ | ˘ ´ | ˘ ˘ ´ | ˎ ´
For the breaking of gold in their hair they halt as a man made lame:

˘ ˘ ´| ˘ ˘ ´ | ˘ ˘ ´ | ˘ ´ | ˘ ´| ˘ ˘ ´
They are utterly naked and bare; their mouths are bitter with shame.

ˎ ˘ ´ | ˘ ´ | ˘ ´ | ˘ ´ | ˘ ˘ ´ | ˘ ´
Wilt thou judge thy people now, O king that wast found most wise?

˘ ˘ ´ | ˘ ˘ ´ | ˘ ´ | ˘ ´ | ˘ ´ | ˘ ˘ ´
Wilt thou lie any more, O thou whose mouth is emptied of lies?

From"The Night Before Christmas," Henry Livingston, Jr. (c. 1822)

˘ ´ ´ | ˘ ˘ ´ | ˘ ´ ´ | ˘ ´
As dry leaves that before the wild hurricane fly,

˘ ˘ ´ | ˘ ˘ ´| ˘ ˘ ´ | ˘ ˘ ´
When they meet with an obstacle mount to the sky.

˘ ´ | ˘ ˘ ´ | ˘ ˘ ´ |´ ˘ ´
The moon on the breast of the new-fallen snow

´ ˘ ´ | ˘ ˘ ´ | ´ ˘ ´| ˘ ˘ ´
Gave the luster of midday to objects below

From "Under The Waterfall," Thomas Hardy (1914)

˘ ´ | ˘ ˘ ´ | ˘ ˘ ´ | ˘ ´ ´ (˘)
. . . And when we had drunk from the glass together,

(˘) ´ | ˘ ˘ ´ | ´ ´ | ˘ ´ ´ (˘)
Arched by the oak-copse from the weather,

˘ ´ | ˘ ´| ˘ ˘ ´ | ˘ ˘ ´
I held the vessel to rinse in the fall,

˘ ˘ ´ | ˘ ˘ ´ | ˘ ˘ ´ | ˘ ´
Where it slipped, and it sank, and was past recall,

˘ ˘ ´ | ˘ ´ | ˘ ´| ˘ ˘ ´
Though we stooped and plumbed the little abyss

˘ ´ | ˎ ´ | ˘ ˘ ´ | ˎ ´
With long bared arms. There the glass still is.

˘ ˘ ´ |˘ ˘ ´ | ˘ ´ | ˘ ´
And, as said, if I thrust my arm below

ˋ   ʼ|ˇ ˇ ˇ ʼ |ˇ ˇ ʼ |ˇ   ʼ
Cold water in a basin or bowl, a throe

ˇ   ˇ ʼ |ˇ ʼ|ˇ ˇ ʼ |ˇ   ˇ ʼ
From the past awakens a sense of that time,

ˇ ˇ   ʼ | ˇ   ʼ | ˇ ˇ ʼ |ʼ   ʼ
And the glass we used, and the cascade's rhyme.

ˇ   ʼ|ˇ ʼ | ˇ   ʼ | ˇ ˇ   ʼ
The basin seems the pool, and its edge

ˇ   ʼ | ˇ   ˋ   ʼ |ˇ ˇ   ʼ | ʼ   ʼ
The hard smooth face of the brook-side ledge,

ˇ ˇ   ʼ|ˇ ʼ|ˇ ˇ ʼ|ˇ   ʼ
And the leafy pattern of china-ware

ˇ   ʼ |ˇ ʼ | ˇ   ˇ ˇ ʼ |ˇ   ʼ
The hanging plants that were bathing there. . .

From "The Lifeguard," James Dickey

ˇ ʼ | ˇ   ˋ   ʼ | ˇ   ˇ ʼ
I wash the black mud from my hands.

ˇ ˇ ʼ | ˋ ˇ ʼ |ˇ ˇ   ʼ
On a light given off by the grave

ˇ ʼ |ˇ ˇ   ʼ |ˇ ˇ   ʼ
I kneel in the quick of the moon

ˇ ˇ   ʼ |ˇ ˇ ʼ|ˇ ʼ   (ˇ)
At the heart of a distant forest

ˇ   ʼ |ˇ ˇ ʼ |ˇ ʼ
And hold in my arms a child

ˇ   ʼ|ˇ ʼ|ˇ ʼ   (ˇ)
Of water, water, water.

Dactylic Meter (/ ˇˇ)

ʼ ˇ ˇ |ʼ ˇ ˇ| ʼ ˇ ˇ | ʼ ˇˇ | ʼ   ˇ ˇ | ʼ   ˇ
This is the forest primeval. The murmuring pines and the hemlocks,

ʼ ˇ ˇ | ʼ   ˇ ˇ| ʼ ˇ ˇ | ʼ ˇ ˇ| ˇ ˇ | ʼ ˇ
Bearded with moss, and in garments green, indistinct in the twilight,

ʼ   ˇ | ʼ ˇ ˇ |ʼ ˇ | ʼ ˇ|ʼ ˇ ˇ| ʼ ˇ
Stand like Druids of eld, with voices sad and prophetic,

ʼ   ˇ | ʼ ˇ | ʼ   ˇ | ʼ   ˇ| ʼ ˇ ˇ | ʼ ˇ
Stand like harpers hoar, with beards that rest on their bosoms.

Loud from its rocky caverns, the deep-voiced neighboring ocean

Speaks, and in accents disconsolate answers the wail of the forest.

This is the forest primeval; but where are the hearts that beneath it

Leaped like the roe, when he hears in the woodland the voice of

the huntsman?

Where is the thatch-roofed village, the home of Acadian farmers? . . .

"Mushrooms," Sylvia Plath (1957)

Perfectly voiceless,

Widen the crannies,

Shoulder through holes. We

Diet on water

"Arachne Gives Thanks to Athena," A.E. Stallings

It is no punishment. They are mistaken—

The brothers, the father. My prayers were answered.

I was all fingertips. Nothing was perfect:

What I had woven, the moths will have eaten;

At the end of my rope was a noose's knot.

´ ˘ ˘ | ´ ˘ ˘ | ´ ˘ ˘ | ´ ˘
Now it's no longer the thing, but the pattern,
(˘) ´ ˘ ˘ | ´ ˘ ˘ | ` ´ ˘ | ´ ˘
And that will endure, even though webs be broken.
´ ˘ ˘ | ´ ˘ ˘ | ` ´ ˘ | ´ ˘
I, if not beautiful, am beauty's maker.
´ ´ ˘ ˘ | ´ ` ˘ | ´ ˘ ˘ | ´ ˘
Old age cannot rob me, nor cowardly lovers.
(˘) ´ ` ´ | ´ ˘ ˘ | ´ ˘ ` | ´ ˘
The moon once pulled blood from me. Now I pull silver.
´ ˘ ˘ | ´ ˘ ´ | ` ˘ ` | ´ ˘
Here are the lines I pulled from my own belly—
´ ˘ ˘ | ´ ˘ | ´ ´ ´ | ´ ˘
Hang them with rainbows, ice, dewdrops, darkness.

From "Goblin Market," Christina Rossetti (1859)

´ ˘ ˘ | ´ ˘
Apples and quinces,
´ ˘ ˘ | ´ ˘ ˘
Lemons and oranges,
´ ˘ ` | ´ ˘
Plump unpecked cherries,
´ ˘ ˘ | ´ ˘ ˘
Melons and raspberries,
´ ` ´ | ´ ˘
Bloom-down-cheeked peaches,
´ ´ ˘ | ´ ˘ ˘
Swart-headed mulberries,
´ ´ ` | ´ ˘ ˘
Wild free-born cranberries,
´ ˘ ˘ | ´ ˘ ˘
Crab-apples, dewberries,

´ ˘ ˘ | ´ ˘ ˘
Pine-apples, blackberries,

´ ˘ ˘ | ´ ˘ ˘
Apricots, strawberries;—

"At Last the Women Are Moving," Genevieve Taggard (1935)

(˘) ´ ˘ ˘ | ´ ´ ˘ |´ ˘ | ´ ˘ | ´ ˘ (˘)
Last, walking with stiff legs as if they carried bundles

(˘) ´ ˘ | ´ ˙ ˙ | ´ ˘ ˘ | ´ ˘ ˙
Came mothers, housewives, old women who knew why they

˘ | ´ ˘ (˘)
  abhorred war.

(˘) ´ ´   ˘| ´ ˘ ˘ | ´ ˘ ˘ | ´ ˘ | ´ |(˘˘)
Their clothes bunched about them, they hobbled with anxious steps

(˘) ´ ˘ ˘ | ´ ˘ ˘ | ´ ˘ ˘ |´ | ´ ˘ ˙ | ´ ˘ (˘)
To keep with the stride of the marchers, erect bearing wide banners.

(˘) ´ ˘ ˙ | ´ | ´ ˘ ˘ ˘| ´˘˘ |´ ˘ (˘)
Such women looked odd, marching on American asphalt.

´ ˘ ˘ | ´ ´ | ´ | ´ ˙ ˘ | ´ ˘ (˘)
Kitchens they knew, sinks, suds, stew-pots and pennies . . .

´ ˘ ˘ ˘| ´ ˘ | ´ ˘| ´ ´ ˘ | ´ ˘ (˘)
Dull hurry and worry, clatter, wet hands and backache.

´ ˘ ˘ | ´ ˘ ˘ | ´ ˘ ˘ | ´ ˘ ˘ | ´ (˘˘)
Here they were out in the glare on the militant march.

´ ˘ ˘ | ´ ˘ ˘ | ´ ˘| ´ ˘ ˘ | ´ ˘ (˘)
How did these timid, the slaves of breakfast and supper

´ ˘ ˘ ˘| ´ ˙ ˘ | ´ | ´ ˙ ˘ | ´ (˘˘)
Get out in the line, drop for once dish-rag and broom?

´ | ´ ˘ ˘| ´   ˙ ˘ | ´ ˘ ˘ | ´ ˘ (˘)
Here they are as work-worn as stitchers and fitters.

´ ˘ ˘ ˘ | ´ ˘ | ´ ˘ | ´ ˘ ˘ | ´ ˘
Mama have you got some grub, now none of their business.

(ˊ ˇ)| ˊ   ˇ| ˊ   ˇ   ˇ | ˊ ˇ | ˊ   ˇ   ˇ | ˊ ˇ
Oh, but those who know in their growing sons and their husbands

ˊ   ˇ ˇ| ˊ   ˇ| ˊ ˇ   ˋ | ˊ   ˇ | ˊ ˇ   ˇ | ˊ (ˇˇ)
How the exhausted body needs sleep, how often needs food,

ˊ   ˇ | ˊ   ˇ ˇ| ˊ   ˇ   ˇ | ˊ ˇ ˇ| (ˇˇ)
These, whose business is keeping the body alive,

ˊ   ˇ| ˊ ˇˇ ˇ| ˊ   ˇ | ˊ   ˇ | ˊ (ˇˇ)
These are ready, if you talk their language, to strike.

ˊ ˇ ˇ| ˊ   ˇ| ˊ ˇ | ˊ   ˇ| ˊ (ˇˇ)
Kitchen is small, the family story is sad.

ˊ ˇ ˇ | ˊ ˇ| ˊ   ˇ | ˊ   ˇ   ˋ | ˊ ˇ
Out of the musty flats the women come thinking:

(ˇ   ˇ) | ˊ ˇ   ˇ |ˊ ˇ| ˊ ˇ | ˊ   ˇ ˇ | ˊ (ˇˇ)
Not for me and mine only. For my class I have come

(ˇ)| ˊ   ˊˇ| ˊ   ˇ | ˊ ˇ   ˇ| ˊ   ˇ ˇ | ˊ (ˇˇ)
To walk city miles with many, my will in our work.

"The Slip," Rachel Hadas

ˊ   ˇ   ˇ | ˊ   ˇ | ˊ ˇ   ˇ| ˊ ˇ ˇ
Empty and trembling, haloed by absences,

ˊ   ˇ   ˇ| ˊ ˇ ˇ | ˊ   ˊ ˇ | ˊ ˇ ˇ
whooshings, invisible leave-takings, finishes,

ˊ ˇ ˇ | ˊ ˇ   ˇ| ˊ ˇ   ˇ| ˊ   ˇ ˇ
images, closure: departures so gracefully

ˊ ˇ   ˇ| ˊ ˇ   ˇ| ˇ   ˇ ˊ| ˊ ˇ
practice their gestures that when they do happen,

ˊ   ˇ   ˇ | ˊ ˋ   ˇ| ˊ   ˇ ˇ| ˊ   ˇ
dazzled with sunlight, distracted by darkness,

ˊ ˇ ˇ |ˊ ˇ   ˇ | ˊ   ˇ ˇ|ˊ (ˇˇ)
mercifully often we miss the event.

"The Denouement," R. S. Gwynn

   ´   ˘   ˘ | ´ ˘ ˘ | ´ (˘)
Who were those persons who chased us?

   ´   ˘ ˘ | ´ ˘ ˘ | ´ ˘ (˘)
They were the last of the others.

   ´   ˘ ˘ | ´ ˘ ˘ | ´ ˘ (˘)
Why must we always be running?

  ´ ˘ ˘ | ´ ˘ ˘ | ´ (˘˘)
We are the last of our own.

   ´ ˘ ˘ | ´ ˘ ˘ | ´ ˘ (˘)
Where is the shelter you spoke of?

(˘) ´ ˘ | ´ ˘|´ ˘ (˘)
Between us. All around us.

   ´ ˘ ˘ | ´ ˘ ˘ | ´ ˘ (˘)
Shall we be safe until morning?

   ´ ˘ ˘ | ´ ˘ ˘ | ´ ˘ (˘)
There is no doorway to enter.

Mixed Meters

"Your World," Georgia Douglas Johnson (19–)

  ˘ ´ |˘ ˘ ´ |˘ ˘ ´ (˘)
Your world is as big as you make it

´ ˘ | ˘ ˘ ´ |˘ ´
I know, for I used to abide

˘ ˘ ´ |˘ ˘ ´ |˘ ˘ ´ (˘)
In the narrowest nest in a corner

  ˘ ´ | ˘ ˘ ´ |˘ ˘ ´
My wings pressing close to my side

  ˘ ˘ ´ |˘ ˘ ´ |˘ ˘ ´|˘
But I sighted the distant horizon

   ˘ ˘ ´ | ˘ \ ˘ ´|˘ ˘ ´
Where the sky-line encircled the sea

˘ ˘   , | ˘ ˘ , | ˘   ˘ ,
And I throbbed with a burning desire

˘ , |˘   ˘ ,| ˘ ˘ ,
To travel this immensity.

˘ , ˘ | ˘ , | ˘ ˘ ,   (˘)
I battered the cordons around me

˘   , | ˘ ˘   , | ˘ ˘   ,
And cradled my wings on the breeze

˘   , | ˘ ˘ ,|˘ ˘   , | ˘
Then soared to the uttermost reaches

˘ , | ˘   ˘   ,| ˘ ˘   ,
with rapture, with power, with ease!

From "Mezzo Cammin," Judith Moffett

˘ , | ˘ , | ˘ , | ˘   ,
I mean to mark the Midway Day

˘   , | ˘ ˘| ˘ , | ˘   ,
With soundings in this verse form. Say,

,   ˘ ˘ | , ˘
Muse, how you hate it!

˘ , | ˘ , | ˘ ,| ˘   ,
I know your taste for excess. But

˘ , |˘ , | ˘ , | ˘ ,
These jingly rhymes must undercut,

, ˘ ˘| , ˘
Counter, deflate it. . .

From "A Hymn For St. Cecilia's Day," John Dryden (1687)

˘ , | ˘ , | ˘ ,| ˘ , | ˘   ,
What passion cannot Music raise and quell?

˘ ,| ˘ , | ˘ ,| ˘ ,
When Jubal struck the chorded shell,

˘ , | ˘ ˘ , | ˘ , | ˘ ,
His listening brethren stood around,

˘   , | ˘   ˘ | ˘ , |˘ ,
And, wondering, on their faces fell

˘   , | ˘   , | ˘ ,|˘   ,
To worship that celestial sound:

,   ˘ |˘ , | ˘   , | ˘   , | ˘   ,
Less than a God they thought there could not dwell

˘ , | ˘   , | ˘ , | ˘   ,
Within the hollow of that shell,

˘   , | ˘   ,| ˘ , | ˘   ,
That spoke so sweetly, and so well.

˘   , | ˘ , | ˘   , |˘ , | ˘   ,
What passion cannot Music raise and quell?

˘   ,   ˘ | ˎ , ˘
The trumpet's loud clangour

˘ , ˘ | ˘ , (˘)
Excites us to arms,

˘   ,   ˘ | ˘ , ˘
With shrill notes of anger,

˘   , ˘ | ˘, (˘)
And mortal alarms.

˘   , | ˘   , | ˘   , |˘ ,
The double double double beat

˘ ˘   , | ˘ ˘   ,
Of the thundering drum

ˎ   , | ˘ ˎ ,
Cries Hark! the foes come;

,   , | ˘ ˘ , | ˘ ˘ ,
Charge, charge, 'tis too late to retreat!

Amphibrachs, Dipodics, and Hendecasyllabics

˘   , ˘| ˘ , ˘ |˘   , ˘ | ˘ ,
The world is so full of a number of things

˘ , ˘ | ˘   , ˘ | ˘ , ˘ | ˘ , (˘)
I'm sure we should all be as happy as kings.
—Robert Louis Stevenson

"The White Bird," Anna Akhmatova (1914)

˘　ˌ　˘　|˘ ˌ　˘|˘　ˌ　˘　|˘ ˌ　˘

So worried about me, so jealous, so tender—

˘　ˌ　˘|　ˌ　　ˎ　|˘　ˌ　˘|　ˎ　　　　ˌ

As steady as God's sun, as warm as Love's breath—

˘　ˌ　˘ |˘　ˌ　˘|˘　ˌ　˘|˘　ˌ　˘

he wanted no songs of the past I remembered.

˘　ˌ　˘|　ˎ　ˌ　˘ |˘ ˌ　˘|˘　ˌ

He took my white bird, and he put it to death.

From Samuel Woodworth, "The Old Oaken Bucket" (1817)

˘　ˌ　˘|　˘　ˌ　˘ |˘　ˌ　˘|˘　ˌ　˘

How dear to this heart are the scenes of my childhood,

˘　ˌ　˘|˘ ˌ　˘ |˘　ˌ　˘　|˘　ˌ (˘)

When fond recollection presents them to view!

˘　ˌ　˘ |˘　ˌ　˘ |˘　ˌ　ˎ |˘　ˌ　ˎ

The orchard, the meadow, the deep-tangled wild-wood,

˘　ˌ ˘|　ˎ　ˌ　˘ |˘　ˌ ˘|˘　　ˌ (˘)

And every loved spot which my infancy knew!

Ernest Lawrence Thayer, from "Casey at the bat" (1888)

˘　ˌ |˘　ˎ |˘　ˌ|˘　ˎ|˘　ˌ |˘　ˎ |˘　ˌ

The Outloook wasn't brilliant for the Mudville nine that day;

˘　ˌ |　˘　ˎ |˘ ˌ |˘　ˎ|˘　ˌ|˘　ˎ |˘　ˌ

The score stood four to two, with but one inning more to play

˘　ˌ |˘　ˎ |˘　ˌ |˘ ˌ|˘　ˌ|˘　ˎ |˘　ˌ

And then when Cooney died at first, and Barrows did the same,

˘　ˌ|˘ ˎ|˘　ˌ|˘ ˎ |˘ ˌ|˘ ˎ|˘ ˌ

A sickly silence fell upon the patrons of the game.

Rudyard Kipling, From "The Galley-Slave" (1886)

ˎ ˘|ˌ　˘ |ˎ ˘|ˌ ˘|ˎ ˘|ˌ　˘ |ˎ ˘ |ˌ(˘)

By the hands that drove her forward as she plunged and yawed and sheered,

ˎ ˘ |ˌ ˘|ˎ ˘|ˌ ˘|ˎ ˘ |˘ˇ|ˎ ˘|ˌ (˘)

Woman, Man, or God or Devil, was there anything we feared?

"The Meter of the Night Sky," Arielle Greenberg

˘ ˊ | ˘ ˋ | ˘ ˊ | ˘ ˋ | ˘ ˊ | ˘ ˋ | ˘ ˊ

I wonder what would happen if the K in knife was said,

˘ ˊ | ˘ ˋ | ˘ ˊ | ˘ ˋ | ˘ ˊ | ˘ ˊ | ˘ ˊ

if part of all the Hs in the book had rubbed away,

(˘) ˊ | ˘ ˋ | ˘ ˊ | ˘ ˋ | ˘ ˊ | ˘ ˋ | ˋ ˊ

changing up the shapes of our ancestor's good white bones.

From "Hendecasyllabics," Algernon Charles Swinburne (1866)

ˊ ˘ | ˊ ˘ ˘ | ˊ ˘ | ˊ ˘ | ˊ ˘

In the month of the long decline of roses

ˊ ˘ | ˊ ˘ ˘ | ˊ ˘ | ˊ ˘ | ˊ ˘

I, beholding the summer dead before me,

ˊ ˘ | ˊ ˘ ˘ | ˊ ˘ | ˊ ˘ | ˊ ˘

Set my face to the sea and journeyed silent,

ˊ ˘ | ˊ ˘ ˘ | ˊ ˘ | ˘ ˘ | ˊ ˘

Gazing eagerly where above the sea-mark

ˊ ˘ | ˊ ˘ ˘ | ˊ ˘ | ˘ ˘ | ˊ ˘

Flame as fierce as the fervid eyes of lions

ˊ ˘ | ˊ ˘ ˘ | ˊ ˘ | ˊ ˘ | ˊ ˘

Half divided the eyelids of the sunset;

ˊ ˘ | ˊ ˘ ˘ | ˊ ˘ | ˊ ˘ | ˊ ˘

Till I heard as it were a noise of waters

ˊ ˘ | ˊ ˘ ˘ | ˊ ˘ | ˊ ˘ | ˊ ˘

Moving tremulous under feet of angels . . .

"The Reemergence of the Noose," Patricia Smith

ˊ ˋ | ˊ ˘ ˘ | ˊ ˘ | ˊ ˘ | ˊ ˘

Some lamp sputters its dusty light across a

ˊ ˘ | ˊ ˘ ˘ | ˊ ˘ | ˊ ˘ | ˊ ˘

desk. Some hand, in a fever, works the fraying

ˊ ˋ | ˊ ˘ ˘ | ˊ ˘ | ˊ ˘ | ˊ ˘

brown hemp, twisting and knifing, weaving, tugging

ˊ ˘ | ˊ ˘ ˘ | ˊ ˘ | ˊ ˘ | ˊ ˘

tight this bellowing circle. Randy Travis

ˊ ˋ | ˊ �“ ˇ | ˊ ˇ | ˊ ˇ | ˊ ˇ
sings, moans, radios steamy twangs and hiccups,

ˊ ˋ | ˊ ˇ ˇ | ˊ ˇ|ˋ ˇ | ˊ ˇ
blue notes backing the ritual of drooping

ˊ ˋ | ˊ ˇ ˇ | ˊ ˇ | ˊ ˇ|ˊ ˇ
loop. Sweat drips in an awkward hallelujah.

ˊ ˋ | ˊ ˇ ˇ | ˊ ˇ | ˊ ˇ | ˊ ˇ
God glares down, but the artist doesn't waver—

ˊ ˋ | ˊ ˇ ˇ | ˊ ˇ | ˊ ˇ | ˊ ˇ
wrists click rhythm, and rope becomes a path to

ˊ ˇ | ˊ ˇ ˇ | ˊ ˇ | ˊ ˇ | ˊ ˇ
what makes saviors; the loop bemoans its need to

ˊ ˇ | ˊ ˇ ˇ ˇ | ˊ ˇ | ˊ ˇ ˊ (ˇ)
squeeze, its craving for the ghost of Negro neck.

"What Could it Be," Julia Alvarez

(ˇ) ˊ ˇ | ˊ ˇ ˇ | ˊ ˇ ˇ | (ˇˇ)
Around the kettle of chicken and rice,

(ˇ) ˊ ˇ ˇ| ˊ ˇ ˇ | ˊ ˇ ˇ | ˊ ˇ
the aunts were debating what flavor was missing.

ˊ ˇ| ˊ ˇ ˇ | ˊ ˇ
Tía Carmen guessed garlic.

ˊ ˇ| ˊ ˇ ˇ | ˊ ˇ ˋ | ˊ ˇ
Tía Rosa, some coarsely ground pepper.

ˊ ˇ| ˊ ˇ ˇ|ˋ ˇ ˊ| ˊ ˇ | ˊ ˇ
Tía Ana, so tidy she wore the apron,

ˊ ˇ | ˊ ˋ |ˊ ˇ ˇ | ˊ ˇ
shook her head, plain salt what was needed.

Credits

D

Emily Dickinson, "The Bustle in a House" from *The Poems of Emily Dickinson,* Thomas H. Johnson, ed., Cambridge, Mass.: The Belknap Press of Harvard University Press, Copyright © 1951, 1955, 1979, 1983 by the President and Fellows of Harvard College. Owen Dodson, "Midnight Bell" from *Powerful Long Ladder* (New York: Farrar, Straus & Giroux, 1946). Hilda Doolittle, "The Walls Do Not Fall," from *Collected Poems, 1912–1944,* copyright © 1982 by The Estate of Hilda Doolittle. Reprinted by permission of New Directions Publishing Corp. John Drury, "Ghazal of the Lagoon" from *The Disappearing Town* (Oxford, OH: Miami University Press, 2000).

E

Russell Edson, "You" from *The Wounded Breakfast* © 1985 by Russell Edson and reprinted by permission of Wesleyan University Press. Elaine Equi, excerpt [8 lines] from "A Date with Robbe-Grillet" from *Ripple Effect: New and Selected Poems* (Minneapolis: Coffee House Press, 2007). Originally collected in *Surface Tension* (Minneapolis: Coffee House Press, 1989). Landis Everson, "Famine" from *Everything Preserved: Poems 1955–2005* (St. Paul: Graywolf Press, 2005).

G

Arielle Greenberg, "The Meter of the Night Sky" from *Salt* (Metrical Poetry Feature, edited by Annie Finch), 2005. Thom Gunn, "The Night Piece" from *Collected Poems* (New York: Noonday Press, 1994). R. S. Gwynn, "The Denouement" from *No Word of Farewell: Poems 1970–2000* (Ashland, Ore.: Story Line Press, 2001). By Permission of the author.

H

Marilyn Hacker, excerpt [first 15 lines] from ["Why did Ray leave her pipe tobacco here"] from *Love, Death and the Changing of the Seasons* (W.W. Norton & Company, 1986) Copyright © 1986 Marilyn Hacker. Marilyn Hacker, "Dusk: July," from *Winter Numbers.* Copyright © 1994 by Marilyn Hacker. Used by permission of the author and W.W. Norton & Company, Inc. Marilyn Hacker, "Untoward Occurrence at an Embassy Poetry Reading" from *First Cities: Collected Early Poems 1969–1979* (New York: W. W. Norton & Company, 2003). Rachel Hadas, "The Slip" in *Halfway Down the Hall* © 1988 by Rachel Hadas and reprinted with permission of Wesleyan University Press. Joy Harjo, "Ah, Ah" from *How We Became Human: New and Selected Poems: 1975–2001* by Joy Harjo. Copyright © 2002 by Joy Harjo. Used by permission of W.W. Norton & Company Inc. Langston Hughes, "The Negro Speaks of Rivers," "Justice," "Casualty," "The Weary Blues," and "Madam and the Census Man" from *The Collected Poems of Langston Hughes* by Langston Hughes, edited by Arnold Rampersad and David Roessel, Associate Editor, copyright © 1994 by the Estate of Langston Hughes. Used by permission of Alfred A. Knopf, a division of Random House, Inc.

Index

Accent 3, 4, 26. *See* Chapter 2: 31–55, 56–58, 60–66, 71–74, 76, 78, 90, 91, 95, 96, 99, 109, 119, 125, 131, 169, 211, 329, 357

Accentual alliterative verse, 41, 55

Accentual meter, 31, 35, 40, 41, 52, 54, 55, 57, 60, 170, 211, 318, 363

Accentual poetry, 3, 26, *See* Chapter 2: 31–55, 59, 61, 72, 77

Accentual-syllabic meter, 35, 40, 57, 58, 62, 77, 318

Adonic, 39, 146, 221, 222

Alcaic stanza, 222, 234

Alliteration, 3, 41, 42, 141, 197, 350

Amphibrachs, 61, 150, 151, 152, 156–58, 166, 222, 270, 401

Anadiplosis, 243

Anapest, 61, 65, 66, 75, 80. *See* Chapter 4: 89–92, 97, 99, 102–4, 105, 109, 111, 112, 117–21, 129; and Chapter 5: 133–43, 145, 149, 151, 152, 166, 345

Anapestic meter, 64, 67, 68, 81, 89, 100, 128. *See* Chapter 5: 133–43, 147, 154, 158, 165, 166, 388

Anaphora, 6, 235–37, 242

Antanaclasis, 243

Assonance, 141, 196, 197, 350

Ballad Stanza, 113, 139, 184, 211, 233, 318

Ballad, 293, 308, *See* Chapter 10: 315–35

Blank verse, 85, 183, 354

Blank Iambic verse. *See* Chapter 4: 85–89, 165

Blues, 3, 4,169, 235. *See* Chapter 8: 244–48, 268, 271, 287, 288

Caesura, 58. *See* Chapter 4: 85–89, 92, 93, 95, 99, 106, 107, 118, 119, 129, 130, 135, 145, 165, 177, 293

Canzone, 244. *See* Chapter 8: 254–64

Chiasmus, 189, 207

Cinquain, 211

Consonance, 197

Couplet, 10, 109, 141, 169, 182, 183, 189, 190, 191, 206, 207, 208, 210, 211, 214, 224, 226, 233, 247, 248, 274, 275, 287, 294, 297, 298, 310, 337, 355

Cup (scansion mark), 63, 72–74, 82

Dactyl, 61, 66, 80, 120, 121, 128–30, 135, 139. *See* Chapter 5: 143–51, 152, 160, 162–65, 217, 218, 221

Dactylic hexameter, 67, 77, 144, 165

Dactylic meter, 65–67, 74, 75, 80, 81, 121. *See* Chapter 5: 143–51, 222, 302, 309, 394

Decima, 211, 230, 233

Deformation. *See* Chapter 9: 306–12

Dialogue, 119, 308, 324

Dickinson Stanza, 211

Diction, 28, 136, 164, 237, 331

Dipodic meter. *See* Chapter 5: 156–62, 318, 320, 401

Double footless line, 128–30, 147, 148, 150

Double iamb, 61, 95

Duple meter, 63

Echo poem, 347

Elegiac couplet, 144

Enjambment, 18, 23, 30, 71. *See* Chapter 4: 85–88, 200, 288

Exploratory poetry, 336, 338, 344, 345, 349, 350, 356

Expressive variation, 97, 100–101, *See* Chapter 4: 105–9, 142, 218, 379

Extra-syllable ending, 98, 99, 104, 111, 118, 119, 128, 152

Feminine caesura, 338

Feminine ending. *See* Extra-syllable ending

Folk meter, 319

Folk stanza, 211, 318

Foot, 63, *See* Chapter 3: 66–68, 71, 72, 75–76, 78, 89, 90, 92, 93, 98–100, 104, 127, 133, 134, 141–43, 147, 148, 156, 158–60, 166, 222, 293

Foot break, 62, 66, 71–73, 81, 88, 104, 158

Footless line, 128–30, 147–48, 150

Formula, 43, 277

Fourteeners. *See* Chapter 4: 109–15, 381

Free verse. *See* Chapter 1: 3–30, 31, 40, 44, 50, 54, 56, 68; Chapter 3: 71–83, 84, 85, 116, 119, 143, 154, 159, 162, 176, 195; Chapter 7: 199–206, 232, 234, 273; and Chapter 8: 280–86, 293, 301–3, 309–13, 338, 346, 349, 355

Galliambics, 412

Genre poem, 336. *See* Chapter 11: 346–50

Ghazal, 169, 244. *See* Chapter 8: 273–76, 287, 288, 312, 355

Haiku, 30, 169

Headless line, 74, 75. *See* Chapter 4: 97–99, 118, 128, 134, 310, 375

Hendecasyllabics. *See* Syllabic Meter

Heroic couplet, 78, 119, 206, 234, 311, 355

Hinge technique, 30

History of Form, 218, 287, 305, 311, 316, 351

Hymn stanza. *See* Dickinson stanza

Iambic dimeter, 67. *See* Chapter 4: 109–15, 153, 301, 381

Iambic meter, 64, 67, 74–76, 80, 81. *See* Chapter 4: 83–119, 120, 121, 125–28, 130, 131, 133, 134, 137–39, 141, 145, 146, 152, 153, 165, 211, 293, 310, 311, 369, 381

Iambic pentameter, 10, 11, 14, 51–61, 67, 71–74, 89. *See* Chapter 4: 83–119, 121, 143, 153, 206, 225, 291, 301, 309, 311, 354, 364

Implied couplet, 294

Ionics, 61, 162

Kyrielle, 254. *See* Chapter 8: 269

Lexical accent, 34

Line break, 3, 4, 6, 8, 13–18, 20–24, 28–30, 44, 58, 68, 71, 92, 115, 135, 178, 235, 349, 355

Line Length, 5, 6, 10, 22, 43, 72, 81, 83, 86, 112, 118, 139, 179, 217, 279, 307, 314, 345

Loudness of syllable, 32

Lyric poetry, 14, 15, 121, 210, 224, 225, 235, 288, 317

Lyric prose, 3, 15

Masculine caesura, 88

Medial pause, 41, 55

Metaphor, 56, 100, 112, 194, 232, 235, 345

Metrical contract, 74, 108, 109, 126

Mixed meters (logodaeic). *See* Chapter 5: 151–55, 399

Narrative poetry, 39, 58, 123, 136, 200, 224–26, 234, 286, 295, 300, 303, 308, 315, 319, 324

Nonce forms, 289, 336, 345, 349

Nursery rhymes, 34, 55, 170, 212

Octave, 292–95, 297, 307, 310

Open field (projective) verse, 11

Ottava rima, 190, 226, 227, 230, 233, 234

Pantoum, 169, 244, 273. *See* Chapter 8: 276–80

Paradelle. *See* Chapter 8: 271–73, 355, 405, 408

Parallelism, 26, 207, 215

Performance poetry, 43, 44, 57

Performative accent, 34, 95

Phrasal accent, 34

Pitch, 32, 58, 91

Projective verse. *See* Open field, 11

Prose poems, 3, 4. *See* Chapter 1: 13–15, 54, 56, 125, 154, 165, 170, 199, 330, 343

Prosody, 50. *See* Chapter 3: 57–62, 75, 77, 78, 109, 143, 354–55

Pyrrhic foot, 61, 74. *See* Chapter 4: 93–97, 99, 104, 118, 126, 141, 222, 373

Quatern, 288

Quatrain, 116, 169, 211, 223, 224, 234, 292–94, 303, 307, 310, 319

Refrain, 3, 235, 244, 269, 274. *See* Chapter 8: 280–84, 287, 288, 308, 316, 317, 319, 327, 329, 330, 345

Repetends, 250, 253, 254, 288

Repetition, 3, 4, 15, 20, 30, 44, 137, 150, 181, 189, 226. *See* Chapter 8: 235–89, 308, 317, 318, 327, 328, 336, 338, 345, 346, 348, 351

Rhyme, 3, 5, 8, 20, 30, 42, 44, 55, 79, 81, 84, 85, 91, 96, 119, 162. *See* Chapter 6: 169–97, 206–9, 211, 212, 214, 215, 217, 223, 227, 230, 234, 235, 237, 246, 249, 250, 254, 264, 267, 269, 274, 277, 287, 294–96, 301, 302, 304, 306–14, 318, 330, 337, 338, 344, 345, 355

Rhyme Royal, 225, 226, 230, 233, 234

Rhythm, 3, 5, 8, 10–12, 15, 18. *See* Chapter 1: 25–30, 31, 34–36, 39, 44, 49–52, 55–57, 61, 62, 64; Chapter 2: 66–68, 71, 73, 75–78, 80–84, 88, 89, 92, 93, 95, 97, 100–103, 105–7, 110, 111, 116, 117, 119–21, 123, 125, 126, 128, 132, 133, 135, 141, 142, 145, 146, 149, 152, 155, 156, 158–66, 170, 195, 198, 214, 223, 235, 256, 293, 302, 319, 330, 331, 344, 345, 351, 354

Rondeau, 254. *See* Chapter 8: 267–69, 280

Roundel, 244

Running start syllables, 128, 129, 146–48

Sapphic stanza (sapphics), 152, 156, 160, 217, 218, 219, 221, 222, 234

Scansion, 52. *See* Chapter 3: 62–63, 66, 72–77, 95, 100, 104, 105, 108, 110, 121, 129. *See* the Appendix: 357

Sestet, 292–95, 297, 298

Sestina, 169, 244, 254–60, 262, 264, 267, 271, 285–88, 341, 345, 355, 405, 406

Shaped poetry, *See* Chapter 7: 199–205, 355

Sonnet, 4, 73, 89, 91, 92, 95, 102, 103, 108, 119, 126, 130, 169, 183, 184, 189–90, 193, 198, 210, 224, 226, 237, 243, 247, 253, 262, 268, 287. *See* Chapter 9: 290–314, 316, 337, 338, 345–47, 350, 355, 377, 380

Spenserian sonnet, 30,

Spenserian stanza, 183, 227, 229, 233, 234

Spondee, 61, 73. *See* Chapter 4: 93–97, 99, 102, 103, 104, 106, 118, 119, 134, 138

Stanza, 36, 40, 54, 55, 85, 126–28, 134, 139, 140, 148, 152, 175, 182, 185, 187, 188, 190–92, 196. *See* Chapter 7: 198–234, 235, 245, 246, 249, 254, 255, 264, 267, 269–76, 280, 284, 288, 289, 293, 294, 299, 302, 306, 319, 324–27, 342, 345, 348, 350. *See also* Adonic, Alcaic, Ballad, Cinquain, Couplet, Decima, Dickenson Stanza, Heroic Couplet, Ottiva Rima, Quatrain, Rhyme Royal, Sapphic, Spenserian, Tercet, Terza Rima, Triplet

Stanza length, 179, 211, 231–33, 248

Syllable Length, 31, 32, 43, 83, 96–97

Syllabic meter (syllabics), 36, 39, 54 (Hendecasyllabics). *See* Chapter 5: 156–62, 164, 166, 401, 403

Syntax, 17, 25, 26, 30, 69, 71, 117, 120, 136, 153, 154, 158, 185, 186, 193, 237, 279, 292, 305, 336, 348

Teleuton, 255–58, 260, 262, 264, 286

Tercet, 183, 208, 211, 233, 248

Terza rima, 209–11, 234, 345

Triple meter, 63–66

Triplet, 208

Tritina. *See* Chapter 8: 267, 270

Trochaic meter, 10, 63, 64, 67, 80, 81, 85, 98. *See* Chapter 5: 121–32, 133, 145, 147, 160, 165, 166, 177, 222, 293, 310, 365, 384

Villanelle, 169, 243, 244. *See* Chapter 8: 248–54, 255, 262, 287, 288

Volta, 292–95, 297, 298, 303, 306, 307, 309, 310, 312, 314. *See also* Sonnet

Wand (scansion mark), 63, 66, 72, 73, 74, 95